Mikhail Bakhtin

Mikhail Bakhtin

The Duvakin Interviews, 1973

EDITED BY SLAV N. GRATCHEV AND MARGARITA MARINOVA

TRANSLATED BY MARGARITA MARINOVA

Bucknell University | University Press

Lewisburg, Pennsylvania

Library of Congress Cataloging-in-Publication Data

Names: Bakhtin, M. M. (Mikhail Mikhaĭlovich), 1895–1975, interviewee. | Gratchev, Slav N., editor. | Marinova, Margarita (Margarita D.), editor, translator.
Title: Mikhail Bakhtin : the Duvakin interviews, 1973 / edited by Slav N. Gratchev and Margarita Marinova ; translated by Margarita Marinova.
Description: Lewisburg, PA : Bucknell University Press, [2019] | Includes bibliographical references and index.
Identifiers: LCCN 2018053290 | ISBN 9781684480913 (cloth) | ISBN 9781684480906 (paperback)
Subjects: LCSH: Bakhtin, M. M. (Mikhail Mikhaĭlovich), 1895–1975—Interviews.
Classification: LCC PG2947.B3 A5 2019 | DDC 801/.95092 [B]—dc23
LC record available at https://lccn.loc.gov/2018053290

A British Cataloging-in-Publication record for this book is available from the British Library.

♾ The paper used in this publication meets the requirements of the American National Standard for Information Sciences—Permanence of Paper for Printed Library Materials, ANSI Z39.48-1992.

www.bucknell.edu/UniversityPress

Distributed worldwide by Rutgers University Press

Manufactured in the United States of America

Contents

Mikhail Bakhtin

FIG. I.1. Bakhtin and Duvakin during the interview, 1973. (Courtesy of the Scientific Library at Moscow State University)

Introduction

SLAV N. GRATCHEV

> Nothing conclusive has yet taken place in the world, the ultimate word of the world and about the world has not yet been spoken, the world is open and free, everything is still in the future and will always be in the future.
> —Mikhail Bakhtin, *Problems of Dostoevsky's Poetics*

The book that you are about to read is a unique one in many ways. First of all, it was not originally intended to become a book; it is a collection of six live interviews with one of the most influential thinkers of the twentieth century—Mikhail Bakhtin. Second, his interviewer, Victor Duvakin (1909–1982), was not an ordinary journalist chasing after some breaking news; rather, he was a professional philologist—a former professor at Moscow State University, who was dismissed from his position for being sympathetic to and supportive of the young Soviet writer, Andrei Sinyavsky (Duvakin's former student), who had been arrested by the KGB for publishing in the West satirical novels under the pen name of a Jewish gangster, Abram Tertz.

Duvakin's dismissal from the university in 1966, while painful, gave him the long-desired freedom to accomplish something that no one in the Soviet Union had ever done before: to create a recorded oral library of reminiscences by leading figures in the arts and sciences from the first half of the twentieth century. He undertook a project whose historical and cultural importance should not be underestimated: in the twenty-first century, as Duvakin himself predicted, these phono-documents would acquire incomparable importance for historians and literary critics specializing in the Soviet era.

Duvakin always described his project as simply collecting materials and recordings of live conversations with people, who should have written their memoirs, but, for one reason or another, never did. It all began in the 1930s when he was charged with organizing an exhibition dedicated to the recently deceased poet Vladimir Mayakovsky. The poet happened to be so akin to Duvakin's heart that from that point on he felt personally connected with Mayakovsky. The ways of the Lord are inscrutable, and forty years later, in 1973, Duvakin came to interview Bakhtin precisely because Bakhtin happened to have known Mayakovsky personally, and thus could provide some additional insights into the poet's life and art.

As we can see, a series of ultimately favorable (although often unfortunate at first) events paved the way for Duvakin's interviews with Bakhtin. The most important event, of course, was Bakhtin's physical presence in Moscow: after spending the previous forty years in different parts of the Soviet Union, and therefore far from the cultural and intellectual centers, Bakhtin was finally allowed to return to the capital.

Bakhtin, who by then had gotten used to being forgotten, banned from publishing, criticized and unappreciated, all of a sudden received the attention that he deserved, but never expected. His fame came with certain benefits: Bakhtin received a nice apartment in Moscow, quality health care at the Kremlin clinic, and a decent pension. Publishers' doors began to open for him; they began to call him at home to solicit work for publication, and he was invited to deliver lectures, to speak about literature at symposia, and to participate in radio programs.

Bakhtin had learned not to be surprised about anything. He knew that something important had happened, but he was too busy to make inquiries and wonder why. Now, in his new, spacious, and sunny apartment in the center of Moscow, every morning he would sit at his desk, light a cigarette, make a cup of fresh, strong black tea, and try to write. . . . But he had lost his desire to work anymore: just two years ago his beloved wife, Elena—his best friend, his Muse—had passed away, and left a big void in his life that nothing seemed to be able to fill. It was hard to find now the strength and desire to write.

It was at that precise moment that Bakhtin received an unexpected phone call: from Victor Duvakin, a former professor of literature who, after a short introduction, asked if Bakhtin would be willing to conduct live interviews with him, and record them on tape. Bakhtin agreed.

So, on the gloomy and very cold evening of February 22, 1973, Duvakin and Bakhtin first met in his apartment. They ended up having six long interviews (totaling more than twelve hours), interrupted only by a cup of new, fresh tea served with the traditional oatmeal cookies. And each interview was not only an exciting journey into Bakhtin's inner world, the world that he never revealed to us through his theoretical works, but was also a unique phono-document that preserved for us "Bakhtin in his own voice."

For Bakhtin scholars, Duvakin's records are invaluable: Bakhtin, for the first time, talks about his life, people who he personally met, and difficult times that he went through. We can "hear" his voice: sad but not irritable—the voice of a stoic who knows that life, no matter how hard it can be, is still worth living. Bakhtin's words are uncensored, so to speak; he feels absolutely comfortable talking to a fellow scholar who is interested in his personal and professional opinions, as well as in the memories from his childhood, his life as a young student and emerging scholar of literature during some of the most turbulent times in twentieth-century Russian history. Among other things, this English translation of Duvakin's conversations with Bakhtin will shed additional light on little known facts from Mikhail Mikhailovich's life, and help correct previous errors and chronological inconsistencies his earlier biographers incurred because of the limited sources of information available to them at the time.

In March 1973, when the conversations with Bakhtin came to an end, Duvakin carefully deposited all the tapes on a shelf in the basement of Moscow State University—ready to be "discovered" again in the twenty-first century, as he had promised Bakhtin. He knew that the "great time" for his interviews with Bakhtin was yet to come. Imagine Bakhtin sitting comfortably in his armchair: he is holding a cup of strong, black tea (a detail that is inseparable from his image), lights a cigarette, and turns his attention to the questions his interlocutor has prepared for him. A dialogue with one of the most remarkable minds of the twentieth century is about to begin.

Translator's Introduction

MARGARITA MARINOVA

> In dialogue a person not only shows himself outwardly, but he becomes for the first time that which he is, . . . not only for others, but for himself as well. To be means to communicate dialogically. . . . Two voices is the minimum of life, the minimum for existence.
> —Mikhail Bakhtin, *Problems of Dostoevsky's Poetics*

Scholars from around the world first encountered Duvakin's taped interviews with Mikhail Mikhailovich Bakhtin during the plenary session at the Bakhtin Centennial Conference held in Moscow in June 1995. The snippet from the recordings of conversations spread over six separate sessions conducted during February and March 1973 was meant as a special treat for the roomful of ardent fans of the Russian philosopher. Finally, here was a chance to hear Bakhtin in his own words, to immerse oneself in the world as he saw it from his own perspective, and to become privy to some never before shared memories. Yet many of the listeners sitting in the auditorium that day had mixed reactions to this unique opportunity. Bakhtin's meandering thoughts—at times interrupted by coughing, laughter, uncomfortably long pauses caused by memory lapses (hardly unexpected from a seventy-eight-year-old man), and the occasional meowing of a cat—led some in the audience to wonder if it was such a good idea to gain this personal access to their idol at a time when both his physical and mental state seemed to be in decline. This enfeebled "emergent image" of Bakhtin captured in the tapes was authentic to the person he was in 1973, but it did not represent Bakhtin in his prime. *That* Bakhtin never had the chance to give interviews and was not even sought out for them. Was the aging, rambling man of Duvakin's tapes the *obraz* (image) of Bakhtin that his disciples and promoters wanted to disseminate around the world? Vitaly Makhlin sums up the reaction to Duvakin's interviews: "Is this forgetful, overly agreeable, despondent old man the same author who impressed us so in the 1960s, and then continued to astound even more after his death, during the 1970s and '80s, before everything finally collapsed? . . . No, that is not Bakhtin!"[1] There is an obvious irony here: the closer we get to Bakhtin, the more unrecognizable he seems to become.[2]

However, to walk away disappointed after listening to these recordings seems to be an inadequate response. It shows a lack of imagination, incurred by a faulty reliance on an image of the Russian philosopher, firmly grounded in the prime years of his life. It also overlooks an important aspect of the event represented by these unprecedented interviews, which should have been apparent to anyone familiar with Bakhtin's ideas about the fundamental significance of interpersonal communication. In other words, rather than obscuring some presumed "truth" about his peculiar way of thinking, and thus somehow giving us *less* than what we came to expect, the interviews with Duvakin reveal *more* fully the inner workings of Bakhtin's mind as it actively responds to an interlocutor in a live speech *act*. If Bakhtin was right to insist that it is in the dialogue with another that the self becomes "for the first time that which he is . . . not only for others but for himself as well," then what we have before us here *is* the real Bakhtin, whether we are willing to accept it or not.

Embracing the emergent image of Mikhail Bakhtin in the recordings—rather than rejecting it on the grounds of some external concept of his presumed authenticity—can be incredibly revealing and beneficial for the dialogues' superaddressee: what Bakhtin called also "the third," and which in this case I use to mean the actual present-day listener or reader, the reader of this book.[3] Ostensibly, we are transported to a very different time and space: Soviet Moscow of the 1970s. Yet our time travels bring us even further back in history, to the Russia of the late nineteenth–early twentieth century, which Bakhtin knew and loved so well. That in 1973 he manages to sound like someone who belongs to a different time (i.e., prerevolutionary Russia) is so remarkable that it, alone, should be reason enough to appreciate the intrinsic value of the taped conversations. A truly "European" philosopher, Bakhtin remains grounded in pre-Soviet traditions and categories of thought that Duvakin is not familiar with, and in response to which can offer only guesses in lieu of proper commentary. The low pressure, congenial atmosphere that results from Mikhail Mikhailovich's monolingual, Soviet-trained interlocutor's inability to grasp much of the European context of his interviewee's ideas, is quite liberating: Bakhtin is free to ramble and relax into reciting poetry. Although Duvakin clearly guides the discussion to topics that best serve his own purpose in undertaking the task of creating an oral history of the Russian/Soviet educational systems (he admits as much himself on a couple of occasions), Bakhtin still manages at times to redirect the conversations in ways that make better sense to *him*, and disclose to us what truly mattered to the person behind the icon. His meandering thought is not a liability; instead, it is precisely there, in the unexpected additions and voluntary diversions that we "find" Bakhtin as he was: a man of a long lost world, "made of a very different cloth," in the phrase he himself often uses when describing the poets and artists he admired the most.

The Bakhtin of the Duvakin interviews is clearly oriented toward the past. On the one hand, his interviewer makes sure he stays focused on the task at hand and records Bakhtin's reminiscences about his early years as a student at various universities. On the other hand, and just as important, Mikhail Mikhailovich appears drawn to the past because that is where he feels most at ease. To him, the Soviet reality of his immediate present seems too boring, too fabricated, and too predictable to deserve his full attention, whereas the future remains obscure and partially accessible only through the notion of the much too abstract "universally human."[4] Far from being the proverbial foreign country, the past for Bakhtin is his only true home, and we are fortunate to have been given access to it through Duvakin's recordings.

There's a lot of interest that we uncover once we allow ourselves to be transported to the past. We "meet" Bakhtin's forefathers as he chooses to remember them: recently impoverished members of the Russian nobility, altruistic, and highly intelligent yet unequipped to handle the pressures of the ever-changing political realities. We "hear" the constant chatter, the laughter, and music that permeate the world of his childhood in Orel. Those were happy times despite the ubiquitous financial troubles, and Bakhtin revels in the memories of his big and lively household. It is there, in his family upbringing in Orel, that he locates the roots of his future interests and the formation of his intellectual foundations. The first two interviews are dominated by the topic of Bakhtin's education in Orel, Odessa, and St. Petersburg (he has so many positive things to say about all the institutions he attended, and the professors he studied with). Yet it becomes clear that for this independent thinker, as for many other great minds of his generation, formal education would always remain deficient, incomplete, and at times dangerously marred by contemporary fads and political struggles.

Bakhtin's concern with the effects of politics on our human existence is of particular interest to us today, as he is often portrayed as nonpolitical in Western criticism. Most scholars agree that his "concepts of dialogue and polyphony, like his concept of carnival . . . are free of everything associated with the practice and distribution of power"[5] because he did not feel he could create positive values within intrinsically restrictive systems of political organization. It is all the more interesting, then, that he does not really shy away from the topic in his conversations with Duvakin. Although he does declare himself to be "apolitical" (Interview 2), he has no qualms sharing his negative opinions of the young Bolshevik "extremists" he encountered during his years of studying at the Odessa and St. Petersburg universities, or stating outright that he "did not welcome the February Revolution," which he thought would "end very badly" because "It was inevitable that the victory would go to the masses of soldiers and peasants in uniforms, who didn't hold anything dear, the proletariat that did not constitute a proper historical class and did not have any values, had nothing to speak of. . . . They had spent their lives fighting for the most basic material needs. They were the ones who would surely seize the power in the end. And nobody would be able to overthrow them, because the intelligentsia was not capable of it" (Interview 3).

Duvakin is so struck by Bakhtin's ability to assess the situation correctly and predict the future so well, that he has to ask if this is simply "revisionist" thinking, a false memory informed by knowledge acquired at a much later time, but Bakhtin insists that he did indeed share those ideas with his circle back in the day, and continues to give even more examples of early predictions that came true in subsequent years. He may be "a philosopher," and "a thinker," as he tells his interviewer in their first conversation, but he is not a "typical" member of the intelligentsia, which he sees as "naïve," "absolutely, and completely naïve" (Interview 1) because they are always too hasty to react without fully considering the ramifications of any specific civic action first. Bakhtin remains grounded in reality at all times and appreciates the struggles of those around him no matter how different from him their interests might be. True intellectualism does not mean being "exotic," different from the rest, according to the contemporary popular belief, and he hastens to denounce this kind of flawed intellectual "exoticism," which he found prevalent in certain artistic circles of his youth.

In general, Bakhtin is not timid about offering his uncompromising assessment of various renowned writers and artists. Duvakin was right to assume that Mikhail Mikhailovich would offer a wealth of invaluable information about the famed Silver Age of Russian culture (circa 1890–1920): his reminiscences of the period read like a "who's who" list of early twentieth-century Russian letters. He knew personally (if not intimately), and had much to say about the likes of Vladimir Mayakovsky (whom he disliked at first, but then grew to appreciate); the Futurists; virtually all the major Symbolists (his caustic remarks about Zinaida Gippius, Dmitry Merezhkovsky, and Dmitry Filosofov will surprise many a reader of this book); Maksim Gorky (whom he perceived as a spineless man who still managed to do some good work); and the poets Marina Tsvetaeva and Anna Akhmatova (he preferred the latter; Tsvetaeva's difficult personality did not meet with his full approval). Bakhtin's views on these, and many other important contemporary figures, are both insightful and controversial in the context of the Russian literary canon, and will undoubtedly provoke further discussions among scholars of Bakhtin's oeuvre, Soviet literature and culture, and Stalin's regime.

However, as critical as Bakhtin can be of others, he is also careful to point out the fact that people always have their own reasons for acting in a certain way, and we should be mindful of that as we look at them from the outside in. In most cases, the theorist of *vnenakhodimost'* (outsidedness) generously bestows the gift of looking at another person from that exterior position in order to reveal unexpected assets in the other's personality, or to admire more fully their creative output. In that respect Duvakin's constant prodding and pushing the conversation toward poetry is especially valuable to us today. In his published studies Mikhail Mikhailovich rarely mentions poetic language, and if he does, it is only as a counterpoint to his favorite novelistic discourse. Talking with Duvakin (an expert on avant-garde poetry and a connoisseur of the Russian poetic tradition), Bakhtin allows himself to explore the hidden potentialities of the poetic word and emerges as much less willing to sustain the binary opposition of poetry and prose on which his published writing often implicitly has to rely. Multivoicedness, he admits, can be found in the oeuvre of some of the best Russian poets, and so can the carnivalesque and the public square. He is especially intrigued by poetry's ability to register the presence of "the end," of death, at all times (there is no great poetry without that, he argues in Interview 4), and by the way the physical performance of poetic works can alter their meaning for good *and* bad (in some cases he remembers being struck by a particular poem when recited by its author, only to be disappointed once he tried to read it himself later). And speaking of poetic performativity,[6] we would be amiss if we did not note the poetic nature of the interviews themselves both in terms of subject matter and actual recitation, which our two interlocutors tend to lapse into any chance they have. In the course of the six recorded sessions Bakhtin remembers (mostly error-free) and recites significant portions by Russian, German, and French poets, both from well-know and rather obscure poems. Throughout the interviews, Bahktin often complains about his poor memory in old age. (If that is what a failing memory sounds like, we should all be so lucky.) In this instance Bakhtin is much more self-critical than he needs to be. The fact is that his famed photographic memory for poetry and prose held him in good stead well into his seventies. We know, for example, that he never used notes in his Saransk lectures, reciting huge stretches of text by heart in ancient as well as modern languages.

Translating the quoted poem excerpts was by far the most challenging part of the translation process for me. With a few notable exceptions (such as excellent English translations of Pushkin's *Eugene Onegin*) most of the verses quoted during the interviews had not been translated into English, or if they were, the quality of the translation left much to be desired. I strove to preserve the original's rhythm and rhyming scheme wherever possible, but of course my talents would never match those of such poetic geniuses as Fet, Blok, Yesenin, or Bryusov. There's nothing worse than when a translator "lowers the level" and "trivializes" the source text, as Bakhtin argues in his impassioned defense of his friend Pasternak's much criticized translation of Goethe's *Faust* (Part I) in Interview 6, and I certainly hope I have not committed that particular sin on too many occasions here. (As a side note, the present text will be very useful to those of us who are interested in Bakhtin's views on translation as such. In earlier works, for instance, in "From the Prehistory of Novelistic Discourse," Bakhtin grants translation a major role in the constitution of literature. His review of the prehistory of novelistic discourse advances the idea that language first becomes aware of itself through contact with other languages and goes on to offer the example of the Roman literary consciousness, which was formed through an interaction with the language and literature of ancient Greece. Although Bakhtin stresses the importance of languages intermingling and animating each other across different cultures and periods, he also contends that "that which makes language concrete" also "makes its world view ultimately untranslatable."[7] The examples of Pasternak and Zhukovsky before him, which Bakhtin offers in his final conversation with Duvakin, suggest a more positive outlook on the powers of translation that should be explored further.)

The language of the interviews themselves did not present any serious difficulties in the process of rendering them into English. Both men use fairly informal Russian, and allow themselves to think as they speak, which is something I endeavored to capture through preserving as many of the repetitions, pauses, and unfinished utterances as possible without making the translation too cumbersome or hard to follow. For the most part, Bakhtin's verbal tics (he tends to overuse certain phrases, such as "we might say," "in short," or "anyway") are still there, though I have elected to leave some of them out in those cases where they distract too much from the main flow of the presented ideas. It is also interesting to note, as far as Mikhail Mikhailovich's conversation style is concerned, that he often repeats the last word or phrase, spoken by Duvakin—ostensibly to express his agreement with him; yet in the very next sentence he would offer a completely different, even opposite idea, which irrevocably changes his interlocutor's interpretation. There's nothing "overly agreeable" in Bakhtin's stance, as some complained upon first hearing the recorded conversations. Instead, we encounter an experienced *mezhdusoboinik* (a "just-between-you-and-me-nik"),[8] well-practiced in the art of philosophical disagreement after decades' worth of debates, carried out in small rooms in various corners of Soviet Russia over perpetual cups of tea and cigarettes.

In addition to being mindful of the fact that we are dealing with a live speech act here, I was also careful to avoid the trap of the over-domestication of the source language into English. I wanted readers to recognize that this text is a transcript of a live conversation conducted in *Russian*. I believe that the culture embedded in the original language should retain some of its "foreignness" to target language audiences, which is why I chose to preserve some specific terms (for example, "gymnasium") that have different connotations in Russian, and then glossed them in the notes. Speaking of all things Russian, it is important to note that the vast number of names and places that come up in the interviews should be familiar to most Russian readers, but can be somewhat of a challenge for their Western counterparts. The latter have to work harder in order to follow the narrative thread at times (the notes provided should help alleviate most of those problems), but their reward will be enormous as well. For among the many generous gifts Bakhtin is bestowing upon us here, is the special opportunity to extend our knowledge of the world of "great time" and great literature. If we are willing to enter the conversation as active participants ourselves (which Bakhtin would surely encourage us to do), we must also familiarize ourselves properly with all the people (Russian, but also French, German, Italian, etc.) and works mentioned in passing during the sessions. In doing so, we are certain to receive the kind of education not easily available through regular textbooks or formal lectures, which Mikhail Mikhailovich prized above anything else.

Bakhtin inspired deep reverence and enthusiasm in all his students during his lifetime. The last twenty years of his life were among his happiest, as he was finally allowed to return in an official capacity to the profession he loved so well: he received his first real academic job in 1946 as chair of the General Literature Department at the Mordovian State Pedagogical Institute, and then, in 1957, when the institute changed from a teachers' college to a university, he became head of the Department of Russian and World Literature. Bakhtin always welcomed his disciples with open arms and an open mind. He thrived on dialogue and welcomed probing questions and comments in public forums and private conversations at his modest apartment. Numerous witness accounts[9] from former colleagues, students, and neighbors in Saransk portray the mature Bakhtin as a beloved teacher and mentor. He continued to attract devoted pupils when, in search of a better medical treatment, he moved to Moscow in 1969. His deteriorating health did not prevent him from talking for hours on end with the many young people who made the pilgrimage to his two-bedroom apartment at 21 Krasnoarmeyskaya Street, or from giving public talks on occasion—S. G. Bocharov describes one such 1972 lecture[10] on Fyodor Dostoevsky for teachers from the Podolskii region as a momentous experience that showcased Bakhtin's talents as an effective speaker and inspirational pedagogue. A teacher to the end, Mikhail Mikhailovich recognized the power of the spoken word to change minds and enrich hearts. My biggest hope for this book is that it will help encourage a new generation of rapt listeners/readers to become enthusiastic students of one of the most original minds of the twentieth century.

Interview One

February 22, 1973

Length of the interview: 100 minutes

DUVAKIN: Mikhail Mikhailovich, so you're telling me that you have a memorial book about to come out?
BAKHTIN: It's a book dedicated to me in connection with my seventy-fifth birthday.
D: I see, that's a little different. . . . So, when was your exact birth date?
B: The exact date . . . 1895 . . . November 4th, according to the old style, the 17th according to the new style.[1]
D: And where were you born?
B: Orel.[2]
D: What was your family like? What sort of family did you come out of?
B: A noble family and very old.[3] We have, let's say, documents dating us back to the fourteenth century. . . . But the thing is, our family was already in a pretty bad state. We had lost almost everything.
D: "And my fierce clan stumbled . . ."[4] Yes?
B: That's it! [*laughs*] The fact is, my great-grandfather . . . was a brigadier during Catherine the Great's time. . . . That is, he was a brigadier general, who gave up 3,000 of his own serfs to create one of the first Russian Cadet Corps. It was still in existence up until the Revolution.

FIG. 1.1. Orel, the beginning of the twentieth century. (Courtesy of the Scientific Library at Moscow State University)

D: Was it named after him? Or not?

B: It did carry his name. So, yes, it was known as the Bakhtin Orel Cadet Corps. At one time, it was called the "Bakhtin Military Gymnasium."[5] So he parted with 3,000 of his own serfs—that's how it was, well, there was a record, a financial account of it. It wasn't as if there were really serfs, they were, apparently, sold, pawned, and so forth, as was always the case back then. There was a financial account of those serfs.

D: Well, yes, I understand. That is, it was still a lot of money.

B: Yes, a big, enormous amount. This was the beginning of our future ruin, that is, the family ruin. He was very rich, had many estates, but still, it was such an enormous sum, it had to have huge consequences. . . .

D: This was your great-grandfather?

B: My great-great-grandfather. Yes. And my grandfather finished the job. Nonetheless, my grandfather had several estates: he still owned two whole counties in Orel province. These were the so-called Sevsk county and Trubchevsky county.

D: I'm especially interested in Sevsk, since that's where Ivan Petrovsky[6] was born. You didn't know that family, did you?

B: No, I didn't know them.

D: It seems like his family also belonged to the nobility and founded a gymnasium in Sevsk . . . not too long before the Revolution.

B: Aha, no, that's already after we sold the country estate.

D: And Sevsk—is that in Orel province?

B: Yes, Orel province. Even now . . . Sevsk . . . Trubchevsk . . . is . . . in the same region where there used to be the country estate of Dimitry Kantemir, the father of Antiochus Kantemir.[7] That's where, I think, Antiochus Kantemir himself used to live. We were even somehow related or connected: in a word, one of my . . .

D: . . . one of your uncles thrice removed.

B: Uncle thrice removed, yes. He was connected with the Kantemir family on my mother's side. How exactly, I couldn't tell you. To be honest, it didn't interest me. My brother, on the other hand, he studied our genealogy, and knew everything about it, while I don't. . . . He was one of our neighbors there and was also somehow related to or connected with the Svyatopolk-Mirskys.

D: Really! Well, it was a huge family.

B: A huge family, yes. . . . But also I don't know much about this genealogy. As a young child I visited those estates. . . . They belonged to one of the Svyatopolk-Mirskys, one of them, I don't know which one. . . .

D: One of the last ones . . .

B: One of the last ones. He used to live in England, but then came back and his life ended here very tragically.[8]

D: Yes. He was, at one point, Russia's number one literary critic. Gorky[9] took him under his wing.

B: Yes, that's true.

D: I met him.

B: You did? I never met him.

D: I met him here. He was a typical member of the intelligentsia.

B: That he was, a typical intelligentsia member, very naïve. Absolutely and completely naïve, one might say.

D: A really nice guy!

B: You understand, he was like . . . how can I describe it . . . I imagine, like English communists from the lords. . . . After all, the English Communist Party is rather peculiar: there are hardly any working-class members in it, just aristocratic lords and the intelligentsia. In brief, for them it's considered exotic to be different from others, and so on and so forth. He was like those communists from the lords, this Svyatopolk-Mirsky. He, too, was a lord.

D: Ah, well . . . Did your father already work somewhere?

B: He did. He was a financier and worked for banks. But he no longer owned any country estates. My grandma and grandpa still did. So yes, overall . . . we

were not doing too badly, one might say. Above all, there was the really big house in Orel, where I was born. It was a lot like a farmstead, that home.
D: Oh, how fascinating!
B: I don't know if it's still standing. It was made of wood, you know, with mezzanines. A big house, with about thirty rooms, with outbuildings, etc. . . . Our house was in one of the most expensive neighborhoods. Ivan Turgenev[10] was born there too, not far from our place at the corner of Sadovaya Street and Georgievskaya Street. But Turgenev's house was already gone by the time I was born. There's now a smallish stone building on the same spot. But everyone knows it's where Turgenev's house used to be. When I was born, the country estate still belonged to my uncle. Tikhon Bakhtin—that was his name.
D: So, your father was an important official from the nobility.
B: Yes, yes, he was a rather important official. You see, my grandfather founded a bank before the Revolution, the Orel Commercial Bank, which quickly expanded with a branch in Petrograd, in Petersburg. But the banks had no luck. My grandfather was, one could say, a decent and unusually gullible man. . . . He served as the Director of the Board, and most of his own capital was invested in that bank. . . . But his colleagues, the other members of the board, were either swindlers, or just dimwits, and as a result the bank collapsed. There was a big suit, a legal trial that became quite notorious, and many ended up on the benches of the accused, including my grandfather. Of course, he was not actually arrested . . . because there was no legal reason for that in his case, but there was a trial nevertheless. A famous lawyer, Plevako,[11] came to defend him at the trial. He represented him at the hearings. It all ended with my grandfather being acquitted of all blame, because it was clear from the start who was a crook, and who was just too trusting and willing to put his signature on anything, not really understanding the nature of the deal that was being offered. . . . So in the end someone else went to jail. But his civic duty necessitated the sale of all those big estates. The whole lot! To tell you the truth, he really didn't have to make full retributions. You know how it works—there were commissions, let's say you gave back 20 kopeks on the ruble, and then that's it. But my grandfather refused to do that, and returned the sums in full, which is why he had to give back an enormous amount of money.

Nevertheless, despite all that, we still had the house, and even a small country estate, and about 100,000 rubles left. But then the funds started

FIG. 1.2. Bakhtin's father Mikhail Fedorovich Bakhtin. (Courtesy of the Scientific Library at Moscow State University)

to run out. . . . However, my grandmother . . . Grandfather died earlier, but my grandmother lived to see the October Revolution, and beyond, she died only toward the end of 1917 or the beginning of 1918, of old age, following a bout of typhus.

D: In her own house?

B: Yes, in her house.
D: She was not evicted, and the house was not burned down?
B: No, no, the house was not burned, and she was not evicted, just inconvenienced.[12] She lived, I think . . . I don't know. . . . My mother was there . . . at the time when she was dying from typhus, but I was no longer there. She still had some money, some remaining capital. . . .

My grandfather, despite the fact that he had chosen to work in finance and commerce, was too easy to fool, a really sweet man. I remember my grandmother kept in the pantry a big suitcase, filled with bills—bills that were never repaid by those who had borrowed money. They would lend money left and right. My grandfather gave away money left and right. To the very end, to the Revolution, there was a designated attorney on our staff, who was supposed to work on recovering those loans. So, he managed to recoup a little once in a while. All in all, it didn't make much of a difference. But there were indeed attempts to recover funds to the last day.

Neither my parents, nor we, the children, lived in Orel any longer, we had already left some time before, but we visited every summer, the children did, myself, my brother, and my sister.
D: Did you also have a sister?
B: Well, I had three sisters, even, strictly speaking, four, because the fourth one was an adopted daughter.[13]
D: So, six people. A big family!
B: Yes, it was a big family. Besides us, there were many other relatives who lived with us, for example, my grandfather's brother, who died very young. He died young, and left a rather big inheritance, some country estates in the Dmitrovsky district. His children, three daughters and a son, also lived with us, because my grandfather, and then my grandmother, were appointed as their legal guardians.
D: How very exciting!
B: Well, of course, they had their own money, because their father left them a large estate. There were also other relatives. . . . We went bankrupt, but we had very rich relatives, millionaires. So . . . They were mostly distant family members on my grandmother's side, but we were still quite close. Very wealthy people. I should say that, of course, they are all gone now, except for one cousin, the daughter of one of those also very rich men, a former mayor . . .
D: In Orel?

FIG. 1.3. Bakhtin family. From left, sitting: Maria, Bakhtin's oldest sister; Bakhtin's mother; Nina, adopted daughter. From left, standing: Natalia, Katerina (Bakhtin's sisters). (Courtesy of the Scientific Library at Moscow State University)

B: In Orel, yes. A mayor. That's what basically did him in. He was mayor before the Revolution.
D: Of course.
B: Yes. When the Revolution happened, since he was a good man, he was arrested but they didn't harm him otherwise. Besides, there were enterprises that only he knew how to handle. . . . And so, he was let go, so to speak, in order to do what's necessary, yes . . . Everything would have been fine, but then the Whites[14] came to Orel. Their slogan was: "Everything as it was before the Revolution!" Everything! So my uncle had to become mayor again. And so he did.
D: Yes. And that's what did him in.
B: Well, as you know, the Whites didn't stay very long. The Reds returned. My uncle had to run. He fled with his whole family, pretty successfully, and they ended up in Kavkaz, where he lived under a different name in Armavir. He lived there for quite some time. All was well. Yes. But then . . .

D: Did he emigrate then? No?
B: No, he wasn't able to emigrate. He was unable to emigrate.
D: So he was liquidated?
B: No, they didn't manage to liquidate him. Here is what happened. There was a cholera outbreak there, in Armavir, and he got infected and placed in a special cholera ward, exactly around the time they found out who he really was. By the way, he was given a death sentence in absentia, back in Orel. So when his true identity was revealed, they came to arrest him. But it turned out he was in the isolation barracks. The idea was that they were going to either move him to the prison hospital, or place a guard from MGB at the barracks. . . . No, it wasn't called MGB back then . . .
D: Cheka.[15]
B: Yes, it was Cheka back then. But the doctors said, "Don't worry, we're not even talking about days, he has only hours to live." He was old, and surviving cholera was, of course, difficult. And he did die. Never realized he had been found out. Of course, he did know he had been sentenced to death. So he died, and the family was left behind.
D: Did they touch his family?
B: The family? No, they didn't touch them. Anyways, who was left? His wife and daughter, an only child, Liza. She now lives here, in Moscow, my only remaining relative, a very close relative, on my uncle's side.
D: So, her dad is your uncle on your mother's side?
B: Uncle, yes. Besides that, her mother is also my mother's sister, so we are doubly related.
D: Ah, I see, an inter-marriage.
B: Yes, but, unfortunately, she is sick. She is younger than me, quite a bit younger, even, but still not young anymore, and with a serious condition—a vascular disease, very widespread now. Anyways, because of that she can't even go out, and walk by herself, she needs someone to help her with that. In general, her life is very hard. So she's never visited me here. The last time I saw her, she came to the Kremlin hospital, when I was admitted there. And now we can only communicate over the phone.
D: OK, you spoke at length and told us many interesting things about your family. . . . You were able to graduate from the gymnasium before the Revolution . . .
B: Yes, I was able to do that.
D: . . . and from the university, too? Or maybe not?

B: From the university, too. Though not quite—I had to pass state exams after the Revolution.

D: Did you graduate from the Orel gymnasium?

B: No. The thing is, [my father] worked, he was a banker, and he had to move around all the time. Well, not all the time, but at least several times he had to move, because he was appointed Director of the Orel Commercial Bank branch in Vilno.[16] So he had to live there for five years, and so did I.[17]

D: And you studied at the Vilno gymnasium?

B: Yes, the Vilno gymnasium. Though I started at the Orel gymnasium . . . Well, then . . . after that the family moved to Odessa.[18] I enrolled at the university in Odessa. But I wasn't there very long, my brother and I transferred to Petersburg University soon after.[19] That's where I graduated from.

D: You studied at the historical-philological department?

B: Yes, at the history and philology department. I majored in classical studies.

D: Did your father have a university degree?

B: My father? No, only specialized training. . . . No, actually, he didn't even have that. At the time nobody cared much about that—as long as one had personal wealth . . . and he had his own bank, we might say. So, he began working at his own bank. But he didn't work there very long. He was transferred right away to serve as director of the Vilno branch.

D: Then you have a pretty good idea about what provincial Russian gymnasiums were like: Orel, Vilno, Odessa—[representing] the Central, Western, and Southern regions. Please tell us a little about those schools, if you would, describe them a bit . . .

B: You see, it's hard to remember it clearly. I'll tell you this—the schools, all three of them, were good. The Odessa gymnasium was especially good. It was an excellent school. And the Vilno gymnasium was great too.

D: Was the one in Orel somewhat worse?

B: Yes, it was somewhat worse, a little worse. But the Vilno gymnasium, the First Gymnasium . . . At the time there were only two gymnasiums in the whole city, and, actually, almost in the whole province. . . . There were many students from the surrounding little towns. . . . Lida, there was a little town called that, and others too. . . . So yes, people came from all around. . . .

D: Did you have to pay for your education?

B: Yes, we had to pay. But it must be said that there were many available stipends. In fact, all good students, and those with financial needs, could almost always depend upon getting a stipend. Yes. That must be said right away. I never heard of anyone being sent away because he couldn't pay the tuition. Because in those cases the parents' association took the necessary measures, and the student was free to continue his studies without paying out of pocket.
D: And these stipends were privately sponsored?
B: Yes, privately sponsored. Yes, yes, privately sponsored. Now . . . the First Vilno gymnasium, where I studied, was housed in the university building—the ancient Vilno University, which was built in the sixteenth century.[20]
D: I know that building. I gave a few lectures there. [*laughs*]
B: Aha! I have the fondest memories of it. . . . Well, my best memories are from my childhood at home, of course, but also from Vilno, the gymnasium, its beautiful building. It's magnificent, that building!
D: A proper castle!
B: It took up a whole block, and everything there was so interesting, it had a special kind of air about it. There were several courtyards. Each one had its own name. For example, the main one, through which everybody enters the building, was called Lelevel.[21]

FIG. 1.4. Vilnius University. (Courtesy of the Scientific Library at Moscow State University)

D: Lelevel?

B: Yes, yes. He was one of the heroes of old Poland. The courtyard was named after him. All courtyards had their special names. Yes. Even Piłsudski,[22] he too went to the Vilno gymnasium (that was before me, of course). In general, many who became famous later went to school there, at the First Vilno gymnasium. The teachers were very good, I must say. Very good!

D: Was that a Russian gymnasium?

B: Yes, Russian, purely Russian. But there were many Poles there. Many Poles.

D: But the instruction was conducted in Russian?

B: Only in Russian. The Poles could take Polish language classes, and only Polish students attended those by personal choice.

D: So Polish was officially taught there?

B: Yes, it was.

D: Polish was offered? It wasn't persecuted?

B: Not at all. People like to exaggerate a lot. Persecuted . . . It wasn't a required subject. It wasn't required. Whoever wanted to study Polish could do so. Yes. Of course, Polish was offered, what do you think! I remember the teacher. . . . I never took his classes, of course, but remember him well—he was such an amazing person! He was so handsome, a typical Pole, with a beard, very handsome and very spiritual. All Poles who wanted to could study with him.

D: Was Lithuanian taught as well?

B: No, Lithuanian was not offered. There were Lithuanians there, but they didn't attend the gymnasiums. But maybe they did after all. . . . There were some other private schools. . . . The teachers were wonderful, really good. That's what I thought, in any case. . . . I can't remember a single instructor who aroused a feeling of dislike in me or in any of the other students. No. Those were all honorable people, very knowledgeable, sometimes even impressively so, well meaning, so I can't complain, not at all. I remember, we loved . . . I especially loved Adrian Vasilevich Krukovsky.[23] I remember him to this day. We called him—of course, as is always the case, teachers had nicknames—"the Artist of the burned-out theater." Because he was all . . . His curly hair was all grey, and there was really something about him that reminded one of an artist from an old, impoverished theater. He was a very knowledgeable man.

D: What did he teach?

B: He taught Russian language and literature. He taught brilliantly, with fervor, I'd say even with passion, a passion that inspired us all. He was also a writer. His views were by no means revolutionary. Nothing like that. One of his published works was titled, "Religious Influences on Russian Poetry." He also wrote about Ivan Turgenev. His last article came out in 1916, in the *Journal of the Ministry of National Education*, if I recall correctly.

I also liked the math teacher, Yankovich. Everybody liked him. He was a bit dry, but very . . . well . . .

D: Exact.

B: Logical, exact. But mostly—logical. He never told you: "Here it is, just memorize it." No, he was able to prove it to you, help you understand. Later, after I left Vilno, he was appointed director of the Novo-Sventsiansk gymnasium. The gymnasium was then moved to Nevel.[24]

D: It moved to Nevel?

B: Yes. I also moved to Nevel.[25] Why? Because a good friend of mine, who played such an important role in my life, happened to be there. His name was Lev Vasilyevich Pumpyansky.[26]

D: I've heard of him.

B: He is included in the literary encyclopedia.

D: He's a famous literary scholar.

B: A famous one, yes. A very talented man, with amazing erudition.

D: Of your generation?

B: Yes, my generation. He's a year younger than me.

D: Is he still alive?

B: Unfortunately, he is long gone, he died very young. He was only around forty-nine when he died.

D: I've read something or other by him.

B: You've probably read his essays about Turgenev.

D: Yes, probably.

B: Right. He worked on the eighteenth century a lot, studied Trediakovsky,[27] in particular the syntax and versification of Trediakovsky's poems. Right . . . He was doing his military service, that is, he fought in the war, and then his regiment was stationed in Nevel. That's where he was discharged. He chose to stay in Nevel because it was very complicated to live in Leningrad (it was Petrograd then) at the time, life was hard there. Well, simply put, there was a food crisis. He didn't go back. His life in Nevel was very good. He was closely connected with all the important people there. He gave many lectures there. So . . . When he came to

FIG. 1.5. Lev Pumpyansky, 1913. (Courtesy of the Scientific Library at Moscow State University)

Leningrad—Petrograd—he stayed with us, in the apartment with my father, mother, and brother,[28] who had been a good friend of his since the gymnasium. . . . My brother escaped to the South. He joined the volunteer army there, and then they all, together with the soldiers fleeing from the Crimea, emigrated abroad, to Constantinople. Then he found himself in the Foreign Legion.

D: In Spain?

B: No, no, no. This Foreign Legion was still . . . that was before Spain, of course.

FIG. 1.6. Bakhtin's older brother Nikolay in his youth. (Courtesy of the Scientific Library at Moscow State University)

D: With whom? Where?

B: The French Foreign Legion, the old Foreign Legion. A long time ago there was a Foreign Legion in Algeria.

D: Ah, in Algeria . . .

B: That's an interesting phenomenon, very peculiar, we might say. He, by the way, wrote about his life in the Foreign Legion in his memoirs. Then he was seriously wounded. They mostly fought with the insurgent Berbers. He was injured several times, the most serious wound was to the

FIG. 1.7. Bakhtin's mother Varvara Zakharovna Bakhtin. (Courtesy of the Scientific Library at Moscow State University)

chest, very near to his heart. After his discharge he moved to Paris. At first he continued working for the army, at some clerical job. As he wrote about it, they didn't have much to do, the discharged, nothing at all: just write letters and shoot the breeze all day long. . . . Very light service. Then he . . . yes, he entered the university. . . . He had almost finished his university studies back in Russia, but he had to get a formal degree there. And he did . . .

D: At the Sorbonne?

B: Yes, the Sorbonne, the Sorbonne. So he graduated. . . . He gave many lectures and published quite a few short articles.

D: What was his degree in?

B: Classical studies, like me.

D: The same?

B: Yes. But while later I moved away from Classical studies, he remained true to it to the end. He defended his dissertation at Cambridge.

D: Did he stay there, or come back?

B: No, he didn't stay in France. There is . . . there's a very famous scientist now . . . Konovalov, he is the son of Konovalov, the minister . . . [29]

D: Minister Konovalov.

B: Yes, Minister Konovalov.

D: I know him. Gudzy[30] was acquainted with him.

B: Yes, Gudzy knew him. He came here for the Congress of Slavonic Scholars. I believe it was the fifth congress . . .

D: Or the fourth—the fourth one, in Moscow, in 1958.

B: He was introduced as "Sir Konovalov." Anyway. He was also my brother's friend, they met abroad. They didn't know each other in Russia. So, this Konovalov convinced him to move to England. He was already in England, had immigrated there from the start.

He [my brother] moved there. At first he was at Cambridge. Not long ago, I was given as a present a photocopy of his last lecture there, on Pushkin. Right. His topic was: Why is Pushkin—such a seemingly clear and simple, classical author—so rarely and poorly translated, so little known abroad? That was his last lecture. It wasn't published while he was alive. After his death, not very long ago, they found the notes for this lecture among his papers.

D: When did he pass away?

B: In May 1950.

D: What were you telling me before, I think the last time we spoke, that something of his is coming out here? Yes?

B: Here? No, nothing of his is being published here.

D: So he died an émigré?

B: In the Lenin Library[31] here you can find his work on contemporary Greek language. But he approaches it through the prism of ancient Greek. His main idea is that there's more to learn about antiquity as it really was—unembellished, free from any externally imposed concepts—from modern Greek, than from archeology, or the known ancient Greek, classical texts. Modern Greek has never been studied from an archeological perspective, so to speak. For example, as you know, this was one of the ideas of the late academician Marr.[32] . . . He worked in paleontology . . .

D: I know.

B: But my brother's ideas emerged independently of Marr and are somewhat different. He wasn't looking for some kind of proto-symbols, some, let's say, proto-elements, he was searching for . . .

D: So he stayed within the frame of the classical Indo-European model?

B: The Indo-European model, yes. He traveled from England to Greece several times, participated in archeological excavations, in particular at the Marathon Field. . . . My mom even had a postcard. He didn't write to me, out of concern for my security: in those years, you were not supposed to correspond with anyone from abroad. That would have been too risky, so he wrote to our mother instead, knowing that she'd pass along everything. . . .

D: Where did your mother live?

B: My mother was already in Leningrad. My sisters lived there. So, she had a postcard of him and his wife (he married a British woman) on the Marathon excavation site. All he has on is a pair of pants. In Greece. Yes . . . There was also another postcard of him in front of the ancient buildings of the Cambridge University. He is wearing a robe, holding a distinctive folio, and there are some other professors and students nearby. He is in the forefront.

D: Did your brother go to the same Vilno gymnasium as you?

B: Yes, of course.

D: Was he a little older than you?

B: Yes, he was a little older. A little older.

D: But you . . . Let's go back to the gymnasium years. Did you graduate from the Vilno gymnasium?

B: No, I transferred to the one in Odessa, and graduated from there.

D: What can you tell us about Odessa?

B: Odessa . . . That was also a very good school. The Odessa gymnasium was very good indeed. I can't complain, not at all. All teachers were good. Maybe there weren't any that stood out, as was the case in Vilno, perhaps the level overall was somewhat lower . . .

D: The level of the students?
B: And the teachers. But also, the students, yes. There was nobody who stood out among them either, to me, at least. But everything was still great! They were excellent youngsters, wonderful, noble. I can't complain. The teachers were good. Nobody was persecuted, harassed. . . . Nothing that our most progressive writers, journalists, and activists are claiming to have happened, actually took place. Perhaps it did happen here and there, who knows, but I wasn't aware of it. And in any case, that would have been the exception. Overall, our gymnasium was very strong, I'd say. Very strong.
D: How was it called?
B: Just gymnasium.
D: The Odessa gymnasium? Was there only one?
B: No, there were several. Ours was the Fourth.
D: So, the Fourth Odessa gymnasium. Did any of the future famous Odessa writers study there with you?
B: No, nobody.
D: Bagritsky?[33]
B: No, they all went to other schools. I didn't know them. Only later . . .
D: No one? Not Ilf and Petrov, not . . .[34]
B: No one, no one. I wasn't in Odessa for very long. I did begin studying at the university there, but then soon after transferred.
D: So, you only finished the last grade, the seventh, at the gymnasium there? Seventh or eighth?
B: Both seventh and eighth.
D: Is eighth grade the equivalent of our tenth now?
B: Yes, it is. There was also the so-called preparatory class. But, like many others, I didn't do that. Usually one prepared at home, and then took the exams during the first year at the gymnasium.
D: And you started attending the university there?
B: Yes, I did.
D: Did they have a history and philology department there?
B: Of course. The Odessa University[35] was then called Novorossiisky after the region. I must say there were some really good, notable professors there, with whom I studied. For example, I remember the amazing linguist Tomson.[36] He was a remarkable linguist, simply remarkable. We used his wonderful textbook to prepare for exams; it is impossible to find it now, I've tried. It's a university textbook, *An Introduction to Language*

Studies, very good. There was also another professor there, very interesting, but somewhat difficult as a person—Lange.

Well, there is a famous German scholar by that name, the author of *A History of Materialism*, etc. I think . . . What was his full name? . . . My professor's name was Nikolay Nikolayevich Lange.[37] He was a student of Wundt's.[38] He had begun his work in his psychology lab. Yes. He had a book, what was it called? *Psychology Issues*, or *Psychology Studies*, I don't exactly recall. It presented some very interesting studies, in psychology. Specifically, he worked on drug addiction, and he even took opiates himself—he had begun doing that already in Germany, while studying with Wundt—opium or hashish, I forget. And as a psychologist, a scientist, he studied his own reactions: how the drugs' influence began, intensified, and spread, etc. Very interesting studies, especially considering that there were very few similar ones in Russia, in fact, there weren't any, nobody worked on that. At home it was mostly literary scholars, who knew about this subject because of Baudelaire's famous book *Les Paradis artificiels*, that is, *Artificial Paradises*. By artificial paradise he meant . . .

D: Getting high . . .

B: The hallucinatory experience, yes. Mostly, he meant hashish. That is a very interesting book, like anything else by Baudelaire. We should note he gives an extensive description there of a book by De Quincey,[39] which we didn't know about, it wasn't ever published in Russia.

D: De Quincey?

B: Yes, De Quincey, a famous classical author, an important figure in the field of classical studies, an Englishman. He was a drug addict, from his early youth to his death. Still, he died very old, despite everything. Toward the end he was able to take such enormous opium doses his doctors, all scientists, couldn't believe it. But it was possible. He slowly increased his intake to such monstrous amounts, and yet he was always fine.

D: And did he enjoy it?

B: Yes, very much so. He described his dreams, his visions. And because he was such an amazing classicist, with a gift for poetic expression, all these visions of his are rendered very poetically, which drew Charles Baudelaire's attention to his work. That's how he ends up giving us De Quincey's biography. De Quincey's book was famous in Europe. It was written in English but translated into French and published in full in several issues of *Revue des Deux Mondes*.[40]

D: *Revue des Deux Mondes?*

B: That's a famous nineteenth-century French journal.
D: It was still published in the twentieth, I believe.
B: Yes, it was. But the *Confessions of an English Opium-Eater User* was published, of course, already in the nineteenth century. I read the whole text in *Revue des Deux Mondes.* Nobody at home explored this issue, few were even interested. And then Nikolai Lange exposed us, let's say, to this scientific psychological method of studying the condition of a person, taking opium or hashish, which of the two I can't recall . . .
D: Well, anyway, we got somewhat side-tracked . . . So the Classical Studies branch of the historical-philological department at the Novorossiisky University in Odessa was very highly regarded, yes?
B: Yes, very highly. Another professor there, Mochulsky,[41] was a rather dull man, he did not leave any lasting impression on me. He was very respectable, though. . . .
D: And you didn't study Russian literature there? Or did you?
B: Of course, I did!
D: In the classics department?
B: Yes, it was all the same, all the same.
D: And Western European literature, too? Were there any general courses?
B: Yes, of course. There were general subjects. Specialization started much later. All in all, at first we studied together, regardless of the specific major.
D: Did the degree take five years?
B: Four, it took four years.
D: And did you already have any knowledge of the ancient languages?
B: Yes, I did.
D: From the gymnasium?
B: Yes, from the gymnasium. Latin was compulsory. I should tell you that was a fabulous course. That Latin class was just marvelous. Ancient Greek was offered as an elective, for those who wanted to take it. I took ancient Greek.
D: So upon entering the university you already knew Latin, ancient Greek, and, of course, French . . .
B: French, naturally. I knew it since childhood. Also German. Since my brother was a little older, we had a German governess. It was a bit early for me, I hadn't learned how to speak Russian properly yet . . . so German was almost my first language. Almost. I even thought in German, and spoke in German for many . . .
D: You learned French later then?

B: Yes, a bit later.
D: No English?
B: No English.
D: At the time it wasn't . . .
B: English was not offered then, not even as an elective. You could study it at the university. You could study any language at the university. There was always someone to teach you. For example, my brother began learning (but dropped it later) Dutch as an elective. There was a Madam Lassen at Petersburg University, she was teaching the language as an elective.
D: When did you study at Odessa University, what years? Was it already during the war?
B: No, before. I was already in Leningrad during the war.
D: In Petersburg.
B: Yes.
D: Sorry, but something doesn't add up here. So you entered Odessa University . . .
B: Maybe I'm mixing things up in my old age, it's possible . . .
D: The war began in July 1914. Even if you spent your freshman year there during the '13/14 academic year, before the war, in Odessa, or even if you moved up directly to second year courses, according to what you told me before . . .
B: Second year, yes, second year.
D: So you were there only one year . . .
B: Only a year.
D: . . . in Odessa. So the courses with Lange, etc.—you were then a freshman?
B: Yes. I finished the gymnasium there and spent only one year at the university.
D: So, then, '14/15, '15/16, and '16/17 were your second, third, and fourth year at Petersburg University?
B: Yes. The University of Petersburg . . .
D: Or maybe it was already Petrograd . . .
B: Yes. I don't remember the exact dates. We have my brother's memoirs, published in English. . . . There are details from our childhood there. . . .
D: That's fine. But what interests us more is what's not there.
B: There are reminiscences about our governess, the German, whom I, for one, simply adored. . . . I called her only "Liebchen" and loved sitting in on her lessons. She was wonderful.

D: So, both your upbringing and education were of very high quality.
B: Yes, very high quality. But I should say that despite the fact that I can't complain about the gymnasium and the university, I learned mostly by myself, independently. That's always the case. Because institutions of formal learning could never give you the education you desire. If you were satisfied with what they offered, you'd end up becoming . . . an educational bureaucrat. Right . . . You'd only know the past, the previous history of knowledge, but as to its contemporary state, where true creativity actually takes place. . . . You had to familiarize yourself with what's going on by reading the latest studies, the newest books, on your own. For example, I told you about Nikolai Nikolayevich Lange. He was a wonderful professor, just wonderful, but once, I remember, I asked him—I had started reading philosophy books in the original, in German, very early—asked him about Hermann Cohen,[42] the founder of the Marburg School. . . . Anyhow . . . His first book, a very important one, *Kant's Theorie der Erfahrung*, that is, *Kant's Theory of Experience*. . . . I asked Lange if he thought it was a significant book, and he said, "It would seem so," that is, he hadn't read it. Besides, I was left with the impression he only knew of Hermann Cohen through hearsay.
D: I also know of him through hearsay—because of Pasternak.
B: Right, right . . . Andrey Bely also mentions him:

> The Marburg philosopher Cohen,
> Creator of dry methodologies . . . [43]

This, of course, is an absolutely unfair assessment: "creator of dry methodologies." He was an outstanding philosopher, who left an enormous impression on me, enormous. We'll talk about it later, when we get to it.
D: OK. All in all, [you've given us] a very interesting history of your initial formation as a scholar. Now we move to the next stage. . . . Who did you want to tell us about?
B: One could say that I started thinking independently and reading by myself serious philosophy books quite early. From the very start I found philosophy most fascinating. And literature, too. I read Dostoevsky when I was eleven or twelve. A little later, when I was twelve or thirteen, I began reading all the serious classical texts. I became familiar with Kant very

early and read his *Critique of Pure Reason* when I was very young. And it must be said I was able to understand everything, really understood it.

D: And did you read it in German?

B: Yes, in German. Didn't even try to read it in Russian. The only work of his I read in Russian was *Prolegomena*. It was translated by Vladimir Solovyov.[44] I read that. *Prolegomena* is a good book, quite interesting, but it's really just an abridged version of *Critique of Pure Reason*. I read also other German philosophers. Very early on. I read Søren Kierkegor[45] before he was known in Russia.

D: Excuse me, I don't know who you're talking about . . . Søren . . .

B: Kierkegor.

D: Kier-ke-gor? Was he German?

B: They write his name wrong here, in Russia: Kerkegaard. It should be "Kierkegor."

D: Was he Danish?

B: Yes, he was a Dane, a very important Dane.

D: And was he also a philosopher?

B: A philosopher and a theologian. Right. A philosopher. He was a student of Hegel's, he studied with the man himself . . . also with Schelling. Later he fought with Hegel, with Hegelianism. He was one of the early founders of existentialism, completely overlooked during his lifetime.

D: What years are we talking about? Is he . . . our contemporary?

B: He is a contemporary of Dostoevsky, they were born in the same year, but he died a bit earlier.[46] Of course Dostoevsky didn't know of his existence, but the similarities in their ideas are astounding, their themes—very similar, the depth—also. Now Søren Kierkegor is considered to be one of the greatest modern thinkers. He went completely unnoticed during his lifetime, though.

D: Was he translated into Russian?

B: He was a great scholar. . . . There were translations. Very few, and of poor quality. You know, in Odessa I met a very well-educated Swiss man, Hans Limbach. He vanished without a trace. . . . He was a fervent admirer of Kierkegor when nobody else had heard of him.

D: That was a real person whom you met?

B: Yes, a real person, an acquaintance of mine.

D: This Swiss man, is he the one who gave you the books then?

B: Yes, yes. He introduced me to Kierkegor. He even gave me as a present Kierkegor's first book, with the author's autograph: "Søren Kierkegor." Later I was able to acquire the collected works. . . . I didn't know Danish, but he was already translated into German in full. "Pieter Verlang," I think, or another very good German publishing house printed his whole oeuvre in ten volumes.[47] Now Kierkegor is considered a giant of modern thought . . .
D: In the West?
B: . . . He is studied . . . In the West, yes. Even at home we already have two published books about him. One of them is especially good, by . . . My memory is now so bad, especially about recent events. . . . I still remember things from the more distant past. . . . Yes . . . She's a philosopher, pretty young. She lives here. Quite famous, her work has been published in *Voprosy Literatury* [Questions of Literature] and *Voprosy Filosofii* [Questions of Philosophy].[48] All her articles are very objective, she doesn't go overboard, doesn't point fingers. Kierkegor was always accompanied by the epithet "retrograde," or something like that, before in Russia. He was a very religious man, as a matter of fact, half philosopher, half theologian. That's why when they wrote about him in Russia, they called him "that retrograde [*mrakobes*] Kierkegor," or, as they preferred, "Kierkegaard." Anyhow . . . But she evaluated him very objectively, with full understanding of his importance . . .

I have the other book, by Lurie, I think. See, my memory is awful! Impossible!
D: You have an amazing memory!
B: "Amazing"?! How can you say such a thing? When I was young my memory was truly phenomenal. I could remember anything I read just once, poetry or prose, it didn't matter. Now my memory is gone, really gone . . .
D: Yes . . . I also used to memorize poetry very easily.
B: I can't recite what I used to know by heart anymore—and I used to know a lot by heart, a lot! Prose, too. For example, I knew by heart a lot of Nietzsche, well, excerpts, of course, not whole works. In the original, of course, in German. I also went through a period of complete obsession with Nietzsche.
D: But that happened later, right?
B: Yes, later. Though not much later. No, actually, I discovered Nietzsche even earlier than Kierkegor.

D: You were born in 1895, so in 1915 you were twenty years old. You were still at Odessa University, but already well versed in philosophy and . . .
B: Yes, of course, I learned a lot about philosophy during that period. Kazansky[49] was one of the professors there. I attended his lectures.
D: There was a Kazansky associated with OPOJAZ[50] later.
B: Ah! Yes, of course. That was his son, my professor's son. In general, the sons of my Odessa professors ended up in Leningrad, with Lange's being the sole exception. Lange's sons, I think, were not very successful, loafers, as they say. But Kazansky's son studied . . . [51]
D: There was a Kazansky even in the LEF[52] issue about Lenin's language. Kazansky.
B: Yes, there was Kazansky there, Boris Kazansky, the son of my professor. Professor Kazansky was a highly regarded man. He translated all of Aristotle from the ancient Greek.
D: Into Russian?
B: Yes. That, of course, was a formidable task. Translating Aristotle is very hard. I think even harder than the poet Plato. Aristotle's terminology is very difficult to translate. But he did an amazing job. However, as an original philosopher himself. . . . Actually, he wasn't an original philosopher at all, and that made his course "Introduction to Philosophy," the first philosophy course one had to take at the university, of rather poor quality.
D: And what is your opinion of . . . I'm asking for a retroactive assessment . . . of Oswald Külpe's *Introduction to Philosophy*.[53]
B: Külpe, Külpe . . . He was German.
D: Aha, German! And I thought he was French!
B: Külpe, you ask? He's pretty mediocre.
D: I had to use his book as a student.
B: I see. Külpe is not an important figure.
D: And what do you think of Sergey Trubetskoy's *A History of Ancient Philosophy*?[54]
B: It's a bit more interesting, but I wouldn't call it a classic. I'd recommend the following (remember I'm partial to the Marburg school).[55] Natorp's *Philosophical propaedeutic*. Paul Natorp was a student of Hermann Cohen's, who also belonged to the Marburg circle. He was one of the purest, most consistent practitioners of the Marburg school of thought. Anyways, he wrote this book, *Philosophical propaedeutic*, which, by the way, was translated into Russian.

D: So, Mikhail Mikhailovich, was the heyday of the Marburg school at the end of the 1890s through the early 1900s?
B: Yes, correct. But the first publications had already appeared in the 1880s. They were by Hermann Cohen. Then came his whole philosophical system in three volumes; the first was called *Logik der reinen Erkenntnis*, that is, *The Logic of Pure Knowledge*. Next followed *Logik des reinen Willens*, that is, *The Logic of Pure Will*. That's his ethics. And finally, the third book: *Logik des reinen Gefühls*, or *The Logic of Pure Feeling*, that's his aesthetics.[56] Well, as you know, that's the Kantian tradition. Only in Kant we have *Critique of Pure Reason*, and here it is *Critique of Pure Knowledge*, and then, let's say, his ethics is called a *Critique*. . . . Excuse me, Kant's title is *Critique of Practical Reason*, and he calls his aesthetics *Critique of Judgment*. Those are the three major branches of Kant's philosophical system. And, following him closely, Hermann Cohen considered his own philosophical system to be a further continuation of Kant's ideas, firmly grounded in Kantian foundations. He never veered away from the heart of Kant's teachings, just developed them further.
D: Now, Mikhail Mikhailovich, you mentioned when we were first talking about Odessa, that there was some kind of linguistic or literary circle there. . . . I thought it was OPOJAZ but you said, "No, Om . . ."
B: "Omphalos."
D: That was in Odessa?
B: No, no, that was already in Leningrad.
D: Petersburg.
B: Petersburg, yes.
D: OK, then, I won't rush you. I thought you simply forgot about that.
B: Later it became famous, in Odessa there was even a publishing house—now all forgotten—called "Omphalos."
D: "Omphalos"?
B: "Omphalos," from the Greek, meaning "navel," "belly button." "Navel." "Omphalos." I can try to recall more about it, and then tell you everything I remember.
D: Sure, when we get there. I thought that was in Odessa and you just forgot to mention it.
B: No, no, this wasn't in Odessa. . . . When I was still in Odessa, it . . . I don't remember exactly . . . It began in 1912–13 . . . We formed a club of sorts. . . . The club mostly consisted of young people, either finishing

up their studies at the university, or in their last year studying there. Right . . .

D: But wasn't that already at Petersburg University?

B: Petersburg, correct. You didn't have to pay membership fees to participate in "Omphalos." It was just a group of friends getting freely together. Two of its members were the brothers Radlov, Sergey Radlov and Nikolay Radlov.[57] They were especially active in the club.

D: Yes, that's already in Petersburg, so—a different topic. What else can you say about Odessa? You told us so much of interest, gave us a lot of background. Could you go back to that time once more, and try to paint a somewhat broader picture? You described your own progress very well, and your philosophical . . . In general, this fascination with the Marburg school, with philosophy, how widespread was it?

B: It wasn't very widespread at all. It was never widespread. Just a narrow circle of people.

D: Who were some of the people close to you?

B: One of them was a man I met much later, but who became a close friend. He had studied in Germany, with Hermann Cohen himself. He went to the grave a long time ago, but his daughter still visits me.

D: Who's that?

B: Matvei Isayevich Kagan.[58]

D: So you didn't know him in Odessa?

B: No, no, we got acquainted much later.

D: I was asking you about the people who shared your interests in Odessa. . . . Who else was there?

B: No one, just my brother, who was there with me, he started his university education in Odessa too.

D: So you were not even a classics scholar yet?

B: No, I was already a . . . I'd say I was a philosopher.

D: You were more of a philosopher than a philologist?

B: Yes, a philosopher rather than a philologist. A philosopher. And that's who I am to this day. I am a philosopher. A thinker. In Petrograd, that is, Petersburg, there was no philosophy department. The thinking behind it was the following: "why bother," they said, "what is philosophy anyways?" Neither here nor there. Best to become a specialist in something. So there was a philosophy department, but not an independent one. If you wanted to get a philosophy degree, fine, but you also had to specialize in Russian or German studies . . .

FIG. 1.8. Matvey Kagan, 1927. (Courtesy of the Scientific Library at Moscow State University)

D: Was that under the umbrella of the historical-philological department?

B: Yes, the historical-philological department, or within the classics department. I, for instance, decided to go the classics route. . . . You had to choose two areas of study; you weren't allowed to focus solely on philosophy.

D: You couldn't graduate with a degree in philosophy only.

B: You couldn't.

D: That's as it should be.

B: I think so. After all, what does it mean to be a philosopher, at the end of the day? Philosophers . . . Most often, they are divided into humanists and naturalists, because some of them specialize in the natural sciences—physics, math, and also philosophy, while others choose to focus on humanist studies. There was another member of the Marburg school, Ernst Cassirer . . . [59] You have probably heard of him?

D: No, I don't know him.

B: He was another remarkable Marburg philosopher. His work is still very highly regarded, and at home his *Die Philosophie der symbolischen Formen, Philosophy of Symbolic Forms*, in three volumes, is widely appreciated and read. The first volume is called *Language*, the second—*Myth*, the third—*Cognition*. . . . That's Cassirer.

D: How about your literary interests during the Odessa period? Were you only concerned with the classics or . . .

B: No, not only with the classics. I was very passionate about contemporary poetry: the Symbolists, the so-called decadents, Russian, French, German. One of my friends in Odessa—he was actually more than just a friend, a second or third cousin—he was also a student at the Odessa University with me, and had an amazing [library], filled with almost everything that had come out by French poets. I was able to use his library, and thus knew the French Symbolists, decadents, very well . . . starting with Baudelaire . . .

D: Baudelaire was translated into Russian only in 1911 . . .

B: No, there were translations of him before that. Valery Bryusov[60] was great in that respect, we should say. Very early on he began to . . .

D: He was already publishing some of his translations in the *Symbolists* poetry anthologies.

B: Yes. The anthology *The Cursed Poets, Les Poètes maudits* also came out at the same time.

D: *Poètes maudits*, that's Yakubovich's work,[61] I think.

B: No, Bryusov was the first to translate those poets. Yakubovich was not interested in them.

D: But he did bring the work out . . .

B: Yes. Under the trendy title *Poètes maudits.*

D: Yes, I am familiar with it. Who were your favorites?

B: Of the poets?

D: Yes.

B: Contemporary?

D: Yes.

B: As for the old ones . . . Of course, I loved Pushkin, who doesn't! I also loved Tyutchev,[62] Baratynsky,[63] Fet.[64] I liked the others less. I didn't like Lermontov[65] too much. Of the French poets, I was especially partial to the first, the founder of Symbolism and decadence, Charles Baudelaire.[66] I knew him, honestly, backward and forward. I knew a lot of his poetry by heart, in the original French, of course. Charles Baudelaire . . . I also thought very highly of José Heredia . . . [67]

D: Heredia, I've heard of him.

B: Yes, Heredia. He had published just one small book, *Trophées*. But despite that, he was chosen . . .

D: *Trophées*?

B: *Trophées*, that is, *Trophies*. A Greek word. It's the same in French, *Trophées*. So José Heredia, even though he had only this one little anthology, was considered very . . .

D: Didn't Éluard[68] also start publishing around that time?

B: No, he came a bit later. Éluard . . . He was and remains, in my opinion, a second-rate poet. He became famous at the time only because of his association with surrealism, and so forth. But when he moved away from surrealism it turned out he was in fact quite empty inside. A hollow man. He even took his old love poems, quite good, honest verses dedicated to his beloved, and later reworked them so they turned out to be about the Revolution. Instead of "beloved" he wrote "Revolution." He swore his love and loyalty to the Revolution. That was, to be sure, contemptible.

D: Contemptible is right.

B: No, he was . . . he became a fool.

D: And what about the Russian Symbolists?

B: What about them?

D: Who did you like?

B: I had a favorite poet among them, who remains my favorite poet in general, Vyacheslav Ivanov. Vyacheslav Ivanov,[69] yes. I also liked Annensky, Innokenty Fyodorovich Annensky, a lot.[70] He, as you know, was not just a remarkable poet, but also . . .

D: . . . a classicist. He translated Euripides.

B: Yes, he did.

D: . . . which was the reason why Zelinsky[71] pounced on him . . .

B: Yes, yes . . . But Zelinsky also edited Euripides's texts. The last volume of Euripides's works was edited by him. To a great extent . . .

D: I have it, I know.
B: Zelinsky was my most favorite teacher, by the way.
D: You studied with him? Personally?
B: I studied directly under him.
D: How about Mikhail Pokrovsky,[72] the classicist, did you know him?
B: Yes, I did.
D: I studied with him.
B: I didn't have the chance because he was in Moscow.[73] All the classicists: Pokrovsky, then Sobolevsky,[74] who died not too long ago, he was almost ninety-five . . . Radtsig . . . [75]
D: Radtsig passed away not too long ago too. But he was quite boring.
B: Boring, yes.
D: He had the mentality of a gymnasist.
B: Pretty coarse . . . What was his way of teaching ancient literature?! It was all so banal, nothing more than a sentimental retelling of the text, the *Iliad*, for example. What you'd expect from a sentimental gymnasist in his last year of studies at the gymnasium.
D: He taught at the university to the end, he was already eighty . . .
B: I know . . .
D: He kept lecturing. He was quite endearing with his devotion, we might say, to university teaching. But the students . . . Freshmen paid attention to him, but later . . .
B: Then they realized that's not scholarship . . .
D: Just fairytales . . .
B: Fairytales, yes . . . That's all he did: told fairytales, and bad fairytales at that.
D: Yes. And then, I'm not a classicist but even I got upset when he talked to me about translations of the classics. . . . I don't know, maybe he was right. . . . It was during the war, we were waiting in line to get some potatoes, something like that. . . . So he began reciting his own translations, which to my ear sounded awful, very bad Russian poetry, and kept comparing them with others: "Bryusov did it like that, so terrible . . ." He especially hated Veresaev's translations.[76]
B: Well, in Veresaev's case he was mostly right, yes.
D: Both Bryusov and Veresaev . . .
B: Concerning Bryusov he wasn't completely justified, no, not completely.
D: His distortion of others was one thing—that didn't matter to me. But his word-for-word translations . . . He had no talent.

B: He was crude, crude not in the sense of how he lived, of course (he was a decent person, as far as day-to-day existence is concerned), but in the way he understood antiquity, how he evaluated poetic translations.
D: I knew Mikhail Pokrovsky myself, I studied with him, though I was so poorly prepared for it that . . . I even wrote an essay for him about the role of the chorus in Euripides's dramas (not Aeschylus, Euripides), how its role becomes less and less important and all but disappears. He gave me a passing grade, but I myself felt it wasn't really my calling. I visited him at home several times. You can imagine what the proletarian university students in 1927 thought of a professor of Antiquity!
B: Yes, of course . . .
D: I went to him just to be different, to show my dissent—because nobody else visited him. There were only three or four of us. For the same reason, I attended Mikhail Pokrovsky's lectures, which were, I understood that later, absolutely brilliant and deep.
B: Petrovsky was a true scholar.
D: A scholar who perished. His brother, Fyodor Petrovsky,[77] also a scholar of Antiquity, is still alive.
B: A wonderful collection of essays in his honor recently came out.[78] A marvelous compilation, very interesting. . . . There was also Losev,[79] but you likely didn't study with him.
D: You're right, I didn't.
B: You should interview him as well; it'd be good to record his memories. He was a very serious classicist.
D: Is he still alive?
B: He is, but completely blind. Blind. Yet despite everything he keeps working.
D: Mikhail Mikhailovich, I try not to interrupt you too much, but my questions, the things I'm asking about in passing, they have a certain . . . [*laughs*]
B: Trajectory . . .
D: Yes, a certain trajectory. You described beautifully your micro-environment, but you also inhabited a macro-environment. . . . For instance, Odessa itself . . . You also didn't discuss Vilno from that perspective . . . As for Odessa . . . Why did you . . . Were you ever in the army?
B: Never.
D: Why?

B: Because of an illness I got as a child, an illness that essentially has been with me to this day. So-called osteomyelitis.
D: Oh, yes, I know about that. Is that why you lost your leg?
B: Ultimately, yes. But not when I was a child. . . . Back then there were many surgeries . . .
D: It affects the bones, this illness.
B: Yes, the bone marrow. Not the bone itself, but the marrow inside. It's an inflammation of the bone marrow. The treatment methods include—even now—surgery, drilling into the bone in order to drain the pus.
D: That's not the same as tuberculosis?
B: No, not at all. Tuberculosis is worse, I think. Osteomyelitis is an acute illness. An acute illness that often comes back later. I got sick when I was nine or ten years old, I believe. It was a very difficult surgery. They cut into my leg all the way through, drilled into my thigh and knee. I was sick for a long time, but still, I started walking again pretty soon after.
D: You could still walk after that?
B: After? Of course!
D: Was your leg amputated much later?
B: Yes, many years later, actually, not too long ago, comparatively speaking.
D: How is that possible? I remember seeing you without one leg already before the war.
B: Before the war, yes. It was amputated two years before the war. Just before.[80]
D: Because of the osteomyelitis?
B: Yes. It came back a few times during that very long period, so I had more surgeries.
D: And the other leg is not affected?
B: It's fine, the osteomyelitis didn't go there.
D: And you can still bend it?
B: I can, but I am no longer able to control it very well because of how long I had to rely upon just that one leg. I could walk very well, with crutches, as well as if on my own two legs—I could run, jump, climb up and down, everything I wanted—but the whole weight fell on that one leg, the healthy one and . . . After a while it stopped serving me at all . . . The cartilages in the hip joint wore out and tore. Cartilages can't be repaired, as you know.

D: So that's what happened, they just wore off?
B: Yes, completely.
D: So walking is very hard for you now.
B: They amortized with time, so to speak . . .
D: Right . . . But back when you were living in Odessa: at that time, you still had both your legs, and were completely mobile?
B: Completely mobile, yes.
D: I am very, very satisfied with the way you described the process of your development as a scholar, but there's more. . . . Besides everything else, you also must have taken advantage of just living in Odessa. There was theater in Odessa, there was literature, the Odessa writers. [*laughs*] You know what I mean? Tell us a little about the pre-war Odessa, the early war years . . .
B: Yes, the pre-war, pre-revolutionary Odessa. All in all, Odessa is a beautiful city. Just beautiful. Very sunny, very happy-go-lucky. It was probably one of the happiest cities in our Union, in Russia. A very joyful city. There was so much laughter . . . always so much merrymaking. I have always been impressed by Moscow, and, especially, of course, by Petersburg. Petersburg was a gloomy city compared to Odessa, though I always loved it more than Odessa. There you have it. Odessa was a happy, sunny place. The locals were very lively but had one unpleasant characteristic—they were quite vulgar.[81]
D: Vulgar?
B: Vulgar. "Mother Odessa," they used to say. "Mother Odessa." There was a lot of vulgarity in that "Mother Odessa." And I think you can sense that vulgarity in the work of all the famous Odessa writers. I didn't know any of them at the time, [though] they were about my age, some a bit older, some a bit younger . . .
D: Most of them younger.
B: Yes . . .

Interview Two

March 1, 1973

Length of the interview: 167 minutes

DUVAKIN: Well, Mikhail Mikhailovich, we ended our conversation last Thursday talking about Odessa. We had to stop there. You were talking about the vulgarity of the locals. Would you like to finish with that, perhaps? The people of Odessa are not all unrefined, right? After all, there are some decent people among them . . .
BAKHTIN: Yes, of course, there are.
D: There's the Odessa Theater . . . [1]
B: I think we talked about that last time. The Odessa Theater was wonderful. Back then they always seemed to host visiting troupes, from our leading theaters, and also from various European countries. Always. In that respect the people of Odessa knew Western European art as well as the northerners, or perhaps even better!
D: Better than the citizens of Moscow and Petersburg. Were you able to hear any of the important singers who came to Odessa?
B: Of course I did, of course I did. It's just that I can't remember right now if I saw them perform there, in Odessa, or somewhere else, later. Let's see, I heard Chaliapin there.[2] But the first time I listened to him was before Odessa. In Vilnius. He came there.

D: Let's move to the next period in your life then: Petersburg.
B: OK. Maybe I can start by telling you about the movement, the circle formed in Petersburg back in 1911–12.
D: Was it already there when you arrived?
B: Yes, it was in full swing. I had already visited them before I moved to Petersburg. . . . Once I relocated there, I joined their circle. Its leader was my brother, Nikolay Mikhailovich Bakhtin. The circle, by the way, didn't have a rigid organization. There was no formal membership. It was a group of friends, similar to Pushkin's circle: they were people connected through common interests and the university, which they all either attended then or used to attend in the past; they were all close friends. The circle was called "Omphalos."
D: What does that mean?
B: It means "belly button," "omphalos."
D: From the Greek?
B: Yes, Greek. I should mention that most participants in the circle were classicists. Yes, classicists. There were also a few Romano-Germanists. Now, let's see, who was there? As I said, my brother Nikolay was the leader. Then . . . Lev Pumpyansky, who had known me and my brother since our days at the gymnasium. Another member was . . . Lopatto,[3] but I forgot his first name and patronymic. He was then a linguist and had just finished his studies at the philology department. He studied linguistics, and later joined OPOYAZ, though he didn't play a major role there, and his name is usually not even mentioned in connection with it. Lopatto was also a poet, but, we should note, not an important one. In 1914, or maybe it was a little later, in 1915, he published a collection of poems. I must say it was not very good. He was not a serious poet.

Let me turn next to what our circle was about, what set us apart. Lopatto was a poet, but also a literary scholar. He published several articles inspired by the early ideas of OPOYAZ. Then following the October Revolution . . . he stayed for the first few years, but then left. He was very rich, let me tell you. His father, right before the Revolution, had bought the famous "London" Hotel in Odessa. He was very wealthy, a millionaire, even multimillionaire.
D: Lopatto was raking it in.[4]
B: Raking it, very true. Yes, yes. [*he chuckles*] In addition, he also married (in 1916, or . . . that's correct, 1916) a very rich woman, with a huge dowry, so that added to his immense wealth too. This is why, as far as I know, he

is still alive and well to this day in Italy. He had a house, a proper palazzo in Florence, bought before the Revolution.
D: What is interesting about him as far as cultural contributions go?
B: He was interesting for this reason: because he had extremely broad interests and was very social, which helped unite the people around him. Well, it helped in the sense that he always had money, while most of us were pretty poor.

Other participants in the circle included the brothers Radlov, Sergey, and Nikolay. Sergey is the future film director, but at the time he was just a linguist, and nobody would have guessed he'd become a director later. He was a young scholar-linguist. His brother, Nikolay, was an artist. Not a bad one at that, and a master caricaturist. But that wasn't the main thing for him. There were also many other members of the circle, whose names I might be able to remember later, but my memory is not what it used to be. Not at all.

So what was the circle about? They were learned jesters, pranksters, or clowns of scholarship, if you will. But we know from history that this is a pretty typical phenomenon. For example, in Poland, there was the so-called "szubrawiec" circle. . . . They, too, were highly educated scholars who got together to write humorous texts, mainly parodies, etc.
D: When was that?
B: The "szubrawiec krzyżówka"[5] existed at the beginning of the nineteenth century. We should note that our baron Brambeus-Senkovsky came from that circle.[6] He belonged to that group back in Poland, before he moved to Russia for good. There were similar societies in other countries, say, in England. There they also had a circle of people who specialized, so to speak, in mockery and satire, not of the vulgar kind but scholarly, almost philosophical. That's where Swift came from, to a large extent. He also belonged to a similar society—already in the eighteenth century so a century earlier. Yes. We should note that although Swift later became, well, extremely serious, a tragic figure even, in his youth he had learned to laugh from his friends in that circle. Later, when he served as a minister of the Irish church, and became an Irish national hero, laughter, of course, survived only in his literature, in a number of pamphlets he wrote then. You're probably familiar with those pamphlets, "A Modest Proposal" being the most famous one.[7]
D: No, I don't know it.
B: It's one of the best pamphlets of the times. The gist of it is that it is presented as written by a completely serious supporter of the (then popular) liberal political economy. He discusses pauperism, talks about

how there are too many children without parents, how too many people just throw out their kids. That's economically unsustainable, unreasonable. Why not put those children to good use? The "modest" proposal is to fatten them up, then slaughter them: their meat, skin, etc., would come in handy. He offers serious calculations: how much a pound of meat would bring, what the skin would be used for, how to use everything properly, what great profit could be derived from it all. Also, how to brine the meat, and so on. And once again he is very specific: how much would the salt cost. . . . A completely serious economic proposal. And, imagine this, when he published it, people took it literally. [*he chuckles*] That's what he wanted, actually, because he wanted to show how this kind of economy, this kind of economic organization advocated by proponents of the Manchester School, would logically lead to cannibalism. Profiteering. Everybody should only be concerned with his own profit, nothing else. Best not think about anything else. Then all will be well. That's it. This pamphlet, by the way, is a stylization, a parody of a serious economic tract, so it's the work of a scholar, someone who knows philosophy very well, in a word, it's satire of a particular type.

D: So the Poles continued this tradition?

B: Yes, but you could also say that they didn't continue this particular tradition, since there was something similar everywhere. They had something like that in France, too, even earlier, in the seventeenth century, the so-called poets-libertines.[8]

D: And your circle, the "Omphalos," was similar in kind?

B: Yes, the same kind.

D: And it was led by the Lopatto you were talking about?

B: No, my brother was the leader.

D: Did Lopatto help organize it?

B: Yes, he did. Actually, it's not that he organized much, he simply financed some of the circle's activities.

D: So, what can you tell us about this club?

B: "Omphalos," which, by the way, we could also compare to Pushkin's Arzamas Society,[9] they were very similar . . .

D: Right. . . . Could we see this "Omphalos" as a precursor to, a sort of an early version of OPOYAZ?

B: No, no. Time-wise, they were almost parallel to each other. Maybe "Omphalos" was a little earlier. . . . But no, no, OPOYAZ was very different. Very different. OPOYAZ didn't have what "Omphalos" had: a deep, critical, but not gloomily critical, rather, cheerfully critical attitude to all aspects of life and contemporary culture. Everybody had his own area of specialization, where his strengths lay. What did the members of this circle do? They wrote parodies of various genres in different styles. They also held mock conferences. We should note that they didn't satirize any particular poets or scholars. No, theirs was a broader parody, in the spirit of, let's say, the Middle Ages: a parody of the most serious and gloomy approaches to life. These poets didn't like seriousness, especially excessive seriousness, and strove to mitigate it with irony and humor. . . . Therefore, these were not parodies or stylizations of particular phenomena in life, of literature or science, no, everything was treated not with stern ridicule but with a sort of light, ironic humor. A good, even a programmatic example of this is my brother's poem, "Omphalos epiphales"—the literal translation from the Greek would be "Omphalos manifested, revealed." As you know, the term is used also in Christianity.

D: In theology.

B: Yes, early theology. "Revelation," "God's revelation"—epiphany, God's epiphany. So, there. "Omphalos epiphales." Here it's as if "omphalos" is compared to . . .

D: The revelation of the belly button.

B: Yes, the revelation of the belly button. It was a very long poem. The action took place in ancient Rome, actually, during the period of its decline. I forgot to mention all those works were written and copied on a typewriter. The editions they put together were all typewritten. Maybe some of them still exist somewhere, perhaps someone still has them. Maybe they are in Lopatto's archives.

D: So nothing was actually published?

B: No, nothing was officially published. Here is the beginning, the introduction to the poem "Omphalos epiphales":

> I came to you—a prophet of the cult
> Of the mysterious and sacred omphalós,
> Who by the stealthy panther was beloved,
> And witnessed all the orgies of Lesbós.
> The women of two hundred and eight tribes
> Caressed me deftly and forever, as it were.
> I knew the vibrant, frenzied dreams of their minds,
> The hazy languor, and the rapture's blur . . .
> Etc.[10]

D: There seems to be a nod toward Bryusov here.
B: Yes, partially . . . and in general toward all the usual prophetic undercurrents of Symbolism . . .
D: As far as the parody goes, it reminds me a little of the famous parodies of Vladimir Solovyov.[11]
B: Yes, somewhat. He loved that sort of thing, Vladimir Solovyov did, that's true. I must say the circle worshipped Vladimir Solovyov. Later on, right before the Revolution, the "Vladimir Solovyov Society" was created. I think there was only one meeting, then the Revolution happened and everything fell apart. But that society was supposed to be quite serious.
D: So, when you joined that circle, did you . . .
B: I didn't write anything. Just attended meetings. Also, when the circle was first formed, I was still in Odessa.
D: Understood. Did you transfer to Petersburg University?
B: Yes, Petersburg University.
D: Give us an idea about the historical-philological department there in 1916, would you? [You were there in] 1915, '16, and '17, right?
B: . . . including 1917, yes. Well, what can I say? I think it was the heyday of the department, really. There were some very original, very powerful scholars working there. There were no stuffy professors there, no bureaucrats, in my department. The biggest stars whom I knew, and took classes from there included . . . Faddey Zelinsky.[12] . . . He was a remarkable scholar of antiquity, translator of ancient works, etc. He exerted great influence on all classicists back then. Besides that, we had Nikolay Lossky[13] in philosophy. In general, the philosophy department was very interesting and lively, the kind of department that can't exist now in Russia. It was chaired by Alexander Vvedensky.[14] He was the author of *Logic as Part of the Theory of Knowledge* (1912), you probably know it. It's really a wonderful work. He has many more books, articles, and the like. He was a strict follower of Kant, not a neo-Kantian, but a representative of pure Kantianism. So that was the department chair. . . . One of the associate professors, who later became a full professor there, was Nikolay Onufrievich Lossky. He was the brightest, most animated figure in the department. He held completely different views. He was a strict follower of Kant, in fact, I'd not even call him a neo-Kantian. He was an intuitionist. His main work was *The Intuitive Basis of Knowledge* (1906). As a result, naturally, those two philosophers saw each other as complete

opposites, enemies even: the chair of the department, and one of its leading scholars, Lossky.

D: Have you read his latest, posthumous, book, which was published abroad: *Dostoevsky and Christianity* [*Dostoevsky and His Christian Understanding of the World*] (1944)?

B: No, unfortunately I haven't.

D: I'm reading it now.

B: I read his autobiography. It's very interesting, very interesting indeed. His reminiscences. He starts with his childhood and finishes almost on his deathbed, so to speak. He lived to be ninety-five, by the way. And worked practically to the end.

D: Did you have a negative opinion of Semyon Vengérov?[15]

B: No, not at all, I had a lot of respect for him, a lot of respect. But he was. . . . He didn't have his own ideas, he was not so well-versed in philosophy. He was a remarkable documentarist. I didn't participate in his famous circle, the one dedicated to Pushkin. . . . [*Addresses the cat*] Here you are again, aren't you? [*To Duvakin*] Is it in the way?

D: Please, continue . . .

B: So yes . . . the third member of the department I wanted to talk about—that's Ivan Lapshin.[16] As a logical intuitionist, he was against Kantianism and any rationalism. He was a proponent of English positivism. In general, he was an anglicized man, an anglicized thinker.

Thus, we had three very different directions there, which coexisted perfectly. The department was very close-knit. Really close-knit. There were arguments, but that only made the work at the department more interesting, nothing else. It seems to me the philosophy department there was stronger, and deeper, livelier, than the one in Moscow, where you had Chelpanov, Lopatin, and so on.

D: Well, Chelpanov was not really a philosopher but a psychologist.

B: Chelpanov? He wrote an enormous book, *Introduction to Philosophy*, which was required reading at Moscow University. He also had many other purely philosophical studies. His dissertation, though, yes, it was purely psychological.

D: I had to use his psychology textbook, not his philosophy one, as a student during those Soviet years.

B: Yes, he did have a psychology textbook. His dissertation was devoted to the subject of visual perception . . .

D: What about the classicists? Who was there?

B: The classicists, I told you already—Zelinsky . . . there were also others. Who was I especially close to? Stefan Srebrny.[17] He was Polish. He was also a student of Zelinsky, and focused on comedy, mainly ancient comedy, and middle ancient comedy. Well, of course he also touched upon the comedy of late antiquity, Greek comedy.

D: How about the Department of Russian and European literatures?

B: I was not very interested in it. I don't think there were any strong people there.

D: What other departments were there? You were talking about the historical-philological department, right?

B: Yes, historical-philological. As for history . . . There were some historians who worked there, of course. Can't even remember who right now . . . I went to some of their lectures. Once I heard the famous Pavel Vinogradov[18] give a lecture. He came from London to do that. You see, he had moved to England, to an English university. Such a remarkable historian!

D: So you missed Klyuchevsky . . . [19]

B: Yes, he was already gone.

D: Was there a linguistics department?

B: Linguistics? Of course! The main figure there was Baudouin de Courtenay.[20] He was an impressive scholar. But as a teacher he was . . . how shall I put it. . . . He wasn't a pedagogue. He got carried away when he lectured. During exams, for instance, they played him: people said you could get a passing grade from him even if you didn't know anything. On a bet some physicists and mathematicians tried to pass an exam with him [*laughs*]—and succeeded. All you had to do was start your answer with a question to him. He got excited, and kept on talking about that question, which he found fascinating, forever. He went on and on, then eventually remembered he had to stop, muttered "Excellent, excellent," and gave you an excellent grade. [*he chuckles*] He gave himself an A, so to speak. Baudouin de Courtenay was in fact the founder of . . .

D: OPOYAZ?

B: Formalism in general. Not OPOYAZ, but formalism as such.

D: Well, Shklovsky[21] was a direct disciple of his.

B: He was, as was almost everyone who studied at Petersburg University then. He was the chair of the Department of Linguistics. There were,

actually, two founders, who established two types of linguistic formalism: Fortunatov[22] in Moscow . . . you probably know him . . .
D: I was his student . . .
B: That was one kind of formalism. The other type, which informed the work of OPOYAZ, that was . . .
D: Baudouin de Courtenay.
B: . . . Baudouin de Courtenay. He was closer to the father of formalism in general linguistics: de Saussure. Saussure.[23] He represented formalism in its purest form, so to speak. . . .
D: Where did Saussure teach?
B: In Switzerland, French Switzerland, then moved to Paris, I believe.
D: Did Baudouin de Courtenay study with him?
B: No, as far as I know he didn't, but he was familiar with his work. He knew it quite well.
D: Was de Saussure a French scholar?
B: Yes, French.
D: But he never came to Russia, never gave lectures here, didn't have actual contacts with anyone here?
B: Never. There were no contacts. What's more, his major work, his introduction to linguistics [*Ferdinand de Saussure's Course in General Linguistics*] (Paris, 1916) was not published during his lifetime. It was put together from notes taken by his students during his lectures only after his death. What he published while alive had no significant impact.
D: And what about that group of young philologists—the linguists turned literary scholars, and the literary scholars turned linguists—which became known as OPOYAZ: did you know any of them personally? You were there during the same years.
B: No, no, we moved in very different circles, very different.
D: So you didn't know the young Shklovsky, the young Eikhenbaum, never ran into them?[24]
B: No, no, I met them later, got to know them much later. Not back then. When they were just starting with OPOYAZ, I didn't know them. I became familiar with OPOYAZ after finishing the university, when I was in Vitebsk. Only then did I get to read the OPOYAZ brochures, which were famous because they were printed on super thin (toilet) paper.
D: I have those. *Poetics*?
B: Not only *Poetics*. There were earlier, separate little pamphlets.

D: They approached literature from a linguistics point of view, so to speak.
B: Yes, from a linguistics point of view, of course. But it was their own special brand of linguistics. There were many very talented linguists among them. I did know one of them, by the way, perhaps the best one. His name was . . . [*A long pause*]
D: Was it Polivanov?
B: Polivanov, absolutely! Polivanov.[25]
D: He was, of course, quite important . . .
B: Very important.
D: Very important. I met him when he was already under attack by the supporters of Marrism.[26]
B: What's interesting is that he had very close ties to the Communist Party. For some reason, he admired greatly Leon Trotsky. In addition, he had served as Deputy Secretary of Foreign Affairs in the first Bolshevik government, something like that. . . .
D: Really? The one in Petersburg? In the "Northern Commune"? Or was it somewhere else, in the FER (Far Eastern Republic)?
B: No, no, no! The one in Petersburg itself. He was Trotsky's deputy, worshipped the man, you might say . . .
D: So that's why later he so quickly. . . . I never understood that before.
B: He was even called "the Bolshevik minister" back then. But, of course, he was not an actual minister, just a deputy minister. Well, I don't know for sure what his responsibilities were to the end, but he got to do a lot because he knew so many foreign languages, which was not something others could boast of.
D: Wasn't he also involved in some shady business, with former expropriators, already before the Revolution? He was interested in criminality, not as an actual activity, but in its language, the language of criminals. In order to study it properly (I heard about that from one of his students), he started to hang out with criminal elements, and became a drug addict. . . .
B: That I didn't know about. Well, I knew he had a drug problem.
D: He was later wounded in the arm, they had to amputate it. He only had one arm.
B: Yes. You see, he took part in the underground movement. But, as far as I know, not the Bolshevik underground, but . . .
D: The Socialist Revolutionaries?[27]
B: Yes, the Socialist Revolutionaries.
D: Before the Revolution?

B: Yes, before.

D: Then he was probably deputy secretary before July 1918, when the leftist SR's were still part of the government. When Kamkov was there, also Proshyan, for whom Lenin wrote an obituary later . . .

B: And Shklovsky, too, was . . .

D: A Socialist Revolutionary, yes.

B: Yes, a leftist. You know what happened: right after the purges had started, and so many SR's got arrested, it was printed in the newspaper that he was a leftist Socialist Revolutionary as well. . . . When he found out about it . . .

D: He left the country immediately.

B: Yes, he fled right away.

D: He spent two years abroad, then came back for some reason.

B: Yes, he did come back, he did. But he hadn't played a big role in anything, it seems.

D: Of course not, it was just one big adventure for him.

B: He was not a politician, but an adventurer. It was just an adventure for him, yes.

D: Did you know Polivanov in those years, as a student, before he lost his arm?

B: Yes, when he still had both of his arms . . . I think . . . It seems . . . I don't remember . . . I also met him later, when he had already lost the arm.

D: He later went to Turkistan for a while.

B: Yes, yes. Then he disappeared from Leningrad, wandered around, spent some time in Constantinople . . .

D: All in all, even if he was not a proper academic, he was still a talented scholar.

B: An incredibly talented man, an erudite. A true erudite, not just talented. That's who he was, Polivanov. He also worked with Shcherba.[28]

D: Shcherba was in Petersburg, and Fortunatov taught in Moscow at the time.

B: Yes, yes. But as far as Petersburg goes . . . Baudouin de Courtenay [was the main figure]. Shcherba, to me, was not a theoretician, he was a . . . His knowledge of French was remarkable. His most significant work was his book about the French language. In addition, he was a true pedagogue. Baudouin de Courtenay was terrible at teaching, as I told you already.

D: You did, yes. . . . And how about the Department of Foreign Languages?

B: The foreign languages department. The most important faculty there was Petrov.[29]
D: So the Veselovsky brothers[30] were already dead?
B: Yes, they were no longer there. But there were others there, like Shishmarev,[31] who continued in the tradition of the Veselovskys. I knew Shishmarev. At one point—briefly—he served as the director of the World Literature Institute. He returned to Leningrad, where he died. But before he passed away, he was able to publish a remarkable book: *An Introduction to Romance Philology.*
D: We should mention that the term "literary studies" didn't exist back then. We had Classicists, Indo-Europeanists . . .
B: . . . Romano-Germanists . . . and Slavists.
D: Who were the Slavists at Petersburg University?
B: I did not study that. Can't remember now who was there. Though I did have to pass an exam in a Slavic language, so I had to have taken classes from someone. I already knew a little Polish, we read *Pan Tadeusz,*[32] portions of *Dziady.*[33] . . . But I was not very interested. It was just a matter of paying my dues, so to speak. I was never interested in Polish.
D: I have to say that the picture you paint of Petersburg University from 1915 to 1916 is much more positive than the one given by Viktor Borisovich Shklovsky. He didn't like Vengérov[34] very much . . .
B: Because he used to be in his Pushkin circle.
D: According to him, the youngsters rebelled against Vengérov. . . . But what else was happening at the university, I got no idea from him, even though we talked on three different occasions.
B: His assessment is quite biased. He [Shklovsky] only knew him as a participant in that one seminar. . . . That's not fair. Vengérov was a true scholar, a proper academician. The young rebels, they were close to the Futurists, for them the most important poet at the time was Mayakovsky.[35]
D: Khlebnikov . . . [36]
B: Khlebnikov, too. But he [Vengérov] was a good scholar—a remarkable bibliographer. You could learn a lot about bibliographic studies from him. . . .

But, to return to "Omphalos," we organized various meetings, loved playing charades . . . I remember how, in someone's apartment . . .
D: So the scholars put on charades, right?
B: Yes, of course, in Srebrny's apartment, he was older than any of us, of course, much older. . . . He was already a *dotsent*[37] and led seminars on

Ancient Greek poetics. Like many other professors, he hosted those seminars at his home. That's what people did back then. For example, Zelinsky's famous seminars took place in his apartment, where his wife also fed us delicious *pirozhki*.[38] So yes, we used to have classes at Srebrny's place, then some people who were not very close to him left right after, while the rest of us, his inner circle, stayed behind, drank tea, and played charades. I remember one of those—we had to act out the name "Burliuk."[39] The first part of the word, "bur" [Boer], my brother represented brilliantly: he held the Bible in one hand, and a weapon in the other, in a word, a stylized Boer.

D: Right. Boers were quite fashionable in the wake of the recent Anglo-Boer War, yes.[40]

B: Yes, that war was still fairly fresh in our memory.

D: There was a little book about it, *Peter Maris, A Young Boer from Transvaal*. Shklovsky mentions it in his memoirs, and I remember it too.

B: And Srebrny, who was an accomplished actor, impersonated Burliuk. Another person we tried to imitate was Vengérov. . . . So Vengérov was acted out by someone else, who was not famous yet, Adrian Piotrovsky. He later died tragically, was executed actually.

D: Really, was he executed?

B: He was executed. And how!

D: When?

B: It was a terrible story. I don't remember the exact date, but it was during the years of that terror . . .

D: During the Revolution or in 1937?

B: It was in 1937, yes, '37. He was very young when the Revolution took place. While doing his obligatory military service in the army before the Revolution, he was taken prisoner by the Germans, but was able to escape like a hero, almost miraculously. Following that, he began his studies at the university. He was so young, so handsome, cut such a dashing figure, and was also a very talented actor. So he pretended to be Vengérov, who decides he wants to familiarize himself with the newest trends in contemporary prose and poetry, and so visits an art café . . . like the famous Stray Dog[41] cabaret or maybe . . . the Comedians' Resting Place did not exist yet, of course . . .

D: At that time, there were the Stray Dog and the Pink Lantern.

B: Yes. So, he goes there and meets a certain poet. . . . This man, he is told, is the leader of modern poetry. His name is Burliuk. And the two start talking. The conversation goes like this: Burliuk explains very seriously the main ideas of Formalism, while Vengérov acts impressed, stunned, keeps asking questions, etc. [*Bakhtin talks to his cat again*] Here you are again. What's to be done with her. Looking for more trouble, I'm sure! Unruly creature!

D: Let's go back to what you were saying earlier if you don't want this to be recorded for posterity.

B: What do you mean?

D: This, your conversation with the cat. [*laughs*]

B: Right.

D: That's OK, it makes everything even more real. I'll keep an eye on it. Go on.

B: So Vengérov, naturally, represented the old, academic, factographic style of literary studies . . .

D: How was the scene acted out?

B: Well, Vengérov acts amazed, stunned by everything, and explains that he feels a little behind the times, which is why what he's been hearing seems very strange to him. That was all true, by the way. But one of Vengérov's main characteristics was that he was a very tolerant man. He was ready to accept anything, even if he didn't understand it well. He was very tolerant. And he absolutely did not attack the younger generation.

D: So he knew some of the Futurists then?

B: I think so. He was, in general, a very serious . . .

D: I wanted to ask you about it, because Viktor Borisovich's reminiscences about the university back then made me a bit suspicious.[42] His views were somewhat partial . . .

B: Yes, or maybe not partial, but, I don't know . . . let's say . . .

D: A little opportunistic, perhaps.

B: No, not that—one-sided, I think. He knew only one side of things. Also, you see, we are talking about university life before and in the early years of the Revolution. There was an internal struggle within the student body: such sharp divisions and in-fighting!

D: Because of politics?

B: Yes, politics. First, there were the academicians, who thought it best not to get involved: "Politics is not our business," they said. "All we need right now is to focus on our studies."

D: That's right.

B: "When we graduate, we'll see. Then we can join different parties, go in separate directions. Now better not get into it. Our main task is to take our studies seriously." Those were the academicians.
D: Did you belong to that group?
B: I didn't belong to any group.
D: You were an academician, though.
B: Well, I sympathized with them, of course, because their opponents created all kinds of . . . obstructions at the university, and so forth. In a word, they were trouble. Big trouble. There were, of course, also other social underlying causes [for the unrest].
D: There were probably also SR's there, and Socialist Democrats there. But the majority of the Petersburg University students must have been liberal Kadets, people of the Kadet party.[43]
B: Of course, the academicians in most cases were children of the Kadet leaders.
D: Professors.
B: Yes. "White collars," as we used to say. The rebel democrats, who couldn't even speak Russian very well, but used some sort of underground slang, they hated the academicians. There were fistfights at the university.
D: Fistfights?!
B: Literally, among students.
D: Actual fighting?
B: In the famous university hallway. There was this hallway that ran the whole length of Petersburg University, a really wide hallway . . . kind of like Nevsky Prospect,[44] which it was usually compared to. Of course, that was an exaggeration, but still, it was very big, and always crowded with students from all departments. That's where the fighting took place.
D: Did they fight in an organized sort of way, say, like old fashioned fistfights among two groups of people?
B: Not really, I'm talking about individual fights, one against another. Not organized in any formal way . . .
D: Someone slaps another in the face, then . . .
B: Like that, yes. Someone supported one person, another was on the opposite side, so they got in a little skirmish . . .
D: What happened in those cases? Did they get kicked out of the university?
B: No, the administration in those cases . . .
D: It didn't intervene?

B: No, it stayed out of it. The students themselves had to figure it out. But when there was a big political demonstration, the administration did intervene. And if the demonstrations actually interfered with classes, some did get expelled. However, I think all who were expelled then, later did manage to re-enroll again. There were really no political repressions at the university before the Revolution. The repressions started afterwards, under the new leadership.
D: Excuse me, but wasn't Kasso[45] in charge back then?
B: He was, yes, he was in charge.
D: Didn't he send some students to the Army?
B: Toward the end of his tenure [as Minister of Education] he did, yes. But I should say that Kasso . . . You know, the revolutionaries writing about Kasso, and in general about the politics of our national university education, they greatly distorted the truth. Kasso was a very intelligent, well-educated man, with a European education. He was a European, a European! His politics were very reasonable. He believed that a university was a place where one went to learn, get educated. After graduation, it was up to you what you wanted to do, but while in school . . .
D: In Moscow, there was a huge scandal, following which all liberal professors left Moscow University.
B: Yes, yes, there was something similar at Leningrad University, but none of the professors we respected left or supported the opposition at all.
D: Were the professors Active State Councilors? Or just State Councilors?[46]
B: Not all of them.
D: They didn't have to have that rank?
B: No, not at all. . . . Some would earn it after a certain number of years of service, but others never got there. Most professors didn't put in enough years of service to be awarded the actual rank of Active State Councilor. Usually they were promoted to that grade right before retirement.
D: Was that the third rank? Active Privy Councilor, Privy Councilor, State Councilor . . .
B: No, Privy Councilor was the highest grade.
D: Was that the rank of the Minister?
B: Ministers were Active State Councilors, but not all of them. Some were just Privy Councilors, and some, as far as I know, even simply State Councilors.

D: So we have: Active Privy Councilor, Privy Councilor, Active State Councilor, State Councilor. What rank was below the State Councilor? Do you remember?

B: Collegiate Councilor, I think. But I can't recall for sure right now.

D: That's perfectly okay. All in all, there were fourteen grades, right?

B: Yes, fourteen.

D: The Table of Ranks was introduced by Peter the Great, correct?

B: Yes, by Peter the Great, it was his idea.

D: And the ranking was done away with only after the October Revolution?

B: Yes, that's correct.

D: The February Revolution didn't get rid of it?

B: They didn't have the time, but even if they had had the time, it's unlikely they'd have messed with it.

D: That February you were a student at Petersburg University? Excuse me, Petrograd University.

B: Yes, but I never participated in any of the movements taking place at the university at the time. I stayed entirely out of that.

D: You were completely apolitical.

B: Completely. I was apolitical, but, of course, I never sympathized with the extremists: the extreme parties, or extreme ideas in the area of our general education. I did not sympathize with them. Not at all. I thought that the existing conditions at the university and in general with our educational system already ensured that anyone could become a scholar and be prepared for life.

I should mention that the Law School at the university was very strong too. I remember attending lectures there, along with everybody else, given by Professor Petrazhitsky,[47] the lawyer. It was hard to follow what he was saying because of his thick Polish accent. And in general, he was not a good public speaker. But his lectures were extremely interesting. He was well versed in philosophy. He tried to approach the law from a new, philosophical perspective. That was very intriguing to me.

D: Now we get to 1917. You said your "Omphalos" was still active. Besides that, what other societies did you participate in?

B: Nothing else, because such associations could not exist. But I did take part in various circles after the Revolution, that I did.

D: What kind of circles: literary? philosophical?

B: Philosophical, and religious, and literary, all unofficial, of course.

D: Did you participate in "Vol'fil," the Free Philosophical Society?[48]
B: I went to their meetings, but never presented anything myself.
D: The society was mainly Andrey Bely's[49] brainchild.
B: Yes, it was his idea. Vol'fil.
D: It'd be interesting to talk some more about it, give your insider's perspective. Did you attend their meetings?
B: Yes, I did, I did. I must say I wasn't a big fan. You see, all they did was babble on and on, the way we Russians tend to do. There were no serious scholarly presentations. It just provided an excuse for some high-flying oratory of the liberal-democratic kind.
D: . . . and also of the mystical, idealist type . . .
B: Yes, partially that, too. I attended some meetings of the Religious and Philosophical Society. Now that was a much more serious business.
D: That was Merezhkovsky's[50] society, right?
B: Yes, Merezhkovsky's. . . . At the time Kartashev served as chair of the society. We had Merezhkovsky, Gippius,[51] there. Then Filosofov[52] played a big role as well. . . .
D: How do you pronounce his name: Filosófov or Filósofov?
B: Filosófov. That's how everybody called him—his personal acquaintances, his friends . . .
D: I am so used to Filósofov.
B: He pronounced it Filosófov himself. So yes, Filosófov is correct.
D: Well, okay, let's now turn to . . . I made you linger on your university experiences because I have an ulterior motive, an assignment, as it were, given to me by the late Rector: to write a history of higher education in Russia. . . . I have collected a lot about Moscow University, but as far as Petersburg University is concerned, except for Shklovsky's rather unreliable accounts, I had very little. In a sense, you were the first to give me a somewhat solid picture of it.
B: I'd like to add a bit more about the university's administration.
D: Please do.
B: There was the Rector and the Prorector, and that was about it. . . . [53] The administration did not interfere at all in academic life. Besides, they were specialists in their particular fields of study. For example, Grevs was a historian.[54]
D: Ah, did you know Grevs then?
B: Of course, I did. Ivan Mikhailovich, if I remember correctly. So yes, they were scholars themselves, not some bureaucrats. They stayed out of

academic affairs. What they wanted to create was an atmosphere of general tranquility, highly conducive to academic work. . . . And they succeeded in that to a large extent in Leningrad, that is, not Leningrad but . . .

D: Petrograd.

B: In Petersburg, no, in Petrograd, they had more or less accomplished that goal. Most students, except for the unreasonable troublemakers, really respected them, and how could you not? The Dean of . . . what did we call him then? . . . Student Affairs, or something else . . .

D: The Provost?

B: No, not the Provost. This was a purely administrative position, dealing with everything student-related. He kept the student archive. His name was Ivan Semyonovich Slonimsky. Such a sweet old man. Almost like a saint. So gentle, agreeable, obliging. He practically ran the office of student affairs.

D: He was the one in charge.

B: Yes, he was in charge. I forgot his title. His son was even my friend. He was older than me. He graduated with a law degree, then enrolled in the Department of Philology, for a second degree.

D: Did you have to pay?

B: Yes, we did. But I should tell you the tuition was not very high.

D: How much did it cost per year?

B: I think about 80 rubles—per year.[55]

D: Were there any scholarships?

B: There were. And it was easy to get one. It was all nonsense, really. Very easy. But, you see, the students themselves thought it beneath them to receive financial help. They tried their best to avoid it. It didn't take much to get one, though—all that was required was a form signed by two of your friends confirming your financial need. Usually it went like this: one went to the office with the required form and asked the first two students who happened to be there, often complete strangers, to sign it. And they signed it, of course. It was tradition. And that was it. All in all, scholarships were easy to obtain. Everybody who had financial need, and didn't feel bad applying for one, got it. But even those who truly needed it, the majority of them, didn't apply. That was also tradition.

D: It was awkward.

B: Yes, very awkward.

D: How much was the scholarship for? Also 30 rubles?

B: No, your tuition simply got waived. There were also other kinds of scholarships, of course—for academic merit. But I can't recall now what . . .

D: Were they externally funded?

B: Yes, they were. The benefactor's name was attached to the scholarship. But I was talking about the possibility of avoiding paying any tuition at all.

D: Well, 40 rubles per semester, that's less than 10 rubles each month.

B: Less than 10 per month!

D: Of course, 10 rubles were quite a bit back then.

B: That was a lot, quite a bit. Still, people preferred to avoid asking for help, also because you could easily earn that kind of money with private lessons, or by publishing something here and there, things like literary reviews or . . . You know, one has to say that we had a great student cafeteria, absolutely marvelous, where for about a . . . I can't remember exactly, but let's say, for a "grivennik,"[56] you could have a wonderful meal.

D: When I went to the university, lunch cost 33 kopecks, and was pretty awful, I have to say.

B: In my time, it was excellent.

D: But you could eat as much bread as you wanted.

B: Bread was not rationed back then, you could eat your fill . . .

D: It was the same in 1926.

B: Lunch was really good. Simple but good. "Shchi,"[57] usually, also with meat, and there was porridge, meat patties . . .

D: Interesting. When I was a student during the second half of NEP,[58] around 1926–30, I supported myself by giving private lessons. I did not have a stipend. Let's see: I earned 1 ruble for an hour-long lesson, sometimes even 1.50, and lunch in the cafeteria cost 33 kopecks.

B: But that lunch was lousy.

D: Terrible. And you had to wait in line, on the stairs, for forty minutes.

B: I don't think there were lines then . . . The so-called queues appeared only later.

D: No, they were already there in 1917, even 1916.

B: All right, in 1916, for certain things, perhaps, but not everywhere.

D: For bread.

B: Yes.

D: You've given us a wonderfully full picture of Petersburg University. Who was its Rector then?

B: Grevs served as Rector.

D: Grevs was a historian. Wasn't he the Dean?
B: He was, for a while, but then became the Rector, I believe. I don't remember all this very well. Students didn't cross paths with the Rector much, I must say. You could graduate, or you could stay at the university for as long as you liked.... There were no time limits. There was a "subject system" in place, that is, you could study a certain subject, then pass an exam on it when you were ready. There were exceptions, of course. For instance, there were subjects that required you to take a particular seminar first, or some kind of a lab. But you had a lot of freedom. You could take the exam whenever. Now the grades from each exam are noted in the student's record-book. Back then, you could try to pass individual subject exams within four years, and then take the finals within five, ten, twenty years.... There were some very old students. There was no limit... you could keep studying...
D: That's ridiculous!
B: Yes. If you could pay to keep studying, that's all that mattered.
D: Don't you think that's ridiculous?
B: There were certainly some minuses, but also pluses to the system. There were some old students, who never really attended classes, but wanted some kind of status in life, so they became eternal students. That's what they were called, "eternal students." It was the same situation in Germany, even more so. You were given a general student gradebook, "a matricula card." You could study one subject at one university, another—somewhere else, a third one at a third, and it was all legal.
D: So there was no concept of "university year"—freshman, sophomore, etc.—and moving up each year?
B: There was, there was, but it was a formality. Usually what mattered was how many years you spent studying—three years meant you were a third-year student...
D: And what if you studied there for eight years? Were you supposed to be an eight-year student?
B: We didn't count beyond the usual years... "He is a perpetual exam taker..." or "This student has a tail...," as we used to say.
D: So there were students with "tails"?
B: Right. For example, someone could study for five or six years, but still have many "tails," that is, exams he hasn't passed. In Germany, you could take exams in any subject at any university you wanted. That was great, because there were different professors at different schools. Everybody

wanted to take a course with the most famous, the best professor at the time, so they went . . .
D: . . . to his particular university.
B: Yes. And moved somewhere else from there. They also had those students, the kind we called "eternal students." But they had a different name for them: "bemooster Herr," that means "hairy face" . . .
D: You mean with a beard?
B: No, wait, here is a better translation. "Moos," "Bemooster Herr." Covered in moss! Moss. Yes. That's the best expression, a mossy student, someone covered with moss. We called them "old students" or "eternal students." I think Leonid Andreev[59] wrote a play called "The Old Student." Or perhaps it was a different title?
D: I think it was different.
B: It was about an old student, who tries to fit in with the new generation, the revolutionary movement, etc.
D: Mikhail Mikhailovich, let's not go there today. . . . Better tell us about the important cultural figures you knew at that time. You saw Chaliapin, you said. . . . Who did you see, who did you know personally or otherwise? You attended performances at the Art Theater.[60] What do you remember about that theater? After all, you see, your opinion . . .
B: The Art Theater? Of course, I was familiar with the Moscow Art Theater. They visited us on tours.
D: Tours where? In Odessa?
B: No, Petersburg. But it's true I saw them first in Odessa, when they came on tour.
D: All right then, let's start with Chaliapin and Sobinov.[61]
B: What about Chaliapin? What can I say? He impressed me greatly. Sobinov—less, somewhat less, for some reason.
D: Well, you're a musical person.
B: Perhaps, but I am not a music specialist. . . . You could say I appreciate music, but I'm no musician. I did teach at the Conservatory, but my subject was ethics. Besides that, there were musicians among my friends. For instance, Maria Venyaminovna, a truly remarkable . . . [62]
D: But that was later.
B: Yes, quite a bit later.
D: We'll talk about her separately.
B: Yes, that was later. . . . Now what can I say . . . I was impressed . . . But how to say something new about Chaliapin, which hasn't been written

about yet. . . . He was recently in the news again. . . . His Jubilee was duly noted. What can I add to that? He left an enormous impression on me. As far as I'm concerned, he was the best bass singer I ever heard. And I heard many extraordinary artists in my time.

Now, as for the Art Theater . . . I first encountered it in Odessa, then again later in Leningrad. I don't recall ever going there in Moscow. I do remember them performing in Leningrad, I remember that very well. Both before and after the Revolution.

D: Did you see it with the principal cast, then?

B: Yes, the principal cast.

D: So tell us what you thought of it, your impressions of the Moscow Art Theater. Of course, I'm mostly interested in . . . Well, Meyerhold—but that, of course, was later.[63]

B: Yes, Meyerhold was later, later. I mainly knew about him from others. We had friends in common, Meyerhold and I. We were acquainted, eventually, but I didn't know him well, not well at all.

D: In Moscow we had the Bolshoi Theatre,[64] the Maly Theatre,[65] and the Art Theater . . .

B: Yes, but the Bolshoi was called Mariinsky back then.

D: That's in Petersburg!

B: Mariinsky Theatre. Now it's the Bolshoi.

D: No, no, the Bolshoi is in Moscow, I was thinking of Moscow. Didn't you live in Moscow at the time?

B: I visited Moscow but didn't live there. In fact, I never really lived in Moscow, never lived there permanently, just for short periods of time. After the Revolution, I resided in Moscow for months at a time. But the Art Theater I knew from Odessa, not from Moscow. It was still the old ensemble. Of course, one of them who came was . . .

D: Konstantin Sergeyevich?[66]

B: Yes, Konstantin Sergeyevich. I remember we went to see . . . "Hotel London" had a restaurant with huge windows to the street, on the first floor. We happened to be there for lunch at the same time Stanislavsky and some others were there. It was easy to get a good look at him . . .

D: Did you like the Art Theater?

B: I can't say I loved it. But I liked it, it left a strong impression. . . . Some things . . . I remember seeing them to this day. *Brand* really shook me.[67]

D: Who played the title role?

B: I think it was . . . Kachalov.[68]

D: What about *The Lower Depths*?[69]
B: I never got a chance to see *The Lower Depths*, imagine that! And since I was never a big fan of Gorky,[70] I never made a special effort to watch his plays.
D: How about Chekhov's?
B: I did see those. . . . But I have to tell you I got the impression that he wasn't staged correctly, that he was misunderstood.
D: Misunderstood? Really?
B: Yes, they didn't understand him.
D: I'd say he was watered down, made to be too touchy-feely.
B: Yes. Also . . . Chekhov himself called his plays farces or comedies. For example, he clearly labeled *The Cherry Orchard*[71] a "farce." That, generically speaking, is not correct. . . . Still, there's no doubt there were certainly farcical, comedic elements in it. . . . But to turn it into a drama . . .
D: Almost melodrama . . .
B: It should have never happened, never. But it did happen.
D: That's really amazing.
B: We should note that later, of course, when the new group of actors came along, and when the theater itself was glorified, turned into a model for all to follow, it changed completely.
D: Completely changed, you say?
B: Yes, completely. The official sanctification killed the old theater. In that sense, the usual happened: as soon as a cultural phenomenon becomes canonized, it dies. It can only exist in an atmosphere of complete freedom, honest competition, and open critique. . . . When a theater is deprived of such an environment, it perishes.
D: I see . . . Theater. Music. How about poetry?
B: Poetry? I knew most of the poets. I was not very close to the really important ones, but I did know a lot of them, almost everyone. I knew best Vyacheslav Ivanov,[72] but we were not intimate friends, even though he was my favorite poet, and I greatly respected him as a person, too. Still, we were not very close.
D: Where did you two meet?
B: In Leningrad, someone introduced him to me at an event . . . I had a dear friend, Voloshinov . . . [73] He is the author of *Marxism and the Philosophy of Language*, a book that is attributed to me. Valentin Nikolayevich Voloshinov. His father was friends with Vyacheslav Ivanov, they used the informal "you" with each other.[74] So he introduced Ivanov

to me at a literary evening in Leningrad. Later, after the Revolution of 1917, we also met in Moscow. I remember most vividly our last two encounters, right before he left for Baku.[75] After Baku, I never saw him. . . . Those were horrible years, hungry years. He lived in a sanatorium on Arbat.[76]

D: I used to visit it in 1920, when my father had to spend some time there following a serious illness. Bunin was his roommate. What was his first name? The brother of Ivan Alexeevich . . . [77]

B: That must have been later. I was there in 1920.

D: 1920, yes. I remember that summer well. That institution always made me think of the book by Gershenzon[78] and . . .

B: Vyacheslav Ivanov.

D: Ivanov: *Correspondence across a Room*.[79]

B: When I visited, Ivanov was still there. So the "correspondence across the room" was about to happen, or had already happened. I saw the room, though. There was also another patient there, a very interesting, remarkable man. He was . . . a poet, I think . . . My memory has gotten so bad! A poet, whose work I love, and also really appreciated his memoirs . . . Khodasevich![80]

D: Ah! He was still in Moscow then? He hadn't left yet?

B: He was still in Moscow. He occupied the second bed in the room. Or was it a different sanatorium? A white, two-storied building . . . I happen to have the book, *Correspondence across a Room*.

D: It's a rare book now.

B: Yes. I happen to have it right now, but it's not mine, unfortunately. But maybe it will be since the owner hasn't asked for it back yet.

D: Did you meet Gershenzon then?

B: I did not. But Vyacheslav Ivanov was there.

D: Did you know him personally?

B: Yes, thanks to Voloshinov.

D: And did you find him to be a little . . . What was he like as a person? After all, you were a member of the Omphalos circle, which I can't picture him ever joining. I see him more as a possible target of Omphalos's ridicule.

B: That may be true, of course, we did make fun of him, but that didn't preclude our respect for him, or his influence on us. Besides, the Omphalos poets did compose using ancient meters . . .

D: Did you value him highly as a poet?

B: Yes, very highly. Especially as a poet. But also as a scholar. His collected essays are very interesting. Some of his articles are truly remarkable. He published three books.

D: Mikhail Mikhailovich, let's turn to Symbolism. . . . You mentioned Vyacheslav Ivanov. I imagine you found his style appealing also because of your interest in antiquity. Did you also meet Innokenty Annensky?[81]

B: No, I was too late for that. He died in 1909. . . . I did know his first book very well, and really liked it. It was called *Quiet Songs* (1904).

D: How about Bryusov?

B: I did know him, yes. We met several times, talked together, but we were not close, though I must say I had a lot of respect for him. Today, when I read how other people remember Bryusov, like that Khodasevich, for example, I am outraged.[82]

D: I haven't read Khodasevich's memoirs. But I am familiar with Tsvetaeva's . . . [83]

B: Also terrible. I believe she wrote . . . described him as someone who managed to "supersede his mediocrity."

D: You know who first said that? It was Aykhenvald.[84]

B: Aykhenvald coined the phrase?

D: "A superseded mediocrity."

B: Perhaps. That was the gist of her essay. Tsvetaeva, too, judged him as lacking any true talent, but saw him as being able to overcome his own mediocrity through hard work, which helped him cover it up, and achieve something.

D: You don't agree?

B: Completely disagree. He may not have been a genius, maybe not even so great, but he was an extremely valuable member of the artistic intelligentsia, a cultural leader. He played an important role in the revival of Russian poetry. After all, he was able to bring closer to us the art of the Western European Symbolists. He did a lot. In addition, he contributed greatly to the proper understanding of ancient poetry through his translations, especially of the late Roman period, which he knew very well. Even as a poet—while not great, or even major—he was a genuine poet, not some kind of a fraud, who had "superseded his mediocrity." Khodasevich paints him very negatively as a person, too . . .

D: And Khodasevich himself, was he an unpleasant man?

B: You know what? He left a dual impression. His appearance was, at least when I knew him, striking. He was very thin. Like a skeleton, all sharp angles. The first time we met, his figure reminded me of the famous paintings that were popular at that time, drawn by Hodler. Ferdinand Hodler,[85] maybe you are familiar with him?
D: Hodler? No, I don't know him.
B: Yes, he is completely forgotten now. He was very popular at the time, though, a Swiss artist. His human figures are like that—all sharp angles. So Khodasevich looked like one of those men. It was obvious right away he was not very kind, but mean, bad-tempered. He was the first to admit it. But, at the same time, he had a certain charm. For one, the sharpness, the meanness he exuded were accompanied by something child-like . . .
D: Really? You are talking about Khodasevich?
B: Yes, him, as strange as it might sound. And that created its own allure. Besides, he was able to rise above all that meanness of his, his own harshness toward everything . . .
D: It's interesting to note that before he became openly anti-Soviet in emigration, even then . . . during the time he lived abroad . . . Gorky spoke of him kindly, with compassion, and loved his poetry.
B: Gorky did, yes. But Kamenev[86] was his real protector, or, I should say, his wife was.
D: Olga Davidovna Kameneva?[87]
B: Have you read *The White Corridor*?[88]
D: No.
B: It's very interesting.
D: Was it written abroad?
B: Yes, but it's about the first year following the October Revolution. The white corridor, where all the rooms of the revolutionary leaders used to be, is in the Kremlin.
D: I haven't had the chance to read it yet. I haven't read much émigré literature. Even now, when it's a bit easier to procure it. . . . I was too young back then, only eight years old.
B: I think it was written in 1926, and published abroad, naturally.
D: Right . . . You described Khodasevich so vividly . . .
B: Vyacheslav Ivanov was a very complicated man. And his judgments . . . Some considered him to be impossible, very rude, etc. . . .
D: Vyacheslav Ivanov? I thought he was supposed to be . . . all grandeur.

B: Well, according to some . . . Who, for example? I believe Bely described him this way, at least partially. At the same time, there also was a certain grandeur about him, no doubt. It was his most important characteristic, I think.

D: "Service to the Muses does not tolerate vanity":[89] these words of Pushkin come to mind when I think of him.

B: Yes.

D: And what about the relationship between Bryusov and Vyacheslav Ivanov? What was it like?

B: They got along well, I believe, they never fought—in poetry or otherwise . . .

D: But still, as you remember, as far as the literary, aesthetic debates of the 1900s are concerned, they belonged to opposing camps: Bryusov was on one side, while Vyacheslav Ivanov, Blok, Chulkov were on the other.

B: Yes, but they still respected each other. Though, naturally, they were very different. . . .

D: How about Andrey Bely?

B: I knew him, too.

D: I have my own impressions of him, but I'm curious about yours.

B: I first heard him at the philosophy meetings of . . .

D: "Vol'fil"?

B: No, earlier, before "Vol'fil." I never heard him present there when I attended. It was before that, at meetings of the Religious-Philosophical Society, when Merezhkovsky still presided. But in general the head of the society was Kartashev.

D: Yes, right, you already talked about that. Could you tell us a bit more about this Religious-Philosophical Society?

B: He [Bely] gave very interesting talks. I heard him speak twice. Can't remember the titles of his talks now.

D: Were they later included in *Green Meadow*?[90]

B: No, no, this was later, after *Green Meadow*, later than that, of course. It was toward the end of 1916.

D: Did the Religious-Philosophical Society exist up until . . . ?

B: Until the October Revolution.

D: Really?! And I thought it was finished by the early 1910s!

B: Not at all! I was present at the society's last meeting, when its chairman Kartashev gave a speech. Kartashev was already Minister of Education, during the Provisional government. So yes . . . He offered some concluding remarks. Nobody said anything about the Society closing down, but it was in the air . . . everybody felt it was the last meeting.

D: Did Bely give a speech then, too? Or were his presentations earlier?

B: No, Bely was not present at the last meeting. I heard him talk before that. Another one who spoke then was Sergey Solovyov. . . . [91] At the time he was already a priest.

D: A priest? I seem to remember that he later had a mental breakdown . . .

B: Even before that, he was sick a lot of the time. He had even tried to commit suicide at some point earlier. Then he was ordained as a priest.

D: Later he embraced Catholicism.

B: True, but when he gave his talk about the white *klobuk*[92] at that meeting, he was still an Orthodox priest, I am sure of it. His topic was the legend of the *White Klobuk*, and how it came to Russia. He offered a very nationalist and extremely Orthodox interpretation.

D: Well, that's exactly how I imagined Sergey Solovyov, more or less. But that's not important . . . I'm curious about everything that happened back then! You are one of the last remaining people who still remember and can tell us a lot about that trio: Merezhkovsky, Gippius, Filosófov.

B: Yes. They always came together and sat together. Okay, let's talk about the meetings of the Religious-Philosophical Society. . . . They didn't have their own space, but were given a floor in the building of the Russian Geographical Society.

D: Was that in Moscow?

B: No, Leningrad, of course . . . I knew the Leningrad people. The Moscow circle—I didn't know them, never visited. But the Leningrad branch. . . . It met on Demidov Street, the second floor. On the second floor landing, there was a big table with books for sale: proceedings of the Religious-Philosophical Society, books published by the Society's members, and so forth. . . . The hall where the meetings took place was very small. Very small. I'd say, 200 to 300 people capacity, at most. If that . . .

D: 300 people is not bad.

B: Maybe so, but there were hardly that many people present at every meeting. So, there were some small tables, benches, chairs. On the left, you had the main entrance, on the right—a long table. That was the main table, the presidium. The podium was next to it, on the left. The members of the Religious-Philosophical Society always sat in front of that table. There weren't that many of them, and few showed up for meetings every time. The rest of those present were not members, but competitors, we might say. I received an invitation. [When I arrived] I was introduced to the chair, Kartashev, we chatted a bit, then he wrote down my name and said, "From now on you'll get the official announcements."

D: Attending meetings was not compulsory then?

B: Not at all, not at all. And indeed, I did start getting regular announcements, typed on very thin paper, about that particular day's agenda: what presentations there would be, and so forth. But you didn't have to show an actual invitation to get in. Outsiders never went there. It was just to let you know what was happening, since there were no official announcements in the press. So, Merezhkovsky, and next to him Zinaida Gippius, immediately followed by Filosofov, all sat at that long table . . .

D: Did you know them personally?

B: Who?

D: Merezhkovsky, Gippius, and Filosofov.

B: We were acquainted, but that's all. We'd greet each other with a nod in passing. I did run into them a lot there, though. It was a small, pretty tight circle of people, everybody knew everybody else.

D: Was the lady striking?

B: Oh, yes, very much so! She produced great effect with her appearance. She really cared about her looks. Besides, she behaved in such a way that she seemed to be of a different world, like a fairy mermaid [*rusalka*]. I'm not sure if it was an affectation, or she really couldn't breathe well on this earth, like a mermaid. . . . She seemed to have trouble breathing . . .

D: Well, she was able to keep breathing almost to the age of ninety.[93]

B: Yes, it likely was just an affectation. Overall, she was very interesting.

D: A redhead?

B: I can't remember the color of her hair now. She was very intriguing, physically very attractive.

D: I've seen pictures. She had a good figure.

B: I've seen pictures, too . . . but in person she left a much greater impression. Perhaps she wasn't as beautiful in real life (portraits always made her look a little prettier), but she was incredibly charismatic, even if artificial.

D: What do you mean?

B: Her charm was combined with a kind of phoniness. . . . That is, she was a fake.

D: Fascinating!

B: Well, she was fake in the sense that she had crafted a particular persona for herself. For instance, her heavy breathing was meant to remind one of a mermaid out of her element. And, in general, her mannerisms were all a performance, something fabricated, deliberate. This left you with a feeling of falseness, artificiality. At the same time, she was very charismatic because she was incredibly smart. Smarter than Dmitry Sergeyevich,[94] smarter than Filosofov. Their relationship . . . I'm sure you know they were in a ménage à trois.[95] And within that ménage à trois Merezhkovsky was . . . how shall I put it . . .

D: The least important . . .

B: Yes, the least important participant. . . . He was not very masculine looking, even if he did have a beard.

D: He was rather frail, we might say.

B: Yes, frail, effete. His skin had a bluish tint to it, like that of a drowned man. Yes . . . I didn't find him appealing. This should be said: they always arrived late, after everyone else was already there. The three usually walked in arm-in-arm, with Zinaida Gippius in the middle, and had to cross the room, go between the rows of seats, since the entrance was on the left, and the table on the right. I remember everybody stood up when they came in.

D: Really? Everybody got up?

B: Yes, they did. Well, maybe not all but . . . It's not like you were obliged to stand up, but my impression was everybody did anyways. But perhaps some did remain sitting. There were some people in the audience who hated Merezhkovsky. . . . So, yes, theirs was a grand entrance, always accompanied by a commotion, shuffling, physical movement . . .

D: The distinguished guests had arrived.

B: Yes. They came in, greeted various people, then sat at the table: Merezhkovsky next to the podium, then Zinaida Gippius, then Filosofov. Filosofov was not always present, I think. I remember him being there once, in particular, because he took part in a debate. Besides that, I'm not sure if he was always there.

D: What was he like, in general?

B: He was not stupid, not at all. He was quite smart, actually, and knew a lot. He was a thinker of sorts . . .

D: I thought he was a literary man?

B: A literary man, of course.

D: But beyond that . . . I have an idea about the type of person Merezhkovsky was, but as for Filosofov—I don't know in what sense he could be considered a thinker.

B: Well, he didn't start a new way of thinking, a new trend of any kind—that wasn't his goal. We could say this: he was a proper gentleman.
D: A gentleman?
B: Yes. Merezhkovsky didn't look like a gentleman. Despite always dressing with great care, and wearing splendid suits, he still resembled a drowned man, just pulled out of the water. . . . Filosofov, on the other hand, he was a real nobleman, so he didn't have to dress that way. He dressed like a gentleman, a person who . . . You remember what they say about the English nobility: What is a gentleman? A person who can wear a really shabby, old collar, and still make it look flawless, as good as new. He could carry off anything. Filosofov, I think, did not dress as well as the other one, but he could wear anything, even the most modest outfit, and still look presentable. He was a gentleman, a real gentleman. That was obvious in everything. And like a gentleman, he didn't feel the need to trouble himself with anything, to have a fully formed worldview, write books that require . . .
D: A lot of work.
B: Yes, he wasn't that type of person. But he was very smart and well educated, and when he spoke publicly (I heard him that one time, when he took part in a debate; he didn't give presentations), he sounded very intelligent, and stayed on topic.
D: Merezhkovsky belonged to the merchant class, not the nobility, right?
B: He wasn't even a merchant. There was another merchant who . . . I used to know him. . . . Another famous poet back then . . . it'll come to me . . .
D: Rukavishnikov?[96]
B: Rukavishnikov, yes, Ivan Rukavishnikov. He came from that class, the merchants, his parents were millionaires, maybe even his grandparents, I'm not sure. Merezhkovsky, on the other hand, was just a shabby member of the intelligentsia. A shabby member of the intelligentsia.
D: I see. If I may, I don't want to use up too much recording tape on myself, but I want to check on something with you. When I lectured at the university, to tell the truth, I offered a satirical picture of . . . There was this book, I think written by Vengérov, from before the Revolution, *Russian Poets of the Nineteenth Century,* with illustrations.
B: When was it published?
D: In 1910, I believe. So yes, there were their pictures in it: Merezhkovsky, Skitalets . . . [97] Zinaida Gippius looked stunning, her hour-glass figure

clad in a white dress, much like you are describing her. Merezhkovsky, though . . . the phoniness . . . I've read much of his work, but I don't like his poetry. So he is sitting there, with his little beard . . .

B: Yes, he had a little beard.

D: . . . in a big armchair, looking very pensive, somewhat like Chekhov, and clearly posing . . .

B: Posing, right, posing.

D: There're also shelves with expensive books there, with gilded spines, clearly old, and a cross on the wall behind . . . a huge cross, compared to his body, and a Catholic one at that . . .

B: Yes, that was . . .

D: . . . then there was something else that caught my attention, a little domestic detail, which seems strange if you're a religious man: the cross touched on an electric bell right next to it.

B: Such a silly thing!

D: You see, electric bells back then were a sign of luxury.

B: Yes, yes, yes.

D: It was the bell used to summon the servants. You see, for some reason that sign of bourgeois comfort, of material and spiritual complacency, left a big impression on me. Is that fair?

B: Yes, very much so.

D: Does that fit your impression of Merezhkovsky as he was in real life?

B: Yes, yes. He, too, liked to pose, to pretend. And he always drew attention to himself, to his own role in anything he happened to talk about. For example, if the topic was Lev Tolstoy, he would say something positive about him, then add: "I have the right to say this, because I used to argue with Lev Nikolaevich a lot, when he was still alive." Why did he need to tell us about it . . . that he had had the "honor" of arguing with Tolstoy?

D: Did you hear any of his talks?

B: The times I was present he never gave a talk himself, but he always felt the need to respond to other presenters—kind of like a discussant. His comments were never thought-provoking. He spoke the way he wrote. There was another interesting figure at the time, Alexander Meyer.[98] He used to be a Social Democrat, but then became a religious idealist. He was of German descent. He was a professor of history at Lesgaft University at the time.

D: Lesgaft—was that the Institute for Physical Education?[99]

B: Yes. [*he chuckles*] But back then they offered philosophy classes there. So Meyer taught there and was very popular and well liked among his students. He was an impressive individual. Truly remarkable. Also exceptional as a human being. Very good looking, too. Very handsome. He had an amazing greyish beard, Assyrian in style, beautiful eyes, and so forth . . .

We were put on trial together,[100] but that was only a formality, since I didn't share his beliefs. But I did know him well, he visited me at home (I never went to his); however, I didn't have the same views. But officially, they had to stick something on us, so they stuck on this. Back then, you know, they didn't care much about the truth.

So he did give presentations. His ideas were very extreme, radical. For example, he thought (that was before October, but after February) that the Revolution had to be broadened further so it evolves into a social revolution. It had to include those at the very bottom . . .

D: Was that after he became a religious idealist?

B: It was, correct.

D: Bely held a similar position. . . . He, too . . . After all, he wrote the poem "Christ Is Risen"[101] . . .

B: True, he did share that view at one point, that's right.

D: Still, he was considered a Bolshevik, which he never really was.

B: No, I don't believe he was considered a Bolshevik, even though . . . He formed his own circle later, after the Revolution, after the Religious-Philosophical Society had ceased to exist; that is, it went underground, if you will, his society did. . . . Its members were mostly young people. At one of their meetings, I was told (I never attended those, because, as I said before, I didn't share their ideas), they discussed the question: "What if Vladimir Lenin were here? What would he think of our meetings?" And they came to the conclusion that he'd think positively of them. That he'd be able to understand how progressive they were, and so forth. That was, of course, very naïve, very naïve of them. . . .

D: Did they consider themselves revolutionaries?

B: Yes, but nonviolent revolutionaries. Still, they did accept the need for revolutionary violence, provisionally, in some form or another, as far as I can recall. Alexander Meyer—a most good-natured, pure individual, who wouldn't hurt a fly—came up with some kind of a formula that didn't exactly justify the use of brute force, but . . .

D: . . . but still made peace with it . . .

B: Yes, made peace with violence, with revolutionary violence.
D: Understood. Let's go back to our couple. Did you ever hear Merezhkovsky or Zinaida Gippius recite poetry?
B: No, never.
D: In general, did Zinaida Gippius give public presentations?
B: Not when I was around. She just liked to show off.
D: Your gallery of Symbolist poets would be incomplete without Blok.[102]
B: That's true. . . . But, you see, I didn't really know Blok personally. I heard him talk—that is, not talk but recite his poetry—twice. But we did have friends in common.
D: Who were those? Were you acquainted with Yevgeny Ivanov?[103]
B: Yes, I knew him well. During our last years in Leningrad, he was a permanent fixture at our home.
D: He was a close friend of Blok's.
B: He also became a close friend of ours and called himself "your red-bearded pal." He did have a red beard.
D: Light-colored.
B: Yes. You wouldn't call him handsome, exactly. Even his face was, if you just looked at it, kind of dumb.
D: Right. I didn't know who he was at all, but happened to go hear him talk once, without any particular reason or interest. Later he, the poor soul, ended up selling discounted albums at the Literary Museum.
B: Yes, yes. He had it rough, really tough.
D: Bonch[104] paid him virtually nothing. I knew him just as someone working in the archives. Only later did I find out he was an important figure.
B: Yes, he was truly a remarkable person. But he had the face of a simpleton. He even seemed always tongue-tied, literally tongue-tied. He did have a speech impediment, and couldn't pronounce some sounds at all.
D: What did he tell you about Blok? And what can you add to it, or change in keeping with your own impressions? He left some letters—I know that.
B: It's hard for me to say anything, after all, I didn't know Blok well at all. But I adored him as a poet.
D: But if you liked Bryusov . . . In a sense, Bryusov and Blok were at the opposite ends of the Symbolist spectrum.
B: Yes, to a degree. Their differences are overemphasized if you ask me. We, Russians, like to collide things, to turn them into extremes, into

opposites and so forth. That's not how things really are. Still, we can't think of Symbolism without Bryusov, its originator, or Blok, who was much younger, of the second generation of Symbolists, or Vyacheslav Ivanov. They shared the same soul, if you will, so there were no real contradictions. They belonged to the same camp, in the deepest sense of the word. The same camp. There had to be some sort of multi-voicedness. It was necessary, such multi-voicedness. And it existed. That's where the real strength of the movement lay: that within its confines you could have a multitude of different talents, diverse viewpoints.

So yes, Blok. He left a strong impression. How so? He was very handsome, without a doubt, well built. What else? He recited his poems beautifully, with the perfect intonation. . . . He didn't declaim them, but read them in his inimitable way. Once upon a time I could emulate him, his way of delivering poetry. . . .

D: Could you really?

B: Yes, if I wanted to. But not anymore.

D: Are you sure?

B: I can't do it anymore. Yes . . . What else can I say? . . . It was obvious right away that he was special, molded out of a different dough, not like you and me, mere sinners. There was something sublime about him, as if he was above it all. . . . That was my impression of him. He was elevated even above himself. The best Blok was to be found in his poetry, though not all of it. Then there was the other Blok, the man, who used to hang out with who knows who, and got involved in who knows what. . . . His obsession with the Bolshevik Revolution, all the nonsense regarding the Russian intelligentsia, the intelligentsia and the common man, the intelligentsia and the Revolution, all of that was that same Blok, above whom soared that other Blok, the creator of true poetry. You felt it immediately: here is the man, and here's something else that transcends him, surpasses anything human. But not always. He could sit in an armchair somewhere, or take a walk, or recite his poems all the while staring in the eyes of his audience trying to gauge the impression he was making. . . . But that didn't seem to be the real Blok, the essential Blok . . . But after all . . . One has to have a body, a social position, a job of some sort, one must get dressed in the morning. . . . When I saw him he was dressed in a shirt . . . the kind that poets used to wear . . . Yes, poets . . . It came from France, that fashion. At first it was the revolutionaries of 1905 who wore that type of shirt, then it became fashionable with the poets, the writers.

D: And you could sense all of that in him back then, is that right?

B: Yes, I could.

D: Mikhail Mikhailovich, given what you were saying earlier, your evaluation of Blok's *Twelve*[105] must be rather negative. I'm just following your logic . . .

B: My assessment is the following: the poem is, of course, amazing, both in terms of talent and ability to represent vividly the Revolution. In general, he is very strong in his poetic depictions. I remember that Petersburg—blanketed in snow, the shots ringing out all around. . . . You're walking down the street, say that same Nevsky Prospect, at night: it's dark, there are strange figures who suddenly appear in front of you, and you hear shots, someone is shooting, the devil knows why or at whom. . . . He was able to capture all of that. The conversations at the beginning between the philistines, and others, those are magnificent! Just magnificent! The old woman, the young lady, the prostitute. . . . "We need a true poet, a visionary," and so on. That's all glorious, of course! But there's also some irony in it. Irony. The twelve Bolsheviks are ironic (but irony there already means something else, we should add). Their depiction is ironic. It may seem like they are portrayed in a purely positive light: the twelve Apostles following Christ. . . . Yes! But that is actually very ironic, the whole situation is presented as ironic. Even Christ himself is a little . . . despite his perfect poetic description. . . . "In the blizzard's swirl . . ." How does it go?

D: [*recites*] Ahead of them—with bloody banner,

> Enveloped in the blizzard's swirl,
> His body never touched by bullets . . . [106]

B: "With sprightly step, pearl-like . . ."

D: No, "the storm below."

> [*B and D together*]
> "In the tender, pearl-like snow,
> His head adorned with roses iced,
> Ahead of them—goes Jesus Christ."[107]

B: That's simply wonderful! Still, the whole picture has ironic undertones. . . . After all, the tones in his depiction of the society of the time, the multi-voicedness of the time—all of that is spoken with irony, not carried through to the end. . . . In a word, that was Blok at his best; as I said, there were "two Bloks": the man and the poet (the elevated one) . . .
D: Apropos of the "supra-Blok." Do you think he had already reached such poetic heights in his first anthology, as many critics believe?
B: The first one?
D: His first published volume, that is, his *Verses about the Beautiful Lady.*[108]
B: Both Bloks can be found in all of his poetry. There's Blok, the poet, the Symbolist, then later the Symbolist renegade, if you will, appears as well . . .
D: And then we have this:

> The scruffy cat on the roof
> Keeps staring at him, with sympathy.[109]
> You think: He saw it, too?
> But there'll be no reply.[110]
> His virtue is in his revelry.

B: Yes.
D: Self-irony. By the way, the essay about irony is great.[111]
B: He knew and understood how irony works indeed.
D: So you knew and loved him as a poet?
B: Yes, I knew and loved him as a poet. I used to know a lot of his poems by heart. But my memory is not the same anymore. I could recite almost everything by Blok, also by Vyacheslav Ivanov. Right. There was something in Blok the man, not in the other lofty Blok, something that—it was probably caused by the internal contradictions, the fact that he didn't coincide with himself, so to speak—something that led to his betrayal . . . a traitor, a renegade of Symbolism, if we can use that term "Symbolism" here, and also of the Russian intelligentsia . . .
D: "Renegade" doesn't quite fit here.
B: . . . there was a time when he disowned the Russian intelligentsia.
D: I still think "renegade" is not the right word.
B: Okay, it doesn't fit, it doesn't.
D: His was an honest casting off . . .

B: An honest casting off, perhaps, but you could also be an honest renegade. Yes. An honest casting off.
D: Yes, but "renegade" also means "traitor."
B: Yes, of course.
D: Did you get that impression from him? What else . . . ? Tell me more, please, which of his things did you find most spectacularly good, that is, from the point of view of the "supra-Blok"?
B: The "supra-Blok"? You know, it's hard to say, there were so many, so many. . . . Let's try to remember them together. First of all, "The Stranger." It's one of his earliest poems, an early work . . .
D: It's from 1906.
B: He recited it first at Vyacheslav Ivanov's literary salon, the famous "Tower."[112] I personally didn't go to the "Tower," because in my time someone else was living there already, but my place was close by, so I frequently passed by the building and remember the "Tower." There are so many other remarkable poems of his. In particular, I love everything about the creative impulse to write poetry: "To the Muse": "In your innermost songs there are hidden . . ."[113] An incredible poem, unbelievable!
D: What's your interpretation of its infernal imagery?
B: Ah, yes, the infernal . . .
D: Above you, all of a sudden, there blazes . . .

> [*B and D together*]
> . . . The circle, dim and purplish-grey,
> Which in the past I glimpsed at in my visions.[114]

B: You see, "which in the past I glimpsed at in my visons" could be interpreted this way: first of all, that the poet himself was already familiar with the infernal element, and, secondly, the color, that "purplish-gray," reminds one of Vrubel's palette. He was an ardent admirer of Vrubel.[115]
D: I imagine the blazing circle as a reflection of Dante's Inferno. The back-shadowings of Hell.
B: Of course, Hell . . . by the way, you can find demons and the demonic in general in Vrubel's art. Blok adored him. Even in that 1912 speech when he denounced Symbolism . . .

D: "The violet worlds" of Symbolism . . .
B: Exactly. In that same speech, he talked about the "the world of your glorious sorrowful shades, O immortal Vrubel." Those were his words.[116]
D: What about his "Italian Poems," "Ravenna"?
B: Marvelous! "Ravenna" is just marvelous! All of his Italian poems are great. But I love "Ravenna" the most. There's something about creativity there too: "In the hot summers and the blizzards of winter . . ."[117] You know it, of course?
D: Yes, but not by heart.
B: Wonderful poetry, simply wonderful!
D: Don't you think . . . I simply can't resist the temptation to continue this discussion, it's so utterly interesting. . . . Won't you say, in all seriousness, no desire to offend, that, together with Blok's tragic dimensions, his high tragedy, there's also a certain decadence, a particular feeling of desolation? Think of the high tragedy of his "Frightful World"!
B: Yes.
D: There's a certain . . .

> "I was accosted by a poor soul . . ."
> —it's from the same cycle,—
>
> "Who followed close, the fool."
> "Where's your money?"—"Left it in the bar hall."
> "Where's your heart?"—"In the dark whirlpool."[118]

Do you remember it?
B: Yes.
D: There's something in this. . . . I agree with Blok's own confession: "The drama of my worldview . . ." then, in brackets, "I never ascended to the realm of true tragedy."[119] What do you think?
B: That's true. But, no, I think there was an utter desolation in him. If you like, I think there is an utter desolation in all poets. Anyone who is not familiar with the internal abyss, who cannot relate to it in some way, cannot understand also the sense of complete fullness, the overflowing so necessary for the poet: "Our world's infinite rapture / Is only known to the poet's heart . . ."[120] This "infinite rapture" can be understood only by the heart that . . .

D: So you don't see any boundaries between . . . the truly tragic . . . and. . . . Tragedy allows for catharsis, after all, but there's also that desolation . . .
B: See, here's the thing. We very much misuse the term "tragic" today.
D: We've lowered it quite a bit.
B: Tragedy in its pure form, the kind created in antiquity, by the likes of Aeschylus, Sophocles, and even Euripides, is in fact naïve, quite naïve. They didn't come in contact with the abyss, weren't really familiar with actual terror, didn't know it yet. Indeed, they couldn't have known it yet. They were, despite their incredible power and stature, children, and that's also where their strength partially came from as well. Our tragedy can never be that pure . . .
D: It's more frightening.
B: Yes. It bears the mark of the abyss, and, besides, it's inseparable from aspects of comedy. Yes, from comedy.
D: That's your main idea in *Rabelais and His World*: carnival.
B: Carnival, of course, carnival . . .
D: I'm out of my element here, forgive me: is it like mystery-bouffe?
B: If you wish, yes, yes.
D: That makes sense.
B: Yes, yes. I am also of the opinion that, if you look at it more broadly, the world that Blok belonged to, together with Bryusov, and also Balmont, Bely, and Vyacheslav Ivanov, was also the world of Mayakovsky, to an extent. Mayakovsky. But Mayakovsky betrayed that world in some of his work, turned into a renegade. Even while he was still alive many considered him a renegade, because of some of the ugly things he did. You know that some people wouldn't shake his hand.
D: It was the same with Bely.
B: Yes, but for different reasons. It was because. . . . Well, as I was saying, he was prone to betrayals. . . . Like I was saying . . .
D: We'll come back to Mayakovsky later when we talk about your encounters with him. There's a little detail we haven't discussed yet. . . . Your depiction of the Symbolists was marvelous. We covered everything, the whole movement, it seems.
B: Yes, all of Symbolism.
D: Plus we covered Khodasevich.
B: Khodasevich, yes, and also Annensky. I very much loved Annensky. I still do.

D: But you didn't meet him personally?
B: No, I couldn't have, he died in 1909. But I met people who knew him well, his students at the Tsarskoe Selo Lyceum.[121]
D: His students from the Lyceum? Did you know his brother, by any chance?
B: No, I didn't. He moved in different circles, in a different world. He was a politician, Nikolay Annensky, a politician of the liberal bent, a member of the intelligentsia. I didn't know him.
D: Did you ever meet Gumilev[122] and Anna Andreevna?[123]
B: Of course, I knew Gumilev. We were not friends, and couldn't have been, but we met on many occasions. I loved his poetry. Of course, I didn't think he was on the same level as Vyacheslav Ivanov or Blok, but I loved his poetry nevertheless. His later poems I value greatly even now. He was an interesting, unusual person. But he lacked depth. That was never his goal; however, he didn't strive to be deep, not at all. He wanted to be brilliant.
D: Brilliant?
B: Yes, brilliant.
D: Physically, he was also a scrawny fellow, correct?
B: No, he was tall, slim, angular. My impression of him was the following: he reminded me of Rilke,[124] the same style, same outward appearance. Only Rilke's eyes were gentler, more peaceful, while his were more manly. Overall, he was a manly man. And he valued his manliness. He loved masculinity. He turned out to be a great army man. Before that he traveled a lot, exposed himself to all kinds of danger. Like many others back then, at one time he looked for danger, and thought it most pleasant to . . .
D: [*recites*] . . . At times we were attacked by lions,

> But there were no cowards among us, in disguise,
> We shot at the lions, aiming between their eyes . . . [125]

It feels like you're drawn into a wormhole—don't you think? Was he also a show-off? Did he like to put on airs?
B: Yes, he liked to pose, if you will. But his boldness, his love of war and military danger were genuine. We might say he was in love with war, in love with it. He felt he hadn't lived before the war. His travels, etc.—all

that was nothing! Amour, the love for a woman, didn't matter. War, that's what really counts!

D: [*recites*] Four days, already, we advance,

[*the two continue reciting together*]
No food in four days, too.
Who needs an earthly sustenance
At this time of passion and of thrill
When God's divine cadence
Our souls, better than bread, will fill.

And the weeks, drenched in blood,
Seem to be dazzling and light . . . [126]

B: By the way, all those war poems written at the time . . . many poets then wrote such hackneyed works . . . right?

D: They were very bad.

B: Terrible, contrived poems.

D: A lot worse than during our war.

B: Much worse, of course. Belabored. Because they were written by people who didn't understand war, didn't love it. Hard to imagine them. . . . People like Merezhkovsky. . . . What would someone like that do on the front? Blok, on the other hand, he was different, very brave. But he never fought on the frontlines, though he got pretty close; he was not afraid of bullets, in any case.

D: It's really incredible: during our war, the last one, there were those insignificant poets, like Surkov,[127] Simonov[128]. . . . They wrote . . .

B: Hackneyed bureaucratism, the lot of them!

D: But they were still able to produce great war poetry.

B: Yes, yes, somehow . . .

D: Whereas back then we had brilliant poets . . .

B: Who produced boring, hackneyed, dead war verse.

D: For example, Bryusov was especially bad.

B: Very bad. His revolutionary poems were terrible, too. He wrote those back in 1905. Horrible verse!

D: Did you hear Gumilev recite his own poetry?

B: No, never.

D: Did he stutter?
B: I think a little.
D: Zenkevich called him a stutterer.
B: No, that's an exaggeration. He was not a stutterer, of course, but he was also not very good at recitation.
D: And did you have the chance to hear him read?
B: No, never had that chance.
D: Where did the two of you meet?
B: We met at . . . I can't remember right now . . . at the meeting of some society. But we didn't know each other then, I just saw him there. Later we were acquainted at the Religious-Philosophical Society. I saw him there, in truth, only once, before the war, right before he joined the army. The second time we met was when he came home from the front briefly on leave. That's when he came to one of the Society's meetings. He was already in uniform, an officer in the guard . . . a guardsman. . . . What were they called? Their uniform had skull and bones on the shoulders . . . The Legion of Death, I believe. A Hussar! A Hussar![129] In any case, he looked magnificent. I remember that day I was standing on the landing with Akhmatova, among others, smoking. You had to go out to smoke, so we climbed to the next landing, above the second floor, because the Society had been given the second floor, and the landing was between floors. . . . So there we were standing and smoking. Then someone, Anna Akhmatova, I believe, cried out: "Gumilev is here!" and she flew down the stairs, like a bird. I followed behind and saw him, too: a man in uniform, simply magnificent! That was Gumilev. Splendid! The splendid Gumilev!

That's when I understood that he was born to be in the military. Though it didn't last long. But despite the short service, he still earned two Saint George Crosses.[130] In those days it was hard to get the Cross of Saint George. Back then connections didn't get you that award. It's all rubbish what they say or write. Here, in Russia, awards are a dime a dozen. I know many people from the intelligentsia, whose job was to write orders, and since they wrote them as they were told by the higher-ups, they were awarded medals, which they didn't deserve. But in those days it was hard to come by a military award. And he earned two! Two Crosses of Saint George! But he was never wounded. He even writes:

> But St. George . . .
> [*B and D together*]

. . . twice graced his breast,
by bullets never scarred . . . [131]

D: Yes, that's from *The Pillar of Fire* (1921) [his poetry collection].

B: I see you know poetry very well.

D: I do.

B: And not just the older poetry . . .

D: Yes, I know poetry. Right. Well . . . It's nice that you can feel that.

We have to stop now. The tape is over, and my time is up. . . . But we are not finished. Next time we'll start with Akhmatova, and then move on to the Soviet times.

B: There won't be much to say about the Soviet years. I want to tell you more about other interesting things: like the salons, which were living out their last days back then.

D: Great! You paint a wonderful picture of the atmosphere at the time. But we're done for today. I'm switching it off.

Interview Three

March 8, 1973

Length of the interview: 124 minutes

DUVAKIN: Mikhail Mikhailovich, let's begin. Last time we ended with Gumilev. How about we talk about Anna Akhmatova now.[1]

BAKHTIN: Ah, yes, Akhmatova. What can I say about Anna Akhmatova. I didn't know her very well as a person. We met several times. We talked once, but our conversation wasn't very interesting. I got the impression that she didn't like to discuss anything other than topics concerning everyday life and love, in particular. She didn't like to talk very much. That's how she was at the time. Of course, that was many years ago, she changed a lot later.

As you know, there are almost no philosophical elements in Akhmatova's early work. Hers was purely intimate lyrical poetry, very feminine. That didn't mean it wasn't very artistically sophisticated, not at all. But it didn't raise any larger questions. . . . There was no depth to her early poems, in the period when I knew her. It was the same in real life, as far as I could tell. She was interested in people. But she related to them as a woman, as a woman relates to a man. She divided people into two categories according to how she felt about them: interesting, and not interesting. That's a very feminine approach. Because of it, I didn't like her very much personally.

Besides that, I found her to be a bit arrogant. She seemed to look down upon ordinary people. I heard the same from others who knew her later. Even in old age she was still arrogant, even more so: for example, when editors went to her home to see her, she didn't even respond to their greetings, didn't ask them to sit down. They stood in front of her while she made the necessary corrections, agreed or disagreed with the proposed changes. . . . I repeat, she didn't treat them as human beings. So yes, she could be like that. But who knows, maybe such recollections are too subjective, random. Perhaps they had caught her in a bad mood: after all, she was persecuted to the end, to her death. Maybe she felt particularly harassed that day. . . . But I should say I heard that from others, too, many people complained about her arrogance and even rudeness.

D: And that happened at her home when people visited on business?

B: Yes, on business, regular folk. With people whom she considered more or less important . . .

D: Those from her circle . . .

B: . . . yes, with people from her own circle, she was very different, of course. That's often the case, though. Gogol[2] made that brilliant observation a long time ago: one's personality changes dramatically depending on whom he is talking with—his superiors or inferiors. But it was actually Thackeray who first described this phenomenon properly in his *Book of Snobs*.[3] He says the snob talks with the shopkeeper one way, like so, and with an aristocrat—completely differently, like this. [*Bakhtin changes his intonation, in the first case he talks condescendingly, in the second comes across as very servile.*] So his personality changes entirely, depending on whether he is looking to the left or to the right, his expression as a whole is transformed every time.

D: Would you say that the snob is related to the petty bureaucrat then?

B: The snob? Not at all.

D: It appears that . . . the bureaucrat is governed by the Table of Ranks[4] in his understanding of who is above and who's below him.

B: Yes, official standing is what determines behavior. But the snob, he is not just a bureaucrat, his snobbism is not defined only by how he treats his superiors and inferiors. It also determines his artistic taste, and how he resolves other questions. For instance, let's imagine that a snob is at the theater, watching a brand-new play. He'd stay quiet and wait to see what the truly influential people would say about it first. Only then would he offer an opinion, attaching himself to an already expressed judgment.

Only then would he "bravely" start to praise, or, on the contrary, to deride the play. What he himself felt watching it, that doesn't matter to him, he doesn't trust his own impressions. In general, he doesn't exist independently, apart from public opinion, apart from the official assessment of high-ranking people, the established connoisseurs of culture, the arts, music, and so on. That's the snob for you. Unfortunately, there are even more snobs in Russia now than there used to be. People in the past still dared to express independent opinions and were not afraid to share them publicly. These days, of course, that's no longer the case.

D: Going back to Akhmatova, would you call her a snob?

B: No, she wasn't a snob. But there was a certain quality about her that one could call snobbish.

D: Like her different treatment of people.

B: Yes. In general, she tended to look down upon those who hadn't distinguished themselves somehow in the arts, literature, science, politics—she looked down on ordinary people.

D: Well, what do you think of her as a poet?

B: I respect her greatly as a poet. Nowadays she is considered to be one of our greatest poets. I think that's going too far, of course. Her range is too narrow, too trivial to merit such a high estimation. Even her temperament, her humanity, does not qualify her for true greatness.

D: Well, you know what the temperament of artists, especially the nervous kind, is like. . . . Besides, you were right to note that despite being persecuted all her life, she behaved with a lot of dignity.

B: Yes, with great dignity.

D: What's your assessment of her as a reader and as a literary scholar? Do you know what Eikhenbaum[5] thought of her? Do you remember his old books?

B: I do. I think very highly of her as a poet. She was without a doubt an important poet, one of the most important ones, even, of her time, of her circle.

D: Do you agree with Eikhenbaum's claim that she brought something new to Russian poetry, turned a new page, so to speak. . . . Do you remember? As far as her use of poetic language is concerned, and so forth. . . . His topic was *Acmeism*[6] in general, but he wrote mostly about Akhmatova. Personally, I don't completely agree with him.

B: He overestimates her importance, of course. His approach to her was Formalist. She didn't create a new poetic language. Certain new modalities, yes, there are those, but they are very specific, feminine. She didn't invent a whole new poetic language, though. Still, she was a good poet, a wonderful poet. We should add that the circle she belonged to, the Acmeists like Gumilev . . .

D: Mandelstam,[7] Gorodetsky,[8] Narbut . . . [9]

B: Yes, she thought very highly of Mandelstam, that I know. Gorodetsky—not so much. As for that other poet, Kuzmin,[10] he also belonged to the Acmeist circle. From an artistic standpoint he was probably the most significant poet of that group.

D: I'd say that was Mandelstam.

B: Mandelstam, too.

D: If we're talking about women's poetry, that is, what Akhmatova's poetry really excelled at, there are three names that come to mind (you already discussed, rather negatively, one of them): Zinaida Gippius, Akhmatova, and Marina Tsvetaeva.[11] Of those three, who do you value the most as a poet?

B: Marina Tsvetaeva, I suppose.

D: I don't doubt that.

B: Yes, Marina Tsvetaeva. Her poetry has the kind of depth lacking in . . .

D: . . . Akhmatova, and which is present even less in Gippius.

B: Ah, Gippius, of course! She was completely artificial: she was fabricated herself, and so was her poetry. As to Akhmatova . . . There was something false about her, true . . . but her poetry was not fake.

D: In terms of your personal connections and sympathies, you belonged to the Symbolist camp, correct?

B: Yes, the Symbolists. The most important poet for me, and not just as a poet but also as a thinker and a scholar, was Vyacheslav Ivanov. Vyacheslav Ivanov, yes. I still love him.[12]

D: As a poet, too?

B: Also as a poet.

D: I confess, I don't get it.

B: His style maybe rather unusual, too learned, sophisticated and so on for some, but still, some of his poems are truly remarkable, just remarkable.

D: Which one of his books do you see as most important?

B: The most important one? *Cor ardens*, which came out in two volumes.[13]

D: I am familiar with it.

B: But the anthologies before and after it are also significant. In truth, I don't know his work from the emigration very well, but I used to have a typed copy of some of his later poetry. You could already feel his decline. . . . The power of his earlier verse, especially in *Cor ardens*, was no longer there. There were echoes of earlier motifs, I suppose, but they were already much weaker. Still, overall, he was a very significant figure. I was able to get the first volume [of his collected works]. The complete collected works are being published in Belgium, in Brussels, right now—an amazing edition. So far, only the first volume has come out. I was able to get a copy, and read it, but couldn't acquire it for my own. The introduction was very interesting—it contained his detailed biography, including information about his last years, his death . . . [14]

D: What year did he die?

B: I believe he was eighty-four when he died. He's buried in Rome. Not too long before he passed away, he was able to get an audience with the Pope, the two of them talked for quite some time. Their conversation has been recounted in great detail. He was buried in the Dominican cemetery.

D: Did he become a Catholic?

B: No, he didn't. He held the same view of Catholicism as Vladimir Solovyov. He embraced all the parallels [between Eastern Orthodoxy and Catholicism], but he also shared Vladimir Solovyov's position that he couldn't—even though he understood the Eastern schism—join Catholicism without his own Church uniting with it as well. Still, he was certain that the unification of the two was bound to happen, sooner or later.

D: The unification of Eastern and Western Christianity?

B: Yes. And he moved toward it himself . . . ahead of time, in anticipation of its coming . . .

D: But he didn't leave his own faith behind . . .

B: He didn't forsake Eastern Orthodoxy, true. The same happened with Vyacheslav Ivanov. All his life, he felt very close to Catholicism. After all, he lived so many years in Catholic countries, in Italy, in France. . . . In the beginning, when he was still a student of Mommsen,[15] he was drawn to German culture and Protestantism, but that didn't last very long; the rest of his life he was connected with Catholicism. He even taught at Catholic schools—in Italy . . .

D: Okay, Mikhail Mikhailovich, let's go back to the Acmeist circle. Did you meet Akhmatova on neutral territory, or did you . . .

B: Completely neutral, over tea . . . I think at the home of Maria Yudina.[16]

D: Really! Another interesting detail in passing.

B: Yes, yes, but that was later. That was our last meeting, I think.

D: So you already knew her?

B: Who?

D: Maria Yudina.

B: I knew her well before I knew Akhmatova . . .

D: Fine, we'll turn to this subject later, toward the end of our conversation. As far as the Acmeist circle goes, did you . . .

B: I was not part of it. Not at all.

D: So you knew neither Narbut, nor Zenkevich . . . [17]

B: I had heard their names.

D: Not even Sergey Gorodetsky?

B: I did meet him, under rather unfortunate circumstances. Balmont[18] was supposed to give a public lecture. Many people came to hear him. He showed up, and sat down at the podium, clutching a book in his hands. He began squirming, twisting, and tipping to one side.

D: Who did that? Balmont?

B: Balmont, Balmont. He was drunk. Completely drunk. He was almost always drunk in those last years. . . . He was so intoxicated, he started to fall off his seat. . . . Suddenly, there appeared the lanky figure of that same Gorodetsky. He grabbed Balmont by the arm and escorted him behind the curtain. Then he came out again, and announced that, unfortunately . . .

D: . . . he wasn't feeling well . . .

B: Yes, Balmont wasn't feeling well, and the lecture had to be canceled. He said something about the tickets, too, I can't remember. That's when I saw him first, that beanpole of a man. But I knew his poetry quite well. Later Gorodetsky changed a lot. He played a role in Vyacheslav Ivanov's biography, back when Vyacheslav Ivanov and the late Annibal, Zinovieva-Annibal,[19] were still with us.

D: She was his wife, correct?

B: Yes, she was. She was his second wife. He divorced the first one. She was his second. According to them, love could not be limited to two people only, a third was necessary, so, put simply, theirs was another kind of ménage à trois. So, they were looking for a third person to join them. That's when Gorodetsky appeared—very young, attractive. . . . They embraced him as the missing third in their relationship. But nothing came of it, after all.[20]

D: It worked in Merezhkovsky's case, but not for them.

B: Well, Merezhkovsky didn't really want that man . . .
D: Filosofov.
B: The whole thing happened against his will.
D: You can build a ménage à trois in many ways. . . . You could have, for example, two women! [*laughs*]
B: Yes, but in this case, they wanted something else. . . . However, it didn't work out. After that, they found an artist to play the role of the third, but that relationship didn't work out either. Then Zinovyeva-Annibal passed away, at a very young age.
D: And he was left all alone, right?
B: Yes, he was left by himself, and he remained faithful to her memory to the end.
D: Yes, but he. . . . His fame coincided with the beginning of Acmeism . . . much like his own Adam: "Forgive you me, enchanting vapor / And universe engulfed in fog . . ."[21]
Do you remember it?
B: I do.
D: It was celebrated as the manifesto of Acmeism when it appeared in *Apollo*.
B: I remember that.
D: "But the translucent wind's so much better / For the new worlds created for us all . . ."[22]
B: However, Vyacheslav Ivanov was never an Acmeist.
D: True. So, these Acemists, who exerted great influence over many other poetic circles, but especially the Leningrad poets . . . did you shy away from them? Did you shun the Futurists, too?
B: The Futurists? Yes, I kept my distance from them. I knew them, and saw them around, but . . .
D: Even Khlebnikov?[23]
B: I didn't know him personally. No, Khlebnikov I never really knew.
D: You never attended any Futurist events?
B: Never. I must tell you my own circle ridiculed and treated them with contempt because to us they represented just another passing fashion, and we believed that their movement would never give birth to anything long-lasting. We did make an exception for Mayakovsky,[24] but only up to a point, up to a point. We didn't think too much of him either.
D: So, who was in your university circle? You are talking about your last years at the university, right? How many years did you spend studying at the University of Petersburg after coming from Odessa?

B: Four more years.
D: Four? So, two years in Odessa and four more in Petersburg?
B: No, one in Odessa.
D: So five all together. That's standard.
B: Yes, five. But that wasn't supposed to be the norm. The course of study was supposed to take four years, but it was rare that one would really [finish in four] . . .
D: Right. Last time you talked a lot about your professors. But you didn't say much about the students. . . . You told us about this—I forget the word in Greek—"Navel" society . . .
B: Yes, that was the circle I moved in. As a group of philologists we approached everything that came from contemporary culture with a healthy dose of skepticism: all those Futurists, Acmeists, and even more so the poets of the revolutionary Left who were the poets of the times.
D: People like Skitalets,[25] they were not your cup of tea . . .
B: Skitalets? Of course! To be honest, I thought some of his work was rather interesting, and read it with pleasure . . . for example, his "Cinders" [Огарки] . . .
D: How about Gorky?[26] Did you like him?
B: Not particularly. Only a few things. I did understand, of course, we all did, his importance as an artist. But we didn't care for him. We didn't like his style.

Besides, since we knew what sort of a person he was, that too didn't make him very appealing to us. He was an astounding person. You know, he seemed completely deprived of willpower, quite effeminate. He was interested in whatever those closest to him at the time happened to be interested in: the Revolution, the Counter-Revolution, whatever. . . . In short, he was a flip-flop. For instance, someone who didn't sympathize with the revolutionary movement would go to him, the two would chat, and Gorky would whole-heartedly agree with everything he heard. Then another one would come, a representative of the revolutionary circles, and they'd have a talk, and Gorky would agree with him, too. He had no willpower at all. He couldn't pick a side, once and for all. No. He would choose one thing, then another, then a third. True, life later forced him to commit to one position, but to his last days he also . . . He kept swinging from one end to the next. And that was caused not by any sort of conformism, no, but by his strange, unusual lack of will. Not conformism, though, no, and he wasn't doing it to derive any personal profit.

D: There was a certain broadness about him. You are suggesting that he didn't find a way to combine different viewpoints, and alternated between them instead?

B: Alternated, yes, that's exactly it. The different viewpoints could not agree with one another. There was nothing consistent to which they could adhere. It's not that he was eclectic. He simply was one person one moment, and someone else the next. You are probably familiar with Khodasevich's reminiscences of Gorky?

D: No, I haven't read them.

B: They are quite good, by the way. Khodasevich[27] presents him in a positive light, all in all.

D: He supported him fully.

B: He did. Still, Khodasevich always stayed true to himself, that is, he couldn't help but exhibit a certain malice. . . . Anyway, he says that Gorky really liked cheating, and cheaters in general. When he was the one deceived, he always showed great compassion and forgave everything. He loved to deceive others as well. He found swindlers, cheaters to be quite attractive. He was with them in spirit, we might say. So, yes . . . That's what he wrote.

D: Who did? Khodasevich?

B: Yes, Khodasevich. He offers many examples from Gorky's life. Besides that, I had an acquaintance who once worked [with him] . . . Adrianov, a historian. He was better known as Zoya Lodiy's husband. Zoya Lodiy—perhaps you've heard of her?[28]

D: No.

B: Really? You never heard of her? Zoya Lodiy was an incredible singer, but not an opera singer—a chamber singer of great subtlety. She performed very rare pieces, then, later on, music from around the world. She spent several years studying Italian folk songs in Italy.

So anyhow, he was Zoya Lodiy's husband. He was much older than her. She died very young, though. She was a hunchback, Zoya Lodiy was, but she had a beautiful face. By the way, her marble gravestone is very famous now. It was carved by the artist . . . I forget his name. But he was one of our best artists. Anyways, Professor Adrianov told me a lot about Gorky, whom he knew very well. The two mostly met at the editorial offices of *Delo*.

D: Ah! Is that the journal *Delo*?

B: Correct. Their paths crossed in other literary venues all the time as well. He, too, had much to say about Gorky's lack of constancy as far as his views were concerned.
D: To be honest, your description matches completely Lenin's account of Gorky. Do you remember it? "As a politician, Gorky lacks character completely."[29]
B: Yes, yes, that's right, but not only as a politician. That was true of his worldview as a whole. His approach to religion is another example: one moment, he was an atheist . . . You have probably read about his meetings with academician Pavlov. . . . Such a complete reversal. . . . But in the end he was, if not exactly a believer, then certainly a religious man. He understood well what religion was. Blok, for instance, recounted how once the two of them got into an argument [about that]. He sided with the atheists at the time, while Gorky argued that, despite everything, the human soul was immortal. It's all true. Blok himself said it. But I don't remember now where, exactly, he wrote about it.
D: Mikhail Mikhailovich, and you didn't have the chance to meet Gorky yourself?
B: Gorky? No. I saw him only a few times, and then (no need to record this), when I was imprisoned Gorky even sent two telegrams to the appropriate institutions.
D: Gorky?
B: Yes, in my defense.
D: Well, that needs to be recorded.
B: He was familiar with my first book,[30] and had heard a lot about me in general. We shared many acquaintances . . .
D: So Gorky sent a telegram . . .
B: Yes, a telegram . . .
D: To NKVD . . . [31] or what was it called then?
B: Speaking on my behalf. It was still GPU[32] back then.
D: What year was that?
B: 1929 . . . I believe.
D: I see. So Gorky . . . Later he stopped trying to intervene.
B: Later, yes. There were two telegrams by him included in the evidence at my trial.
D: You don't say!
B: But later he did stop trying to intervene.

D: His wife, Ekaterina Pavlovna,[33] did a lot of good.
B: Ekaterina Pavlovna, yes. I didn't know her, but my late wife visited her several times. They were acquaintances and liked each other a lot. She was then the head of the so-called . . .
D: The Red Cross.
B: Yes, the political Red Cross. Vinaver was its official head, while she served as vice chair. But she was really the heart and soul of the organization.
D: Yes, she received a lot of praise for her work at the time. But then . . . their work became less and less meaningful later, and gradually fizzled out.
B: Yes, it was absolutely useless.
D: Your thoughts about Gorky are very interesting. There are many conflicting emotions here, though, because, on the one hand, although what you're saying can be interpreted as negative . . .
B: But not entirely negative.
D: At the same time, he helped so many different people, in various ways. Who could be intellectually further away from Gorky than Vasily Rozanov?[34] And yet, he threw his weight behind him in 1918!
B: Yes, yes.
D: This shows he had a really big heart, despite everything.
B: A big heart, yes! Also, a genuine goodness, which he without a doubt possessed. An unconditional goodness. And another thing, you probably know the literary scholar Gachev.[35] He might have been one of your students. Gachev.
D: No, I only know him by name.
B: He belongs to the same group of literary critics as Kozhinov,[36] Bocharov.[37] They worked together on the three-volume edition, *Literary Theory* . . .
D: Of the three, only Kozhinov used to be my student.
[*A cat is heard meowing*]
B: Poor kitty!
D: What should we do? Who are we supposed to be recording: the cat or you? [*both laugh*] Seems she's now quiet again.
B: Anyway. Gachev wrote a very interesting study (which hasn't been published yet, but will be, in its own time) about Gorky, in particular his "tramp" period, his play *The Lower Depths*, Gorky's work in general. He claims Gorky embodies the origins of the carnival.

D: So he's developing further your ideas.
B: Yes, yes. Gachev, you might say, is a student of mine, but not in the usual sense, as he studied at Moscow University. Anyway . . . [He claims Gorky] embodies the origins of carnival, because he is only interested in life once it parts ways with the ordinary. The serious, day-to-day existence that took place in between carnivals didn't concern him. It was the carnivalesque life, life outside the norm, that made him feel as if he truly belonged. The analysis of Gorky's Italian stories is especially intriguing. For instance, he wrote about the strike of tram workers—I think that was it, do you remember?
D: Yes, I remember, that was it.
B: What he is describing in that case is pure carnival: He is looking for disruptions to the regular course of life.
D: But on the other hand, we have *The Life of Matvey Kozhenyakin*.[38]
B: There were other aspects to his writing, of course, but at its heart . . .
D: Consider also *The Life of Klim Samgin*.[39]
B: Gachev sees even *Klim Samgin* as an expression of carnival, an internalized carnival.
D: Well, carnivals are happy, festive . . .
B: Yes, festive. There may not be much festivity and joy there, but still—we are presented with a parade of masks, a parade of masks. . . . There are no individual faces. By the way, there's a type of person that Gorky didn't like—I call them agelasts[40]—in real life . . .
D: What kind of people?
B: People who are too serious, who don't appreciate laughter, jokes, pranks, mystifications. He didn't like them. And so, in *Klim Samgin* there are no positive characters of that sort. All those heroes, the communists, and Kutuzov[41] most of all . . .
D: Ah, the positive characters in Soviet literature! What a joke!
B: No, no, Gorky didn't present him in a positive light. It was quite negative. . . . He is such a dry character. He is a singer, but his singing lacks feeling. It's all a formality to him. And, in general, he doesn't really understand people.

Moving on. His analysis of the play *The Lower Depths*[42] claims that, as a matter of fact, the actual hero there, the real positive character in the work, is Luka (Luka has been completely misunderstood), and he claims that Gorky himself saw him as the protagonist. That's how it turns out to be in the play. As soon as he appears . . .

D: The play may intend it this way, but then, later, in 1933 . . .
B: Later, you say! What came later was a result of that lack of willpower in his worldview. . . . He was persuaded that Luka[43] is a liar. . . . True, he is a good person, and tries to help others, but how? He offers people illusions, falsehoods, which may be helpful in life, but which are actually unacceptable, degrading in the long run. So he bought into this interpretation and started to see his own work in this light.
D: Very interesting. . . . But let's continue. . . . Could you please talk a little about yourself, about your own life at the time? So, you finished the university . . .
B: Yes.[44]
D: Then February came.
B: Let's see. February, yes, the February Revolution.[45]
D: Were you still a student then?
B: I was. I was just finishing up. Here, in Leningrad . . . no, not Leningrad, it was still Petrograd. . . . [46] The famine began . . .
D: The famine started right after the October Revolution.
B: True. But February was also very difficult.
D: Following that February. . . . Do you have any interesting memories from the summer of 1917? We always skip over this period, as if it didn't happen.
B: I'll tell you this, but there's no need to record it . . .
D: We can erase it later. . . . Or we don't have to transcribe it, if you prefer.
B: I did not welcome the February Revolution. I thought, or I should say in my circle we believed that it'll all certainly end very badly. We knew well, by the way, the leaders of the Revolution . . . of the February Revolution, that is, those who in part made the February Revolution happen, and then . . . well . . . those who were promoted by the February Revolution.
D: The Kadets?
B: Yes, the Kadets, and also the . . .
D: The SR's?[47]
B: Yes, the Trudoviks. It was the party that Kerensky[48] himself, and others of his ilk, belonged to. We were of the opinion that all those intellectuals were utterly incompetent to govern, they were incompetent to defend the February Revolution (that is, if it would have to be defended). So, inevitably, the extreme left, the Bolsheviks, would take over. And that's what actually happened. We were right in our predictions.

D: There weren't many highly notable Bolsheviks at the time.
B: True, they were much less known to us. We were better acquainted with the left SRs, also the extreme leftists among them, who later collaborated with the Bolsheviks. Then there were also people with the most left, radical convictions in the circle of SRs, and in the circle of social democrats too, who then . . . joined the Communist Party, and so forth. Trotsky[49] was the most famous among those. . . . Zinoviev,[50] too, to an extent . . .
D: Trotsky joined the Bolsheviks only in May.
B: Yes, there were many like him. Dzerzhinsky . . . [51] No, Dzerzhinsky was not a party member, I think he didn't belong to any party, he was simply an extremely religious person, and was preparing to enter a monastery.
D: You don't say!
B: Yes. A Catholic monastery. He was a religious fanatic, a Catholic, who then crossed over to the other side. . . . But he was the exception, so to speak, very atypical as far as the Bolsheviks were concerned. . . . An unusual person, cut from a different cloth. . . . Vyshinsky[52] was a Social Democrat who later became a Bolshevik . . .
D: He was a Menshevik until 1921.
B: Really?
D: Yes. He was anti-Bolshevik all through the Civil War, and joined them only after they won.
B: Yes. He even gave a lecture (I wasn't present myself, but friends of mine went and told me about it later) after the February Revolution, but before the October one—or maybe not, it could have been after October—in which he welcomed the advance of the Volunteer Army in the south and talked about some kind of a plan to fight the Bolsheviks.

So yes. I thought at the time that the most extremist party would take over, that we would end up with either a monarchy or the most extreme ochlocracy[53] in Russia . . .
D: Excuse me, but are you sure that these aren't these retroactive memories, seen in light of what happened later?
B: No, no, I really thought so back then.
D: You already sensed that in February—that the choice was between monarchy and absolute extremism?
B: Yes. And that the monarchy, in short . . . that the victory of the extreme elements was unavoidable. We were very pessimistic. We thought it was the end. Of course, it would be impossible to resurrect the monarchy.

There was no one left, and nobody to back them up. It was inevitable that the victory would go to the masses of soldiers and peasants in uniforms, who didn't hold anything dear, the proletariat that did not constitute a proper historical class and did not have any values, had nothing at all to speak of. . . . They had spent their lives fighting for the most basic material needs. They were the ones who would surely seize power in the end. And nobody would be able to overthrow them because the intelligentsia was not capable of it.

D: So you never went to mass meetings and protested, then?

B: No, I never did. I stayed home and read or went to the library when it was still heated. Never joined any of the protests in the streets.

D: Did you ever hear Kerensky speak?

B: Twice. I immediately saw that he was an insignificant person, who somehow managed to climb too high, and was completely unqualified for his job. . . . By the way, there was a family I was very close with: the husband was my friend, then I became also close with his wife, a former baroness. She was Kerensky's last love. He came to her every night, spent his evenings at her place. . . . His last love. Though who knows, maybe later he fell in love again.

My friend, who completely shared my views, once said to Kerensky, "What are you talking about? They'll get rid of you at first opportunity!" And Kerensky replied, "Excuse me, but we know everything, we are watching the Bolsheviks closely, don't you worry, they can't do anything to us. . . ." That was literally the last time we saw each other, just days before the coup and Kerensky's escape, maybe three or four days before. I must tell you that Kerensky was very much liked by the masses. . . . He had quite a bit of authority.

D: I'd rather say he was popular.

B: Popular, yes. But it was all very superficial. I remember my friend telling me how, the first time Kerensky came to their place (he lived at the time at the Polytechnic Institute, in Petrograd), the doorman teared up: "Kerensky was here! Kerensky was here!" He was moved to actual tears.

D: How about you? Weren't you moved yourself by his remarkable eloquence?

B: He was never that remarkably eloquent. That's all just a made-up story, the myth about his oratory talent. I heard him give a speech twice. His style was very crude, vulgar, the style of a demagogue, I should say.

D: He, too, was a carnival character then.

B: Yes, but not by choice, and not even by nature. There was something of the carnival in him, though . . .

D: So he didn't captivate you at all?

B: Not at all, not at all.

D: How about Pavel Milyukov?[54] You must have had some respect for someone like him?

B: I did have a lot of respect for him, absolutely, but I considered him powerless. People like Milyukov, it seemed to me back then, could not govern Russia.

D: He didn't have what it takes to govern. . . . How interesting!

B: Yes, yes, that's interesting indeed.

D: But you understand that the circle governing Russia then was actually powerless . . . and that's why they were overthrown, tossed out, because they themselves, one could say, were already dispersed all over the place.

B: That's correct.

D: After all, besides Stolypin,[55] there wasn't anyone else who . . .

B: Yes, nobody . . .

D: . . . could be considered a prominent force.

B: Yes. Stolypin was a very important player, a much greater force than he's given credit for, and quite far-sighted. He thought that the only way to save Russia from an impending revolution (his ideas, most likely, did present the correct solution to our problem) was creating out of the peasantry a prosperous middle class of smallholding landowners. He believed that only private property made a person respectable and . . .

D: . . . stable.

B: Stable, yes. But nothing came of it, he was not able to implement his ideas for a reform of the peasantry. So there you have it . . .

D: His ideas were incongruent with the nature of the Russian people.

B: Do you really think so?

D: Our history as a nation would suggest so. . . . In this case Gorky was far more attuned to the Russian national character.

B: Well, let's look at the kolkhoz[56] then. The collective farms are not working out very well—and not just here, but everywhere else, too, in all the other Slavic countries. It's the same everywhere. But that's not the point. I'm trying to remember how things were back then, today I don't even. . . . Even back then I didn't give those problems much thought, though. It was obvious that the old regime was in decay. That whole story about Rasputin was[57]—how should I put it—truly fateful and prophetic.

D: That's very interesting. But let's go back to the official taping and our philological concerns. So, the February and October Revolutions came and went . . . Then 1918 rolled around . . . On the one hand, those were hungry times, but on the other, we had the so-called "café" period in Russian poetry.

B: Why "café period"?

D: Because poetry was no longer to be found in literary journals, but was now . . .

B: . . . shared in cafés, I see!

D: Did you have the chance to experience it, or did your solid academic ways prevent you from lowering yourself to their level?

B: Of course, I didn't stoop to that level. By the way, I was already familiar with that kind of artistic activity. . . . But it was very different before the Revolution . . . "The Stray Dog"[58] Cabaret, for example . . .

D: Did you go to "The Stray Dog"?

B: Yes, sure, but as a guest, nothing more. I didn't know the scene very well.

D: In the capacity of a "pharmacist" . . . [59]

B: Exactly.

D: . . . as they were called?

B: I also sometimes went to "The Comedians' Resting Place."[60]

D: What are your memories of "The Stray Dog" and "The Players' Rest"? I'm very curious. I've heard from the bohemians that you were called (well, not you in particular, but people like you) "pharmacists" . . .

B: True, I was considered a "pharmacist" there, which is why I did not go there often.

D: Who did you get to hear there?

B: All kinds of poetic scum. The only really remarkable poet I heard there was . . . Kuzmin![61]

D: At "The Stray Dog"?

B: Yes, I heard him recite his poetry there.

D: And that was still during the war?

B: Maybe it was at "The Comedians' Resting Place," I can't recall for sure. Probably both cafés.

D: Both "The Stray Dog" and "The Comedians' Resting Place" were in Petersburg, right?

B: Yes, in Petersburg. I think I also visited another similar place on the Nevsky Prospect:[62] "The Poets' Café."[63] I went there only once. Inside, there were some bearded men wearing berets, like the French poets. I didn't like any of it. It wasn't very serious.

D: Do you remember Rukavishnikov?[64]

B: I do. I did know him.

D: He sounded like a scholar, though he really wasn't one, but still, like Shengeli . . .[65]

B: Shengeli, yes.

D: He never missed a single opportunity to perform.

B: But what kind of a poet was he?

D: He wasn't a poet at all.

B: He was terrible even as a translator. . . . He also turned out to be a bad scholar.

D: That's the sort of environment Yesenin[66] joined and took shape in.

B: Yesenin? Yes, that's where he took shape. . . . We are in murky waters with Yesenin. Kozhinov looked into this issue. It turns out that Yesenin. . . . Usually, the story goes as follows: a primitive, pure Russian peasant moves to Moscow, Leningrad, and the atmosphere there ruins him, turns him into a drunkard and a womanizer, and so forth.

But Kozhinov told me something very different: that Esenin had embraced high culture even before he arrived in the big cities, that he had friends he corresponded with there, and so forth. So he had formed his views even before he fell under the influence of the bohemians. So the bohemians replaced the more serious trends in his thought, and his poetry.

D: The Symbolist salons, like the one run by Merezhkovsky and Gippius, were far more serious.

B: Merezhkovsky and Gippius, that's partially true, yes. There was also someone else, whose name is not well known. But Kozhinov unearthed that, too. His name was . . . It'll come to me. . . . My memory, ugh! In her memoirs, Tsvetaeva talks about visiting someone's home, where she listened to Kuzmin. . . . Do you remember?

D: That's in her prose?

B: Marina's, yes, in Marina Tsvetaeva's prose. She describes this person's home there. The host was a very anglicized man, the famous builder of a well-known battleship, whose name is not mentioned, and his two sons were there, too. One of them was a poet. Or maybe one was the son, and the other was his friend. . . . One was a poet. So, this poet knew Yesenin and exerted great influence over him. But Marina Tsvetaeva doesn't say who he was, that poet.

D: But Kozhinov was able to unearth it all?

B: He did.

D: I'll have to ask him. Though he doesn't call me anymore . . .

B: Were you able to record Kruchenykh, too?[67]

D: He died before I had that chance. He seemed afraid of something. I have no idea what. He was a very suspicious man.

B: I met him toward the end of his life. Well, maybe not that late, actually. The last time I saw him was twenty years ago . . .

D: So you did know some of the Futurists, after all?

B: Yes, I found him really impressive. . . . He was sixty at the time . . .

D: He looked younger.

B: Yes, much younger, kind of short, and quite lively, extremely lively! His manner of speaking was so interesting. He told me about the work of one of his friends, who was studying Dostoevsky's character names. He spoke so well, made everything sound so fascinating.

D: In general, he was a man of great talents—not necessarily academic, but philological talents.

B: Without a doubt. Even though the analysis of the names in Dostoevsky wasn't his own work, he was able to present it very convincingly.

D: It seems to me that given your own ideas, you shouldn't have too negative an opinion of Kruchenykh's *zaum*?[68]

B: I'm not against it, not at all!

D: It's just that earlier you said that . . .

B: Yes, I was trying to remember . . . We certainly underestimated . . .

D: You told me there was nothing of interest there . . .

B: True, but you see . . . It's not that there isn't anything interesting, it's more that it was all one big . . .

D: Bluff.

B: Vulgarity, I'd say.

D: Bluff.

B: Both. But no, I am not against it [Futurism] at all. Not at all. I consider Khlebnikov to be a remarkable poet.

D: So your attitude toward Khlebnikov has changed. Now you . . .

B: Even back then I. . . . Even then I put him in a separate category, and later—even more so.

D: What do you find interesting about Khlebnikov?

B: Everything. His type or style of thinking fascinates me. He is a deeply carnivalesque man. Deeply carnivalesque. In him, carnival is not superficial, an exterior mask. No, it resides within, underlying his subjective experiences, his thought expressions, and so forth. He could not be contained within any frames and did not accept any existing foundations. He understood perfectly what reality, realist thought, meant. Least of all could you accuse him of being short-sighted and playing games. . . . No.

D: But he seemed very distant from everything.

B: Not at all. He understood reality, people, very well. He understood everything perfectly, but he did distance himself from it, if you will, though not because of some abstract ideas, like others, no. His detachment was the result of the desire to pursue symbolic, even somewhat mystical ideas. He had almost prophetic visions. But you couldn't contain those within the limits of the type of mysticism that was popular then.

D: Symbolist mysticism.

B: Yes. He was different. His was a peculiar mystical vision. Mysticism without being mystical, we might say. His thought had enormous, cosmic dimensions, but it was not abstractly cosmic.

D: I don't understand.

B: He was able to—and this is why I claim his nature deep down was purely carnivalesque—move away from the particular, and capture the boundless, endlessly universal, the whole world, we might say. He was one of the presiding chairmen of this world, of the whole Universe. He was able to experience that within himself, and then put it into words. But you can't interpret those words the same way you interpret ordinary language about personal things, individual experiences, private people. You just can't. If you're actually capable of entering the stream of his cosmic, universal thought, then you'd be able to understand everything, and everything would become interesting. He was a remarkable human being. Truly remarkable. All the rest of the Futurists are dwarfed in his presence. Dwarfed. Little, insignificant people. This Kruchenykh, for instance, and the rest of them. They were talented enough, quite capable. David Burliuk[69] and . . . that other one . . .

D: Vladimir?[70]

B: Vladimir. Vladimir was also probably quite talented.

D: Did you know them personally? Did you run into them often?

B: I met [David] Burliuk, but I just saw him around, we were not personally acquainted. However, I knew people who told me a lot about him and his work. He was an interesting man. Quite interesting.
D: There was a third brother, Vladimir, an artist.
B: He was an artist, yes, but I don't really know him. As for David Burliuk, he was rather insignificant as a writer and an artist. He turned out to be quite the businessman later. He became rich in America. There he ran a salon, which attracted the American ultra-left, radical intelligentsia. Each year he celebrated very solemnly the anniversary of the October Revolution with a reception at his house, and so forth. He was quite the character.
D: Now it's time to turn to Mayakovsky. Did you meet the young Mayakovsky at all?
B: Not once. After all, he lived in Moscow then.
D: He was in Petersburg during the war.
B: We never met.
D: Not even at "The Stray Dog"?
B: No, we didn't run into each other there at all. Or perhaps he was there, but, you know, back then. . . . Now Mayakovsky is the "great Mayakovsky." For us at the time he was just another loudmouth we didn't think much of.
D: So you have no personal impressions of him?
B: No. Only when . . .
D: Okay, then tell us about the two times you met him after the Revolution. Then we'll chat more generally.
B: The first time we met was on Stoleshnikov Street, at the literary offices in a ten-storied building, I believe.
D: Ten floors, you say?
B: You're right. Where today there are the "Soviet Writer" offices, "Roman Theater," etc. Valery Bryusov was head of the Literary Department then.
D: The Literary Department of the People's Commissariat of Education, which Bryusov chaired. Was that in Nirnzee's House?
B: Yes, it was, at the time.
D: We are talking about 1920–21.
B: Yes, that period, 1920–21. I used to go there. Once there was supposed to be a poets' evening. I went into Bryusov's office. He wasn't there. His second-in-command, Pyotr Kuzko,[71] was there, though. Kuzko served as Bryusov's deputy at the People's Commissariat, and was one of the "old"

Bolsheviks, even though he was still quite young at the time. He was a handsome man, a redhead, very pleasant and kind. We spent some time together just sitting and talking. We were already acquainted, can't remember where. Maybe it was at the Academy of Fine Arts. But we barely knew each other. We chatted for a long time, he told me a lot, especially about his encounters with Vyacheslav Ivanov. He also spoke at length about Bryusov. He had great respect for him, as a poet and a scholar. Kuzko himself was very well-read, quite knowledgeable without being a proper scholar. He was modest, kind, and very liberal in his views, despite the fact that the Party had given him the assignment to shadow Bryusov.

D: So, he acted as his deputy?

B: He did.

D: And Bryusov had just joined the Party?

B: Yes, correct. . . . So, according to him, Bryusov was petty by nature, and seemed fearful all the time. . . . "He comes to my place," Kuzko told me, "supposedly to play chess, but keeps asking me about various Party business, what people think of him, whether he has any chances of keeping his job or if he'd be sacked soon, and so forth." In a word, he was displaying a certain small-mindedness, a certain paranoia—and he'd never be able to rise above that.

We were waiting for Bryusov, but he never came. Other people kept barging in with questions and requests for Kuzko in his official capacity. One of them was a very tall man. I immediately realized it was Mayakovsky: I had seen his picture, maybe even seen him somewhere before. He was dressed very fashionably, at a time when most had pretty shabby clothes. He was wearing a flared coat. That was very trendy back then. In general, his clothes looked all new, fashionable, and it was clear he was very aware of that himself, that he was dressed like a dandy. Like a dandy. [*chuckles*] But a real dandy doesn't show any awareness of his attire. This is, if you like, the first sign of dandyism, to wear your clothes as if you're paying no attention to them at all. Instead, Mayakovsky seemed fully aware and proud of his flared coat, his trendy clothes, his whole stature. . . . In short, I didn't like him.

Kuzko then gave him the newest issue (fresh off the press) of, if I remember correctly, the journal of *LITO*,[72] a special edition. Journals were hard to come by in those days. . . . Anyway, some of Mayakovsky's verse was published there. So, he grabbed the journal, and immediately tried to find his own poems. It was clear he relished seeing them, savored the fact that they were now in print. A published author! It left a very bad impression on me.

I should say that such behavior is quite normal, but I expected more of Mayakovsky, who was, after all, a man of carnival, and was therefore supposed to be above such things, and should not have cared about his costume or whether his poems were published or not. Instead, I saw the opposite: like any small-minded person, he was thrilled to see his work in print, even though he was already famous and widely published. Just like the clerk in that short story by Chekhov, the one who fell under a horse, and then was so happy to read about his own accident in the paper. So yes, I didn't like that about him. I don't remember what he said. He talked with Kuzko, not with me. He then left, and soon after I did, too.

D: Is this the only time you saw him?

B: No, we met one more time—at a Poets' meeting, if I am not mistaken. Poets recited their work and each poet was supposed to represent a different movement. At the time there was, as you know, a whole gloomy obscure mass of such movements. Everybody and their mother read their poetry. Then it was Valery Bryusov's turn. I never saw him privately anymore, just in public, on the stage. He read his poem . . . I can't recall the title, though. I do remember these lines:

> Is the Klassische Walpurgisnacht
> Taking over Soviet Moscow . . . [73] and so on.

"Klassische Walpurgisnacht" means "the classical Walpurgis night."[74] Many poets I'd never heard of read their work. There were also representatives of the other arts. I remember when the group of Neo-realists in sculpture was established. They created some kind of small sculptures out of newspaper. I thought it was all very interesting, everybody was quite talented, but there was no future development possible, no continuation. . . . And indeed, that's where it all ended. So Mayakovsky also recited one of his poems . . . "An Extraordinary . . ."

D: "The Unusual Adventure."[75] A conversation with the sun.

B: And this time I did like him. I liked him on the stage. He behaved very modestly. His reading was brilliant! Brilliant! He didn't gesticulate much. Others said he gesticulated too much. That's not true. "I said to him,

'Take a seat, luminary' . . ." He extended his arm as he read, "Take a seat," as if . . .

D: He was inviting in the sun.

B: I liked it. I liked him then, and also liked his poem.

D: Did you read much of his work at the time?

B: I did, quite a bit. We used to read everything back then, we just gulped it down, even the trash. But Mayakovsky—of course I read him.

D: Did you read "A Cloud in Pants,"[76] "War and Peace"?[77]

B: I did. I read them. I remember liking his "War and Peace" very much. There were some very interesting verses there, quite good. But there were also, of course, fake, fabricated, inauthentic lines there. To the very end he couldn't get rid of that falsity, deliberateness, even in "At the Top of My Voice."[78] Still there were some splendid lines too, simply splendid!

D: What in "At the Top of My Voice" feels to you as fabricated and inauthentic?

B: I don't remember the exact lines. . . . But there's a lot that's good there. . . . For example, this:

> I know the power of words, I know how they alarm,
> These words are not the kind that crowds would applaud . . .[79]

What follows is simply magnificent:

> [*B and D together*]
> Such words make coffins burst out from the earth,
> And march forward on their own four oak legs.
> Sometimes they'd be thrown out, left unpublished, not in print,
> And yet those words would still pull forth under the tightened saddle . . .

B: "Centuries ring, and trains crawl / To kiss poetry's . . ."[80]

D: "To lick."

B: Excuse me?

D: Not "kiss," but "lick" . . . stylistically . . .

B: Forgive me, "lick poetry's . . ." Yes, I remember, "lick poetry's calloused hands." What do you think he meant by that?

D: Do you like it or not?

B: I actually do like it.

D: So, "the trains crawl to lick poetry's hands" . . . Mayakovsky announces clearly that poetry is above everything. The trains will lick . . .
B: That's powerful. And then: "trifles . . . seeming trifles"
D: Yes, that's another fragment:

> I know the power of words: seeming trifles
> That fall like petals under a dancer's heels,
> But man has a soul, lips, bones . . . [81]

That poem's not finished.
B: That's very, very good: "man has a soul, lips, bones." It's not bad that the poem cuts off here. It's completely clear. There's nothing left to prove. That's so good!
D: You, of course, were not like him, your broad cultural background produced a very different artistic and stylistic sensibility.
B: Yes, a very different artistic sensibility. But I should also note the following: I was very familiar with the literature of the Left in the West, especially in France. They went as far as our Futurists, if not more. Our Futurists seemed like children by comparison and used to be simple copycats at first. That was true even of Mayakovsky, to an extent.
D: Very interesting.
B: But he did forge his own poetic language.
D: Do you really think Mayakovsky created a new language?
B: I do. That is . . . What do you mean by "new language"?
D: Well, I mean it in the sense that he introduced a new "principle" in poetry rather than new formal characteristics.
B: Yes, absolutely. I believe he created . . .
D: How do you see it? How would you define this principle?
B: That's hard, after all, I am not a theorist of poetry. Usually, it's defined as a new tonality, not as it was before, not syllabo-tonic.
D: If before poetry was, let's say, syllabo-tonic, now it became intonation-based.
B: Yes, intonation-based. . . . A new tonality, which he brought as close to declamation as possible, the type of declamation that is familiar, populist—the way the orators of the French Commune used to speak, almost like a scream. Mayakovsky himself used to say that he "yelled." Not "wrote," not "sang," but "yelled." Somehow, he was able to transform that scream into poetry.

D: We are back to your favorite topic, carnival. . . . But you invest this term with so much content.
B: Yes.
D: I didn't get it at first, but then I read, three years ago, your excellent book about Rabelais. It was still new back then. I didn't understand what carnival was at first. . . . But you see the carnivalesque as a common characteristic of all artistic activity, of all great art.
B: That's correct.
D: That's why you choose Rabelais, and then, at the opposite end, Dostoevsky. . . . The unity of these contradictions . . . In that context Mayakovsky can also be seen as an extremely important author.
B: There are many carnivalesque moments in his work, true.
D: "Mystery" and "bouffe" are everywhere in his poetry.
B: Yes, everywhere.
D: Even, you understand, when he engages in such carnivalesque nonsense as using advertisements and so on, there still emerge serious undertones there, and vice versa. I'm so glad you see it this way, your interpretation is very clear and truthful . . . It goes against the general trend, but . . . This is the right context. . . . That's how I imagine it really was. . . . We're talking 1921, right?
B: Yes.
D: Not later than 1922?
B: Definitely not later.
D: If it was in the fall of 1922, he had already come back from his first trip abroad, to Latvia.
B: I think it was before that.
D: Possibly before. So, in 1920, '21, '22, he worked at ROSTA.[82] He used to sit in his office, fully dressed, in a quilted jacket and army headgear . . .
B: Must have been quite cold.
D: . . . in boots, etc.
B: Though it was already summer then. Or spring, perhaps . . .
D: He used to dress very poorly in his childhood and youth. . . . But according to many witnesses, and one photograph in particular, there was a certain . . . not dandyism, exactly, but a carnivalesque quality to his outfits later. . . . Especially once he started wearing a top hat.
B: Burliuk used to wear a top hat, too.
D: Burliuk gave him the idea. Then came "A Slap in the Face of Public Taste,"[83] and VHUTEMAS,[84] the school for painting, sculpture, and

architecture. . . . There was that one time when everybody at that school ran out of their classes to take a look at Mayakovsky, when he dared to walk back into the same place that had expelled him earlier. . . . They were used to seeing him in rags, and now all of a sudden, there he was, all fancy. I have it on record. Everybody rushed down to gawk at him: "My goodness, who is this?! Mayakovsky?!" "In a top hat!" "Ragamuffin!" He loved it! Yes, he'd do stuff like that from time to time . . . But that wasn't dandyism. It wasn't who he really was.

B: Not dandyism, not at all.

D: You are absolutely right about that. It was just another prank, play-acting.[85]

B: Play-acting, you say? Yes, quite possibly.

D: It was all an act . . .

B: In the end, that's what I saw: a moment of play-acting, rather than a series of deliberate acts. I would have understood immediately the carnivalesque nature of his behavior then.

D: It's like a stain on the wall.

B: Yes, yes.

D: In fact, he was ready to do just about anything, he was acting all the time. He was a gambler by nature.

B: A gambler, true.

D: And how he played cards! Such passion!

B: Really? Was he any good?

D: He was fierce. Fierce! When they started playing cards, it was to the bitter end, to the last piece of underwear!

B: Playing cards is . . . Gambling is a deeply carnivalesque event.

D: All right, then, let's move on. Mayakovsky is just a small episode in your life. Your life and literary development didn't overlap with his very much.

B: Not much.

D: That's what I thought. I imagined, based on what I had heard about you before, that you had crossed paths with some of the youngsters from Marshak's circle.[86] To begin with, what were you doing at the time? Were you an independent literary scholar?

B: At that time? Yes, I was.

D: That was right after you graduated from the university?

B: Not quite. After I finished my university studies . . .

D: How were you supporting yourself in Petersburg during that period, from 1918 to 1921?

B: No, no, I left Petersburg in 1918. This is what happened: one of my closest friends, Lev Vasilyevich Pumpyansky,[87] whom I already told you about, was doing his army service in a small town, Nevel. Nature there was so enchanting! Such a beautiful place! Anyhow, he was serving there, and knew everybody, and everybody knew him. He visited us in Petrograd, where we were all starving, there was nothing to eat. He talked me into going to Nevel with him: one could find work there, he said, there was plenty of food, and so on. So that's what I did. That was in 1918.

D: What was your job there?

B: I'll tell you. The Novo-Sventsyansky Gymnasium[88] had been moved there. The school principal turned out to be my former math teacher, white-haired, an old man already. And thus, I was able to get a position teaching at the Sventsyansky Gymnasium. But I didn't teach there very long, maybe two or three months. The gymnasium was then turned into a state school. But everything stayed the same: the students were allowed to finish their studies, the teachers remained the same, my old friend, my former teacher, Pavel Adamovich Yankovich, was still there, too. But he wasn't the headmaster anymore, I don't remember who took over that role. Still, he continued to work there.

D: Did you spend all of 1918 there?

B: 1918 and 1919. I spent two years there.

D: Now I understand. . . . At first I wasn't sure why you have such gaps in your memories, why you couldn't remember the literary cafes. . . . That was all happening during the same period you were away. So, you left Petersburg, and waited out the famine years in Nevel.

B: The hunger years, yes. I spent about two years there. . . . Then my friend Pumpyansky and I moved to Vitebsk,[89] which wasn't very far; it was the regional center. There was a cultural renaissance in Vitebsk then: because of the famine many people from Petersburg moved there temporarily.

D: Chagall[90] was there, too.

B: He was there, yes, but he was a local. He had such long legs . . .

D: Did you meet him?

B: I did, but we didn't know each other well. I can't remember how many times I visited him before he left . . .

D: So you were there in 1920 already?

B: 1920, '21, and '22.

D: Forgive me, but how about 1921, in particular?

B: You see, I traveled to Moscow and Leningrad, but only briefly. Just visited. I never lived in Moscow. I came from Leningrad, and then returned there.
D: Ah, now I understand.
B: I didn't like Moscow at all.
D: You didn't like to go to Moscow?
B: I had visited Moscow earlier, of course, after all, I am from Orel . . . [91]
D: But you didn't like it?
B: I didn't like Moscow. Anyway, I spent about two years in Nevel. . . . There was something very interesting there, quite typical of the times: the Nevel Learned Society. It was no joke, but a very serious organization. I served as its Chair, by the way. The members included Pumpyansky, Matvey Kagan,[92] the philosopher, the chemist Koliubakin. . . .[93] But let's go back to the Society. We all got a little salary from it . . . not much, of course, it didn't even pay for . . .
D: So you did get some sort of compensation for your work there?
B: Yes, a small salary. I must say that the year and a half or two I lived there were quite good in terms of food. We had everything.
D: So, you didn't really experience the Petersburg disaster?
B: Not really. I even sent the family some food from Nevel.
D: Were you already married at the time?
B: No, not at that time.
D: Who do you mean by "the family"? Your parents?
B: The family? My father, mother, sisters. I should say my mother and sisters died during the blockade of Leningrad.[94]
D: Because of starvation?
B: Starvation, depression . . . It happened during the siege. My mother was already very old.
D: Was your father still alive?
B: No, he had died earlier. He had a fairly easy death, comparatively speaking.
D: And how long were you in Vitebsk for?
B: Vitebsk was such an interesting place to be, I must say. Why, you might ask? Because many representatives of the Petersburg, Petrograd intelligentsia ended up there. They founded a great, world-class music school in Vitebsk.[95] I used to teach there, at the conservatory. Malko[96] served as head of school. He used to be the lead conductor of the Mariinsky Theater.[97]

D: Amazing!
B: A truly distinguished man. A remarkable musician, remarkable. Another really impressive figure there was Dubasov.[98] He was the lead piano teacher. Such a wonderful pedagogue! Many of his students became prominent musicians later.
Presnyakov[99] was there as well. He used to be the chief ballet master at the Mariinsky Theater. He owned a little country estate in the Nevel region. There were many other good people there. It was a real conservatory, and a magnificent one at that. . . . What else? There was also an arts school. Its director was none other than Kazimir Malevich himself.[100]
D: You don't say!
B: Yes, the founder of Suprematism.[101]
D: That's the period of his "Black Square," right?
B: Probably, yes. He was the school principal. The building was marvelous. It used to belong to a wealthy banker by the name of Vishnyak.[102] The architecture was quite unusual. So, this house became an arts school. Malevich was its heart and soul. He was an extremely interesting person.
D: Did you know Malevich personally?
B: Yes, I did. We were very close back then, the two of us, when we both lived in Vitebsk. My wife loved him. She just adored Malevich. We often spent time at the school together.
D: Your wife? So you were already married?
B: Yes, I was already married.
D: Did you get married in Nevel?
B: No, in Vitebsk. My wife was from there. Yes. He was also interested in astronomy.
D: Malevich?
B: Yes, Malevich. He had a small . . .
D: Maybe it was Khlebnikov's influence?
B: . . . telescope . . . Yes, partially Khlebnikov's influence. At night, he would gaze at the stars with such interest and intensity . . . He shared Khlebnikov's deep understanding of the Universe. He could express his insights as an artist very well, with great clarity. He was an original thinker, though he lacked formal education. As an artist, he was well educated, of course, but other than that . . . He was an incredibly discerning, refined person.[103]
D: So, he had his own aesthetic ideas?

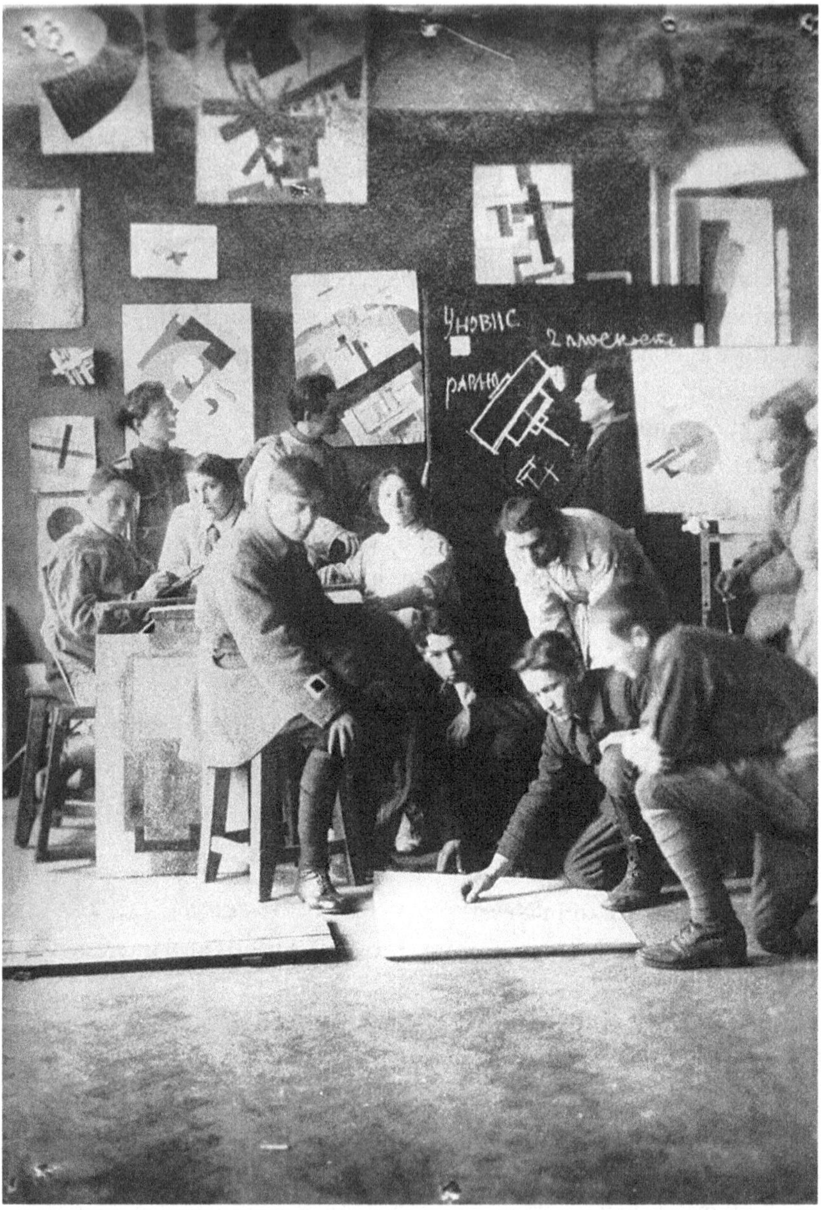

FIG. 3.1. Kazimir Malevich in his class (Malevich is standing next to the blackboard). (Courtesy of the Scientific Library at Moscow State University)

B: He talked about them all the time. He even produced a small brochure, which later disappeared.[104]
D: Is he the founder of what we call "Abstractionism" in Russia?
B: Yes, but his version of it was his own.
D: What is the essence of "Suprematism"? "Supreme" means superior.
B: Suprematism? No. The idea is that it's the highest form of art.
D: "Supreme."
B: Yes, supreme, Suprematism. Here is the thing: in contrast to the Abstractionists, he was somewhat . . . He continued Khlebnikov's tradition, his concern with the Universe . . .
D: I see. Internationalism and Universalism . . .
B: Universalism, yes. He was interested in the Macrocosm, the Universe.
D: That's what he got really excited about . . .
B: He used to say that our form of Art exists in a tiny corner of the three-dimensional world. Just a small corner . . . a tiny space, nothing more. The big Universe doesn't fit in it, and never will. And since you're limited by the little corner you exist in, you can't ever understand the Universe. But he was doing his best to penetrate it.

I remember meeting him for the first time. I went with someone, can't recall who now, just to meet him and see the school. He welcomed us warmly, and showed us around, explaining things along the way. I remember his first explanation. He came up to a certain sculpture and said, "Here we have a sculpture; it's as if there is three-dimensionality but here . . ." He pointed it all out . . . He could do it in a very straightforward manner. "Take me as an example. I am the artist who produced this. Where am I? After all, I am outside the three dimensions, which I have created. You'll say that I, too, exist in three dimensions. But they are not the same, not the same at all. I perceive the work, and as an artist I am able to view the three dimensions from without, from a fourth dimension, if you count arithmetically. But you can't view them arithmetically. You can't say there are just three dimensions. There are thirty-three, three hundred and thirty-three, etc., there's no end. As an artist, I position myself, my gaze, within cosmic, universal dimensions. As a human being, I, of course. . . . You can hit me, physically strike my body, sure, but you can't get to me as an artist. . . . My vision is beyond yours."
D: My eye is beyond all your influence, correct?
B: Yes, exactly. You can't do anything to me. He was very persuasive because this was a person who . . . He wasn't making things up, or trying

to show off. He was sincerely convinced of what he was saying. He was a bit of a maniac. He ended up in an insane asylum, by the way.[105]

D: Really?

B: He died in an insane asylum, in dire poverty.

D: Where?

B: I think Moscow.

D: He never left Russia, did he?

B: No, he didn't. His art traveled all over the world, of course. Even during his lifetime his constructions, the so called "Supremats,"[106] were very popular in America. But he used to say that the "Supremats" were not exhibited properly: they should have been placed horizontally, not vertically, as was usually the case. It's not a big deal, he'd add, because they'd always be Supremats no matter what; their placement would not ruin the artistic intent. Still, their full impact is revealed best if they're exhibited correctly. He was very famous in America at the time.

D: Already back then?

B: Yes, already back then. His constructions were shown around America. . . . They were used to . . .

D: How about here, at home? You said he taught at the school for a while, and then what?

B: He fell on hard times and ended up in a psychiatric hospital. Very soon after he left Vitebsk. I don't know what his official diagnosis was. It could have been . . . who knows. . . . At that time it was all very poorly . . .

D: . . . poorly understood.

B: Severe psychosis . . . or neurosis, not psychosis, perhaps. Besides, he was completely depleted.

D: How do you mean, "depleted"?

B: When we were living in Vitebsk . . . Well, you could actually buy anything to eat there. He was a big man, quite solidly built, you could say. His face was so . . . resolute . . .

D: Is he roughly of Mayakovsky's generation?

B: Yes, the 1890s. He wasn't old. Perhaps a little older than me, can't recall now. I didn't know his exact age. He was a bit older, I think. His students treated him like a priest, worshiped him, so to speak. They gave themselves over to mystical contemplations of the depths of the Universe, etc., and believed they could escape reality through their art. They sincerely believed that was possible. And it was all genuine, I repeat, there were no games, no falsities.

D: What an unexpectedly splendid portrait you're giving us!
B: Yes, you see, he was such an interesting person, talking to him was so interesting. And he was completely honest, completely unselfish. He was not after success, career, money, fancy food—he didn't need any of it. He was an ascetic, if you will, totally in love with his ideas. He was certain he had discovered something completely new, that he was the first to have been able to look into, discern the depths of the Universe.
D: Who else was there, in Vitebsk? Malevich was the director of the art school, you said, right?
B: He was, yes. The best professor teaching there was considered to be. . . . Pen. There was such an artist, Pen.[107] He was famous but not particularly original.
D: He was fairly ordinary then?
B: Yes, ordinary, a Realist in the style of the Wanderers.[108] Nothing special. . . . He was quite good, of course . . .
D: I think Chagall was one of his students.
B: It's possible. He was the only painter you could study with there.
D: I know about him thanks to Azarh's, Alexandra Veniaminovna Azarh's reminiscences about Chagall. Did you know her—Alexandra Azarh,[109] later Granovskaya (though maybe her maiden name was different)?
B: I don't remember.
D: She told me about Chagall . . . also Mikhoels![110] Wasn't he there too?
B: He was there as well, but I didn't know him.
D: There was no drama school there then?
B: No drama school. But there was a theater club at the music conservatory.
D: He must have participated in it.
B: Mikhoels? Probably.
D: So, even though it was a small town, not everybody moved in the same circle.
B: The thing is, it wasn't a small town. It was actually a big regional center, and very refined. Even before that period, many important people had come from Vitebsk . . .
D: Yes, true, the Kagans—Lilya Brik,[111] she had just graduated from the gymnasium there.
B: Lossky,[112] the philosopher who was my professor at the university, also graduated from there.

D: The one who died in 1965?
B: Yes, him. I learned not too long ago that the father of Delvig (Pushkin's Delvig)[113] used to live in Vitebsk, too, and Delvig visited him there. There was a whole series of such people, too . . .
D: Then we could say that Vitebsk was one of the cultural . . .
B: . . . hubs. Yes, absolutely. At the time, it was . . . Later, of course . . . When things settled down, people left: Malko left, and Presnyakov too, and others left Vitebsk. Malevich, too, left . . . and then died.
D: So you're saying that Vitebsk was a cultural center, which gave birth to such artistic powerhouses as Chagall. While Petrograd was suffering, Vitebsk was flourishing.
B: Yes, it was flourishing.
D: How long did you stay there, in Vitebsk?
B: A long time, almost to 1923, so three full years. In the fourth year, I left to go back to . . .
D: So, let's get this straight, you arrived in 1918, '19, and stayed through 1920, '21, '22?
B: Yes. In 1921 I got married, in May of 1921.
D: Your wife was a local girl?
B: Not quite.
D: What was her maiden name?
B: Her father was an important county official before the Revolution, and they also had a small country estate near Polotsk.[114] I spent two or three years living with them. Her parents were still alive then. She was born on that country estate near Polotsk. It was a stone's throw away from Vitebsk.
D: What's your wife's name?
B: Elena Aleksandrovna Okolovitch.
D: Okolovitch?
B: Yes, Okolovitch. Bersh-Okolovitch.
D: Where does the "Bersh" come from? Is it Jewish?
B: "Bersh" is like "von" or "de," the French "de," or [the German] "von." Noblemen added it to their names. "Bersh" is not a surname. "Bersh-Okolovitch" . . . that's because . . . I can't remember right now. . . . She was of Bulgarian descent. The Bulgarian roots went way back, though, her mother and father were pure Russians.
D: Ah, now I get it. You only visited Moscow occasionally. . . . Then in 1923 you moved to Petrograd and lived there until 1929?

B: Correct, until 1929.

D: You were not . . . I remember your book but . . . You were not very famous.

B: I was only famous in very narrow circles. The one around me is now called the "Bakhtin Circle." Lately, they've been writing a lot about it. It included Pumpyansky, Pavel Nikolayevich Medvedev,[115] Voloshinov.[116] I should note that everybody, except for Medvedev, was also in Nevel.

D: Medvedev is the one who later wrote about Blok, right? Or was it about Bryusov?

B: He worked on Blok, yes. His first book was titled *Blok's Creative Path.*

All three were in Vitebsk, where we lay the groundwork for the circle that was later set up in Leningrad. While there, I gave lectures. . . . I offered, at home, completely informal courses in philosophy, Kant at first (I was so stubbornly devoted to Kantian ideas at the time), then more general topics.

D: Did you ever teach at Petersburg, at Leningrad University?

B: I did not, never had the chance. I was supposed to, but it didn't happen.

D: Did you ever run into Bogatyrev's, Shklovsky's circle?

B: No, never.

D: You were never in contact with them?

B: No, I don't believe I ever was . . . Nikolay Borisovich.

D: And the famous Baudouin de Courtenay?

B: Yes, that's it, Baudouin de Courtenay.

D: Was Baudouin de Courtenay still there when you were there?

B: Yes, he was. I attended his lectures. One more thing. I left Petrograd but returned to Leningrad.

D: How do you mean? In 1924? It was still Petrograd in 1923.

B: Correct. Then it immediately became Leningrad.

D: Right, it was renamed in May 1924.

B: 1924, yes. Anyway, my life from then on took place in Leningrad. There used to be some literary salons there. The Shchepkina-Kupernik[117] salon was nearing its end. I attended evenings there during the last years of its existence.

D: What was interesting about this Shchepkina-Kupernik salon?

B: I didn't like it very much . . . There were some very old-fashioned people there . . .

D: Much like Shchepkina-Kupernik herself.

FIG. 3.2. Pavel Medvedev, 1913. (Courtesy of the Scientific Library at Moscow State University)

B: True. Former Russian generals, state attorneys, quite old, previously prominent solicitors. At the time, it was not so much Shchepkina-Kupernik's salon any longer as much as it was her husband's, Nikolay Borisovich Polynov. He was a distinguished state attorney . . . a very gentle, refined man. He was quite interested in philosophy, aesthetics, art, poetry. I gave talks there, lectured on various topics, and so forth.

FIG. 3.3. Valentin Voloshinov, 1913. (Courtesy of the Scientific Library at Moscow State University)

D: So, you gave presentations there?

B: I did.

D: On philosophical topics?

B: Philosophy, but mostly aesthetics, philosophical aesthetics.

D: As a Kantian?

B: Yes.

D: You allowed yourself the luxury—I'm being ironic, of course—to read lectures on Kantian philosophy in Leningrad in 1924?

B: Kantian philosophy, correct.

D: Was that the reason you were sent to distant regions before too long?

B: Yes. But it seemed like there was nothing to worry about at the time. . . . Then the article appeared, the anonymous one . . .

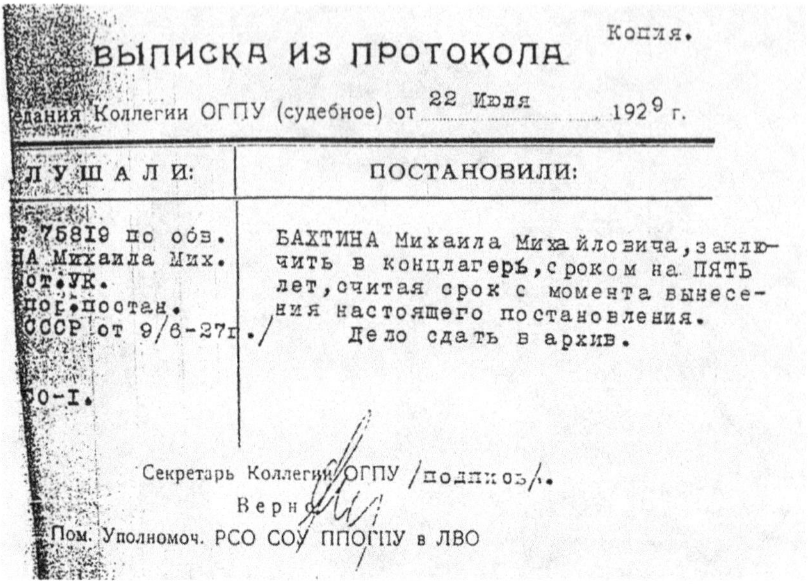

Копия.

ВЫПИСКА ИЗ ПРОТОКОЛА

...дания Коллегии ОГПУ (судебное) от 22 Июля 1929 г.

...ЛУШАЛИ:	ПОСТАНОВИЛИ:
...75819 по обв. ...А Михаила Мих. ...от. УК. ...пор. постан. ...СССР от 9/6-27г./ ...0-I.	БАХТИНА Михаила Михайловича, заключить в концлагерь, сроком на ПЯТЬ лет, считая срок с момента вынесения настоящего постановления. Дело сдать в архив.

Секретарь Коллегии ОГПУ /подпись/.

Верно:

Пом. Уполномоч. РСО СОУ ППОГПУ в ЛВО

FIG. 3.4. A copy of Bakhtin's prison sentence. (Courtesy of the Scientific Library at Moscow State University)

D: Was it anonymous?

B: Well, it wasn't signed, but we knew who the authors were . . .

D: Was it a feuilleton?

B: A short article, yes, like a feuilleton . . .

D: With material about that salon?

B: Yes, then the GPU got involved . . .

D: Wait! Are we still talking about 1924?

B: No, that was already 1929 or 1930. No, 1929. It talked about my past, about those Kantian lectures. They accused me of giving informal talks on topics of an idealist nature. . . . Actually, I wasn't even formally accused of anything. . . . There was an investigation. At the time, the GPU continued to operate according to Dzerzhinsky's[118] traditions. So, I can't really complain: I was treated quite well.

D: You were not abused in any way?

B: Not at all, no. At the time, Chief of the Second Department was a man called Ivan Petrov, a former minor writer. He was very proper and treated me with obvious sympathy as a fellow literary scholar. Stromin-Stroev[119] was the chief investigator, and he was also a decent man. Later both were shot in connection with Kirov's murder.[120] They apparently knew something, so they had to be killed, annihilated.

D: I understand.

B: So, yes, the article's title was "The Ashes of Oaks."[121]

D: "The Ashes of Oaks"?

B: Yes, "The Ashes of Oaks." The Oaks were Kant, Vladimir Solovyov, and so forth, and the rest of us . . .

Interview Four

March 15, 1973

Length of the interview: 124 minutes

DUVAKIN: Let's continue, Mikhail Mikhailovich. Could you finish up the last topic we were discussing before the end of our last session: the article about you.
BAKHTIN: Okay. The article published then in the evening issue of the *Red Newspaper* (which we all called *Birzhevka* [the *Stock Exchange*] because it greatly resembled the pre-revolutionary *Stock-Exchange Gazette*), was signed with a pseudonym, "the brothers Tur," and titled "The Ashes of Oaks." The persons mentioned in the article were being actively persecuted by the GPU. Many different circles and representatives of different generations were included in that group. The article managed to refer to all of them, one way or another. To be fair, it only talked about "this kind of people" and "that kind of people," without naming anybody in particular. Mostly, it targeted the older generation: like the academician Platonov . . . [1]
D: Platonov? The same one who was later accused during the Industrial Party Trial[2] of preparing to take on the post of Minister of Foreign Affairs?
B: A Minister, yes. The same one.
D: The whole thing was put together without his knowledge. He probably wasn't even aware of it.

B: It's all complete nonsense! Someone, probably while sitting drunk in a Parisian bar, decided to jot down a list of people who could get government appointments in the event that the Bolsheviks fail. . . . Just for fun, nothing else!
D: Not really. This same Industrial Party . . .
B: I know, I know . . .
D: According to the newspapers, they did put together a possible Cabinet. They were not émigrés. I think (I was wrong earlier), Platonov was supposed to be Prime Minister, Ramzin[3]—something else, and Tarle—Minister of Foreign Affairs.
B: Fine, but the thing is the whole affair was presented very differently: as though the list was created abroad, in emigration. And Ramzin just took it from there.
D: That might be true, I don't know exactly.
B: Whatever. In the end, it's not that important.
D: It doesn't concern us directly.
B: Such a stupid made-up story! Neither Tarle nor Platonov had any idea about their so-called Cabinet appointments. Another person, who was mentioned as a possible Minister of Culture, was Kartashev,[4] the chairman of the Religious Philosophical Society. He did serve as a Minister of Religion in . . .
D: . . . Kerensky's government.[5]
B: Yes, in one of the first provisional governments. I attended the last meeting of the Religious-Philosophical Society. He gave a presentation as the Minister, no longer as the chairman.
D: Let's go back to the article.
B: All right. So . . . The article claimed that there were certain members of the Soviet intelligentsia, who continued the old, pre-revolutionary traditions—the traditions of certain people, scholars like Kant, Hegel, Vladimir Solovyov,[6] and others.
D: In short, people who continued to affirm philosophical idealism.
B: Philosophical idealism, religious obscurantism, and so forth. All those ideas had no place in Soviet society anymore. They were completely useless. Kant and the rest of them were like old oaks, and their followers were like ashes because nothing would be left in the wake of such people: the soil where those trees were originally planted was no more. That's the gist of it.
D: So, the ashes were supposed to be their ideas?

B: Yes, their ideas. The authors wanted to suggest that even the ideas had no foundation any longer, and so the people who espoused them were to be viewed as nothing more than mere ashes.
D: And the brothers Tur wrote this?
B: Yes, the brothers Tur. I think they are still alive, I run into their names occasionally. But they are not actual brothers, I believe, or maybe they are, who knows. . . . In any case, one of them is Tubelsky, the other—Ryzhey. Tubelsky and Ryzhey.[7]
D: I didn't know that. So, that's who was behind the pseudonym. Like the Kukryniksy?[8]
B: Yes, like the Kukryniksy. They were from Odessa originally. But at the time they were, of course, already in Petrograd, and connected with the GPU. They also published articles using GPU materials. The GPU willingly shared information with such "leading," "progressive" journalists as the brothers Tur.

Following that, many people, including myself, had to go, were sent away, exiled.
D: How did that happen? If nobody was actually named . . . The people implicated in the article, were they already under arrest when it came out?
B: Yes, they were already arrested, and some had even been sent away.
D: They were already sentenced.
B: Yes, sentenced and already sent away according to the sentence.
D: Okay then, how long were you held in detention? Were you locked up in the Lubyanka[9] for a long time?
B: Not the Lubyanka, I was held in the DPZ ([ДПЗ], the House of Preliminary Detention).[10] That was in Leningrad, on Shpalernaya Street. And the MGB was on Gorokhovaya Street.[11]
D: You mean the GPU.
B: Yes, the GPU. It was on Gorokhovaya. I should say that we (or at least I) were treated well there, by the MGB, the GPU. Let me tell you a little joke, but don't record this. "Someone comes for a visit and asks: 'Where is your master?' The servant responds: 'The master? What master? He goes to America all the time: one time to CHEKA-go, another time to GPU-go . . .'" That is, they kept putting the master away! [*chuckles*]
D: Good one! Let's continue.
B: So, yes, we were treated well, nobody ever abused us. In fact, people there were very civil and knowledgeable, especially about literature. I won't mention any names.

D: Is that true? Come on, why not name them? You must! Was that under Dzerzhinsky?[12]

B: No, it was already under Menzhinsky,[13] but they still followed Dzerzhinksy's tradition, and he, as you know, didn't allow any mistreatment of prisoners. He was a very gentle person, very polite.

D: So, what was the verdict in your case?

B: Well, there were several . . . The most important one . . .

D: Who was there anyway? Could you tell me who fell into the "ashes" group? Was there an actual club?

B: No, there was no such thing. There were groups, but . . . In short, there was no actual organization . . . The GPU didn't uncover any organized activity, or the sentence would have been very different. At that time it was very important if there had been an actual organization or not. They didn't discover anything like that. There were just different groups of people, friends. Besides, the lectures were given at private residences. For example, I gave many presentations at home.

D: So, who was there? You mentioned Tarle, Platonov . . .

B: Yes, Tarle, Platonov, and also . . .

D: Kartashev?

B: No, he was not there. He was already abroad. Komarovich.[14]

D: Who was he? A historian?

B: No, he was a literary scholar. A very talented man, very talented. He wrote a book in German: *Die Urgestalt der "Brüder Karamasoff"* (1928) [*The Sources of "The Brothers Karamazov"*]. That's a huge work, published in Germany. Besides that, he wrote and published another very good book at home: *The Legend of the City of Kitezh*. In it, he reviews in detail the history of the origins and variants of the legend of Kitezh.[15] He also has many articles, especially valuable ones about Dostoevsky, published in the collection on Dostoevsky's works, which was edited by Dolinin. In particular, he wrote an essay about *The Adolescent*: "The Structure of the Novel *The Adolescent*."[16]

D: Yes, I am familiar with it.

B: I'm sure you are. He returned quite quickly. I think he was sentenced to just three years, and was sent to Gorky.[17] His father was a prominent doctor in Gorky, so he was sent home, as it turns out. [*laughs*] When he returned, he continued to work at the research institute, and published a few more articles. I even have them. . . . A good Samaritan sent me those texts, as well as offprints of his works, and a complete bibliography of

everything he's published. I don't know who sent them to me, someone from Leningrad, it was a long time ago, the atmosphere was different back then. Then he died during the Blockade, just like Engelhardt.[18]
D: Engelhardt was one of them too?
B: No, he wasn't part of that group. He was persecuted a bit later.
D: So, he also suffered repression?
B: He did, yes, and his arrest was connected with a terrible incident. His wife was Garshin by birth. . . . Her maiden name was Garshin.
D: Was she Garshin's daughter? Or niece?[19]
B: I think a niece. She was . . . She suffered from the same illness as Garshin: once in a while she would have a seizure and become unhinged. So, when he was being taken away . . . They lived on the fifth floor, I think, there was only one staircase, because back then all the main stairways in the big mansions were destroyed. . . . She followed behind, as he was being taken down from the fifth floor. . . . And then she jumped over the parapet and killed herself. So, when they got to the bottom of the stairs, they found her mangled body waiting for them there.
D: What a nightmare!
B: A horrible, nightmarish story. Later, when Engelhardt came back, he found another wife, from among his former students. Then he too died in the Leningrad Blockade.
D: So, we have Platonov, Tarle, Komarovich. . . . There were others. . . . Though they were from Moscow. . . . Did anybody from Moscow fall into that category, the "ashes," the idealist philosophers? For example, Frank,[20] or Ilyin?[21]
B: No, because they had already left Russia by then.
D: So, they had left a long time before, in 1922, or 1923. . . . Were people still being exiled abroad in 1923 then? Were there also internal deportations . . . or concentration camps? Did Solovki[22] already exist?
B: In our case Solovki was certainly an option. . . . We could have been sent to Solovki, Kem,[23] Kazakhstan . . . [24] places like that. I ended up in northern Kazakhstan, Terle—in southern Kazakhstan. As for Andreevsky,[25] he was sent to Solovki. There were other members of my group who ended up there, too.
D: Let's go back to our, as it were, main agenda.
B: Okay.
D: So, you came back to Petrograd in 1924. Was that before or after Lenin's death?

B: It was after. He died at the very beginning of that year, in January . . .
D: January of 1924.
B: And we arrived in the spring of 1924.
D: So, we are talking March–April?
B: Let's say April. I think it was April.
D: Okay, April. So, from April 1924 to December 1928 you lived in Leningrad. Petrograd had just been renamed Leningrad.
B: Yes, Petrograd was just renamed Leningrad.
D: That happened in 1924. When you arrived, it was already called Leningrad.
B: Correct. I came back to Leningrad.
D: The name was still new and fresh. And you found yourself in the midst of fervent literary activity, took part in it yourself, began working on your first projects, became acquainted with some notable figures. . . . Well, maybe they were not all that notable yet, but they were to become important later, people like the OBERIU poets,[26] Konstantin Vaginov,[27] or some others. . . . Do you by any chance remember anything about Zabolotsky?[28] You know what, I'll stop breaking up the conversation with my questions now, and just give you the chance to tell me anything you want about those five years. I'm listening.
B: In Leningrad, I met several members of the older generation, in particular Fyodor Sologub.[29] At the time he was the Chairman of the Leningrad branch of the Writers' Union.
D: It wasn't called the Union of Poets then?
B: No, it was known as the Writers' Union.
D: Yes, you're right. There used to be such a thing
B: There was, there was . . . There were many prose writers among its members—such as Sologub himself, who was more of a prose writer than a poet.

Sologub was a figure to be reckoned with then. A heavyweight. A difficult person. There was a certain bitterness about him, mostly for personal reasons. Not because of politics, though, not that. He lost his wife. As everyone knows, she drowned herself, threw herself in the river . . .
D: Do you know why? Was she unbalanced psychologically, or . . .
B: Most likely. In any case, she . . . She was not insane, not at all, it's just that due to some very unfortunate circumstances she decided to put an end to it all. . . . Her body was not found for a long time. Then the water brought it back to shore . . . all mangled up. . . . In short, he had to go

identify her body, and he did. . . . He was very close to her, apparently loved her a great deal . . .

D: That was Chebotarevskaya, right?[30]

B: Chebotarevskaya, yes.

D: And she threw herself into the Neva?[31]

B: Yes, the Neva. So, he [Sologub] was always in a terrible mood. Besides, he was a pessimist anyway, a singer of Death, Smertiashkin [Deathman], as he was called by . . .

D: . . . Gorky.

B: Yes, Gorky. Still, he gathered around himself many young writers and literary scholars. Some of them even presented their research at his place. For example, my friend Pumpyansky read out loud two or three of his articles at Sologub's apartment. I remember he especially liked a piece about three poems, all called "The Monument." It was written by Lev Vasilyevich, and never published.[32] The three "monuments" were by Horace, Derzhavin,[33] and Pushkin—a historical literary comparative analysis.

At the same time, despite that deep pessimism of his, he had a soft spot for pretty young women. Maybe it's better if we don't record this?

D: Is that really true?

B: He did. Despite everything. And even though he was a singer of Death, he didn't want to die, not at all.

D: But he died soon anyway.

B: That he did, yes.

D: In 1927.

B: Yes, quite early. As Chairman of the Union he acted very independently, very independently. At that time, there were already many Communist, Marxist critics joining the organization . . .

But still, Sologub continued to act quite freely. Nobody could touch him, of course. At that time people like him were reckoned with, nobody bothered them. Though his attitude was well known. At the same time, it was also public knowledge that he was apolitical, deep down, at his core: he may have expressed his irritation with certain things openly in some cases, but politically he was indifferent, neutral. He organized a public literary evening once, and even Volynsky[34] participated in it.

D: He was still alive?

B: Volynsky was still alive, I knew him personally.
D: Akim Volynsky?
B: Yes, Akim Volynsky. We used to run into each other at one of the salons. That one time he gave the introductory talk, I remember it well; he started out like this: "When Fyodor Teternikov[35] was a mere teacher, he wore a filthy frock-coat . . ."
D: Akim Volynsky said that?
B: Right. Meaning, that's how he used to be, but now. . . . And Sologub immediately reacted, not directly, addressing the audience, but off to the side, where I was standing, [*whispering*] "When did I ever have a filthy frock-coat? What is this lie. . . . My clothes have always been spotless and well made." [*both laugh*] And he was trying to present himself as a populist, so to speak. [*laughing again*] Akim Volynsky was such a wise old man, but life was very hard for him at the end. . . . He used to complain, "I can't work without strong tea, and you need sugar for strong tea, but there's no sugar to be had . . ." He'd say things like that. That's Volynsky for you. He was trying to acclimate himself a little, adapt himself somewhat.
D: He wrote a book about ballet during that period.[36]
B: Possibly, yes, I don't know what he was writing about back then.
D: During that time Sologub produced several books: *The Enchanted Goblet . . . Only Love . . .* [37]
B: Yes, yes. He wrote more poetry later, which now exists only in manuscript form, as it wasn't published back then . . .
D: Do you know if it's true—perhaps it's just false rumors—that, in 1926 or '27, right before his death, Sologub asked for permission to leave the country, and go abroad?
B: I believe he asked for permission to go abroad before his wife's death. The denial, or more correctly, the delay of the travel approval was one of the factors contributing to her suicide.
D: So, *she* was the one who really wanted to leave?
B: *She* was the one who wanted to leave, yes. That was one of the reasons for her death. As for later. . . . I don't know, I don't think so. I haven't heard anything about him asking for such a permission later.
D: He died in 1927, and his wife about two years earlier . . .
B: That was before I knew him. I met him for the first time after his wife had already passed.

D: I met his wife's sister. She used to work at the House of Writers, as director of the library. Her name was also Chebotarevskaya . . . not Anastasia but Anna,[38] I think, I can't recall her first name.

Anyhow. . . . As for the older generation, you described them all so well, so captivatingly. . . . What's your assessment of Sologub as a writer and a person?

B: Sologub? I always considered him to be an extremely talented poet, and I greatly valued his poetry. I also think that his novel, *The Petty Demon*,[39] is one of the best novels of the twentieth century. It's a wonderful work, very deep, and also almost prophetic . . .

D: Such a disgusting story . . .

B: Well, yes . . . though I believe his last work, *Nav's Spells*,[40] is even worse, even more repulsive . . .

D: Yes, absolutely!

B: His first novel, *Bad Dreams*,[41] is not bad, not bad at all. But *The Petty Demon* is excellent. His Peredonov[42] is among the most remarkable characters in our literature.

D: I'll have to re-read it then. It's in the tradition of Dostoevsky, of course, but there's something of Shchedrin[43] there, too, don't you think?

B: Yes, a little of Shchedrin, perhaps.

D: His Little Judas character, in particular.[44]

B: He resembles Little Judas, to be sure. Still, he is a character of a different epoch, I'd say. Whereas Peredonovs are a dime a dozen these days. . . . Teachers, too. . . . Almost all of our middle school teachers used to be Peredonovs, and there are so many of them still around. The Peredonov-type has become very widespread. . . . In the novel he is still an exception, and the school director, Khripach, hates him, and wants to get rid of him as soon as possible. But now the Peredonovs are well-regarded in Russia, esteemed much too highly, and are setting the tone in schools around the country, especially in the provinces, though also in Moscow and Leningrad . . .

D: I'll definitely have to re-read it. But the author's position, taken by itself . . . After all, Peredonov, we might say, is in a way like Little Judas, but in another sense, he is just a rascal.

B: A horrible rascal. That's how Sologub depicted him, to be sure.

D: And Sologub seems to be in awe of him, in a way.

B: No, Sologub knew this type very well. . . . After all he used to be a teacher himself, and a teacher at a trade school at that. . . . At least I think it was a trade school, in Leningrad. He was also a School Inspector at one time . . .

D: I think he lived in Velikiye Luki.[45]

B: At first, yes, but then he moved to Petersburg. He was already a known poet then. Once a week, I believe on Wednesdays, various writers, poets, dramatists, Meyerhold in particular, gathered at his apartment. That was later, but still before the Revolution. Anyway. He knew Peredonov's world very well, he belonged to it himself, and was perhaps infected by it somewhat, though he was never a Peredonov himself, of course. He was simply a man with a difficult character, a rather unattractive person, though you were always aware of his intelligence, his talent, and superiority over others. You could never call him an ordinary Philistine, he was certainly extremely smart, an important person. One could always sense one was in the presence of a man of great importance when he was around. But he was not very likable. He was a difficult man, Sologub was. Still, he behaved very independently, which caused others to respect him, of course. His poems were wonderful, just wonderful. He was a masterful poet, as I am sure you know. That's what I can tell you about Sologub.

D: [*recites*] My old good friend, my faithful Demon,

> Once sung this little song to me:
> All night the sailor sailed through the wilderness,
> But drowned by the morn in sea.
> Around him waves loomed like domes,
> They fell and rose again above,
> Before him, whiter than the foam,
> There flew his one unrivaled love.
> He heard the call, as he was drifting,
> "I'll not deceive you, trust in me."
> Remember,—said this Demon, witty,—
> He drowned at the morn in sea.[46]

That's Sologub.

B: Also, this:

> Oh Death, I'm all yours. Your guise
> Is all I see. And I despise
> the earthly charms . . .[47]

This is also a marvelous poem, very powerful. It ends like this:

> It's not for me (something) . . . engulfed in the secrecy
> Of your extraordinary beauty,
> It's not for me to fall at its feet.[48]

He means "at Life's feet."

> When your cold tear,
> So crystal clear,
> Has already dropped down from above.[49]

Beautiful lines. Very dark, but beautiful.
Or this poem about Death by suicide, which apparently he once used to dream about himself:

> I touch the water with my bloody
> Lips, dried up from thirst.
> What used to be, will be again.
> What used to be, won't happen only once . . . [50]

There were also such lines:

> They'll stoke the furnace,
> While you sit, waiting, by the tub . . .

And then:

> And indolence will then invade my oozing veins . . .

Then it ends again in the same way:

> What used to be, will be again.
> What used to be, won't happen only once . . . [51]

Gorgeous poetry, but very dark, of course.
D: You know, I think Sologub offers the most concentrated representation—as far as the word is applied to art, of course—of the term "decadence."

B: You see, this term, though. . . . He didn't consider himself decadent, not at all.
D: Who would be considered one, if not him?!
B: He was the least decadent person ever. He was a man of considerable stature: a teacher, an important school inspector—a position that gave him a lot of power. He even used to run reading circles in his school's auditorium, had people gather in his own home, that sort of thing. . . . That was before Chebotarevskaya.
D: No, if we were to consider the poetry he wrote . . . For me, the term "decadent" would cover all of it. I can't think of anyone whose work would fall under that category quite as clearly.
B: I'd say that among all the decadent and Symbolist poets of his time, including Bryusov and Vyacheslav Ivanov, the least decadent, and the most reliable, was Sologub. Would you agree with that? You could never expect any decadent stunts, any surprises from him. . . . He was a solid, respectable man.
D: But that's a different matter. You see . . .
B: His poetry was . . . pure. Pure poetry. It's impossible to call it decadent, no, it wasn't.
D: Well . . . decadence . . . In the French sense of the word that was real decadence.
B: Perhaps . . .
D: . . . That is, the poetry of decline, of withdrawal from life, of death. "Decadence," as a term . . .
B: I should tell you that as a theorist, a literary historian, I don't accept this term. It was singled out, and advanced by some petty poets, mediocre artists, who understood the word "decadence" to mean a certain posture, a particular style, which they found to be very interesting, beneficial to them, and so forth. They used to go around dressed entirely in black, and so forth. Take, for instance, Dobrolyubov,[52] who was then a notable representative . . .
D: Alexander?
B: Yes, of course, the poet.
D: I see.
B: He always wore black gloves, and never took them off. He'd sit in the living room with his black gloves on.
D: I heard about this already from someone else, too, but I can't remember who.

B: Yes, that's a well-known story, very striking. Those were our decadents, our so-called decadents. The serious poets were not decadents. You can't apply the term to them, it smacks of pretension, of black gloves. . . . It just doesn't make sense!

D: That's an interesting question. The term has two meanings, which. . . . It has entered our language.

B: It has, true.

D: Modernism is mostly a matter of style, we might say.

B: Well that's maybe a bit . . . That term is also not acceptable to me. We call Modernists those who . . . This is an abusive word for us: "Modernist" is a term of abuse. To call one of our poets a "Modernist" should be, as a matter of fact, considered a compliment.

D: Let's take the term "decadent." If we reflect on what you've just been saying . . . and remember Chekhov's words . . . Do you recall his opinion? Bunin, I believe, reports the following exchange with him: "Anton Pavlovich, what do you think of the Decadents?" "The Decadents? What sort of Decadents are they?! They are all robust, healthy men. Better to send them to the convicts' squads."[53]

B: Well, you know . . .

D: That's his own personal evaluation, of course . . .

B: Yes.

D: So, Decadence [according to you] should be understood as pure pretense. Could we apply the term to Merezhkovsky then?

B: Well, that would be a stretch.

D: Okay then, how about Gippius,[54] as you described her?

B: That would probably work.

D: And Dobrolyubov?

B: Yes. Though he was less of a Decadent, and more of a religious seeker.

D: On the other hand, we could understand the term "decadent" to mean something more serious, a worldview that's close to the word "tragic," but doesn't coincide with it; that trend in our literature which starts, so to speak, with Minsky,[55] with a concern with the non-existence, with disintegration, with a certain philosophical . . . not theory, but a certain type of emotion.

B: A whole worldview, yes. . . . But then, you see, you can't include . . . Or perhaps too many would fall into this category, because an obsession with a dark, pessimist outlook, with one's future deterioration, with life's end, can be seen as present in many great poets of the past. You could view Leopardi[56] as a true Decadent poet then. Byron would be one, too; in fact, you could even hail him as the clearest example of Decadence.

D: Decadence is considered to have begun in the twentieth century with Baudelaire's *Flowers of Evil*, of course.[57]

B: That's also wrong. Still, it might be acceptable, because there was in Baudelaire—together with the fact that he was a great poet, indeed a remarkable poet—a certain element of affectation, which was typical of this poetic style, of the circle Baudelaire belonged to at that time. Théophile Gautier[58] also belonged to that group, but you can't call him decadent, even though toward the end of his life. . . . Théo, as he was called in those circles, was a very dark person, a pessimist through and through. But nobody would consider him "decadent." That's a completely different thing!

D: In Russia, if we are to use this term . . . Although, of course, it's everywhere in the poetry of that epoch. If you remember, Blok wrote, I believe in a letter to Bely, or maybe it was in his diary, I forget: "I hate my own decadence, and abhor it in others. . . . I punish others for it, though they may be even less decadent than me." But there is . . .

B: Yes, however, here Blok partially has in mind the decadent poets of his time, but he is also using the term (which had just entered our language) in another sense, following Nietzsche. Nietzsche spoke about decadence all the time, and denounced all Decadents, whose existence he saw in a negative light, as being in sharp contrast with the true Übermensch of the future. He, as you know, called Wagner[59] "decadent" as well, especially because of *Parsival*. He condemned the decadent in himself and tried to overcome his own decadence. He celebrated the boundless joy of life, embraced all existence—existence, not life. His "Eternal Return," I think, should be understood most of all in an emotional sense: I accept everything and am ready to repeat my life as many times as you want. That's Decadence, but, again, it's something very different. A different kind of Decadence. Nietzsche himself, who was a Classicist, had in mind a different epoch—Ancient Decadence, and Rome's decay in particular. By the way, there's a poem . . . how does it go, damn it . . . by Annensky[60]:

> I am a pale Roman of the epoch of Julius Apostate.
> In the lull between Barbarian attacks on my abode,
> I keep on composing acrostics, in a languid mode,
> As the glow of the last sunset perishes behind the gate.
> No longer light, my soul is overtaken by ennui . . . [61]

and so on.

That's the kind of decay, decadence, that Nietzsche had in mind. . . . Anyway, how is that connected with Alexander Dobrolyubov? What does that have to do with Sologub and so forth? Nothing. His worldview was very pessimistic, but that's different, very different. That other pessimism was of a different kind. . . . That pessimism was lyrical, and partially philosophical. Yes. Lyrical. That's a good way to describe it. . . . Who was it among our composers who said: "Do you know any happy music? I don't know any." Maybe it was Tchaikovsky. And if you must know, there has never been, and cannot ever be, happy poetry. If there's no hint of the end, of Death, a kind of bad premonition, there can't be real poetry, because poetry must be . . . Otherwise it won't be actual poetry, just stupid delight for the herd.

Take Blok, for example. He understood perfectly what delight really was, but not primitive delight:

> The endless joy of this world
> Is known to the singer's heart . . . [62]

He follows with: "Joy and suffering are one and the same," etc. Then comes the final demise. And

> Still, I accept you.
> I know all about decline and the end.
> Still, I accept you completely, Death.[63]

This is from his famous poem, "Oh, spring, without an end and a beginning . . ." Is that Decadence?!

D: . . . "Spring without an end and a beginning!"[64]

B: Would you call that Decadence?

D: "I know you, Life! I embrace you, / And I welcome you ready for battle!"[65]

B: Yes. That's poetry! All poetry in its various formal expressions is like that. It embraces life, but not like sheep; no, it welcomes it fully understanding that life must also include Death, and that there's no end to the end. That's very important.

"*Respice finem*," as the Romans used to say. "Respect the end," "consider the end." "The end crowns the work," as we say in Russia. So that element is always present. In that sense, all poetry is like that, and all music, too . . .

D: Do you mean all of art then?

B: Well, Decadence . . . Yes, I suppose so, all of art. All art if you like. In any case all the arts, as far as we know, are always connected with the memory of our ancestors, the dead, the grave, with mourning, and so on. Because we have to fortify the living. . . . But what's living doesn't need to be immortalized or celebrated while still alive. We shall commemorate it once it's gone:

> In order to become immortal in a song,
> One must first fall in this life . . . [66]

That's Zhukovsky.[67] From his translation of "Greek Gods."[68] It's a bit different in Schiller,[69] but it doesn't matter.

D: Mikhail Mikhailovich, but isn't the opposite also true . . . I understand your deep-rooted beliefs but . . .

B: Yes.

D: But, to the contrary . . . Do you really mean to say that if there's no awareness of the grave . . .

B: Exactly.

D: . . . there's no art?

B: Yes, if that's how you want to put it. But not in this very primitive sense.

D: But the opposite should not be viewed from a primitive perspective and seen only as a delight for the herd either. I disagree that there can't be a happy poetry. You see . . . There are, of course. . . . I don't know, some uninspired attempts. . . . For instance:

> I have traveled all over the world,
> And life is good, and it's good to be alive![70]

And this was written by a man who was obsessed with death. This type of poetry allows the reader to . . . the message stays with you longer.

B: Life-affirming poetry.

D: Yes. Its effect, you see. . . . As Mayakovsky very aptly said somewhere else, "It's the eternal argument between the pessimist and the optimist: is the auditorium half full or half empty."

B: That's very well put.
D: So, art, including tragic art, the highest form of art, always sees it as "half full," because life goes on, so to speak. . . . What you were talking about just now seems to exclude what you yourself specialize in . . .
B: Not really.
D: . . . both ambivalence, and catharsis. I think that Decadence is a tragedy without catharsis.
B: Yes.
D: You can still find catharsis in Blok here and there.
B: Of course! But still, catharsis is . . .
D: . . . It's there. . . . As for Sologub (I know him less, perhaps), I just don't see it because where there's emptiness there can't be strength.
B: Well . . . I don't know if we can say that. If there's only emptiness and no strength, there can't be real poetry either. As for the kind of optimism you find in your Mayakovsky example: "And life is good, and it's good to be alive," . . . "but our lively mayhem" . . . how does it continue . . . "is even better"[71]—there's something very trite, very false here. Very much so! Despite everything, Mayakovsky's poetry was predominantly pessimistic. Yes . . . Of course, in his last period, when he became a eulogist. . . . There's so much falseness there. . . . Take this line, for example: "My militia is looking out for me"[72]—doesn't it seem that way?
D: Excuse me, but I see carnival here!
B: No, there is no carnival in "My militia is looking out for me." So . . .
D: "Protects me . . ."[73] "The street is mine, the buildings—too . . ."[74]
B: "My buildings." And yet he couldn't get a decent apartment for himself, and couldn't help his friends find homes for themselves in those buildings of his . . . [*he chuckles*]
D: He couldn't get an apartment?!
B: He never did.[75]
D: So that means that he was false, then? Because if he hadn't been truthful, he'd have received all of those perks. In that environment . . . It'd have been the exact opposite of what happened to him.
B: Perhaps, but his language here is insincere nevertheless. Still, his falsity was not obvious, and yet he was not one of the "guys," never became chummy with those in power, those who could actually say about themselves: "These are my buildings. Sure, they belong to others, but they are still mine."

So. "My militia is looking out for me . . ." What is that?! Akhmatova put it best: "Take Tyutchev, for example," she said, "You can't find a bigger monarchist than him, yet he'd never have said that 'the Tsarist militia is looking out for him.'"

D: "Keeps me safe . . ."

B: Yes, he'd have never said that. Such words would never have crossed his lips. With Mayakovsky it's different. It's just not there. There might be an element of irony, but this irony, as is often the case . . .

D: There's more irony later, for example, here:

> Beyond the city
> there are fields;
> in the fields, there are villages.
> In the villages,
> there are peasants
> with brooms for beards.
> Each grandpa just sits there,
> shrewd and scheming.
> They tend to the land first,
> then tinker with poetry.[76]

He is not being serious here!

B: Of course he's not! You see, there's much that's carnivalesque in Mayakovsky. But it wasn't noticed back then, wasn't appreciated. The force of carnival is most powerful in his poetry. It's most evident in his earliest, Futurist, period.

D: It's there until the very end, everywhere!

B: Until the end, okay. That's true. Yet he ended up poisoning himself. Why? Why did he all of a sudden want to be a government poet, a government authority, and so on?

The same thing happened with Meyerhold,[77] who I believe was even prepared to have anyone arrested who disagreed with him about anything theater-related. I think he even used to threaten people (I can't recall any particular names right now): "I'll have you arrested because you are against the Soviet state!" When in fact the person was not against Soviet power, but against his theoretical approach! And who was a better representative of carnival than him?!

D: Well, there was a more refined decadence in Meyerhold . . . Mayakovsky's weaknesses were different. He may not have been very sophisticated, but he was never fake . . .
B: I think that he was, though . . . Under those circumstances. . . . He must have understood what was happening all around, he must have. He must have known that you can't accept everything unconditionally.
D: There's a certain poeticism here, which brings Mayakovsky close to, say, Tsvetaeva! You remember her words: "What am I to do with my excess in this world of measures?!" He, of course, must have known . . . You are right . . . But as a poet, he proclaimed, "My revolution," and embraced it completely.
B: Yes, he embraced it fully, I understand that.
D: He did. That was a widespread, we might even say very common philosophical mistake back then: to see the end as justifying the means. He shares that offense with many other great minds in this world.
B: Yes.
D: So, of course, his death . . .
B: We must note that there was a lot of carnival in the Revolution he knew, the one he wrote about and claimed as "his." A lot of carnival for sure! And he sensed that. But when . . .
D: There was real greatness there!
B: There was, there was to an extent . . .
D: And he identified with that greatness, that buffoonery. . . . The buffoonery gave birth to his poetry. He did play with language. . . . He played with words when he composed his poems, and when he said things like, "Despite all the poetic jibber-jabber, I consider 'Everything for everyone—at Mosselprom'[78] to be poetry of the highest quality." Why? Because to be a poet is to be a wordsmith, and poetry can be about anything! He took this idea to its logical . . .
B: . . . conclusion. Correct.
D: Logical conclusion, yes. He was a complicated, multilayered person. As a poet, he couldn't. . . . He was not an artist of half-tones.

Anyhow, I can't agree with you that poetry cannot be happy. As far as music goes, I don't know . . .
B: Happy, you say . . . Well, poetry can never be just "happy." It just can't. There's always in it something that we can call "the frozen tear."
D: [*recites*] Now, the mazurka. Long ago,

At the mazurka, floors would quake,
Heels pounding on the wood below,
Enough to make the ballroom shake,
The windows rattle in their frames.
Not now: we like more polished games,
Glide smoothly over lacquered boards,
Though a provincial town affords
A sight of the true original,
Heels, and leaps, and long moustache,
As some old squire cuts a dash,
All still the same as we recall;
No sign of the fevered tyrant, Fashion,
That plague of every modern Russian.[79]

I think this qualifies as happy poetry!
B: These lines are very joyous, true. But poetry as a whole, and the complete oeuvre of a poet, again, in its totality, cannot avoid incorporating also . . .
D: Ah! Now I get it. On that we certainly agree.
B: But all in all, in the end . . .
D: We are in agreement here. I'll respond with Mayakovsky:

Off you go, my thoughts, and never stall,
Better hug, depths of my soul and sea!
If your mind is always as clear as crystal
I'm afraid you're just a victim of stupidity.[80]

That's it! Now we're somewhat on the same page, so to speak.
B: Yes, yes.
D: It's time to take a break. . . . And we only had the chance to talk about Sologub . . .
[*interruption in the recording*]
D: . . . Is that Blok you're talking about?
B: Yes, he was a man cut from a different cloth. We are all made very differently from him. He was the exception. When you saw him on the stage—his appearance, the way he read his poetry, which, from the perspective of proper recitation, was quite poor—you could feel that he

was not of this world, that there was something outlandish about him. Not of this world in the sense that . . . In short, we are all little people, and he is very different—immense, cut from a different cloth, in possession of a voice unlike ours. He could be uttering simple, ordinary words, but he'd make them sound unusual, and acquire new meanings. That's the impression he left on me. We never did become acquainted, though. I had already left. . . . And later, when I came to live in Leningrad permanently . . .

D: He was already gone.

B: Yes, he was gone by then. There's something else I remember. While we were in Vitebsk, we received news that Blok was living in the most horrible conditions. And indeed, he was starving to death then. How could you not make sure somebody like him had enough to eat?! What utter nonsense was that?! When others were eating their fill in the Kremlin! And not only in the Kremlin. I remember, but in Vitebsk, where I lived, nobody went hungry at the time. Everybody had enough to eat, nobody was starving.

D: Well, in Vitebsk . . .

B: Why couldn't they take care of people like Blok? There was such horrible indifference everywhere, a lack of understanding, a lack of concern from his friends and, most of all, from the authorities . . .

Anyway, we heard the rumors, and organized a fundraiser in his honor. There was a speaker from Petersburg who gave a talk that evening—a famous journalist, very important . . . I'll think of his name in a minute . . .

D: A journalist from before the Revolution?

B: Yes, from before, before the Revolution. An older man . . . Anyway, he gave a speech, and so did Pavel Nikolaevich Medvedev . . .

So he [Blok] died from a heart condition. This heart condition took a turn for the worse once he was afflicted with scurvy, which, as you know, is the result of poor diet.

D: Is that recorded somewhere, that he died from scurvy?

B: Scurvy? That he died from scurvy? I think it's a matter of official record.

D: I never came across it.

B: Really? I think he even mentions it in his diary, where he writes about the effects of scurvy . . .

D: Scurvy has very clear clinical symptoms.

B: Yes. That's what he had, it seems. Yes. So, when this rumor reached us, we organized that fundraiser.

D: That happened while you were living in Vitebsk, correct?
B: Yes, in Vitebsk. The auditorium was full. We collected a lot of money, and were ready to send it all to Blok. But then I think we decided to buy the food in Vitebsk because you could find everything there. After all, it was a Jewish city. The Jews managed to survive the most difficult times thanks to their connections, their vigorous entrepreneurship, their persistence; they were always able to procure anything. So, we decided to send him some supplies. And that's when we received the news about his death. We were too late! And we ended up not sending anything.
D: What did you do with all the food supplies?
B: I don't remember anymore. We most likely sent everything to his family, to Lyubov Dmitrievna.[81] I didn't pay much attention.

I read some poetry that night . . . Actually, no, I gave a talk . . . I think I gave a little lecture on the "Nightingale Garden," I discussed that work, I believe. Then I recited his poem. . . . It goes like this:

> When you're broken and plagued often
> By people, work, and desolation;
> When everything you held in veneration,
> Now rests beneath, protected by a coffin;[82]

And so on. Gorgeous poetry!
D: "Then you can be proud of your happiness!"[83] That's from the same poem, isn't it?
B: No, no, that's not right. It goes like this:

> When, having crossed the urban desert,
> In deep despair, sickened to the bone,
> At last you reach your home, alone,
> Your eyelashes frozen from the cold,
> Just pause, then, by the door,
> And listen to the music of the night:
> You will discern . . . that different life
> You failed to realize before;
> You'll look around and see as if anew
> The snowy streets, the bonfires' fumes,
> The night, so still, awaiting morning to resume
> Its reign in the dim white gardens in your view,

And the sky—a single book among so many;
The image of your mother, kneeling down,
In the recesses of your soul will now be found,
And at that moment, all things together—
The patterns on the lanterns made of glass,
The chill that turns your blood to ice,
Your cold old love in paradise—
Will shimmer in your grateful heart at last.
You'll bless it all then, as you'll realize
That life is infinitely more, still,
Than the *quantum satis* of Brand's will,
And our world's beauty never dies."[84]

A remarkable poem, just wonderful!
D: Yes, wonderful. And you recited it beautifully.
B: Well, you know. . . . I used to be able to recite poetry really well, but not anymore. . . . I don't have the voice, the lungs, anymore . . .
D: Still, your intonation is perfect.
B: I remember reciting this poem back then.
D: You forgot to mention it when we were talking about Vitebsk.
B: Yes. . . . Now, in regards to Blok . . . My closest friend then, Pavel Medvedev, returned to Leningrad almost right after [that evening]. He went back earlier than I did. He, together with Pumpyansky,[85] prepared our return there. He became close to Blok's widow. Rumor has it that they were lovers. Besides, I heard not long ago that . . .
D: Who? Medvedev?
B: Yes, Medvedev. I heard that he even became her husband officially. But that's not true. I knew Medvedev very well, very well indeed. I can't vouch for sure that he was not her lover, of course, but they were never married. He was the first to study Blok's archives. Blok's notebooks, his diaries, were first published by him, although not in the best possible way, quite carelessly, in fact.
D: Yes, the publication was quite sloppy.
B: Sloppy, true, but at least he published them. He wrote a book about Blok, titled *Blok's Creative Path*. A very silly book.
D: Really?
B: Total junk. Rubbish. Here's an interesting detail: there's a big disagreement about the cross on Blok's grave. Have you heard about that?

D: No, I don't know anything about it.
B: Now there's no cross there. Of course, it's a well-known fact that his remains were moved to another grave. But at the first gravesite, where he was buried before the exhumation, was there a cross or not?
D: I have no idea. Why was he moved?
B: His remains were moved to the "Writers Corner," to be with the rest of the literary figures.
D: At the Volkovo Cemetery.[86]
B: Yes. He was moved there.
D: And where was he buried first?
B: In the Smolensky Cemetery.[87]
D: So, in Petrograd, but in a different cemetery?
B: Yes, a different cemetery. But not anywhere near other literary figures, he was buried in a random spot. So, because of all that confusion, people—abroad, naturally, not here—are arguing if there was a cross at his grave or not. In Russia, we are convinced that Blok was an atheist. But others say he was never an atheist. He was a theomachist, they claim; there can't be a poet in this world, their reasoning goes, who would not be a theomachist, and who would be a true, natural-science-driven atheist. That's rubbish, of course. Anyway . . . They are trying to prove that on his deathbed Blok was not an atheist, that there used to be a cross at his grave, as per his own last wish. I don't know who's right about that. But I'd like to find out for sure. Pavel Medvedev visited the old gravesite. When he returned to Leningrad, he immediately went to the cemetery and took a picture of the grave. It's published in his book, in *Blok's Creative Path*. But I can't remember if there was a cross there or not. I think there was, but I'm not certain.
D: But if there's a picture, what are they arguing about?
B: Everybody has completely forgotten about that book, it's such drivel.
[*another interruption in the recording*]
D: Mikhail Mikhailovich, we talked about Blok last time as well. Today, we covered a new topic: Sologub and his circle. What other important literary memories would you be willing to share with us in the remainder of our session?
B: Before I start talking about my other literary encounters from that period, let me say a few words about where they took place. We had several options back then. . . . First of all, we had the literary circles, or clubs. Of course, in that era there couldn't be any salons in the traditional

sense of the word, but the same function was performed by various clubs, societies formed around their members' interests, personal connections, and so forth. So, what salons or clubs did I frequent during that period, and where did I meet literary figures?

First, we have to mention Rugevich's club. The hostess, Anna Sergeevna Rugevich,[88] was not a writer, she was a doctor, but she was very closely connected with the literary, artistic, and musical circles there, since she was the granddaughter of the late Anton Rubenstein, and one of his heirs.[89] Every time *Demon*[90] was performed, she got a little money. She was the only heir of his, still living in Russia.

Her husband, Rugevich, was an engineer, also very well educated, very refined. His father used to be Deputy to the Finance Minister before the Revolution. He was Polish, and afterward returned to Poland, where he served in the same capacity in the Polish Republic.

A group of people connected with literature, music, and the other arts gathered together at their place. It was there that I used to meet poets like Klyuev.[91]

So yes, Klyuev. He made a very positive first impression on me. By the way, the first time I heard him speak was back in 1916—no, it was 1917, after the February Revolution, but before the October one, at a meeting of the Religious-Philosophical Society, where he followed Andrey Bely's talk. He presented his "Russian Alphabet" that time—his interpretation of different letters, the poetic metaphors embedded in each one of them. I didn't like him then, not at all. He was too stylized: wearing makeup, all oiled up, literally, which left an unpleasant impression. . . . But many years later, when we met under completely different circumstances, I liked him a lot. First of all, he read his poetry beautifully, and the poems themselves were most wonderful.

D: Was *The Copper Whale*[92] already out? Or not? *The Copper Whale* was the title of his poetry collection.

B: It was probably after it came out. *The Copper* . . . What was it, you say?

D: *The Copper Whale*. That's the title of his book.

B: Yes. I don't remember this book now. What of his did I like best? His poem . . . His poem "The Angel of Ordinary Human Acts" had just come out:

> The Angel of ordinary human acts
> Flew into my hut on a lark . . . [93]

Then it goes on to describe a traditional Russian hut in all the usual ways you associate with the immortal Russian village style of life. By the way, such contemporary writers as Belov today . . . [94]
D: Is that the one who wrote about the ancient fortress?
B: No, you're thinking of the one from Vologoda: Belov, the peasant author. I don't recall the titles of his works . . .
D: I am confusing him with Belyaev.[95] That's different from Belov . . .
B: Belov, yes. He [Klyuev] wrote a number of poems, many dedicated to the February Revolution. He didn't write anything about the October one.

> My heart—a bell jingling
> under a wedding rainbow—
> Absorbs the birds' cries . . . cries
> And . . . the golden air . . . [96]

and so forth . . .

He recited his poems beautifully. But I should say that when I read them in print later, they didn't impress me as much as when he read them himself.
D: They said the same thing about Mayakovsky: when he recited . . . Wait, the opposite is true: if you read the work with your own eyes—it's all quite strange, confusing, stupid, even. Yet if you were to hear the same thing in person you'd be impressed. But to go back to the text after hearing it first, and then find it less appealing—that I've never heard from anyone else before. . . . I myself . . . I didn't know Mayakovsky yet, and didn't like him, but then I heard him recite "Tamara and the Demon," and later, when I read the same poem in a journal, so much was opened up for me. . . . As for poems that, when read by the author . . .
B: . . . seem good, but then turn out to be quite bad?
D: Yes.
B: That is, not exactly bad, but less vivid . . .
D: There were so many poets back then . . .
B: Yes, very many. Anyway, Klyuev was like that. Still, he was a real poet. A real poet. Though there was much that was fake in him, too, very stylized . . .
D: Especially the latter.
B: Too many inconsistencies. For example, he presented himself—during that last period when I knew him—as a man to whom the culture of the

urban intelligentsia was completely foreign. For instance, he'd go look at a bookcase and ask, "In what language are your books written?" They were German books. And he could read German perfectly. It's true that his pronunciation was terrible, but that's different. He could read and understand it well but pretended to be someone who couldn't even tell in what language the books were written. He was lying, of course.

D: Yes, lying, naturally.

B: He was lying, lying.

D: Blok thought he was an actual peasant.

B: While in reality, he was . . .

D: But of course!

B: . . . nothing of the sort. He was plenty intelligent, and well read, too!

D: He was an educated man of provincial background, who, even though he had become a member of the intelligentsia, still wanted to preserve his roots.

B: Yes, his roots.

D: I met him once.

B: He genuinely believed that those roots were the real thing, and what we have now is just made up, extraneous, and bound to be short-lived. He was fully convinced of that. But I don't think he believed we could go back to what he called the true Russia, the Russia of village huts, and so forth. He thought there'd be something else in the future, which would be somehow closer to the original, old Russia, instead of what he saw as the messy existence of the kind of modern life that was promoted by the intelligentsia.

Besides that, he had very strong preferences and aversions. He hated Bryusov . . .

D: He hated Bryusov?

B: He did. "Byusov violated everyone with his pen . . ." Those are his exact words.

D: He loved Blok.

B: Yes, he loved Blok. They corresponded with each other. There's many letters, I'm not sure how many exactly, but a lot. For a time, while he was researching and writing his essay, "The People and the Intelligentsia," Blok was obsessed with this kind of nationalism. Klyuev was a representative of the people for him. But that was not true at all. He later figured it out himself, Blok did. He understood everything.

D: Klyuev also detested Mayakovsky.

B: He did hate Mayakovsky, of course. There was a lot that he . . .

D: Did you meet Klychkov[97] in that same circle?
B: I think he knew Klychkov, but what his opinion of him was I am not sure.
D: It was the same . . . Do you remember Esenin's poem: "He chose his nickname—Klyuev, the timid Mikolay . . ."[98]
B: Yes, but I never talked with him about Klychkov.
D: Did you ever meet Klychkov?
B: No, I don't remember him.
D: Didn't he belong to the same group of friends?
B: I think so. In any case, they were close friends, but I don't remember him.
D: You don't remember seeing them together?
B: No, I don't. Not when I was there, at least . . .
D: So, in Rugevich's circle, there was Klyuev, but not Klychkov . . .
B: Correct. He had his own likes and dislikes, he most certainly did.
D: And would you say that the members of this club were respectable people, no bohemians among them?
B: Yes, very much so, no bohemians among them. Let me tell you this about Klyuev: he was, in particular, a remarkable teller of ancient fairy tales, the kind that were never recorded or published. . . . He would hear a folk story once from someone in his native village, and then he'd re-tell it himself, make it his own. He was a remarkable storyteller! Just remarkable! His storytelling was much more genuine than his . . .
D: Poetry.
B: Poetry, yes. But he would only narrate those stories orally, in person. He'd just sit down and begin telling his tale. . . . He was brilliant at that.
D: Was he really born in a wealthy peasant family?
B: Yes, he was.
D: Did he go to school anywhere?
B: I don't know. He always pretended to be a simple peasant, and never discussed that topic, I believe. I asked him once and his reply was, "I didn't go to school. All I know, I've learned from the common folk, and from books I found lying around." That's what he told me.
D: Who else was there?
B: Let me tell you a bit more about him, just to finish. So . . . he was a splendid storyteller . . .
D: We've established that fact.
B: Once when we were at the Rugevichs', he told us a rather coarse folktale. . . . He told it beautifully, but it was very obscene.

D: Oh, do tell it!
B: After that he was not invited anymore. That was pretty unfair, I thought.
D: Was the tale really good?
B: Very good.
D: As fairy tales go?
B: Yes.
D: Please tell us.
B: I can't remember the details. . . . If I were to retell it in my own words, not in the language he used, it wouldn't be the same. Particularly because he also did various noises, voices, especially when he was talking about wood goblins, about mermaids . . .
D: Oh, how interesting!
B: It was remarkable, really amazing! But they stopped inviting him.

The other salon where I used to run into him, they didn't chase him out, never. They didn't throw him out at the first place either, just stopped inviting him. Maybe there were some ladies present, you know, of the type who couldn't handle that kind of language . . .
[*he chuckles*]
D: Was his tale in the style of Kirsha Danilov's obscene stories then?[99]
B: Yes, that's right . . . Now let's turn to the second salon or club, the one hosted by Pavel Nikolaevich Medvedev, about whom I've already told you a lot. A group of minor writers used to go there. Klyuev went as well. He even read his poetry—his new poetry—there. I remember his wonderful recitation of his poem on Yesenin's death:

> Let's commemorate, little devil, Yesenin's life,
> With funereal rice studded with pieces of used-up bathhouse soap . . . [100]

Do you remember it? I think I've left a word out . . . [101]
D: Funereal rice?
B: ". . . with pieces of used-up soap."
D: ". . . with pieces of used-up soap . . ." I see. The boiled rice with raisins and honey, traditionally served at funerals, here is made with bits of leftover bathhouse soap,[102] and will be used to commemorate . . . [103] And it's the Devil who will be honoring Yesenin?
B: Yes, that's right.

D: That's pretty neat!
B: Very neat, yes! It continues in the same vein. Some of his poetry was very lyrical.
D: What did he look like? Physically, I mean.
B: He used to wear something resembling a long, tight-fitting peasant coat. I never saw him in a proper jacket or a tie. He tried to look like a peasant, but at the same time his garments were not really what a peasant would wear.
D: Was his hair shoulder-length?
B: Yes, trimmed in the shape of an inverted bowl, like a peasant's. He had already stopped styling it in any special way (he used to sleek it down with kvass) by the time I met him. He looked well combed, presentable.
D: Was he already balding?
B: I suppose so; he had already begun to lose some of his hair by then.
D: So the two of you went on meeting until the very end? Until 1929?
B: Yes, until the very end.
D: Was he sent away before or after you?
B: I think a little later than me.
D: Did he die in exile?
B: Yes, he did.
D: He never came back, correct?
B: Yes, he never came back.
D: Do you know if he's been rehabilitated?
B: I can't say. Most likely he was. He was sent to the camps not for political reasons, but because of the recently begun persecution of homosexuals.[104]
D: Poet? Zubakin?
B: Not.
D: But who else was famous for this?
B: But really, after all—Zubakin is a very minor poet, and I'm thinking of a very major poet.
D: Was he inclined in that direction?
B: Very much so.
D: We are talking about the 1930s already.
B: Yes. He didn't try to hide it either . . . much like that other amazing poet . . .
D: Ah, Kuzmin!

B: Kuzmin, of course. Right. Kuzmin. Klyuev also didn't hide his orientation. He didn't talk about it openly, naturally, but he also didn't keep it a secret. I remember the visit of an important specialist on this matter, a very serious German doctor, can't recall his name now, who happened to suffer from the same affliction. He published a huge volume on the topic, which I skimmed through once, since I knew about . . .

D: Did you really?!

B: . . . about such perversions. His position was that we shouldn't treat homosexuality as a crime, that it's completely natural, that in fact no types of sexual behavior should be forbidden, or persecuted.

D: What, even rape shouldn't be persecuted?

B: Of course it should be, that should be punished. But homosexuality shouldn't be persecuted. He provided a ton of scholarly support for his ideas; it was an extensive study, beginning with antiquity and taking it all the way to the present day. It turns out there were many poets, musicians, important cultural figures, who were homosexuals.

D: Starting with Tchaikovsky[105] in music . . .

B: Yes, starting with Tchaikovsky, of course. Anyway, his was a very thorough study of the issue, very German in style . . .

D: As thorough as only a German can be . . .

B: Very meticulous, and so forth. So, when its author came here, he was naturally introduced to . . .

D: . . . Klyuev.

B: Yes, Klyuev. They met several times. I wasn't present at those meetings, of course, but I heard reports about them from others. Klyuev, apparently, used to claim that "even our God, Jesus, was a homosexual."

D: Are you serious?!

B: Yes. "He was involved with apostle John, his favorite student, who was a very effeminate man." And he'd continue in the same vein . . .

D: How could Klyuev . . . a man who considered himself to be a . . .

B: . . . a Christian . . .

D: . . . an Orthodox Christian . . .

B: Yes.

D: . . . and also a proper peasant. . . . How could he . . . ?

B: Yes, a peasant. Nevertheless, he would say things like that.

D: I didn't know that . . .

B: Well, you probably read Kuzmin's *Wings*?[106]

D: I don't have the book.
B: It is a very interesting work, very original. But also very open as far as homosexuality is concerned, completely honest . . .
D: I don't remember the book very well.
B: In the end many people—Kuzmin was already dead—were forced to leave because of that reason; they were sent far, far away. Klyuev was among the officially accused [of homosexuality], of course, and sent away presumably because of his writing, but his attitude toward the Soviet authorities was also very well known, so perhaps that was the real reason for his exile.
D: Right, you told us all about those two literary circles . . . Were there any other members of any significance you can remember?
B: Significant? To be honest, there weren't any major figures there. Let me try to remember. There were some writers who came to Pavel Medvedev's home, but they were later completely forgotten. For example, there was Kozakov, Mikhail Kozakov.[107]
D: I remember him. He was an important prose writer, quite well known.
B: He was a famous prose writer, yes. He also ended up in the camps.[108] He came back later, after the rehabilitations, but didn't live much longer, and didn't write anything else, I think. He was, by the way, another one of Medvedev's close friends. It is true, though, that at the very end something happened that drove them apart. . . . Right . . .

There was also another writer, pretty famous in his day. . . . But I can't recall his name now. . . . What do you expect. . . . It'll come to me later.

There were also poets there. Chief among those in Medvedev's circle was Vsevolod Rozhdestvensky,[109] who was very, very young at the time. He had just finished his military service, which he spent in the Navy. He served on a submarine, but, of course, he was at the lowest rank. He enjoyed very great success at that time. They used to say there was an official Leningrad school of poetry.
D: Yes!
B: And at the head of it was . . .
D: Vsevolod Rozhdestvensky, that's correct . . . He is still alive.
B: He is, I know that. Back then he used to perform his work quite often at Pavel Medvedev's home, and, if memory serves, he also frequented Shchepkina-Kupernik's salon.[110] He read his poems there, too. The poems

he presented back then were very good. Pure lyricism, pure lyricism! There were no, let's say, civic motifs in them, almost none. And again—he recited them beautifully! Beautifully! Later, when I read them in print, they didn't have the same effect on me.

D: Do you remember any of his poetry?

B: Of his early poetry? No. . . . You know, he was not that great of a poet, after all . . . I remember his poem "On Blok's Death," for example. That was a good poem.

D: What was his behavior like? Do you remember anything about him in particular? Did you meet him at Medvedev's often?

B: We met at Medvedev's, yes. He took part in the literary debates of the time. Today, of course, I can't remember any of his poetry. I think he published a collection, *Ursa Major* [The Great Bear], I believe it was called. There were some individual poems about Russia there, for example, I remember this line: "There used to be this huge, primitive nation . . ." (That's what they'd say in the West):

> There used to be this huge, primitive nation,
> But to sing, the way it was able to sing on occasion,
> You'll never succeed, despite all your grand aspirations![111]

Good, strong words!

D: "There used to be this huge, primitive nation, / But to sing, the way it was able to sing . . ."

B: ". . . to sing on occasion . . ."

D: "You'll never succeed, despite all your grand aspirations!" This is addressed to the West, correct?

B: Yes, of course. Or take this poem, for instance. Let me remember . . .

> In the fields, suffused with starlight,
> We sing on, in sorrow and travail.
> And for this, on their earthly trail,
> Angels lend to poets their might.
> Led along by hand, like children or the blind,
> We, indefatigable, humble drifters,
> Heed the signs transmitted by the fingers
> Of the fellow travelers by our side.[112]

That's very good.
D: Yes, it is.
B: [*recites*] Angel mine, so simple and demure,

So very mindless of all needs, and of desire,
You shall be my wife, I know for sure,
Playful child still clothed in girlish attire.
For our earthly days, each one unique,
You'll forsake the joy that your piano brings,
And in my room, so absurd and bleak,
You'll just dust and rearrange my things.

But when . . . (something, something)
You'll turn into a human lyre . . . [113]

You see, I'm already lost.
D: Well, that's understandable.
B: By the way, I tried to recite the poem the way he did it, somewhat at least, though of course I can't reproduce his intonation now . . .
D: There's a bit of Pasternak,[114] of Yesenin, here.
B: Yes, there's a little of both in it. There's also a bit of Blok . . .
D: He began writing when Blok was still around, I think.
B: Yes, Blok was still alive.
D: He [Rozhdestvensky] published his memoirs . . . I must try and find him. Is he still alive?
B: He is, he is. He's a Pushkin scholar, works on Pushkin.
D: Does he still live in . . . ?
B: In Leningrad, yes, just as before.
D: He stayed?
B: Yes.
D: You see, you're sitting on a real treasure!
B: Well . . . What else . . . I remember this on Blok:

For the first time . . . such Russia . . .
With depots, telegraphists, at night,
With mines and dawns . . .
For the first time . . . [115]

How did it go:

> At night . . .
> You were his sweetheart sworn . . .
> That errant night . . .
> Your cross was missing
> For the first time . . . (something) in the snowstorm . . .
> Caught in an eternal kiss . . . [116]

That's also very good.

D: Is this Rozhdestvensky writing about Blok?

B: Yes, about Blok. That's real poetry. I think it ends like that: "Caught in an eternal kiss." And then, "The muddy green of the eyes in the faint candlelight . . ." And there was also something like this: "Like broken wings, arms caught in that black frock-coat . . . ," etc. Beautiful verses![117]

D: Did you just gather together to read poetry at those salons?

B: We read poetry, yes. But we also drank tea, and sometimes had wine, snacks at Medvedev's place.

D: Did people read papers as well?

B: Sometimes they did.

D: What did you do there? Did you also read poetry?

B: No, I didn't. I was there more in the capacity of. . . . At the meetings in Medvedev's apartment there were also some paper presentations. People recited poetry, and the prose writers read their short stories. Then there was a discussion.

D: So you just took part in the discussions . . .

B: I did, but I didn't say much. I preferred to listen. I participated more at Rugevich's gatherings.

D: Did you read any papers there?

B: I did, yes. I gave some talks. Also. . . . Vsevolod Rozhdestvensky read his poetry. Vaginov[118] did as well.

D: OK, tell us about Vaginov. We'll end with that.

B: By the way, there was also a third salon, or at least something like a salon—at Maria Yudina's place.[119] Vsevolod Rozhdestvensky presented his work there, as did Vaginov and Valentin Voloshinov.[120] He wrote poetry then, and published some of his verses, but later gave that up completely because he understood that his talent was not very large and decided it's best to stop writing altogether, especially since he was also a musician and a composer. I should tell you there used to be a lot of music at Maria Venyaminovna's gatherings, naturally. She herself played, sometimes all night long. She played there in a way I never heard her perform in concert!

D: Let's leave Maria Venyaminovna for next time. How about Vaginov . . .

B: Perhaps I should tell you about him next time as well. Galina Timofeevna[121] will burst in any minute now. So . . . [*he laughs*]

D: There's something about Vaginov that you want to . . . how should we say . . .

B: I'll tell you about him a bit more, in more detail, because he is completely forgotten now—undeservedly so. . . . He was not even included in the encyclopedia. Nothing . . .

D: Nothing at all? Do you mean there was nothing about him in the literary encyclopedia?

B: Nothing. He was not included in it.

D: Well, that's unfair.

B: Completely unfair.

D: About Rozhdestvensky, I wanted to ask you. . . . Since you saw him in person, tell us a little about his looks, his appearance . . .

B: You see, he was a pretty tall person, very well-built, I'd say he was rather handsome, but his features, much like some of his poetry, were rather undefined. There was no firmness there. None whatsoever. He was, to use the evangelical language, like "a reed swaying in the wind." That's how he was. You could sense it in his attitude toward the [contemporary] literary debates: He always evaded providing a clear answer, and preferred to dance around everything. In short, he lacked determination, and, I think, he lacked courage, too.

D: He lacked courage?

B: He had no courage at all. None. Many liked him, especially when he read his poems, which he did very well. I always listened to him with great attention and pleasure. But when I read his verses in print later, they didn't have the same effect on me anymore, though I wouldn't call them bad . . .

D: Let's see, between him and Antokolsky,[122] who do you think is better?

B: Hard to tell. Antokolsky was much more refined, with broader reach . . .

D: Than Rozhdestvensky?

B: Yes, more refined. Antokolsky was a very cultured man. The other one—he was not as sophisticated. He was a lyrical poet. But when the topic was something different, like civic concerns, or politics, or even philosophy, he ceased being a true poet.

D: So, as a type, he was closer to Yesenin?

B: Yes, closer to Yesenin.

D: As a poetic personality?

B: As a poetic personality, yes.

D: As far as style goes . . . Is it fair to say that the group of Leningrad poets, led by Vsevolod Rozhdestvensky, was stylistically mostly influenced by the Acmeists?[123]

B: Yes, by the Acmeists.

D: Really?

B: And by Blok, to a degree.

D: That's what I think as well.

B: Right, right. But mostly they were influenced by the Acmeists, that's correct.

D: By Gumilev,[124] Akhmatova . . . [125]

B: Yes, yes.

D: Would you say that Vaginov was an important poet?

B: Not necessarily important. . . . Well, perhaps you could say that, but . . . As a poet he was noteworthy, but he was also a significant prose writer.

D: He was?

B: Yes. He was unfairly forgotten later. He was a remarkable prose writer, very interesting, innovative. To this day he is misunderstood and underappreciated. As a poet he was respected in the West even back then. They used to say that he was such a unique poet, that nobody understood and valued him properly in the Soviet Union.

D: All right, we'll leave Vaginov for next time. . . . Did you know Zabolotsky?

B: No, not then. I met him only after his return from exile but didn't know him very well. He used to be neighbors with Maria Venyaminovna; they lived in those cottages on Begovaya Street.

D: Well, rather than just you sharing your memories, we had more of a conversation today. It's all so interesting!

B: Yes, yes, yes.

D: Are you tired, Mikhail Mikhailovich?

B: No, not one bit.

D: Many thanks, Mikhail Mikhailovich!

B: You are most welcome.

D: I'll turn the tape recorder off now, even though we haven't gotten to the very end . . .

B: Then we'll only have Maria Venyaminovna left.

D: No, we still have to talk about Vaginov, Zabolotsky, including the late one, also what you remember about the OBERIU's folks,[126] and your opinion of them in general. Then we'll talk about Maria Venyaminovna separately. I'll stop here.

Interview Five

March 22, 1973

Length of the interview: 121 minutes

DUVAKIN: Mikhail Mikhailovich, let's begin our fifth, most likely last interview.

BAKHTIN: The last one, yes, certainly, that's fine.

D: [*laughing*] And you thought you had only an hour's worth of memories to share! I knew from previous experience that you'd have a lot to tell us. So we decided we'd finish our interviews with your recollections about Yudina. But first let's go back to what you were saying about . . .

B: . . . Vaginov.[1]

D: About the Leningrad poets and writers of the 1924–29 period. Konstantin Vaginov. I remember his last name well. I also recall his little book *The Goat's Song*, but, to be honest, I don't have any memory of what he was like as a poet.

B: Right. Well, let's see . . . Konstantin Vaginov was one of the most interesting and outstanding representatives of the Leningrad circle of poets. He was still very young then and had just finished his studies at Leningrad University. He was a philologist, an extremely well-read person, and a passionate bibliophile. He had a remarkable library, a collection of mostly Italian poets from the seventeenth century.

D: Amazing!

B: In general, he loved . . . First, not the era of Classical Greece per se, but Hellenism as such. He even wrote a poem called "Hellenists." It started like this: "We are all Hellenists . . . ," and so on. Then he was also a fan of the seventeenth century, that is—the Baroque era, the Italian Baroque, people like Salvator Rosa,[2] and others. He had books by these authors from the seventeenth century. Very precious and rare materials . . . [*interruption in the recordings. Static noise*]

D: Please.

B: Was that recorded?

D: No. The part about the patrons of the arts, too.

B: Okay. So, yes, there were some patrons of the arts who invited him to lunch.

D: He had his own sponsors?

B: Yes, there were such people back then. . . . Like . . . Ilya Gruzdev.[3]

D: He was Gorky's biographer, correct?

B: Yes, that's the one. He worked at the Lengiz[4]—the Leningrad branch of the State Publishing House—and wrote a lot. His article about authorial masks was very interesting, quite innovative for the times, as far as literary studies go. He was an imposing figure, who was able to secure good positions for himself, but who was also willing to help the many young and starving writers of the time. It was very common to be a young struggling artist back then. They usually hung around Lengiz or visited each other's homes. If, for example, someone managed to get some tomatoes, he'd say, "I have tomatoes, come eat at my place!" and they'd all go to eat tomatoes together. And that was considered a luxury, because many people didn't even have tomatoes. Nikolay, I should say, was very much like them, though not quite as hungry all the time.

D: Nikolay Tikhonov?[5]

B: Tikhonov, yes. He always wore his old army coat and lived a very bohemian life. He had a teapot, and would offer his writer friends tea whenever they came to visit—sometimes with bread, and sometimes without . . .

Vaginov, on the other hand, as I already told you, kept to himself. He was not closely connected with any of those writers. He made some money from publishing his poems, and helped young authors by editing their works, or by offering them his advice. He used to print his poems and short articles in a journal called *The Notes of the Traveling Theater*.

The Traveling Theater[6] was quite successful then. It was founded by Gaideburov,[7] together with Skarskaya.[8] Gaideburov was a very well-known actor at the time. Skarskaya was also an actress. She was Vera Fyodorovna Komissarzhevskaya's sister.[9]
D: Really? Her actual sister?
B: I think so. Skarskaya was her stage name, I believe. Are you familiar with that theater?
D: No.
B: That theater is completely forgotten now, though it was very successful in its time.
D: So it was a Petersburg theater . . .
B: Yes, a traveling theater.
D: And where did they travel?
B: You see, the name was borrowed from the traveling artists, *The Wanderers*,[10] who exhibited their work all around the countryside. Those Moscow and Petersburg artists wanted to share their achievements with the periphery, as we say now. It was the same with Gaideburov's theater. Although originally from the capital, the theater took its performances to the provinces, in order to introduce the local audiences to all the newest dramatic trends. And they were quite successful at that, up to a point.
D: What kind of a theater was it, stylistically speaking? Was it similar to Maly,[11] to the Moscow Art Theater?[12]
B: Yes, it was. . . . But the dominant trends came from the left: the Symbolists staged their plays there. They also chose to perform some little-known works. For example, they put on many Scandinavian playwrights.
D: That was the fashion back then. It started with Ibsen.
B: Yes, with Ibsen. Of course, they also staged Ibsen. But mostly they put on lesser known plays. It was not a bad theater for its time, not bad at all. It was quite lively, just like Gaideburov himself, and Skarskaya, too. So, they published their own journal, called *The Notes of the Traveling Theater*. Its main editor was Pavel Nikolayevich Medvedev. He was one of my closest friends at the time.
D: Yes, yes, you talked about him already.
B: He was the journal's editor. He was a very capable man, who was able to circumvent all kinds of roadblocks, of which there were many in literature and the arts even back then. He was very brave and ambitious.

He published Vaginov, when other journals wouldn't do it. He printed poetry that is now hard to believe actually came out in those days. One of those published poems by Vaginov, an autobiographical piece, went like this:

> I live like a hermit—at Catherine Canal, #105 (that's his actual address).
> Through the windows I see daisies, wild clover growing outside,
> And hear Georgian, Azerbaijani cries
> Coming from behind demolished gates of stone.
> The temple of the body is destroyed.
> The hordes sing in the steppe,
> Meekly chasing after the red flag . . .
> . . . it tamely flies . . .
> Today, you stink to high heaven, Rus',
> And in your Kremlin Mohammed ascends the stairs.
> Ascending the stairs is Mohammed Ulyan:[13]
> "Either-or, either-or, Rahman!"
> And the regiments stand to order and run . . .
> . . . Calling to China to raise its dashing crimson flag . . .
> [*he pauses, then corrects himself*]
> . . . and gallop ahead,
> Calling to China to raise its dashing crimson flag.[14]

Then it continues in the same vein. . . . You see, to publish such a poem. . . . It was printed in that journal.

D: In nineteen twenty . . . what? What year, exactly?

B: It was probably nineteen twenty . . . hmmm . . .

D: Probably 1923?

B: No.

D: Ulyanov is mentioned as still alive. Was he still alive?

B: No, it was after his death.[15]

D: Why are they climbing the stairs? Or are they the stairs of the mausoleum?

B: Yes. . . . No, actually, it was before he died. It was likely 1924,[16] the year we returned.

D: Yes! Well, it's not surprising that he was, we might say . . .

B: Right. Then it went on like this:

I am still young, my soul is restless and alive.
Yet the demise of the Empire, so great and wide,
Reveals itself to me, and thus my life . . .

That's one of his favorite themes—the demise of the great empire.
D: "And thus my life . . ."—what? "Is reflected in it?" Or what?
B: It's quite simple: that's also his life. You don't need a verb here: "Yet the demise of the Empire, so great and wide, / Reveals itself to me, and thus my life . . ."
As you can see, his poetry is very original, unusual. The address he provides is absolutely correct. He really lived . . .
D: Yes, you mentioned that.
B: Then he is describing perfectly the Leningrad of that time: the demolished stone gates, the street cries of Georgians, Azerbaijanis, all those members of different minorities who were literally flooding Petersburg . . .
D: Why?
B: Well, because they were able to expand, to flourish. . . . They were able to live here very well. The Russians turned out to be much worse at getting acclimated to the new living conditions. Plus, there were many advantages that came with having a minority status . . .

Another thing: there really were daisies and wild clover growing there. I went to his place many times and can testify to that . . .
D: Yes, that, once again, is the period of Leningrad's, that is, Petersburg's total destruction. But I don't feel the presence of the NEP here.[17]
B: It wasn't there yet, that's why. That is, the NEP was officially announced, but you couldn't feel its consequences yet.
D: You can't sense it at all. . . . And this particular method of exposition already existed. Mayakovsky was the first to use it, then others did it after him, too: "I live on Bolshoy Presne, #24. A peaceful place. And quiet. So?"[18]
B: That's true, yes. But I believe that was after Vaginov.
D: No, no, for a long time . . .
B: Sure, sure, that's right, of course.
D: It was still at the beginning of the war . . .
B: Yes, the beginning of the war . . . [19]
D: Besides the openly counter-revolutionary poem you mentioned, does he have any other, more neutral works? After all, he lived a long life, and kept publishing his poetry . . .

B: You see, he didn't have anything completely neutral because life was not neutral, there wasn't a neutral corner left to write about left. He was a loner, and a deeply neutral person by nature, but life was not neutral at all. Hmm, what were some of his other significant works? . . .
D: Do you remember anything else by heart? It'd be interesting to hear more . . .
B: Here, for instance, is the beginning of another poem. It's coming back to me . . .

> Oh, do transform me into
> a speaking monument!
> So that, free at last,
> I could rise up and sing
> About my precious life,
> And my other wild friend,
> Standing at the gates of Babylon . . . [20]

There are many such mythological reminiscences in his poetry, which . . .
D: They are reminiscences of reminiscences.
B: Yes, they are . . .
D: There are echoes of Bryusov here.
B: No, I don't think so. Perhaps of Vyacheslav Ivanov. The poem is about the statue of Memnon.[21]
D: I don't mean specific references, but a more general . . .
B: The general tone, yes.
D: The tone in general, yes. Very similar to Bryusov's. Only Bryusov applied it to the Revolution, while here it's the opposite.
B: Very true.
D: Besides his book *The Goat's Song*, did he publish anything else?
B: I was talking about his poetry, not *The Goat's Song*. He published two volumes of his collected poems. But I can't remember their titles . . .
D: Is he included in the literary encyclopedia, the short, contemporary edition?
B: He is not, not at all. I don't understand why he isn't in it. He is completely forgotten now. I was talking about his poems.
D: How about his prose?
B: His prose is far more important. Although his poems are also very important, very important and original. As for his prose . . . He wrote two

novels, quite big ones. The first was called *The Goat's Song*, the second—*The Life and Works of Svistonov*.[22]

D: So, *The Goat's Song* is not a collection of his poetry?

B: No, it's a novel. A novel.

D: What was the title of his poetry collection?

B: I don't recall that now.

D: You can't remember either one of them?

B: I can't remember either.

D: How about *The Goat's Song*, is that a historical novel?

B: No, not at all. You see, the very title, *The Goat's Song*, is a direct translation of the ancient Greek word for "tragedy." That is, the song of the goat. The main character of his novel is called Teptelkin,[23] a very unusual, interesting man. Teptelkin. Teptelkin appears in his poetry as well. He chose the name carefully.

D: The tragic hero Teptelkin.

B: The tragic hero Teptelkin.

D: It can already be viewed as the sign of a certain stylistic . . .

B: Yes. A tragic hero, who is both tragic and not tragic; he is funny, strange, awkward, yet at the same time deeply tragic. That's Teptelkin.

So this Teptelkin is endowed with just such a biography. But not beginning with his childhood or youth, no, beginning with the October Revolution. Teptelkin is an extremely learned man, completely immersed in his studies. During the hungry years, he moves to the countryside, and we are given an account of his life there. He is a scholar, an enthusiast who doesn't know or understand anything about the world around him. Then the novel describes his life when he's already in Leningrad. He gives lessons, every hour of his day is spoken for, he barely sleeps, and works and teaches all the time. His lessons are free of charge, and on different subjects, but especially on foreign languages—Italian, Spanish—though he also teaches Egyptian, ancient Egyptian language. Anyone interested, anyone who wants to learn, is welcome to study with him for free, as his only goal is to preserve Russian educated culture, Russian philological culture at the highest possible level, so that it doesn't dwindle out and disappear. And then for him it's absolutely . . .

D: . . . not lacking in topicality, shall we say . . .

B: . . . our modern obsession with technology, with efficiency and so forth, is very negative. He finds such things repugnant and incomprehensible.

D: You're talking about Teptelkin, right?

B: Teptelkin, yes. It's all very foreign to him. He lives in a separate world, the world of a philologist, completely detached from life. What else? We follow his attempts to get published, his literary activity. He can't get published because nobody understands him, or acknowledges the value of his work. Next, we learn about his marriage. A woman who's not able to understand him, and so forth. So Teptelkin is, from one perspective, an important, serious, tragic hero, who is not given a proper chance in life . . .
D: He is not accepted.
B: Rejected from life, correct. But he also doesn't accept the surrounding world. Still, his attitude toward life around him is very amiable—he never judges people, the whole emotion of criticism is foreign to him.

Then we are also presented with descriptions of his various quirks. For example, he lives in a tower; a wooden tower in the old Peterhof village.[24] So he is renting this tower, completely unsuited for human residence, and goes there every day. There's a small room there, in which he works. We must say that Teptelkin has a real-life prototype.
D: Clearly, he is based on the author himself, he is an autobiographical character.
B: No, not at all. There was another person living in Petersburg then, whose life and characteristics were depicted very faithfully in the novel. His name was Lev Vasilyevich Pumpyansky.[25] You know him, of course.
D: Yes, I've heard of him—and from you as well.
B: You've heard of him, yes. Now about his articles—he produced many studies of literature. . . . He was a man of incredible, almost supernatural erudition. He knew a huge amount and spoke many languages. It was all true: the free lessons, his attempts to keep philological knowledge alive under the most unfavorable conditions. His style of life was similar, too. He was always starving, of course, never had enough of anything. Despite the fact that he was an important scholar, nobody tried to help him. He was surrounded by various characters, who are very well described by Vaginov. Some of them were living in Leningrad at the time . . .

There *is* an autobiographical character in the novel, though—the nameless poet. He is present in the story all the time, as he is a friend of Teptelkin's. There's also another hero, Kostya Rotikov, who is based on Pavel Nikolayevich Medvedev, the one who studied Blok's poetry, and published several books on him: *Blok's Creative Path.*
D: I have that book. It's not very original or important.
B: An insignificant book, quite bad.

D: His writing fizzles out. The beginning is interesting but then. . . . He wrote an interesting book about Bryusov. The first coherent study of Bryusov.
B: Really? About Bryusov? I don't remember that.
D: The one about Blok was not as good. I always saw him as a specialist on Bryusov and recommended his book. . . . We didn't have anything about Bryusov then . . .
B: He was a literary theorist.
D: Yes, somewhat.
B: He studied Blok, and knew his wife; apparently, they were lovers.
D: Lyubov Dmitrievna?[26]
B: Yes, Lyubov Dmitrievna.
D: Was that after Blok's death?
B: Of course. She allowed him access to Blok's archives. That's how he was able to publish so much: Blok's diaries, his notebooks; also, some unfinished pieces, fragments from his plays. He published a great deal of Blok's literary legacy.

In the novel, the character Kostya Rotikov is doing research on a certain poet (the poet is supposed to be Gumilev) and is trying to figure out who his lovers were in order to have affairs with them himself. Rotikov believes that if one really wants to understand a certain poet, his life and work, to comprehend his soul properly, one must get to know all the poet's mistresses as intimately as possible. He is such an original, yet at the same time very typical character!
D: Kostya Rotikov?
B: Kostya Rotikov, yes.
D: And he is modeled on Medvedev?
B: On Medvedev, correct.
D: And Pumpyansky is the prototype for . . .
B: Teptelkin.
D: Teptelkin himself. And who's the autobiographical hero again? The nameless poet, right?
B: The nameless poet, correct. Everything in the novel is based on real-life events and people. This is where we discover, as I said before, Vaginov's true originality: on the one hand, such acute precision, attention to detail; on the other—remarkably broad horizons, almost cosmic in nature. It's all thrown into a sharp relief there. His uniqueness is also revealed in Teptelkin's character. We begin with a description of Leningrad: "At that time there was a strange creature by name of Teptelkin who lived in the

city." "A strange creature"! Then we read about Teptelkin's everyday life: about his room, the blanket covering his bed, which was an exact replica of the one his prototype had in real life. . . . Since Pumpyansky and I were close friends, I was very familiar with his blanket. All of it was rather well known anyway, and everything was reproduced very closely. At the same time, Pumpyansky's strength, depth, and tragic qualities were perfectly reflected in the character, too.

Overall, I would say that we have here a very peculiar type of literary tragedy—let's call it "the tragedy of the ridiculous man."[27] The ridiculous man. The tragedy of the eccentric, but not in Dostoevsky's manner, in its own style. A very interesting, strange story.

D: I believe at one time I had that book.

B: It's not hard to find. *The Life and Works of Svistonov* is his other novel. Here, by the way, Svistonov is based on Vaginov himself, so it's a more autobiographical work. There were many contemporary figures, very typical of the times, who are depicted in it. The chief one among them is Kuku.

It should be said that this Kuku—a peculiar creature of the times—is someone who's been left without anything of his own. Whatever he used to have (not in the materialist sense) has been taken away from him. The only thing he has left is the ability to appropriate other people's lives, to perform their identities in order to be someone. So he dresses himself in the style of Pushkin's era. And when he goes out for a walk in the park, for instance, the kids always shout: "They'll be shooting a movie here, a movie!" They expect movie cameras, because he looks like someone from the 1820s or early 1830s . . .

Everything about him is like that—contrived. There's an emptiness about him, but it's also an emptiness that at the same time attracts other forces, other epochs, different interests. He dreams of being a man of literature, yet he can't write anything himself because he is empty within. The only thing he can do is imitate other styles. In the end he does find himself in a novel, the one you're reading, *The Life and Works of Svistonov.* At first he is delighted that he'd been depicted in a work of art and would thus enter history. But then, after he reads the novel, he is horrified and flees the city, because he is ashamed to show himself anywhere after the way he has been described in the text.

It's all written in the peculiar Vaginov style. I'd say his writing is truly unique in world literature, exceptional. It's a shame he is forgotten now, that nobody knows him anymore.

When I was about to leave the city, Vaginov was already lying sick: he had the early signs of tuberculosis. Not too long after my departure he passed away from the disease, all alone, with no support from anyone.

However, I do remember there was a special meeting of Leningrad writers dedicated to his poetry. Benedikt Livshits[28] presented a paper about his poetry. He was very enthusiastic about Vaginov's poems. By the way, Medvedev, too, gave a speech, in which he praised his poetry and analyzed its specific characteristics. There were other poets at the meeting that I didn't know, who spoke against his individualism, etc. Fedin[29] served as the chair at the event. Fedin offered the concluding remarks, in which he also profusely lauded Vaginov's poetry, and defended him.

D: When did that meeting take place, do you remember? What year?

B: In 1925, I believe.

D: Who was at the meeting? Who were some of the presenters? Was Shengeli there?[30]

B: I think he was there, and even gave a talk about something. Pumpyansky also presented on his [Vaginov's] poetry.

D: That evening turned out to be the conclusion of his literary [career]. . . . Did its end come abruptly, or little by little? Was he arrested?

B: He was already sick then. Afterwards he left. Here is what happened next: he couldn't get through anywhere, couldn't get published; very little of his work saw print. He needed the money, he was practically starving. But the 1930s had begun, and it was impossible for him to survive that era. Nothing worked out for him. Even Fedin, who was one of his most passionate supporters, turned away from him, and I even heard that Fedin said about him that he "had gotten tired of life, didn't want to keep up with the times—what's one supposed to do about him?" In those days, phrases like "gotten tired of life," "doesn't keep up with the times," were very common. And by "life" they meant, of course, the official government direction, which was being implemented by all possible ways and means.

D: Very well then. That's Vaginov. . . . You gave us a pretty detailed account of him. . . . Do you remember any other poets of those times?

B: Not really, I can't recall anyone else anymore.

D: Nothing about Marshak,[31] Yesenin . . .

B: I didn't know them personally, no. I did see them on occasion, though—Yesenin and . . .

D: How about your relationship with Antokolsky,[32] did you two become closer with time?
B: No, no. I met him only recently, last summer, in fact, in Peredelkino.[33]
D: Was Anna Akhmatova actively involved in that . . . sort of life?
B: No, she wasn't, not at all. She stayed out of it. As for Gumilev—he was already dead.
D: Yes, I realize that, it's a well-known fact.
B: But Vaginov used to be a part of his circle, and respected and loved him very much.
D: You mean Gumilev's circle?
B: Yes, he was their leader.
D: Right. Mikhail Mikhailovich, let's turn to another topic now. Did you go to the theater in Petersburg back then?
B: I did, but not very often, because in my opinion the theater then was not very good.
D: Why? It was still excellent in the second half of the 1920s.
B: Yes, but you see . . . Of course I went to the theater. I was most impressed by Meyerhold's[34] productions, I suppose. Meyerhold, yes. I was very intrigued by him and saw many of his plays. I remember I especially liked *The Government Inspector*,[35] and also *The Forest*.[36] *The Government Inspector* was very interesting. Of all the productions I saw at the time, I remember it best. Khlestakov, the main character, was played by Chekhov, Mikhail Chekhov.[37]
D: You don't say! You saw Mikhail Chekhov as Khlestakov?!
B: I did, yes. Mikhail Chekhov . . .
D: There is a book about him that just came out . . . But it's a little boring.
B: He was an incredible actor! His performance in the title role of *The Government Inspector* left a great impression on me. I never saw him on the stage after that, just on the screen. He also starred in *The Man from the Restaurant*.[38] And not too long ago I saw him in an American movie. He's already very old, and played a very small part, that of the director of a music conservatory. So yes . . . He didn't impress me as much anymore.

I also saw some visiting actors, in particular, I remember I saw—it was absolutely amazing!—Sandro Moisiu[39] when he came here on tour.
D: That would be 1924–25.
B: Yes, in those years. He was an incredible actor, simply astounding.
D: He was a tragic actor. In what language did he perform?

B: In German. He spoke only in German. The others . . . Since he came alone, the other actors, from the Alexandrinsky Theater,[40] performed in Russian. The atmosphere that created was very strange: as if he was of a different world, the real, wide world, and all the rest of the cast were just . . . pygmies, barbarians.

I had already seen him on the stage once before—when he had come with Reinhardt's Theater,[41] and they had staged *Oedipus Rex* at the circus.[42] They performed it in a way that . . .

D: I tried to see it, the performance of *Oedipus Rex* at the theater.

B: Reinhardt's? When would you have been able to . . . ?

D: No, not Reinhardt's production. I mean, classical plays were later staged in the Tchaikovsky Concert Hall[43] in the style of Ancient Greek theater.

B: Ah, yes, but that's quite different. Reinhardt's productions were very original. So yes, they performed at the circus. That time I saw Moisiu in the company of other actors from the Reinhardt Theater. They only spoke German, only German. So, that was the first time I watched him on the stage. . . .

D: What is his nationality?

B: His nationality was . . . I think he was . . . maybe from Yugoslavia . . . not a Croat but . . .

D: Sandro Moisiu?

B: He was not a Hungarian. . . . Sandro Moisiu, yes. He was a small person, very short and pretty scrawny, with the face of a monkey, incredibly animated. Of course, when he was performing, it was absolutely . . . He was able to hide his soul completely, his identity disappeared, even his appearance and height looked very different. The only thing you saw was the larger than life character on the stage, he seemed to tower over everybody around him even though he was actually much shorter than them. He was truly a remarkable actor, one of the greatest that I've ever seen. We didn't have such actors in Russia. . . . Nobody could compare with him.

D: I only remember the playbills. I never saw him on the stage myself. I recall the playbills in Moscow: "Sandro Moisiu" . . .

B: That's the theater I used to go to. I also attended performances at the Traveling Theater, but they didn't leave any vivid memories . . .

D: After all, Moscow was the theater capital of the times, of course.

B: It was Moscow, yes, of course. When I saw Meyerhold . . . He visited on tour, too . . .

D: What did you see of Meyerhold's?

B: *The Forest* . . . Then also *The Government Inspector* . . . yes.
D: So, Meyerhold's company went on tours?
B: It did, it did, quite regularly. I remember it visited two or three times. Sandro Moisiu came only once. I saw him once before, in *Oedipus*, I was still a boy when I saw him that first time. . . . He was very young . . .
D: Excuse me, but was he a considered to be a German actor?
B: He was, yes.
D: Of what was then Weimar Germany?[44]
B: Yes, Weimar Germany. But I believe he started performing with the Reinhardt Theater during the time of Kaiser's Germany.[45]
D: Were you familiar with Kaiser?
B: Do you mean the playwright Kaiser?[46]
D: Yes.
B: I saw something of his. Wasn't *The Unfortunate Eugene* one of his plays?[47]
D: That I don't recall. But I know his work was hotly debated here, too. I wanted to find out what the fuss was all about.
B: Yes, it was widely discussed. Back then those German dramatists . . . they were all Expressionists . . . Kaiser was staged . . . He was also an . . .
D: Also Toller.[48]
B: . . . an Expressionist. I saw that play, I think it was by Kaiser, *Unfortunate Eugene* . . .
D: I remember the title, but alas, all I can recall now are the playbills . . .
B: I remember it well, that play. It was very striking, very theatrical, quite original. It's about the tragedy of a man, who has lost in the war his sexual potency, so to speak, and because of that is doomed to be sexually starved forever. Everyone around him lives their lives solely through their sexuality, and he alone, this "unfortunate Eugene," has no way to relate to them, and so forth and so on.

It was such an unusual play, and very unusually presented, this *Unfortunate Eugene.* There was a lot of talk about it, many discussions, I remember. Most of the time they were very superficial, as nobody truly understood it. At the time our knowledge about such things was all wrong, no one was familiar with psychoanalysis, even though there were already publications about it. As it happens, Freud's works, as well as the studies of his students, were being published here in the 1920s.
D: They were quite vulgar, weren't they . . . I remember . . . or maybe they are regarded differently now . . . I once attended a lecture by Professor Ermakov[49] on this topic.

B: I see! I know him. He has several books . . . One of them . . .
D: He published on Gogol in particular . . .
B: Yes, about Gogol, and "The Nose,"[50] in particular. He also has a book about "The Little House in Kolomna,"[51] in which he reads the house's "columns" as the author's phallus. [*he chuckles*] So yes, you can see Ermakov almost as a parody of Freud, of course.
D: Unfortunately, back then I didn't look into this topic very seriously . . . Only now . . .
B: Yes. . . . You see, Freud's *Collected Works* were being published at the time . . .
D: Here, in Russia?
B: Yes, here, at home. His collected works were being issued while he was still alive and working, of course. But we should note that Freudian ideas didn't take root here. We didn't have proper, serious followers of Freud in Russia then.
D: What do you yourself think of Freud?
B: Well, what can I say about him? In any case, he was one of the very great minds of the twentieth century, a genius who broke new ground. . . . You could compare him to . . . Who, exactly? My goodness! . . . Einstein. The two are usually put in the same category. He was remarkable! You might not agree with him, that's a different matter altogether, but there's no doubt that he was able to reveal things that before him we knew and understood nothing about. He was a discoverer, and a great discoverer!
D: But still . . . from your position of, as I understand it, a twentieth century reformed Kantianism . . .
B: Kantianism, correct.
D: For you, then, he must be . . .
B: From that perspective he's quite alien to me, of course.
D: Alien?
B: Yes.
D: That's why I asked.
B: That's the reason his views didn't affect my own position directly in any way. Still . . . There's a lot about him that, even if not directly . . . Well, any new discovery—albeit not something you yourself would commit to—enriches the world in some ways, broadens it.
D: That's interesting. What else can you tell us about your past? We have some time before we have to take a break . . . and after the break, we'll turn to Yudina. There was something else I meant to ask you about . . .

B: Please do. I can't think of anything else from the past to add.

D: Before Yudina, I asked you to tell me more about . . . Vaginov, I believe . . .

B: Yes, about Vaginov. As for other poets or writers . . .

D: Okay. So what other poets do you recall? Tell us a little bit about your relationship with Zabolotsky.[52]

B: Nothing to tell, really. I simply read his work before his exile . . . before my exile . . . that's all. Later I saw him a few times, but we didn't talk much, and I didn't hear him speak publicly very often . . . I did hear him recite his poetry . . . At Maria Yudina's cottage. That's about all. And then there was this, that he used to drink a lot . . .

D: Oh?

B: Maria Venyaminovna kept a bottle of vodka with his name on it: "Zabolotsky's vodka." She herself, naturally, did not drink vodka, and nobody who came to see her, none of her friends and acquaintances, drank vodka either. For example, I didn't drink it, of course. That's why she kept a bottle just for Zabolotsky: in case he happened to stop by . . . "Zabolotsky's vodka," that's how we called it. [*B and D both laugh*]

D: Mikhail Mikhailovich, let's go over the rest in broad strokes . . .

B: How do you mean?

D: I want to reconstruct the rest of your life. So in December of 1928 you were arrested. . . . Did you leave soon after?

B: Not all that soon. I was arrested, then released . . .

D: They released you?

B: Yes, but I was still under investigation. I was released because of illness and was admitted into the hospital.

D: Did you still have your leg?

B: I still had it, it wasn't amputated yet, but it was already ailing. Besides that, there was an abscess in the hip joint of my other leg.

D: So you were released because of illness, for humane reasons, we might say?

B: Yes, for humane reasons. I was treated humanely, overall. Besides, there existed at the time the Political Red Cross, headed by . . .

D: Peshkova.[53]

B: Peshkova, yes.

D: So, did they later ask you to leave?

B: Yes, I was simply asked to leave.

D: And go where?

B: Kustanay.[54] Kustanay back then was just a regional center.
D: Everything somehow has a different name today.
B: Yes, now it's different. Back then there wasn't yet any virgin soil. . . . Kustanay was indeed a very dark corner, very dark.
D: In the bare steppe?
B: It was surrounded by the steppe, there were very few villages there. Just the barren steppe. . . . The climate was horrible: bitter cold in the winter, brutal dust storms in the summer. The winds blew loose sand around and made it impossible to walk—you couldn't breathe . . .
D: How did you support yourself there?
B: I had a job.
D: Doing what?
B: I worked as an economist[55] for the duration of my sentence. That was normal back then: those exiled to a place like Kustanay had to serve. . . . So, I served as an economist for a trade organization.
D: How long was your sentence for? Five years?
B: Five years, correct.
D: So, 1929, '30, '31, '32 . . . The sentence was completed in 1933, yes?
B: Yes, that sounds correct, 1933. I can't remember exactly right now. But I didn't leave then.
D: You didn't have anywhere to go . . .
B: There was nowhere to go because I was already a persona non grata, marked negatively, with a "minus" sign. There was no way for me to be in a regional town center, or any big city with an institution of higher education. . . . So, yes . . .
D: Did your wife accompany you in your exile?
B: She did, yes.
D: And you didn't have any children?
B: We didn't have children.
D: Did your wife also work?
B: At first, she worked at the library, but then no, I was the only one with a job.
D: So, we might say, you had to go through a lot. . . . Then where did you go? Did you stay in Kustanay?
B: We did, yes. I should say that at the time Kustanay was . . . Kustanay was always used as a destination for exiles, even during the time of the Tsars . . . Yes . . . And the locals got used to treating the exiles well. . . . As

strange as that seems, the tradition continued. We were treated very well, at least in the beginning. I was amazed by that, actually. There were already food shortages, everything was rationed, but we always got a bit more than the rest. You go to the store, and they'd give you four, sometimes even eight portions of tea. If you asked, they gave you two or three of everything . . . We were treated so well by the trade organizations . . .
D: And you didn't teach anywhere at all?
B: I did, I did, especially during the last year. There was a pedagogical . . . pedagogical . . . not institute but . . .
D: Pedagogical technical college?
B: Yes, a pedagogical technical college. I worked there for a time. I also taught various courses—for businessmen, on topics pertaining to economics.
D: What's this—did you teach them about Hellenism? [*he laughs*]
B: No, about economics. I learned about that there, quite quickly. You know, it's a subject that . . .
D: Yes. So, did you move to Saransk[56] from there?
B: Yes, I did. This is how it all happened . . .
D: That's after 1934, correct?
B: Yes, I . . .
D: In 1934, did Kirov's assassination[57] affect the fate of the people exiled there?
B: Did it affect us? A little. . . . Even a bit earlier. . . . Yes, it did affect us. Mostly, there was a whole new wave of exiles afterwards. They were, for the most part . . .
D: Communists.
B: Yes, communists. In general, everything changed after that. All the privileges and benefits we used to have—as strange as that sounds, we, the exiles, did have certain privileges and benefits; for instance, nobody would ever dream of asking us to sign off on a loan. Then—we had our salaries. As those of us exiled were for the most part well-educated, highly qualified people that were hard to come by there, we were allotted very different salaries. For instance, if the regular salary was a hundred and fifty, we were given 250–300 just because we were exiled. Of course, you had to justify that kind of money. Everybody there understood that nobody else had our qualifications. After all, those were very poorly educated people, naturally intelligent and capable, for sure, but uneducated.

FIG. 5.1. Bakhtin and the students of Saransk Pedagogical Institute, 1955 (Bakhtin is the third from the left, in the third row). (Courtesy of the Scientific Library at Moscow State University)

D: OK. And where is Saransk?

B: Saransk is relatively close to Moscow, a twenty-hour drive from there. In Mordovia, the independent Republic of Mordovia.

D: That's in the south, along the Volga River?[58]

B: It's not on the Volga, no, it's way south of the river.

D: Not on the river itself?

B: No. You see, there . . .

D: And when did you find yourself in Saransk? Before the war?

B: Before the war, yes. Before that.

D: So, during the harshest years—1936, '37, '38—you lived in that same Saransk? And nobody touched you while you were there, you were not given a second sentence?

B: No, no . . . That was . . . Excuse me, Saransk, I'm starting to get mixed up. So, yes, I went to Saransk, that's correct . . . But I didn't spend the difficult years there.

D: Where were you, then?

B: The thing is, they started in . . . I was in Saransk in 1936 and '37, the very beginning . . . Then living there became absolutely impossible. All around people were being arrested, grabbed up, and so forth. It was horrible, incomprehensible.

FIG. 5.2. The house in Saransk. (Courtesy of the Scientific Library at Moscow State University)

D: That was happening everywhere.

B: Totally incomprehensible.

D: So you left?

B: I managed to leave there in time.

D: Where did you go?

B: Moscow and Leningrad. I lived in Moscow and Leningrad for short periods of time.

D: Without an official residence permit?[59]

B: Without a permit, that's right. I had family in Leningrad: my mother and sisters were there. My married sister lived in Moscow. So yes. I also had friends in Leningrad.

D: So, you started living illegally, we might say, without a residence permit?

B: Illegally, correct.

D: You ran away from the place of your exile.

B: Yes.

D: And that saved you, because . . .

B: It did save me, yes. Apparently, nobody went looking for me. There were so many strange things back then: a person got arrested, and so forth, but if, for some reason, he were to leave his place of confinement, nobody chased after him, nobody went looking for him.

D: Because he had already fallen out of the work plan of the local "organs."[60] They had their own plan too.

B: Yes, they did have their own plan, of course. So that's how I lived at the time.

D: I saw you at the Institute for World Literature[61] in 1939 or thereabouts . . .

B: Well, at the time I was already . . . I continued to live . . .

D: Did the Institute for World Literature let you give presentations without asking what you were doing in Moscow?

B: Yes. Here is what happened: I left Saransk, we might even say, ran away. . . . Not literally, of course, I simply got on the train and . . .

D: Didn't you have to report to the authorities every month?

B: In Saransk?

D: Yes.

B: No, I didn't have to do that in Saransk.

D: Hadn't you already served your sentence?

B: I had served my sentence, yes, that's why I didn't have to report to anyone.

D: You were just considered to be "with minus status."

B: "With minus status," correct. During my last year in Kustanay, I was already declared a "minus." I was told: go ahead, you may travel now, but here's a list of towns where you're not allowed to live. So, I thought, "I'm already here, why change one Kustanay for another?" And I stayed there another year. During that last year, I received a letter from Pavel Medvedev. He had gone to Saransk for a while. He simply went there to make some money on the side. There was a big pedagogical institute in Saransk, and its dean was one of Medvedev's students. So he went to earn some extra cash. He liked it there; he liked it in the sense that it was very peaceful and quiet there, everything seemed fine. At that time, that was still the case. . . . And he advised me to move there.

D: To go back to Saransk?

B: No, not go back, but move there for the first time. I was still in Kustanay then . . . Yes. He told the people at the institute about me . . .

D: So what did you do? You were in Saransk . . .

B: I was there for a year. I spent two semesters there.

D: Did you get a job teaching?

B: Yes, I taught at the institute.[62]

D: You were telling me before we started recording that you found that very boring . . .

B: It was boring, yes.

D: It was boring to teach there?

B: Yes, it was boring because everyone was very dim-minded: the students and the teachers. But the pay was good. The thing is, we were paid by the hour. Quite a bit . . . . I was able to bring back from there about 10,000 rubles, even though I'd only worked at the institute for two semesters. When I bolted out, I had 10,000 in my pocket. [*he chuckles*]

D: Hmm. . . . Well, yes, that's possible.

B: Yes. . . . That's how we lived . . . [63]

D: And where did you and your wife wander off to then?

B: We spent time traveling between and living in Leningrad and Moscow, and whenever possible tried to pass the night in different apartments while we were there. We had friends, many friends, everywhere, and they took us in when we needed a place to sleep . . .

D: That's fortunate . . . Back then people were scared to allow undocumented visitors in their homes . . .

B: That's true, but nevertheless . . .

D: Did you have a Saransk residence permit?

B: Yes, both my residence permit and passport were from Saransk.

D: So here we are. You couldn't join the world of scholarly endeavor, so to speak, because you were not . . .

B: Well, yes, I was living, we might say . . .

D: Were you yourself working on anything serious at that time?

B: Yes, I wrote, worked, and read a lot.

D: What were you writing then? When did you begin working on *Rabelais*?

B: I had begun working on *Rabelais* already back in Kustanay. Then I continued . . .

D: But there were no books back then!

B: Well, let me tell you about that now. I had a good friend in Leningrad, a close friend, the only one of my old friends who is still alive. He is a year older than me. He is alive and still very active. Professor Ivan Ivanovich Kanaev.[64]

D: Kanaev? Never heard of him . . .

B: He's published a lot. He is a biologist. He was a geneticist, and because of that . . .

D: He suffered under Lysenko . . . [65]

B: Of course. They used to call him "the entrenched morganist," "the entrenched morganist Kanaev."[66] [*chuckles*]

D: Did he procure books for you then?

B: The thing is. . . . One of his close relatives happened to be the Director of the Saltykov-Shchedrin Library[67] (the former State Library) in Leningrad. In general he had many family connections in that world.

D: So he got hold of books for you?

B: He could get me books from anywhere. From any collection.

D: And they found their way to you in Saransk?

B: They did, yes, and later . . .

D: That's great to hear! There are decent people everywhere.

B: True. I had this box, with my address written on one side of the top, and Kanaev's on the other. All I had to do was turn over the top. He'd send it to me, and I'd open it, make use of the books inside for as long as I needed, and then turn the top over and send the box back to him. That was all.

D: And he was the one who borrowed and returned them. Did he do it in his name?

B: Yes, of course he borrowed them in his own name.

D: Because you needed some pretty rare literary works in order to . . .

B: Very rare, yes. The thing is, he could even send me manuscripts. In short, he had great connections at the library. And because of that he was able to . . .

D: So you began working on your wonderful book about Rabelais in Kustanay?

B: Yes, though the bulk of my work on it happened later, of course. In Moscow, I lived without being officially registered, and so on, then I moved from Moscow and Leningrad to a more permanent place of residence: that was Savelovo.[68]

D: You were allowed to move there?

B: To Savelovo? I was no longer asking anyone for permission, I had "minus" status, but Savelovo—it was just a district town.

D: Yes, more than 100 kilometers from Moscow . . .

B: More, it's 130 kilometers away.

D: Right, and it wasn't a regional center.

B: Yes, which is why everybody could obtain official residence there.

D: It was the end point of the Savelovo railway line.
B: Yes, yes, yes. It's the closest place on the Volga from Moscow. The Volga was right there. There were very few internal exiles there, very few. Personally, I didn't know any exiles living there.
D: You yourself were no longer exiled, just expelled.
B: Expelled, correct. "Negatively marked," a "minus-nik" [*minusnik*] as they said back then, expelled from home. I have to tell you that there used to live . . . Oh my lord . . . He was a poet, a poet . . . But he had already safely left by then . . . You know, I don't feel very well today . . . Not at all . . . My memory, and everything . . . I can't get the right words out . . . I have no idea why . . . Maybe it's the weather, or something . . . Mandelstam! Yes, that's the one!
D: Mandelstam! Of course, he did live in Savelovo . . .
B: Yes, yes, he did, though very briefly.
D: Did you meet him in person? How about Nadezhda Yakovlevna[69] and . . .
B: No, I found out that he used to live there only after he had left already. So we never met.
D: Yes, he up and moved to Moscow; then he . . .
B: Yes, that's correct. I believe he first moved to Alexandrov,[70] while it was still beyond the border. . . . Then he went to Moscow, yes.
D: OK. And when did you . . . Were you able to become "legal" again only after Stalin's death?[71]
B: Yes, after Stalin died.
D: So, you moved from Savelovo to Moscow?
B: Yes. While I was living in Savelovo I traveled to Moscow quite frequently and spent quite a bit of time there.
D: When did you lose your leg?
B: I lost it . . . in Savelovo, yes.
D: The surgery was done there?
B: Yes, it was.
D: That's pretty terrifying.
B: It was.
D: You were told they had to do it to save the other leg, correct?
B: Yes. I was operated on there. I should say the surgeon was excellent, simply wonderful. Quite old, an elderly man . . .
D: Did you try to have your "minus" status officially lifted?

B: Not at all. It would have been completely useless at the time. In general, I am against all the . . .

D: . . . activity . . .

B: . . . activity—the silly bureaucracy, the worthless exchange of paper . . . I was never officially rehabilitated. Never applied for rehabilitation myself.

D: What are you saying?!

B: Why should I bother? I never thought I was investigated or sentenced legitimately, since I don't believe you could call what we had back then a real justice system. Everything was sort of . . .

D: Still, you should have tried to overturn that decision . . .

B: Why should I? What good would that do me? Almost everyone who was arrested and put on trial with me was officially rehabilitated, but I didn't even apply. I don't need this. Not at all. Why bother?

D: So, you returned from Savelovo . . .

B: From Savelovo I went to Saransk.

D: Saransk again?

B: Saransk again! Yes.

D: And that's when you began to receive "pilgrims"?

B: People started to come see me, yes . . .

D: Vadim Kozhinov[72] told me he went to visit you.

B: He did, that's correct. He came to visit several times. Then . . . that man . . . Vladimir Turbin[73] visited quite often.

D: I know.

B: With Lialechka.[74] He brought Lialechka with him; she was his assistant at the time.

D: Who's this Lialechka? The same one taking care of you now?

B: The same one, yes.

D: I must tell you my attitude toward Turbin is rather ironic.

B: Yes? Why is that?

D: I find him disappointing. . . . Take that book of his, *Comrade Time and Comrade Art* . . .

B: Well, that book is very old; it was published a long time ago, when he was very young and enthusiastic about technique for its own sake, that sort of thing.

D: But in my interactions and conversations with him he struck me as . . . But yes, I haven't read any of his later things, so maybe I am not being fair. I don't want to insist, but my impressions of him were that he was a very superficial, pretentious young man.

B: He was back then, but he is not like that now. Now he's different. I should note that his book, *Comrade Time and Comrade Art*, was adequate for its time.
D: It was quite lively.
B: It was fresh, original, animated, very well written, with style.
D: But overall, he's just babbling.
B: He himself acknowledges in the introduction that he's not a scholar or a researcher, but a journalist. It's a book of journalism. At the same time, he is a highly educated man. He's been teaching for fifteen years now.
D: I remember him from when he was still a post-graduate student.
B: Right. His famous study group on Lermontov existed for the longest time. He is already . . . The members of that circle still get together once in a while, there are some PhDs, and many mid-career academics among them already.
D: That's possible. I am behind. He was very . . . On the one hand, he seemed to be forward thinking, but on the other, he was . . . He behaved in a very orthodox way. You see . . . He comes from a family of the old intelligentsia. I even know his mother a little bit. She used to teach children French.
B: Aha. He is from a very well-educated family, yes. His father was an engineer. In addition, he thinks that Bulgakov[75] borrowed the name Turbin[76] from his father. . . . In truth, his father did live in Kiev,[77] and lead a big regiment of engineers there . . . Some of the stories Bulgakov describes in his work are very similar to what happened to him, as he was the one who told Bulgakov about them.
D: All right. So, this is where your autobiographical narration is nearing its end, we could say.
B: That's where it ends, yes.
D: After that you moved to . . . For a while you lived in . . .
B: . . . I went back to Saransk . . .
D: Why did you go back there?
B: Where else could I go? Nowhere!
D: So you lived there then?
B: Until Khrushchev[78] came into power. While Stalin was still alive.
D: After the war?
B: Yes, after the war.
D: Between 1948 and 1953?
B: Yes. All this was still during that era. Traveling to Moscow or Leningrad was no problem. I visited both all the time, but couldn't live there,

couldn't register my residence there. So I went to the Ministry of Enlightenment, as it was called back then . . .
D: The Ministry of Higher Education?
B: Yes. I wanted to ask for an appointment at a provincial university somewhere. And as it happens, I discovered that my former dean from Saransk was now in charge of the department for all pedagogical institutes. When he saw me he said, "Go back to Saransk. I'll give you the official appointment letter right away, and I'll write to the director there. You'll be provided with everything you need. It's best for you to go to Saransk." So I went there.[79]
D: And how many more years did you spend there?
B: I was there for quite some time, quite some time. I stayed there up until . . . almost until I moved here.
D: But you also . . . Didn't you and your wife spend one summer in Peredelkino, at the sanatorium there?[80]
B: Yes, that's true, we did spend time at the sanatorium. . . . That was earlier . . . Yes . . .
D: So, it wasn't until the 1970s that you were given your Moscow apartment?
B: No, the official Moscow residence permit I received only at the end of last year, actually no, this year. So, no. Back then the hospitals didn't require registration, and neither did the sanatorium. They didn't even ask to see your registration.
D: I think you were simply too passive in all this. You should have been officially rehabilitated in 1957, of course . . .
B: But what's the point . . .
D: You would have been issued an apartment . . .
B: Yes . . . Well, I don't think so . . . Maybe . . . I don't know . . .
D: Times had changed.
B: But I had a good life in Saransk, as far as living conditions go. I had a nice apartment. We were given one, a separate one just for us.[81] It was just me and my wife, nobody else lived there. We had two rooms. The apartment was bigger than what I have now: the rooms were bigger, the ceilings were higher, it was in an older, very nice building in the town center. The main government buildings were across the street from us: the House of Government, and the Saransk regional party quarters. Also, the attitude toward me at the university was [very positive]. . . . True, every time the boss changed, the attitude changed as well, but then things went back to

how they were before. So, you see, it wasn't bad. Not bad at all. I wasn't mistreated there. No, I can't say that I was.

D: No one treated you poorly there?

B: No, nobody.

D: How about your book about Dostoevsky—did you write it before you were arrested?

B: Yes, before the arrest.

D: In 1928?

B: Yes.

D: So, when you left, your name was already known to people. The book was generally noticed.

B: Yes, it was, it was noticed.

D: There were articles about it. And the second edition you prepared while living in Saransk?

B: Yes, I revised it for the second edition in Saransk. Kozhinov, my editor, came to see me, and also Sergey Bocharov.[82]

D: Ah! Bocharov came too!

B: Yes . . . he was also a friend . . . he came to see me in Saransk as well . . .

D: He's such a good lad . . .

B: Very good indeed. A remarkable young man.

D: Vadim Kozhinov was also one of my students, and very close to me . . . It was hard to rely on him. I have to say that I did hear from him. . . . He is a very capable person.

B: Yes, a very capable person.

D: Very capable, but rather unprincipled. Unfortunately. I don't know. . . . He used to boast to everyone that he's my student, etc., and then, all of a sudden, he up and disappeared. All of that became rather unpleasant . . .

B: Do you think it was because of what happened to you?

D: Yes![83]

B: No, that can't be. You don't really know Kozhinov then! He would never do such a thing! He is absolutely fearless. No, you're mistaken! And as for his attitude toward me? At that time, I was still a *minus-nik*, not known to anybody. My book about Dostoevsky was completely forgotten. . . . He did everything. Without him . . .

D: Did he push your book through?

B: Yes, it all happened because of him! I wasn't planning on publishing it again.

FIG. 5.3. Bakhtin in his office, February 1973, during his conversations with Victor Duvakin. (Courtesy of the Scientific Library at Moscow State University)

D: Are you serious?!

B: Yes, I wasn't planning to. And *Rabelais* was sitting on my desk, already finished, but I was not thinking about publishing it, and considered that impossible even. . . . Then he showed up—and got it all done.

D: So he was the one who pushed it all through?

B: He was, yes, and did such a brilliant job of it.

D: Well, that, of course. . . . And the more honor to Vadim, if that's what happened.

B: Yes. I know him quite well by now, and he is truly fearless. How can you think that?! There's no way he got scared because of your reputation.

FIG. 5.4. Victor Duvakin in his office, late 1960s. (Courtesy of the Scientific Library at Moscow State University)

No way! He always gets himself involved with people whose reputation is not exactly stellar. He is a very active person. He is not satisfied with writing only. He wants to act, to play an important role in life. He's not interested in making a career, no, he is not a careerist! He needs action, deeds, that's what he needs.

D: Yes, but what turns up here . . . and these anti-Semitic . . .

B: Yes, but you see. . . . He's a person . . . no, no, he's not an anti-Semite, not at all, not anti-Semitic, anyone who thinks that, it's a misunderstanding. You see, what's the matter here is that . . . He's a person who's always active. He is not satisfied with writing only. He wants to act, to play an important role in life. He's not interested in making a career, no, he is not a careerist! He needs action, deeds, that's what he needs.

D: I am so happy to hear good things about people I used to associate with, but in whom I had some doubts.

B: No need to have any doubts at all. In any case, what you're talking about is out of the question. That sort of thing could never have had any influence on him.

D: Perhaps he just lost interest in the whole thing.

B: He would have felt even more sympathy, it seems, etc. . . . He would have supported you in any way he could. Yes. Because no . . . he is not that kind of person!
D: People reacted in very different ways to what happened back then, and I was, of course, always on my guard.
B: No!
D: Well, let's hope for the best. See how much our lives are intertwined! By the way, I wanted to ask you, is your last name very common?
B: It's not very common, no.
D: Are there many people who share your last name?
B: I don't think so . . . I knew only of . . .
D: The thing is, there are people with the last name Bakhtin in my wife's family. I got interested in genealogy because of what you said at the beginning: that you come from an ancient family . . .
B: Ancient, yes.
D: . . . and that you have extensive information about your family tree.
B: I do, yes. That is, I don't have it myself, since I wasn't personally interested in it, but my brother was. He knew our genealogy . . .
D: And you come from nobility?
B: Yes, of course.
D: From Orel.[84]
B: From Orel, yes. The family had a Moscow branch. In that branch, there was one Bakhtin, pretty famous: not a literary scholar, but an important official (he was at one point a State Secretary during the reign of Alexander II).[85] This Moscow family connection—the Bakhtins—can be found even in Pushkin's life, and in Lermontov's and others. There were girls from the Bakhtin family who knew Lermontov, and he even courted one of them, I believe. That was one of the family branches, so to say. They belong to the same family tree, but we are not true relatives. My relatives are all from Orel, and most of them were military men, generals. One of the most prominent of these, we might say, founded the first Russian Cadet Corps.
D: The one you told us about?
B: Yes, that one, in Orel.
D: Was that your grandfather?
B: My great-grandfather, yes.
D: Very interesting. Now we'll take a break, you need to have lunch, then we'll talk about Maria Yudina. By the way, I wanted to ask you . . . I

FIG. 5.5. Bakhtin in his apartment, 1974. (Courtesy of the Scientific Library at Moscow State University)

became very curious . . . Maybe I am wrong. After all, no one is a prophet in his own land. What have you read by Yulian Sergeevich?[86] He is my cousin. Did you read his work yourself, or did he read it out loud to you?

B: Both: I read it myself and listened to him read out loud. That was a long time ago. He wrote very short . . .

D: Very short, short stories?

B: Yes. Like the one about the Fly, which you know.

D: And you've been following those stories for a long time?

B: For a very long time. We met through Maria Yudina, a long time ago.

D: Do you think his work was important?

B: I think that in any case it is very interesting, very subtle, and yes, in the end I believe it to be quite significant. Very significant. But his literary style, this type of writing, is not well known in Russia. It's not appreciated, not understood at all. If you take any Asian literature, let's say, Japanese . . .

D: You can find it there.

B: Yes. Only one image is provided there, the smallest detail, even the tiniest detail is still perfectly refined. We don't have anything like that, but his writing has it.

D: The thing is, I'll tell you the truth. . . . I find him oppressive. . . . It's as if he knows he is a genius, someone who's opened up a new era in art, and he's angry with me because I don't acknowledge that . . . He sees himself as an innovator, a pioneer . . .

B: Well, he is right, up to a point. You see, as far as his genius goes . . . In general . . . that word . . . I think that you can talk about someone's genius only a hundred years after his death—or fifty, at the very least. Time has to have the chance to verify him and properly separate him from the others. But there's no question that he's an innovator, and that his work, his short stories, broke new ground in our literature. . . . It's too bad that his style has not taken root . . .

D: And why not?

B: It's all too . . . incongruent with our reality.

D: You see, there's nothing political in it, but . . . Why? Elena Guro[87] wrote similar impressionistic pieces. Prishvin[88] did as well.

B: Hmmm . . . That's very different . . .

D: How is his writing so distinctive?

B: It's different.

D: I can't argue with what you're saying. Of course, it's very subtly done, the individual details are so . . . There's the little piglet he wrote about . . .
B: Yes, there was. A sick piglet.[89]
D: Yes, a sick piglet. That stays with you, it's really good. And then the story about the Pioneer leader known as "Potato," who drives a tram—that's quite nice . . . But he claims to achieve a certain depth in writing that I personally can't see at all. . . . I value your opinion greatly, of course, and should perhaps revise my own views about him, but it seems to me that if you're really dealing with something of lasting value, then every time you read it you would find something new in it. And your comparison with certain trifles . . . As Chekhov used to say, one can write about anything, "even an inkwell."
B: True, very true, and he did write . . .
D: Here you have the inkwell and the pen, that's all you need. In general, what can be said about all this? . . . But after all, it wasn't him that discovered this style. And, for me, that inkwell or pen fails to reveal, as it were, the greater world . . . I just don't feel it. At first I used to listen to him all the time, but then I got bored, especially since he loved to read his work out loud a little too much. I listened for a while . . . What you were saying before about Rozhdestvensky applies here: yes, it's interesting the first time you read it, but then you start thinking about it, and it becomes less interesting. Of course, that would also depend on the reader's overall responsiveness to the text. . . . Maybe the problem is with me, I don't want to insist that I'm right, no, not at all, but . . . I put my trust in the kind of great art that I can keep going back to . . .
B: Many times.
D: Yes, many times, and discover something new every time. You remember . . . well, the two of us differ in our recollections here, but my experience with Mayakovsky is like that. With Pushkin, too. And Dostoevsky as well . . . Though I have to say I don't go back to Dostoevsky a lot. Because of your books I recently began re-reading him. Some of his works I haven't read at all, ever. I do want to read everything, from cover to cover . . . Starting with the first volume . . .

So yes . . . As for his style of exposition . . . In fact, he put a lot of emphasis on narrative style, he considered his writing to be poetry in prose.
B: Well, that the term could be applied in part.

D: But I think it's not right to do so. Personally, I believe that poetry in prose is impossible, absurd. Poetry . . . it's poetry because it has particular formal features.

B: Well, yes.

D: Verses have their own specific qualities. And by the way, those "Verses in prose"[90] by Turgenev I don't like at all. When all is said and done, there's some little thing there, "some sort of oversalted cabbage soup" . . . taken as something small in itself . . . So taken by itself, after those "verses in prose" of Turgenev, after Chekhov, after Guro, and off to the side, purely in a formal sense, comes Rozanov.[91] Although I completely agree that Rozanov was an entirely different tonality.

B: A completely different tonality.

D: He's a paradoxicalist.

B: Yes, and it's not the thing itself but the specificity of thought, the distinctive experience you find in his writing. Everything else is just objects, things, natural phenomena.

D: And here things, you see . . . What do we have here, after all: a thing or, if it's a poem in prose, a lyrical hero? If it's a lyrical hero, then I don't feel it at all . . .

B: It's not a lyrical hero, not at all. It's a thing, a thing, an occurrence, a phenomenon of some kind. But it's something usually depicted only as a small detail in literature, something that doesn't have any significance by itself, that acquires meaning only as a part of the whole, of the plot, and is only necessary in the context of a given problem or character. In short, it's not an independent entity but just a detail, a part of the whole.

D: Do you think it has the right to its own independence then?

B: It does, yes, it has that right, definitely.

D: It's not for nothing that he always tries to present his works in cycles.

B: That's another matter. You could create such cycles, but every entry stands on its own, it's valuable by itself.

D: Then some of Chekhov's working notebooks can also be read as literature.

B: Yes, but that's very different, very different. After all, those are Chekhov's notes toward future stories, his future writing material.

D: He [Yulian Sergeevich] is, of course, very capable. His father was also a writer.

B: He was?

D: Yes, he was. He wrote some pretty decent short stories. He was a talented teacher, a great pedagogue, who distinguished himself as such. He was of a democratic, even of a slightly nihilistic turn of mind, and a biologist. Yulian also studied biology, became a good observer of things. By the way, it was Lidia Evlampievna[92] who put him on that path: she advised, encouraged him to write. And as he couldn't devote himself to it completely, for forty years he . . . Now he has turned to writing about Dionysius. He also read here several times. He thinks the public readings were a success. But that wasn't actually the case at all, I've asked around about that. I got answers like, "Oh, well . . ." People fell silent, they didn't want to offend him, and yet they had sensed in him a certain—and perhaps that's unfair—dilettantism. But his powers of observation . . .
B: I think it was the dilettantes themselves who viewed him as a dilettante. It seems to me that a real art professional would be able to appreciate his writing.
D: I don't want to argue . . . It's just that . . .
B: I, too, am not a specialist in frescoes, icons, and so on. That's another matter. Nevertheless, I believe that his method is very original, interesting, and successful in accomplishing its goals. In the end, I trust that he'd be able to carve out a new path. Maybe not while he's still alive, but later. In any case, he will be . . . important.
D: God willing. . . . You see, he is my first cousin, and is like a brother to me. I don't have anyone closer to me left . . .

I have a brother who also wrote poetry all his life. He wrote in the Acmeist style, like an epigone of Acmeism. "You, after all, can't . . . you don't write poetry," he used to tell me. I believe that if a person knows that he doesn't *have* to write poetry, he is better off if he stops trying altogether. I don't write poetry because I understand that I don't have the talent for that. He wrote—from the time he was ten until he turned sixty—all his life he kept writing poetry. From time to time he'd make the rounds of some editorial offices, and was even able to push a few things through. But it was all very amateurish, of course. . . . My brother was a mathematician. Yulian, of course, is much more talented than him . . .
B: He has talent, yes.
D: More subtle . . .
B: Yes, of course.

D: More subtle. But his tone when he talks is sometimes quite impossible. . . .
B: What do you mean?
D: I mean that there's a feeling of . . . I'd say, delusions of grandeur. Very strange . . .
B: Well, that's true, delusions of grandeur are typical for certain epochs. In general, as the inspector from *Crime and Punishment* says himself, "Who doesn't think he's a Napoleon these days?!" There are times when everybody thinks they are. . . . Back then, it was Napoleon. With the rise of Symbolism, Decadence, Futurism, everybody, all of them considered themselves to be geniuses.

Back then they thought it had to be so. Bryusov decided to call his insignificant collection of poems *Masterpieces*. And when people asked him, "Isn't it immodest to call your own work a 'masterpiece,'" he answered: "If I am publishing it, then I think it's good. Those who say my poems are weak are lying." If he is published, if his writing is published, then he believes in the genius of his work. That was his response to the publication of *Masterpieces*. Later, of course, he matured, and spoke and behaved himself very differently, but . . . Back then they were all "geniuses," all those members of various circles. . . . Among the Futurists . . .
D: Yes, of course: "I'm a genius, Igor Severyanin . . ."[93]
B: Exactly!
D: But it was all in a sense a kind of a game, a certain pose. In real life Yulian is a very modest person . . . He was a serious biologist, studied the specific classifications of ticks or mites, etc. He had such bad luck! His main advisor—who was, by the way, a high school teacher with university aspirations, a young man—drowned. He was left to fend for himself at a crucial time, at the age of nineteen. His father was already dead, too. . . . He attended lectures at the university even if he wasn't officially admitted yet. . . . Of course, he had to study at the university . . .
B: Of course, yes.
D: But he decided to stop trying to go to the university and went to the Zootechnical Institute instead. And when the Institute was re-structured and split into two, he ended up in the veterinary school, purely by accident. Anyways, he became a professional, and very well regarded, veterinary doctor, but . . .
B: How old is he now?

D: He is two years younger than me. I turned sixty-four already . . .
B: So he is sixty-two.
D: He is sixty-two, yes. Sixty-two. We like each other a lot, but I am scared at times . . .
B: No, no, he is definitely not a graphomaniac . . . I am positive he is not. . . . There's real value in his writing.
D: So he is right to pursue this?
B: He's right, absolutely.
D: Well, that's one thing. Everybody has the right to write, if he is so inclined. Every literate person . . . When I finish recording other people, I'll record also myself. I haven't done that yet. There's a lot I can talk about. He thinks that publishing his work will have a great impact on the

FIG. 5.6. Bakhtin during an interview with Victor Duvakin, 1973. (Courtesy of the Scientific Library at Moscow State University)

world. I don't doubt his talents. You see, if he were twenty-five and were to ask me, "Am I talented or not?" I'd reply, "Yes, of course, very talented!"

B: It's easy to be talented when you are twenty-five.

D: Yes. But when he's sixty-two, and you say, "You're talented! You must write!"—that's like killing the person. You shouldn't do it. You should be asking, "Have I accomplished anything? What am I leaving behind?" It's the time for a final reckoning. Do you understand? You seem to suggest, if I understand you correctly, that for him there will be . . .

B: A positive outcome. That's my opinion. Of course, that depends on a host of different circumstances. Perhaps that will happen much later, many years after his death, it might happen.

D: I think that if he now were to . . . But . . . You see, it's one thing to have the right to write, and quite another—to find stark discrepancies in the assessment of one's own work. . . . I believe that if he were to publish his writings now . . . I think he can publish them, it's possible to do so today . . .

B: Yes, of course.

D: . . . but nobody would take notice.

B: That's completely understandable. There're no eyes or ears to appreciate his writing today.

D: There are many contemporary attempts to write in that style: very short stories, or what you find in the literary encyclopedia . . .

B: Sure, but we are not talking about simple short stories—it's something else altogether.

D: It's the genre of the miniature.

B: Yes. His style lacks sharpness, but I think that's not a bad thing. Still, if he were a bit edgier he'd have better luck finding publishing venues today.

D: Well . . . Excuse me, that's all beyond the official scope of our interview, so to say . . . but this discussion has been very moving for me.

B: I completely understand.

D: We are talking about someone very near and dear to me. . . . Maybe I have really been unfair. . . .

Interview Six

March 23, 1973

Length of the interview: 133 minutes

DUVAKIN: OK, Mikhail Mikhailovich, let's turn finally to our last topic: Maria Venyaminovna Yudina.[1]

BAKHTIN: Yes. I met Maria Yudina when I moved to Nevel because of my friend Lev Pumpyansky.[2] Lev Pumpyansky had been living in Nevel for two years as he was doing his compulsory military service there. Or maybe not, he wasn't there because of that, actually, but because his regiment was stationed there. By the time I arrived he had already been discharged. So yes . . . He knew very well everyone who belonged to the local society, including the family of Dr. Yudin.[3] He was the most respected physician in Nevel, Dr. Yudin. In addition, when there were elections for the Legislative Assembly, he decided to run.

D: Run as a representative of which party?

B: Here is what happened with him, it's an interesting story. All his life he had been a Kadet. Overall, of course, he belonged with that party because of who he was—his character, predilections, his solid career as a medical doctor. But since he'd figured out that you had to be more to the Left to be elected, and the Kadets therefore stood no chance, he all of a sudden became a Menshevik.[4]

D: A *Menshevik*?

B: Yes. It happened almost literally on the eve of the elections. . . . So he was listed as a Menshevik on the ballots.

D: And was he elected?

B: No, he wasn't. Even as a Menshevik he was not elected. After all, this was Vitebsk county. He didn't get through. There were so many Mensheviks there, the list was very long, his name was way down the list. In general, as far as I can remember now, the Mensheviks didn't do very well in Vitebsk. The SRs were more popular.[5]

D: Ah yes, for sure he would have been better off transferring his allegiance from the Kadets to the Socialist Revolutionaries! [*chuckles*]

B: True, but for some reason he decided to go with the Mensheviks. . . . Anyway . . . So one of his daughters . . . He had a big family.

D: A big family?

B: Yes. He also had two sons, one of them, also a prominent physician, died not too long ago. . . . No, there were three sons, forgive me. . . . Wait, no, two sons, just two, and several daughters. There were many of them. I only knew . . . Well, I probably knew everybody, but can't remember them all now. I was close only to Maria Yudina and her sister.[6]

D: Were they Jewish on both sides of the family?

B: Yes, the whole family was Jewish. The mother was Jewish, too. But she had died. By the time I got there, she had already passed away, a year before that, I believe. So I only knew Maria Venyaminovna's father, brothers, and sisters. Later, in Vitebsk, I also met her uncle.

D: Was their family wealthy?

B: They were comfortable but not really rich because they were not merchants or industrialists. He was a physician, who earned quite a bit, and his brother—Yakov Gavrilovich—was a lawyer, a renowned lawyer who also made a good living. Right. Perhaps they, like many other Jews, did have a little capital once, but at the time that didn't matter anymore: nobody had any capital anymore. He had his own house. It was in the center of the city, there was a garden: a beautiful home where he lived with his family. It was a huge house. Right. Lev Pumpyansky had made his acquaintance and met his youngest daughter some time before. That's Maria Venyaminovna. She was sixteen when I arrived.

D: So that was in 1919?

B: No, 1918.

D: And she was sixteen years old?

FIG. 6.1. Maria Yudina, 1930s. (Courtesy of the Scientific Library at Moscow State University)

B: I think, so, yes. But I'm not completely sure. . . . When was she born?
D: I don't recall the exact year, but I thought she was born before 1900.
B: I believe she was four years younger than me.
D: And what year were you born? I forget.
B: 1895.
D: 1895! How could she have been sixteen then? If you were born in 1895, then she was born in 1899. That's what I remember. And if that's correct, then in 1918 she was not younger than nineteen.
B: No, no, that can't be! She was younger. Perhaps seventeen, or eighteen at the most, I don't know exactly when she was born. Also, I say I was older than her by four years, but maybe it was five, certainly not less than four, though. She was still a girl, still not entirely grown up, when we met.

I taught a brief philosophy course there. The local intelligentsia showed great interest toward everything, but especially toward philosophy. So I gave a series of lectures on philosophy. Maria Venyaminovna was among those who attended. I noticed her right away: a girl, still very young, rather big, I must say, quite plump, dressed all in black. Her look back then was rather . . . monastic, in sharp contrast to her young face and eyes. Yes . . . She used to dress like a nun, or, if not like a nun, exactly, very similar to that.
D: Had she already converted to Christianity then?
B: I believe she had, yes.
D: It didn't happen when you were there?
B: No, it had happened before my arrival.
D: So, she grew up in a Jewish family, and then decided to become Christian in her early youth?
B: Yes, she got baptized when she was very young.
D: Just her? Had the whole family adopted Christianity?
B: Just her. The family was not baptized. The father was . . . Well, he was a doctor, so . . . He was a bit cynical. . . . He was a very intelligent man, I must say. Very smart. A strong person. Quite extraordinary. But his worldview was rather cynical. He didn't care one bit if his daughter embraced Christianity, Islam, or any other religion—it was all the same to him. . . . Anyways . . . She came to my lectures and listened very attentively. . . . .
D: Were you lecturing on the history of philosophy?
B: My course was an introduction to philosophy. That's history, to be sure, though not presented in a chronological manner, but in the order of main ideas, as is often done.
D: I understand.

B: Yes. An intro to philosophy. The problems we covered were ordered chronologically.
D: Well, the issue of human knowledge . . .
B: Right, exactly!
D: . . . in antiquity . . . and the classics . . .
B: Right. I mostly focused on Kant and Kantianism. I considered that topic to be fundamental to philosophy. Neo-Kantianism[7]—that is most of all, of course, Hermann Cohen . . . Natorp . . . [8] Cassirer.
D: I know a little about Natorp and Cassirer[9] because of Bely.[10]
B: Of course, you'd be familiar with them. Do you remember Cassirer's famous three-volume work *Philosophie der symbolischen Formen* [*The Philosophy of Symbolic Forms*]? It's a remarkable book, still very relevant, people still quote it in Russia today. Back then, that book was the main topic of my philosophy course.

Now, when I met Maria Venyaminovna first, she was very much under the influence of Lev Pumpyansky. Maybe she got baptized because of him too. He also comes from a Jewish background. He was half-Jewish: his father was Jewish, and his mother was French, so he was half Russian Jew, from the Western regions, and half French.[11] His cousins on his mother's side were French: one of them was a French officer, and one was even—if I am remembering right—later a member of the French government. I believe his sympathies were with the Right.
D: But that has nothing to do with her family . . .
B: It does not, correct. So yes, she had fallen under his influence, also in terms of philosophical ideas. He, too, liked to philosophize. He was not a real philosopher but enjoyed philosophizing nevertheless. He also exerted his literary influence over her. I must say he was a real erudite as far as literature, and especially foreign literature, was concerned. He knew many languages and read very quickly. He could read a whole monograph in one evening, and then discuss it with great precision, we might say, in its entirety. In this regard, Lev Vasilyevich's abilities were exceptional. In general people of mixed blood are often very gifted. I don't know what was the more dominant side in him: whether it was the Orthodox, the Russian, or . . . He loved Russian culture, Orthodoxy, he was an ardent Russian Orthodox himself, but at the same time Catholicism came to him through his mother, too. So yes . . .

And as he was a very unusual person, he exerted an enormous influence over Maria Yudina. For a time—actually, not only then, but, I'd say, always, as Lev Vasilyevich's sway over her continued till her death, even though later they went their separate ways and ended up very distant from each other, because Pumpyansky toward the end of his life embraced Marxism and communism. Well, he didn't become a communist, of course, he would have never been admitted to the Party, but still, he became a staunch Marxist and Stalinist. Maria Venyaminovna's attitude toward all this was . . . I wouldn't say negative, exactly, she just didn't share his views.

D: They strongly disagreed on this.

B: Yes, disagreed. So then, this Orthodoxy, the Slavophiles,[12] whom he knew well and loved dearly, and so forth—even Khomyakov,[13] and not only Khomyakov, of course . . . He valued and loved Khomyakov very much, and not just his theological and philosophical writing, but also his rather weak poetry. He was a poet, this Khomyakov! And by the way, his poetic works, nothing else, were just published in the *Biblioteka Poeta* series. Yes. His poems are of poor quality, but they are very religious.

Those were influences on her. Her mood and overall worldview—to the extent to which we can talk about a worldview in such a young person—were shaped by Russian Orthodox and Slavophilia ideas.

D: Even then?

B: Yes, even then.

D: She held on to those beliefs to her death.

B: To her death, yes. In that sense, she remained true to them to the end. Besides, apparently toward the end of her life she took secret monastic vows.[14]

D: That I didn't know about.

B: You see, I'm not sure about it myself, she never told me. I can't confirm it.

D: And was such a formal ritual possible?

B: Yes, it was.

D: You could take secret vows?

B: Yes, secret vows. You could still remain living in the outside world but be a monk or a nun as well. Yes. You just had to observe the monastic order, accordingly adapted, of course. That's what I was told.

I was struck by the following at her funeral: when she died and was lying in state, some bishop, one of the church leaders, came and sat by her side for a very long time, which is not something that ordinarily happens when regular believers pass away. Then, there was a special service at her gravesite, a *panikhida*,[15] in the cemetery . . .

D: I was present.
B: You were there? A monks' choir performed during the service, I believe . . .
D: No, that's all exaggerated.
B: Exaggerated?
D: Yes. Here's the thing . . . Buses are not allowed in the cemetery. The coffin had to be carried by hand for quite a great distance, not less than 500 steps . . . They were mostly young people . . . Disheveled and green youngsters, the lot of them, very similar in appearance to the disheveled youth of today. . . . In front, carrying not a fancy church cross, but a simple wooden one, walked a bearded, funny looking old man, who began chanting anew every time the choir stopped singing. It was already getting dark, and the cemetery was almost empty. We found the right spot in the dusk, and they began to lower the coffin in the grave. And at that point a quid pro quo, we might say, happened: it turned out the grave had not been dug long enough. The coffin got stuck. They had to deal with that . . . I was standing very close by, and was watching everything very carefully . . . It's so good we are recording this . . . They managed to fix it . . . The whole thing took about an hour, it was quite a job . . .
B: Yes . . . making a grave longer is a big job.
D: Yes! They didn't start digging immediately either. At first they kept saying, "You lower it . . . you lift it up . . . ," "No, you lower it on your end . . ." So . . . The elderly sexton kept chanting the whole time. At times he was the only one singing . . . There was, apparently, a priest standing nearby, they kept trying to get him involved, but he seemed frightened to do so.
B: Yes, because that's completely forbidden by the Patriarch: you were not supposed to perform a *panikhida* at the gravesite. Never!
D: So, technically, there was no *panikhida* at her funeral. I don't know, exactly, the proper texts of the Orthodox funeral service, but I think you were supposed to repeat over and over again the same psalms: "Dear Lord, God Almighty" . . . and also . . . "Sanctus, sanctus . . ." The whole text . . . I can imagine it pretty well: I remember the funeral of my father . . . I don't think there was an actual service performed at that time, it was just . . . We could say there was only some Church singing, led by the sexton . . .
B: The sexton, yes.
D: They sang some kind of . . . They say even—excuse me, I'm trying to remember better and be more precise—they say those young people who

sang at the funeral were not members of a choir, but former students of hers from a certain music school . . .

B: Most likely the Gnessin School.[16]

D: Either from there, or from the Conservatory, I don't know for sure. There was, by the way, another, civil *panikhida* held in the main hallway of the Conservatory . . .

B: That's a whole other matter . . .

D: It had taken place earlier. I must say her burial left an enormous impression on me. . . . It was so cold, I froze to the bone—such an incredibly cold day it was . . . I think it was November 30, or something like that . . . Toward the end of November 1970, that's for sure. Afterwards, everyone who wanted to come to the wake, so to speak, was taken there by bus . . .

B: Were there many people?

D: Many people, indeed, but only about sixty came to the wake.

B: Oh!

D: The wake took place in the studio of the artist Efimov,[17] the one who used to make sculptures of animals. He had already died. The whole thing was organized by his son, whom I knew by sight. At this point Zlata Konstantinovna[18] and I went our separate ways. She was very close to Maria Venyaminovna. She herself was not a religious person. She's friends with my wife and Maria Venyaminovna. So anyway, I don't know if we could call that a "wake."

B: That's true, yes. But you might be right anyway, and perhaps there was a *panikhida*, a secret one [*chuckles*], the performance of a secret wake of sorts . . .

B: She was buried next to the mother of her fiancé.

D: Yes. Forgive me, please continue, let's go back to Nevel again. So, she was already the type of girl that . . . already then . . .

B: She already looked like a nun. She dressed like nobody else did. The first time I saw her I was struck: what a figure she cut! Because, let me repeat, she presented such a contrast, almost absurd: a young, ruddy, healthy face (she was quite strong), but all the time, always this black clothing. Then we became closer, and I started to spend more time at her house. Pumpyansky left Nevel soon after. I stayed, but he left because he was given a job in the military intelligence. He was simply drafted.

D: Was that during Soviet times?

B: Yes. It was Soviet Intelligence. But it was still seen as an extension of the old one.... All the officers in it were pretty old.
D: Who did they collect intelligence against?
B: Germany.
D: Still against Germany?
D: Right, this was before ... before the battle of Pskov?[19]
B: Yes, obviously, though I don't remember exactly. In any case, it was Soviet Intelligence. They were all officers, brilliant officers, all wonderful people, very good people. They engaged only in military intelligence. Just military counter-intelligence. Lev Vasilyevich was needed to serve as a translator during interrogations of German prisoners, and so forth.
D: So that was some kind of remnant of the old army, still separate from the Red Army ...[20]
B: No, it was already considered part of the Red Army.
D: Then that was after the battle of Pskov.
B: Naturally, after the battle of Pskov, yes.
D: So already around the middle of 1918.
B: They advanced very quickly on the territory, formerly occupied by the Germans. So Pumpyansky joined them as a translator. But he didn't stay with them very long.
D: That's a very short period of time we're talking about.... Well, let's keep the topic closer to Maria Venyaminovna.
B: All right. So, we became close friends. She was very interested in philosophical questions, and then it became obvious that she had the rare gift of philosophical thinking. As you know, there aren't many true philosophers in the world. Many people like philosophizing, but genuine philosophers are very rare. And as it happened, she was one of the few who could have been the real thing.
D: That's especially rare among women.
B: Yes, even rarer. She also showed great interest in languages in general, and in Latin and Ancient Greek in particular, in literature, too. Later, already in Leningrad—no, it was still Petrograd then—I gave her lessons in Ancient Greek for a year, maybe even two. But not back when we first met, back then we only had philosophical discussions. By the way, her father, the doctor, also showed interest in philosophy, and culture in general. He was an intelligent, open-minded man, despite his rather cynical outlook on life, very typical of the old medical intelligentsia,

which still harbored traces of the nihilism of the 1860s, and so forth. Moving on.

We often went on long walks. Nevel's surrounding countryside is lovely, and the city itself is beautiful. It's located near lakes, it's lake country. The lakes and countryside are just marvelous. We walked a lot—Maria Venyaminovna, Pumpyansky, some other person once in a while, and me—and we talked the whole time.

I remember discussing the earliest beginnings of my moral philosophy, sitting on the banks of a lake, about . . . it must have been about ten kilometers from Nevel. We even named that lake "the lake of ethical reality." [*smiles*] It didn't have an actual name.

There were beautiful hillocks there, but not ancient ones, just from 1812,[21] for the most part. This was the road Napoleon's army took in its retreat. So we deliberated different topics there: religion, theology, but mostly, since I was interested in philosophy and neo-Kantianism in particular, that was our main subject of discussion. And, I repeat, I was amazed by her philosophical abilities.

Besides, at the time she was already a musician, and had performed in Nevel . . . We used to have a People's House in Nevel, and she performed at events there. I remember one evening dedicated to Leonardo da Vinci. I gave a talk, and then she played Liszt's "Funérailles."[22] It's a remarkable piece. A funeral hymn . . . It's an unusual musical work, very dark, but very powerful. She played it marvelously. I remember being impressed by the incredible strength of her hands, so rare in a woman. Yes.

Our close relationship lasted for a brief period of time: the summer and beginning of fall that year, after which Maria Venyaminovna left to study at the Conservatory in Leningrad. I think she was already enrolled there and went back to her studies at the start of the semester. I stayed in Nevel a while longer, and then moved to Vitebsk. I went to live in Vitebsk.

D: How did she start learning music? Or is that beyond the limits of what you know about her?

B: I don't know. She was already a remarkable musician. Although, of course, she hadn't finished her studies at the Conservatory at the time, but she was an incredible pianist.

D: Where had she studied before the Conservatory, do you have an idea?

B: I don't know anything about that. She probably learned to play at home, after all, Nevel was such a . . . Jewish town. So yes . . . There were many musicians there, many musicians. Some were very good, obviously, so . . .

D: How about you, at that time did you already have a good understanding of musical culture?
B: Well, I was a dilettante. I didn't play anything, but of course I knew my way about in music. Then in Vitebsk I offered a course at the Conservatory on aesthetics, with an emphasis on the aesthetics of music, naturally.
D: Could you explain—not for me, but for posterity—the basics of your ideas about the aesthetics of music, which she must have heard?
B: You see, that'd be very hard for me now, I've already forgotten everything. . . . It was so long ago! Today I don't subscribe to those ideas anymore. In general, I could say that my aesthetics of music, which Pumpyansky was inspired by later, relied heavily on Hegel and especially on his Hegelian follower. . . . My memory is now so indecent, just indecent! . . . He was also a great philosopher. . . . Lived longer than Hegel. . . . The philosophy of revelation . . . [23]
D: I don't know. Keep going.
B: But how can I? That's not acceptable. How terrible! Next I'll be forgetting Kant perhaps. . . . I even have his book here but will have to look for it.
D: You'll remember his name later.
B: He had written a lot on music, a whole philosophy of music. And, in general on the philosophy of mythology and the philosophy of art.[24] The same ideas are now being developed by Levi-Strauss, who many find to be very original for some reason—the notion that music and myth are so close to each other that they should be considered the same thing . . .
D: Music and myth?
B: Yes. That idea already existed back then. Pumpyansky developed it in his many courses on the philosophy of music. I also advanced it in my aesthetics of music. Who was he?! What was his name?!
D: It'll come to you.
B: Of course, it will, it has to! It's as close to me as my own name. How could I forget it?! I loved this philosopher very much and used to know his work backwards and forwards. Back then I studied philosophy very seriously, very thoroughly, and knew all that very well.
D: I don't want to get in trouble, so I don't dare suggest any names . . .
B: No, no, everyone knows him, even students know his name. . . . What can you do . . . I'm blanking on it! But what can you do?
D: Is he after Hegel?
B: Yes.

D: Is it Schelling, perhaps?

B: Yes, Schelling, of course![25]

D: Really? I should have said that sooner, the name was hovering on the tip of my tongue. [*chuckles*]

B: Schelling's philosophy, of course.

D: I remember that in the '40s of the last century, after Hegel and the Hegelians, there were the Schellingians, too.

B: Yes, Schellingism, Schelling, yes!

D: I know this not because I am a philosopher, but simply as a historian of culture.

B: Of course, it's him! So Schelling . . . Schelling's outlook, his famous, somewhat religiously tinted *Philosophy of Revelation*, his theory of aesthetics—they were all very close to me and Maria Venyaminovna. You could say she was a follower of Schelling's thought . . . and partially of Hegel's, but only partially because she was not at all interested in the theory of cognition, or dialectics—I don't believe she was ever concerned with dialectics, ever.

D: While you, on the other hand, are?

B: Not really. . . . For me, too, dialectics is not the main thing.

D: But your concept of ambivalence came out of dialectics, didn't it?

B: It was derived from there, but it's not dialectics per se. It's such an old story: dialogue and dialectics, the relationship between the two in terms of theory and history. There was even . . . How many years ago was that? It was a few years ago, no, maybe ten. . . . There was an international symposium in Athens on the topic of dialogue and dialectics. Opinions diverged a great deal, naturally. I hold the view that dialectics is born out of dialogue, and then, later, dialectics again gives way to dialogue, but dialogue at a higher level, a much higher level.

However, none of that really matters. Back then the question had not yet been posed or discussed. But Maria Venyaminovna was close to Schelling's attitude. In addition, she was extremely interested in Romanticism, German Romanticism, Novalis . . . ,[26] and . . .

D: Hoffmann . . .[27]

B: Hoffmann, yes . . . though less. I'd say she didn't like Hoffmann very much, despite his musical spirit, his Kreisler, etc.; she preferred the Romantics who were more religious in nature, people like . . . eh . . . Tieck . . .[28]

D: Tieck and Novalis, the two names always go together.

B: Tieck and Novalis, yes, but there were many others, too. Brentano,[29] Arnim,[30] all the Jena Romantics.
D: Did she read German?
B: She did, yes. The whole family—well, it was a Jewish family after all—knew German very well.
D: So, she read everything in the original?
B: Of course, in the original, especially as most of them were not yet translated into Russian. She knew German fluently, and spoke it at home.
D: So, you spent the whole summer with her?
B: The summer, yes.
D: And the two of you were very close friends?
B: Yes. We saw each other every day: we took walks together, I visited her at her house, or she came to mine. That's how it was. Afterwards she came back several times to see her family in Nevel, and again we got together. But she would come only for a few days, just for a short visit.

After that I left for Vitebsk. She also came to Vitebsk, to spend time with her uncle, and she stayed at his house. He was well off, had his own house, a very nice one.... Then we saw each other again, and again spent many hours in conversation.

At the time, then, she was living in Petrograd, where she continued her studies at the Conservatory. She studied with Nikolaev.[31] He was a very important music teacher, a pianist. He had many great students—for example, Shostakovich was also Nikolaev's student. Many great students. I knew a lot of them.
D: Did he teach in Petersburg?
B: Yes.
D: Which school did he work at?
B: The Conservatory. He was a professor at the State Conservatory. So yes, she studied with him. He was considered to be the best pedagogue at the time. He wasn't a virtuoso performer himself. He was a pedagogue. That's usually the case: the best teachers are not virtuosos, and don't perform publicly themselves, or at least very rarely do.... There are exceptions like Rubenstein.... Anton Rubenstein himself was a virtuoso ...[32] His brother, on the other hand, the one who founded the Moscow Conservatory, Nikolay Rubenstein,[33] was not a virtuoso at all, though he was a musician, too, an incredible musician. Anyways, that's how Maria Venyaminovna and I first met. Then later ... Well, later Lev Pumpyansky went back to Leningrad.

D: It was still Petrograd then.
B: Of course it was, Petrograd. And I stayed in Vitebsk. I stayed in Vitebsk for two more years after his departure.
D: Did Maria Venyaminovna come to visit during that period?
B: She did come to visit me in Vitebsk. Yes. Several times. That is, she didn't stay with me, of course, she stayed with her uncle, but she came to my place several times; our relationship, much like her relationship with Pumpyansky, was never completely broken off. She was very close to him in Leningrad. Besides, those first years after she finished the Conservatory, Maria Venyaminovna rented an apartment in Leningrad—a nice place, she had two rooms, though they were part of a bigger communal apartment. . . . She later found another place for herself, something more suitable, and left her two rooms to Pumpyansky. He lived there. Maria Venyaminovna somehow—I don't know how—procured a wonderful apartment for herself on Dvortsovaya Naberezhnaya,[34] right across from the Peter and Paul Fortress.[35] An amazing apartment! Before the Revolution a certain high-ranking general used to live there. It was a big, marvelous flat, with a terrace, no, not a terrace—a balcony, overlooking the Neva. She lived on the second floor. Above her lived Tarle, the academician.[36] They saw each other often, and became good friends. That was in Petrograd, that is, it was Petrograd then, and later Leningrad.

Anyhow . . . Let me tell you about another episode from her life. Her very close relationship with Pumpyansky led people—even her family at first, that is, her father and sisters—to believe that they were husband and wife.
D: But he was not married?
B: He wasn't married, no, he wasn't married. He got married just a few years before his death.[37] He was a bachelor most of his life. Anyway. He did propose to her, but she didn't accept, she wanted to think about it. Her family, her father and sisters, were against it because at the time they thought that Pumpyansky didn't belong to this world and was not fit to be a husband. They were absolutely right, by the way. He was not of this world.
D: Even more so than her?
B: Even more. And, of course, he was unfit to be a husband. Though at the end of his life he did become one. . . . So anyway. For a while he took it really hard—that happened during that first summer of our acquaintance—and suffered greatly because of it. In addition, he was very

hostile toward her father, once he almost slapped him in the face. I tried to find ways to calm him down. Then the two of them became friends again, and the whole thing ended well. He finally understood himself that a marriage was not necessary, it wasn't the right time.

But his influence over her continued for a very long time, even in Petrograd, when she lived there—his impact was powerful and long lasting. She also took lessons from him. I taught her—that was already in Leningrad—Ancient Greek, while Lev Vasilyevich, as a Frenchman, gave her French lessons. He knew the French language perfectly, after all, he was half French; clearly his mother's influence was greater than that of his Jewish father. His father was not, shall we say, an orthodox Jew, and apparently was not very religious at all. He was a pharmacist, like many other Jews then.

D: A medical pharmacist?

B: Yes, at a place somewhere out in the western regions . . .

D: Did he have his own pharmacy?

B: I'm not sure. I didn't know him personally. Besides, he died very young, very young. Pumpyansky and I were friends from school.[38] We attended the same gymnasium, but his father had already . . . No, he was still alive at first, and then died. His mother was the only one left.

D: Mikhail Mikhailovich, what was Maria Venyaminovna's fiancé like? Or was that later?

B: That was much later. Much later. He was a young composer, who had already finished studying at the Conservatory, and had already acquired a little fame.[39] True, he hadn't composed anything significant yet. Mostly, he adapted to fortepiano the works of Bach and other composers—he took pieces composed for an orchestra or an organ and adapted them to piano. He wrote adaptations for fortepiano. He was a young—I knew him myself—an utterly charming young man, very slender and handsome. A charming young man! And his parents . . . True, I only knew about his father through hearsay. . . . He came from the family of . . . eh!. . . . Again with the name . . . Can't remember it now. . . . It was a very famous family, very well known. He was even somehow related to the Romanovs.[40]

D: So, he came from the Russian nobility?

B: The Russian nobility, yes, and one of the oldest noble families at that . . . His mother came from the very noble Kurakin family . . .[41]

D: Was it a family of princes?

B: No, it wasn't—it was an ancient noble family, but not titled. Right. A very old, distinguished family.
D: But you can't recall his last name?
B: I can't remember. I tell you, one of these days I won't be able to recall my own name!
D: I am afraid I can't be of much help here.
B: Saltykov! There!
D: Ah, Saltykov!
B: Saltykov, yes, Saltykov! They were not related to Saltychykha[42] or the Saltykov-Shchedrins.[43] The Saltykovs belonged to—they were connected, I believe, to Alexey Mikhailovich . . . [44]
D: There was a Saltykov family during the reign of Ivan the Terrible.[45]
B: Yes, the Saltykovs are an ancient clan. Yes. So, this Saltykov . . .
D: Were they engaged then? I seem to remember he died in a climbing accident.
B: Yes, they were engaged, but hadn't married yet. There had only been an official engagement. She became his betrothed, when his father was still alive.[46] Then the father passed away . . . He was a man of the world. I don't know what job he had, I think he didn't work, he was just a man-about-town. They had some personal wealth, country estates, and so on. Later he became an artist. He painted many pictures, I saw most of them. His still lifes were especially good, but his portraits were not bad either. He was quite talented. So his son became a musician. And then . . . They were engaged for about two or three years.
D: Why so long?
B: I don't know why. He was still very young.
D: Was he younger than her?
B: Much younger than her, yes! Much younger! He visited us with her all the time. At the time I lived in Savelovo, near Moscow, and usually the two of them came to see me there together. He used to bring along books, some wonderful books for me. Right. . . . For about two years they came to see me as a husband and wife-to-be. Then he left for Nalchik.[47] He was an alpinist, a mountain climber. He went to climb some new summit, together with a group of alpinists, and they all died there, everyone, not just him.
D: The whole group?!
B: The whole group. They were all tethered to each other, trying to climb that summit, which was very difficult and few, if any, had managed to

take it before. They were tethered to each other and fell all together; their bodies were never found. So, he never got a proper grave.[48]

Maria Venyaminovna remained faithful to him to the end and lived with his mother. She moved in with her, with his mother. They lived together for a while. Then she found another apartment for the mother. She was a diabetic, his mother, and was already quite blind and deaf; her life was extremely hard. So Maria Venyaminovna took good care of her: she found her a home, and a good woman (who earlier had been her own housekeeper and secretary) to take care of her. I knew her well; she was in general a cultured person. So, she took care of her until the end.

D: And so she never had a family, a woman's life?

B: She never had a family, though she dreamed of one her whole life. Well, perhaps not her whole life, but when she was young . . . back then . . .

D: Did she have any stormy love affairs when she was young? You met her when she was very young, and she was already showing monastic tendencies . . .

B: Yes. Well, there was no actual romance between her and Pumpyansky.

D: Well, that's just it, she was, in fact, a girl . . .

B: Neither he nor she were made for such affairs. They were enthralled by something else entirely. Their friendship was purely spiritual.

D: At the same time, she was human. . . . She left the impression of being of such a passionate temperament . . .

B: Temperament!

D: . . . that it's hard to imagine that she . . .

B: Well, just imagine that . . .

D: . . . she was also a girl.

B: Imagine that, she was a girl yet had no romantic relations with anyone. Her father, on the other hand, was a real Don Juan, a powerful, strong man. [*laughs*] He had countless love affairs, most likely. But not her—she was a nun, a proper nun by nature.

Her fiancé, Saltykov, was the sweetest, kindest person ever. I completely understand how she could fall in love with him. But the difference in their ages was huge. Still, it's possible that . . .

D: What was the difference in their ages? Maybe ten years?

B: No, not ten. I am afraid it was more like twenty. She was . . . It happened not too long before she died.

D: What I had heard was that . . . the whole affair took place in the 1930s . . .

B: Yes, it happened during the 1930s.
D: The 1930s. When I first met her, I remember I heard, not from her, of course, from someone else, that her fiancé had just passed away. I remember her as an old woman already . . .
B: Yes, she was already quite old. But she looked much younger. She was very strong. As a pianist, she flourished during that period. But he was still a young boy. A very charming youth. Yes. He was very capable, and not only in music. I am not familiar with his musical compositions, and have never heard them, but the two of us talked a lot . . .
D: It's very strange that, if there was an official engagement . . .
B: Yes.
D: . . . Why did they postpone getting married?
B: I think the parents were against it at first, because of the age difference, but then changed their position completely, and wholeheartedly supported the marriage, especially the father.
D: You mean his parents?
B: Yes, his. Especially his father, who felt that Maria Venyaminovna had a very positive influence over his son. But the whole family . . . I must say that the family . . . You know, they were an old aristocratic family, very kind, good, refined folk—they were high society, but always treated strangers, people who were not like them and especially members of the intelligentsia, with great respect.
D: And there was no whiff of anti-Semitism in their behavior at all? Is it possible that . . .
B: No. I must state it clearly: we have the wrong idea about that. The Russian nobility, especially the ancient families, were never infected with anti-Semitism.
D: That's more typical of the bourgeoisie.
B: Yes, that's a purely bourgeois phenomenon! Anti-Semitism was not typical [among the nobility].
D: Well, there was a hint of it among the Slavophiles, and even Dostoevsky . . .
B: Then, you see . . .
D: Yids, Polacks . . .
B: Only . . . it's all very specific, yes. That might be true, but Dostoevsky, in fact, was never an anti-Semite, and could never have been. The Hebrew religion, the Old Testament, the Bible . . . After all, the entire Old Testa-

ment in Christianity . . . What can you say? Prayers for Jews are offered in every service. There's no religious service that doesn't mention Abraham, Isaak, Jacob, and so on. There. Even in Orthodox funeral services they sing: "Give them rest in the bosom of Abraham, Isaak, and Jacob." It's in their bosom that the departed Christian souls will find rest. In general, you can't separate Christianity from Judaism, that is, not Judaism, but from the ancient Hebrew testaments. So there. Overall, there can't be any anti-Semitism here, of course.

In practice, our clergy, for example, the Catholic clergy, never exhibited any anti-Semitism. You typically find anti-Semitism in people who are not religious at all, who see religion only as a kind of a ritual, as part of everyday life. The Black Hundreds,[49] let's say, for the most part they were also clergymen, but for them the Church was part of their everyday existence: the Church holidays and so forth were part of everyday life. But the real representatives of religious thought in Russia were never anti-Semites. It's a well-known fact, everybody knows it, that on his deathbed Vladimir Solovyov prayed for the Jewish people, for their salvation, and read psalms as he lay there dying.

D: Did he pray for their salvation as sinners against Christ?

B: No, no, not as sinners against Christ. For their salvation . . . In general, it's a commonly shared view that . . .

[*interruption in the recording here*]

D: I was dumbfounded by the idea that sooner or later . . .

B: The Hebrews will unite, recognize Jesus, join in. . . . How and in what form that would happen is another question.

D: They'll accept Christ?

B: Yes.

D: So, it seems that the Israeli Zionist movement stands against all that, so to speak?

B: Against it, yes. We should say that even though there's a lot written about Zionism, people are up in arms about it now, but we don't really understand it. It's very complicated. Right now, Zionism is in a state of disintegration. There were two general trends in it from the very beginning: one came from Herzl,[50] the other . . . I can't remember the other name now. Some believed that Judaism should never be a matter of state organization, but rather only a way to create a sense of community, of social unity. They did not acknowledge the need for statehood.

D: That was Pasternak's position.[51]
B: Yes, Pasternak thought so. Well, he later became an Orthodox Christian, and a zealous Orthodox at that. This position is shared by some of the Zionists too. Let's not forget that the Israeli government is now socialist, though their socialists are different from the communists. They have their own communists, sure, but those are not very successful. Actually, there aren't that many communists there. And—imagine that!—their own government is at war with the synagogue, the Jewish church. And that's happening at their home, in Israel!
D: I see! Forgive me, we went off on a tangent, of course; I just thought that Maria Venyaminovna was a glaring exception. . . . Well, when I was a kid [*chuckles*] I came across the monarchy brochures you mentioned. After all . . . Take John of Kronstadt, for example.[52] He was at the center of the anti-Semitic movement, John of Kronstadt was.
B: Yes, he was, but even he was not completely that way.
D: He came out in defense of Beilis,[53] back when the famous trial took place . . .
B: Yes, it's a very complicated question. By the way, I met John of Kronstadt when I was a child. My great uncle, who was an enthusiastic fan of his, invited him to his house in Orel. He performed a service there.
D: He was clearly an important man . . .
B: Very important. My impression of him was . . . Well, I was a young child back then, of course; how old was I? About seven, I believe. He left an enormous impression on me.
D: One of the relatives of Shklovsky[54] served as a deacon with John of Kronstadt.
B: Yes, yes, you see how . . .
D: It was either his mother's father, or . . . something like that. I can't recall now, but it's been recorded.[55] Well, John of Kronstadt is a special case.
B: Yes . . .
D: What do you think of Maria Venyaminovna as a musician? What was so special about her art?
B: You see, I think that . . . You should talk with other musicians, who as specialists would be able to tell you better than me. I am not, I must stress, a musician at all, not in the least a professional in the field. I valued her music very highly. I also considered her to be our best pianist at the time. I preferred her to Neuhaus,[56] and others.
D: Even Sofronitsky?[57]

B: Without a question! Sofronitsky, he was . . . He had wonderful technique, he also had a genuine soul, but he lacked real power. He was a bit . . . Maria Venyaminovna, on the other hand . . . What was the most impressive thing about her? That she loved and performed very powerful music: Bach, Liszt, Beethoven, then some of the modern composers, too. The kind of music that had great power, and seemed to verge on something much higher, something mythical or religious. So, here is what I think: Maria Venyaminovna's main characteristic, as a person and as a cultural figure, was that she couldn't fit herself into a *Fach*,[58] that is, into some specialization, she couldn't restrict herself to music only. She was always striving to break out into something broader: first through religion, then through public service. She just couldn't stand to be constrained by the frame imposed on professional musicians, she couldn't bear it! People like that find any kind of "professionalism" foreign to them. So she brought into music everything that lies on the border between music and the other arts, and especially poetry, Romantic poetry. She was very passionate about Romanticism. And Romanticism [in music] has always existed on the boundary with literature, poetry; it strove to escape its confines and transform itself into something akin to religion. That same impulse drove her as well. She chose to play music that was close to Romantic poetry, to an aesthetic or religious revelation. She could never be contained within the limits of what we think of as your typical career in music.

That's what determined both her musical selections, and her original interpretations. Her interpretations were always very much her own. She also, naturally, did not like any musical clichés and defied all expectations. That's why many thought her musical interpretations were too subjective, too individualistic. But that's exactly what I liked about her performances—her ability to amplify the most powerful moments in the compositions of her chosen composers.

Here is what I remember: when I moved, that is, when I returned to Leningrad, Maria Venyaminovna and I saw each other almost every day. I'm not talking just about the lessons she took from me, we were at her place all the time. . . . She lived in a spacious, marvelous apartment, by herself, or sometimes with her younger brother. She had a wonderful study, a grand piano, and so forth. We often spent the night there listening to her play. She played until morning. Until morning! And how she played! I must say I heard her perform at concerts, but the way she played those nights, for her closest friends, she never played like that anywhere else! It was amazing! Her power was given free reign then.

Of course, we also discussed various problems—philosophical, poetic. We recited poetry. For a while we were obsessed with Rilke,[59] then with George.[60] He was such a remarkable poet, very little known in Russia, though he had his school, his circle of fellow poets—I'm talking about the *George Kreis*. Then, *Blätter für die Kunst* was also connected with George. That was the name of the publishing house, which issued so many brilliant books.

D: "Kunst" is "Art." Does "blätter" mean publisher? "Verlag" is publisher . . .

B: "Blätter" means leaves, leaves.

D: Like pages?

B: Well, yes, printed pages for . . .

D: Leaves of Art.

B: Yes, "Art pages," yes. Gundolf[61] was also published there, and many others. . . . One of their books, about Friedrich Nietzsche, was simply remarkable: *Versuch einer Mythologie* [*An Attempt at Mythology*], that was the title of the book about Nietzsche. . . . I loved it and used to have it in my library.[62]

D: Was Maria Venyaminovna ever interested in Nietzsche?

B: No, never.

D: That fad passed her by . . .

B: Yes. Even I accepted Nietzschean thought, although not in its totality but. . . . Those aspects, which were singled out later by the Fascists—of course, in a distorted, twisted form—those aspects, naturally, were very distant from me even then. Anyhow, I must say the following: the notion of Nietzsche as a philosopher of Fascism is of course nonsense, a misunderstanding that could only be based on the complete perversion of Nietzsche's ideas. What did he have in common with those people, who completely lacked any serious philosophy? Nothing, of course.

D: Mikhail Mikhailovich, did you listen to Maria Venyaminovna play both before and after the war?

B: Yes, I did.

D: So what do you think: did she perform better in her last years, or, to the contrary, was she worse then?

B: I don't think she was worse, no. She was good to the end. Then she . . .

D: Of course, I don't count the last year following the accident with her hand.[63]
B: Yes, her hand was injured, her fingers . . . Of course not. But before that happened . . . That was really the period when she really strove to break through the boundaries of music, we might even say, to leave music behind. She dreamed of social activism, on a grand scale. She even dreamed of . . . For example, when the Suez Canal crisis started . . . [64]
D: We are talking about 1956 then.
B: Yes, and as we began to organize an army to send in support of the Arabs, Maria Venyaminovna announced she wanted to go to Egypt herself and join in the fight against the British. All her life she wanted to play an important role in something big, big, but non-musical. Music alone could not satisfy her, musical recognition and fame alone, no, this could not satisfy her. That was not enough. She wanted to become famous for . . . Well, not "famous," really, that's the wrong word, it's too crude. She was not ambitious in that sense, she didn't seek fame; in short, she wanted to become something truly valuable, big, important, she wanted to serve higher powers than Art. In that sense she was, of course, close to the Symbolists who also thought Art should become life, and so forth. Their idea that Art must be at the service of life was . . .
D: You know, it just occurred to me that this is quite different from what Marina Tsvetaeva[65] claimed toward the end of her wonderful essay "Art in the Light of Conscience."[66]
B: I don't know that essay.
D: It ends like this (I remember it by heart): "The doctor and the priest are more needed than the poet." And when the Last Judgment comes, we'll all be asked . . . something along those lines . . . "But if there's a Last Judgment for words, then my conscience is clear." That is, admitting to her human weakness, she nevertheless thinks that her Art absolves her of everything.
B: Her poetry.
D: Yes. So, would Maria Venyaminovna have also said, "If there's a Last Judgment . . ."?
B: No, she wouldn't have said that. She would not have said that. . . . Still, she was never able to escape music completely.
D: I am asking you this because I have an ulterior motive, so to speak. I told you already that I myself don't know much about music, which is why

I can only repeat what others have said. But as a person, Maria Venyaminovna interests me and impresses me a great deal.
B: But of course!
D: I did try to observe her from afar, even if I didn't have the chance that often. Her funeral made a huge impression on me. Some music specialists claim that she used to play better earlier . . .
B: Well, overall they are right, that's true. I would agree with that.
D: And then later she . . .
B: The way she played in those early years in Leningrad, on her own grand piano at home—and what an amazing instrument it was!—I never heard her perform the same way in a concert.
D: Let me continue. Later, when she became obsessed with that same religiosity so admired in her by a certain portion of her Moscow audience, the intelligentsia, which felt itself very close to it, that's when she started to play worse.
B: She did begin to play worse, but not because of that. . . . She was attracted to religion even during her best years. If you like, she was most religious especially during those years when she used to play the piano all night for her closest friends—at that time she was even more in tune with the Church, that is, with religious experience.

And there's something else. It's one thing to be religious, and quite another to want to take part in the work of the Church. That came later, and that's also when her music suffered. But not really because she was participating—even indirectly—in some Church business, no, it happened for completely different reasons. In general, music alone was not enough to satisfy her anymore. For example, that's when she began to read poetry at her concerts.[67]
D: That is to say, the professional musicians and musicologists criticize her for her departure from . . .
B: From professionalism.
D: . . . from professionalism, yes.
B: From professionalism narrowly defined—yes, that's completely understandable, completely understandable. Those same music specialists who criticized her the most, were after all very limited people themselves, who couldn't comprehend Maria Venyaminovna's drive to . . . This drive that was present throughout her life. . . . She had this thirst for something much higher that couldn't be contained within the framework of a single profession, or within professionalism as such. It couldn't be confined to

just poetry, music, or philosophy alone. She was larger than all that. She understood that that wasn't all there was, that that wasn't the most important thing, that what was most important is something else.

D: On the one hand, your observations confirm this, from a factual standpoint . . .

B: I don't think that . . .

D: But on the other hand, there's this contradictory assessment. Actually, no, not just the assessment. . . . First of all, you refuse to acknowledge that her religious beliefs . . .

B: No . . .

D: You don't see a connection there at all then?

B: None at all, because . . .

D: Because she was like that from the start . . .

B: Of course! Philosophy, mythology, religion, and music are the closest to one another in this world—and the most alike. Music, by its very nature, is both philosophical and mythical. It is religious not in the narrow confession-based sense of the word. . . . By its very nature it is, of course . . . [*coughs*] religious and . . .

D: Denominational?

B: No, not that, not denominational at all.

D: Really?

B: Yes. It's not important whether it belongs to . . . Protestantism, Orthodoxy, Catholicism . . . That doesn't matter. When you are dealing with true religious belief, like you find in the mystics, the great mystics, people like Böhme . . . [68] Religious belief cannot be contained by a certain denomination . . . narrowly understood . . .

D: A particular faith.

B: Yes, absolutely. That's why mystics like Böhme . . . He was remarkable! The mystics, who were they anyway?

D: Jakob Böhme?

B: Yes, he was one of the greatest mystics. So, who were they? Protestants? Catholics? Russian Orthodox? In terms of denomination, they might have been Protestants, but at the same time they are equally at home in Catholicism and Russian Orthodoxy. That is where their religious impulse transgresses the narrow boundaries of an individual confession.

D: Still, some fellow musicians and music critics claimed that her playing suffered.

B: She didn't play as well anymore, that's true, and she didn't perform as often, but not for this reason, no, but because of . . . There was a certain weakening of her internal, authentic, grand religious and philosophical predilection, accompanied by the strengthening of external forces—like ecclesiasticism, ritual, and so forth. Yes, that's what it was.
D: As a whole, do you see her as a performer inspired by religious belief from the very beginning?
B: Yes, from the very beginning, correct.
D: And the interpretation I laid out for you, which I'd gotten secondhand, what you think of it?
B: It's factually true, up to a point, but the explanation offered is wrong. . . . First off, she was no longer satisfied by her work as a professional musician . . .
D: No, that interpretation is not . . . If I understood you correctly, you see it as a superficial explanation for . . .
B: It's very superficial, yes, superficial and nothing else.
D: There's a lot being written about her now, and they will continue to . . .
B: Yes, yes. That interpretation is, of course . . . And how could our music critics possibly be able to arrive at a deeper, more meaningful interpretation? Only one of them was a real musicologist that was leaning toward the formal method. . . . By the way, Maria Venyaminovna used to respect and hold him in great esteem . . .
D: Who's that?
B: Yavorsky.[69] He already died. A musicologist by the name of Yavorsky. He created his own school, but he wasn't especially an official person, he was never recognized. Now he's all but forgotten, and yet he was, of course, an important, and very profound musicologist.
D: And she thought he was different than all the rest of them?
B: She did, yes, though they disagreed on a great deal.
[*pause in the recording*]
D: But this opinion of her abilities, her so-called professional deterioration, which I heard expressed by some . . .
B: Well, there's truth to that. In the end, such a deterioration is unavoidable at a certain age for an artist of Maria Venyaminovna's type. . . . As I mentioned before, the basic trait of her art was its enormous power. Her power! Not tenderness, not intimacy, but a great force—not a brute force, of course, but a power of the spirit, which, I should stress, she possessed to a very great degree. When translated into music, that power of the spirit

required strong hands and a strong body. She simply couldn't hold on to it past a certain age . . .

D: She was around seventy when she died.

B: Yes, that sounds right, seventy, yes. As for her spiritual powers . . . She was remarkable in that respect. For instance, she could bear the most excruciating pain without batting an eye, without flinching at all.

D: You mean physical pain?

B: Physical, yes. She could withstand things that normal people could never bear. Everyone who knew her was astonished by her superhuman powers of endurance, her immense spiritual strength. Burning at the stake did not scare her. All her life, she dreamed of being burnt alive, in the metaphysical sense; she wanted to experience true suffering—like Avvakum,[70] and others. So yes . . . She really wouldn't have even flinched at the stake and would have silently burned to ashes. She was that kind of a person. And that quality of hers impressed and fascinated enormously everyone who was familiar with it. Unfortunately, not many people knew her from that side of her nature . . .

D: She was better known for her many other quirks . . .

B: Quirks, caprices, whatever word you want to use. That's true. She was quite eccentric. . . . But nobody really understood her peculiarities and impulses well, they were completely misconstrued. There are whims and there are whims. The caprices of a genius are nothing like the caprices of a simpleton, even if they are called the same. Beethoven's whims (he was also very capricious) and those of someone with no real talent, are separated by a chasm.

D: All her animals . . . She tried to help so many. . . . She was totally unable to . . .

B: She was totally selfless.

D: Selfless, yes, but also completely incapable of living a normal life, so to speak. She gave without restraint, but she also took without keeping score.

B: She did borrow, true, and yet she never had any money. She borrowed and gave it away, borrowed and gave away. In the end, she borrowed so she could give it all away. Even though she borrowed money when she herself needed it the most. She lived from hand to mouth almost all of her life.

D: All right, you gave us a very complete picture of Maria Venyaminovna. Perhaps you can add some other, private episodes, more detailed, the kind of thing that might later go into your memoirs. That could be very useful.

B: What else could I say? She helped others a lot, especially those who had suffered somehow at the hands of the government, people like me. When she . . .

D: She helped you then? You didn't tell me about that.

B: She helped me, of course. She helped as much as she could. Later, toward the end of her life, the roles were reversed, and I helped her with money a little. Otherwise I couldn't assist her in any other way. . . . But all that doesn't really matter. She helped me much more in her time. She also intervened when I was to be sent into internal exile. You see, I was initially sentenced to five years in Solovki . . .

D: How was she able to help in that case?

B: She pleaded with the authorities. You could still do such things back then. She had connections. She petitioned on my behalf. Of course, that didn't decide the case, but still had a certain effect on the outcome.[71]

D: And did you . . . Were there any army officers at her concerts? No? Or were you not in Moscow then?

B: I didn't go to her concerts at the time. She traveled to the front, as you know. And to Leningrad, when the city was under siege and going there was not without real danger. She was attracted to anything that seemed dangerous, that was "threatened with destruction." So she traveled there quite often, and performed . . .

D: Yes. In general, she was like the poet says: "And all that threatens with destruction, / sends man's beating heart in such mysterious raptures."

B: You could say so, yes. But not only. Pushkin, of course, had in mind a more pagan kind of experience . . . which wasn't the case with her. She believed that man exists in order to burn out, give himself up completely, sacrifice everything. That element of self-sacrifice is absent from Pushkin's "Song of Walsingham."[72] Instead, there's a certain hedonism there . . .

D: I agree, certainly there's hedonism there.

B: A rapture. . . . It's well known that grave danger can produce great elation. I am not a military man, but I can tell you that when there were bombardments, or when we lived close to the front, I found the sound of shooting to be very exciting. [*D and B laugh*] Very exciting. What can I say, there's something beyond our consciousness and will that. . . . Bravado or aggression have always been foreign to me, yet I am excited by gunshots. [*chuckles*] But that's different, of course. There's no sacrifice or sense of duty in that. It wasn't like that for her.

D: Where were the bombings you're remembering? Were you in Leningrad then?
B: No, I was not there. Moscow was bombed as well. I believe I witnessed one or two of those attacks. Then later we lived almost on the front line. The front was about forty kilometers away from our place.
D: Was that in Savelovo?[73]
B: Savelovo, correct.
D: I see! When they advanced on Istra,[74] and overtook Iksha itself.[75]
B: Right, right. It was just a stone's throw away. . . . The enemy kept coming at us, then the bombs started falling . . . But there weren't that many bombardments, mostly machine gun fire. Still, we were bombed multiple times.
D: Well, Mikhail Mikhailovich, we can say I've completed recording your odyssey now. I'm so glad I was able to induce you to talk about your biography. At times you simply took a detour and offered some historical, literary, aesthetic, and philosophical digressions . . . In addition to your recollections, though not that numerous . . .
B: But what recollections could I possibly have!
D: . . . I also managed to record a wonderful depiction of the man Mikhail Mikhailovich Bakhtin, for whom I have the utmost respect. The only thing is, we ran into some problems last time, so we have to correct a few things.
B: It's my fault because . . . I don't know why . . . I got very tired toward the end for some reason. I literally . . . I literally forgot some ordinary words . . .
D: I was not a very good listener either. Our last interview, the fifth one, was not too successful, but the rest were very interesting, really very good. Are you planning to write your memoirs?
B: Not at all. By the way, another thing about Maria Venyaminovna. Her whole life she never had a proper apartment. She lived here, there, and everywhere, and suffered all sorts of inconveniences. That's one thing. Another was that she never had real furniture. Of course, it was different when she was still living at home, or later, in Leningrad, when she had that luxurious apartment—there used to be some kind of furnishings there, but nothing that belonged to her, I don't think. She never had proper furniture, never. And she was never associated with the official authorities. She found everything official to be a burden. I am the same way, by the way. I also can't stand bureaucracy. That's why she absolutely

was unable to advance her career. She both couldn't and didn't want to. You see, she was such a visible person, and yet she never received any kind of government award all her life.

D: That was her form of protest.

B: Not only that. Why protest? It wasn't just that. She wasn't even as vocal in her criticism as some of those who were nevertheless given various awards. How about Shostakovich? Didn't he also voice his discontent in his time? Very much so.

D: Yes, but his . . .

B: Right. By the way, we used to have a common friend from our time in Vitebsk, remarkable musicologist who died too early—Ivan Sollertinsky.[76]

D: Sollertinsky?

B: Yes, Sollertinsky.

D: I've heard of him, yes.

B: He is one of our most influential scholars of the arts. His book about Mahler, and all his publications, though quite slim in most cases, were always brilliant. In general, he was an exceptionally gifted man. He studied with Pumpyansky, and also with me for a time. I met him when he was still a young boy. There you have it.

D: And he's dead?

B: He died very young. He worked as a professor at the Leningrad Conservatory as well. He taught theory of music and aesthetics, too, so yes . . .

D: Who else did you know from the so-called leading scholars of music, musicology?

B: Besides Sollertinsky, I didn't know well anyone else. But I was acquainted with many of them. Primarily . . .

D: Sofronitsky?

B: I knew him. We were acquainted, but I don't remember anything about him in particular.

D: How about Neuhaus?

B: Him too. I knew him as well.

D: Were you acquainted with Pasternak too? We didn't get to talk about him during our poetry discussions.

B: I did know Pasternak, certainly, I knew Pasternak.

D: His friendship with Maria Venyaminovna . . .

B: Right! We ran into each other at her place a lot. I especially remember one evening when he read to us at her small cottage, which I shared with her for a while . . .

D: And did he read his prose to you then?
B: No, I never heard his prose. There was the time when he read his translation of Part One of *Faust*[77] to us . . . I should say that . . .
D: Wow! We are talking about a momentous event here!
B: Yes.
D: And you and Maria Venyaminovna were his audience?
B: Yes, and others too. There was Favorsky,[78] and another artist, a little older than Favorsky . . . He even designed the covers of the Symbolists' publications quite often . . . err
D: . . . Yuon[79] . . .
B: Exactly . . .
D: The artists associated with *Mir Isskustva*. The covers . . . Who designed the covers?
B: The covers, in particular . . . Bryusov's collection, *Mirror of Shadows*.
D: I remember that cover.
B: He designed it.
D: Well, never mind . . . So you were there?
B: Yes. There were others, too. There was this man, Schultz[80] was his name, a Classicist.
D: Schultz?
B: Schultz, yes, Schultz. You probably don't know him.
D: I don't.
B: He was a Classical scholar, but since the field of Classical studies was pretty neglected in Russia then, he mostly worked as an archeologist. So, he was on archeological expeditions to the south of Russia most of the time. Because he knew Greek, and so on. He was involved in the Greek colonies' digs, by the way. That was Schultz. A very cultured, highly educated man, he was. Who else was present that night? . . . Pasternak's wife was there.
D: Which one? Zinaida Nikolaevna Neuhaus?[81]
B: Most likely, I don't remember. I didn't know his first wife at all. The second one I did meet, yes. I ran into her, with him, somewhere else, too. So yes. . . . Who else was there? A few others . . . Some other people involved in the arts . . .
D: And how was the reading received?
B: As it should have been . . . Everybody appreciated the quality of the translation. . . . As a whole . . .
D: What is your opinion? Don't you find that his translation doesn't much sound like Goethe?

B: A little, yes. But all translations . . .

[interruption in the recording]

D: And, on the contrary, let's take Byron and Zhukovsky—"The Prisoner of Chillon"[82]—those are, people say, two different works.

B: That's true. Still, I prefer that kind of a translation to the work of someone with no talent, a person who is not a poet himself.

D: But of course.

B: A translator who is not a poet himself. Zhukovsky was a poet. His translations were, after all . . . Even when he moved away from the original author, he didn't sink below him, but stayed on the same level, just a little bit to the side. There's nothing worse than when the translator lowers the level . . .

D: Naturally.

B: Talentless translators lower and trivialize the original text. One can never say that about Pasternak.

D: Well, Goethe reached such poetic heights, it's a complicated matter . . .

B: Right. Overall, I thought Pasternak's translation was very good.

D: Quite powerful, right?

B: I liked his translation very much. I heard it that one time, and then never had the chance to read it again.

D: For a while that's how he was able to survive—by doing translations. And did you ever have any conversations with Boris Leonidovich [Pasternak]?

B: We talked a lot that night, quite a lot. There was a special bottle of dry wine set aside just for him. He drank all of it. Nobody else helped, because no one present drank wine. I didn't drink, the artists didn't either. He drank it all by himself. Afterwards he became very chatty and talked about all sorts of things: about poetry in general, about poetic language. I remember that conversation as being very interesting. I participated in it, too, as did everyone else. Then he also talked about the Writers Union, the Union of Soviet Writers,[83] which he severely criticized for not defending the true interests of writers . . . He thought that it defended the interests of . . .

D: Did you remember anything he said about poetry?

B: I remember this in particular: according to him, poetry, poetic language, should be as close to regular spoken speech as possible, but not close to the practical aspect of the speech act, but to the element of freedom so characteristic of it. . . . Spoken language fears and shuns literary clichés—which is the main thing, the main thing . . . There can't be any clichés, any literary, "correct," we might say, learned elements in poetic language. Poetic language must be as unrestricted as possible—language set free, and in that sense close to ordinary conversational speech. So, there you have it.

D: Mikhail Mikhailovich, we could have traveled further down that path, and talked more about Pasternak. This is all so interesting, and I am so grateful to you, but . . . I have enough tape left for another ten minutes or so, and I want us to put together a quick auditory vignette here . . . [*chuckles*] Please excuse the simplistic expression. In the remaining ten minutes, I'd love for you to end by reciting a few poems.

B: Well, nowadays I'm not able to recite.

D: But you're so good at it! Just try to remember some of the poems you love the most. Just a few, your most favorite ones.

B: Well . . . I love so many poems, but nowadays I can't recite at all, not at all. I used to be able to once, when my voice was better . . .

D: You recite marvelously! You even recited Blok! Of the classical poets, who do you like the most? Because that will . . . The right intonation adds so much . . .

B: Well, what can I . . .

D: Well, one of your favorites . . . You could also recite in other languages—German, or French . . . Anything you like. Something from Fet?

B: I could do that, yes.

D: Right. That'd be great.

B: No . . . I don't even know what to . . . It's been such an infinitely long time since I've recited any poetry . . .

D: What do you mean, "an infinitely long time"? You recited some during our recent interviews. . . . Anything you'd like . . .

B: I can't right now . . .

D: Just try!

B: [*recites*] The night was shining. Moonlight filled the garden.

Its rays lay at our feet by the extinguished fire.
The strings of the exposed piano shuddered,
As did our hearts, after your song expired.

•

You sang till daybreak, tears streaming,
About love that happens only once in life.
And how I wished I could devote my being
To loving, holding you, and crying by your side.

And many years pass—so tiresome, so painfully banal,
And lo, your voice arrives again one silent night,
And, as before, the wonder of your sounds
Reveals that you alone are Life, that you alone are love.

That there are no insults, no real heartaches left,
And life is everlasting when its only meaning
Is trusting those weeping sounds, so bereft,
And loving, holding you, and crying by your side.[84]

Such wonderful poetry! But I can't recite it very well . . .
D: Is that by Fet?
B: Yes. I remembered it in connection with Maria Venyaminovna and her music. . . . Marvelous poetry, simply marvelous!
D: Certainly. As it happens, I don't know or understand this poet very well.
B: But you have to agree the poem I just recited is splendid.
D: Do you like Tyutchev?[85]
B: Tyutchev? What about him? I . . . Well, of course I know him, how can I not . . .
D: Perhaps you can recite something by Vyacheslav Ivanov then?
B: Vyacheslav Ivanov? It's kind of hard to recite his poetry. What can I recite? Maybe this: from *Songs from the Labyrinth.* Do you know it?
D: No. *Songs from the Labyrinth*, you say?
B: ". . . *from the Labyrinth*," yes. "The Labyrinth" stands for the memories of our childhood, and even further back. Vyacheslav Ivanov believed that the memory of a person reaches far back into an endless distance, that they are limited by nothing.
D: I would agree with that! [*laughs*]
B: As you know, many philosophers share his ideas . . .
D: I don't know what the philosophers have said, but . . . [*laughs again*]
B: Plato, for example, and then Bergson,[86] too, of the more recent philosophers. He has a remarkable book—his best one, in my opinion—*Matter and Memory*, in which he posits that our memory has no limits but that

we remember only what we need and forget everything else, yet under certain circumstances—in our dreams, or under the influence of drugs or some illness—we are able to recall more. Or, as Gumilev claimed, there's such a thing as the "memory of the body," and that this memory . . . How did he put it?

D: "Only dragons shed their skin . . ."[87]

B: Yes. "We change our souls, not our bodies . . . ," etc. So, about the *Songs from the Labyrinth* . . . They are very peculiar, those poems, with an irregular, somewhat broken rhythm. [*coughs.*] Well, my expression, my voice and diction are pretty awful these days . . .

My mother sat next to my father.
Neither he nor she said a word.
Night peeked in through the window . . .
"That's the chime," they said, "that we heard."
Then mother whispered in my ear,
"It's still very far. Don't breathe."
My soul felt the silence so near,
My soul sank in the silence beneath.
And all of a sudden I heard it for real:
The sound of Noiselessness (I was three.)
And my heart was finally free
To absorb those eternal peals in my dreams. [88]

I think that's a remarkable poem.

D: Yes, I felt it too.

B: Remarkable for its depth and tonality. Or here is another one from *Songs from the Labyrinth*. . . . I may get things mixed up, though . . .

Arches of delicate marble
Protected my meadow.
Was it hours or years I played among
The butterflies—my weightless companions?
[*pauses for a while, trying to remember*]
. . . I was able to catch in my hand,
Those winged brilliant rays . . .
To them I ran . . .
[*another pause*]

Mother and father sat there waiting . . .
I ran to them, carrying my treasure,
Eager to share my latest triumph.
But all I could find in my fist as I unclenched it,
Were some ashes, like you find in a tomb.
Mother and father gazed at them.
Was this a mute reproach?
Mother and father gazed at them:
Their motionless gaze grew dim.
    And I dream of my old grief,
And the tears keep flowing, . . .
And the fluttering of those rays, full of life,
    Beats within that dark heart of mine.

[С отцом родная сидела.
Молчали она и он.
И в окна ночь глядела . . .
"Чу,—молвили оба,–звон."
И мать, наклонясь, мне шепнула:
"Далече звон. Не дыши."
Душа к тишине прильнула,
Душа потонула в тиши.
И слышать я начал безмолвье
Заветных звонов сны.

Мой луг замыкали своды
Истонченных мраморных дуг.
Часы ль там играл я иль годы
Меж бабочек—легких подруг?

. . . Далось мне рукой проворной
Крылатый луч поймать . . .
И к ним . . .

—Отец и мать сидели . . .
. . . И к ним пришел я богатый
Поведатж новую быль.
Серела в руке разжатой,

Как в урне могильной, пыль.
Отец и мать глядели.
Немой ли то был укор?
Отец и мать глядели:
Тускнел неподвижный взор.
И старая скорбь мне снится,
И хлынет слеза из очей ...
И в темное сердце стучится
Порханье живых лучей.]

A wonderful poem! Wonderful! I must say people just don't seem to understand Vyacheslav Ivanov.
D: Yes, he is difficult ...
B: His poems are deeply symbolic. But at the same time, they are full of completely real-life experiences. Nobody understands that. People find his poetry artificial. How can it be artificial? It's about remembering childhood dreams that later leave a mark on a person's whole life. Take this: "I dreamed of an ancient grief..." He was able to understand that. He caught a ray, but it turned out to be just ashes: "ashes, like you find in a tomb ..." You cannot express that in prose, you need poetry, a childhood dream, for that ... That's marvelous ...
D: Could you recite an excerpt, even if very short, from *Faust* ... or any poem by Goethe in German?
B: I am afraid I won't get it all right. Okay, let's try something from Goethe then. How about the famous "Zueignug," the "Dedication" to *Faust*?

Ihr naht wieder, schwankende Gestalten,
Die früh sich einst dem trüben Blick gezeigt.
Versuch ich wohl, euch dismal festzuhalten?
Fühl ich mein Herz noch jenem Wahn geneigt?
Ihr drängt euch zu! Nun gut so mögt ihr walten,
Wie ihr aus Dunst und Nebel um mich steigt;
Mein Busen fühlt sich jugendlich erschüttert
Vom Zauberhauch, der euren Zug umwittert.
Ihr bringt mit euch die Bilder froher Tage,
Und manche liebe Schatten steigen auf;
Gleich einer alten, halbverklungen Sage
Streigt erste Lieb und Freundschaft mit herauf ...[89]

D: Well, that's enough.
B: It ends like this: "Was ich besitze seh' ich wie im Weiten, / Und was verschwand wird mir zu . . ."[90]
I've forgotten . . .
D: How about something in French?
B: I do remember a few things in French, of course, but here's the thing . . . What would be suitable to recite in French for you?
[*the taping is interrupted*]
D: Go ahead.
B: [*recites*]

> Das ist die Sehnsucht: Wohnen im Gewoge,
> Und keine Heimat kennen in der Zeit.
> Das sind die Wünsche: leise Dialoge
> Täglicher Stunden mit der Ewigkeit.
> Und das ist Leben. Bis aus einem Gestern
> Die einsamste von alien Stunden steigt,
> Die anders lächelnd als die andem Schwestern,
> Dem Ewigen entegegenschweigt.[91]

Magnificent! Just magnificent!
D: And in order to finish . . .
B: [*recites*]

> Nous aurons des lits pleins d'odeurs légères,
> Des divans profonds comme des tombeaux,
> Et d'étranges fleurs sur des étagères,
> Ecloses pour nous sous des cieux plus beaux.
> Usant à l'envi leurs chaleurs dernières,
> Nos deux coeurs seront deux vastes flambeaux,
> Qui réfléchiront leurs doubles lumières
> Dans nos deux esprits, ces miroirs jumeaux.
> Un soir fait de rose et de bleu mystique,
> Nous échangerons un éclair unique,
> Comme un long sanglot, tout chargé d'adieux;
> Et plus tard un Ange, entr'ouvrant les portes,
> Viendra ranimer, fidèle et joyeux,
> Les miroirs ternis et les flammes mortes.[92]

That's a sonnet.
D: Is it a sonnet by Baudelaire?
B: Yes, that's Baudelaire.
D: And now for the very last thing . . .
B: Yes?
D: What are your favorite lines from Pushkin?
B: It's very difficult for me to answer that question. But you know, I can say this . . .
[*the taping is interrupted again*]
D: Please, start from the beginning.
B: But I won't remember all of it.

> When the noisy day of mortal men grows still
> And half . . . half . . . (transparent) shadows of the night.
> Engulf the silent city streets . . .
> And sleep, that reward of daily labors . . .
> Remembrances unfurl their long parchment . . .
> And I, repulsed, review in it the story of my life . . . [93]

No, that's not how it goes. I wish I had glanced at it ahead of time. I'd have remembered it all.
D: I am afraid of your housekeeper, or we would do that. Maybe just a small piece. . . . I want to get a complete fragment. How about a portion of "The Bronze Horseman"?[94] I'm sure you remember it.
B: Something from "The Bronze Horseman"? How about the beginning?
D: Go ahead.
B: [*recites*]

> O'er darkened Petrograd there rolled
> November's breath of autumn cold;
> And Neva with her boisterous billow
> Splashed on her shapely bounding-wall
> And tossed in restless rise and fall
> Like a sick man upon his pillow . . .

D: [*recites*] "'Twas then that young Yevgeny came / Home from a party . . ."

FIG. 6.2. Bakhtin's grave. (Photo by Slav N. Gratchev)

B: [*recites*]

'Twas then that young Yevgeny came
Home from a party—I am going
To call our hero by that name,
For it sounds pleasing, and moreover
My pen once liked it—why discover
The needless surname?—True, it may
Have been illustrious in past ages,—
Rung, through tradition, in the pages
Of Karamzin; and yet, today
That name is never recollected,
By Rumor and the World rejected.
Our hero—somewhere—served the State;
He shunned the presence of the great;
Lived in Kolomna; for the fate
Cared not of forebears dead and rotten,
Or antique matters long forgotten.

[*As he recites, Bakhtin makes some mistakes, like saying "Rabelais" instead of "rodne" [forebears], laughs, and corrects them himself.*]
To do something like that . . . yes. No, I can't really . . .
D: But really, it's all fine. . . . Mikhail Mikhailovich, I simply don't have the words to express my gratitude to you.
B: No need to thank me! You must forgive *me* for the way I told things all mixed up and out of order. . . . This memory of mine being what it is . . .
D: I want to turn off the tape recorder before Galina Timofeevna[95] bursts in and throws me out. That's all. We are done. This was the last, and final interview with Mikhail Mikhailovich Bakhtin.
B: Thank you. . . . It was a pleasure to talk with you.
D: That's all!

Afterword

Six Interviews about the Death and Resurrection of the Word

DMITRIY SPOROV

Twenty-five years ago a journalist from England visited our Department of Oral History at Moscow University. He had heard that we have audio recordings of conversations with Mikhail Bakhtin and wanted to translate and publish them. Disheveled and overexcited, he charmed us with his enthusiasm for Bakhtin's spoken word. But, as it often happens, his excitement fizzled out, or perhaps was simply replaced with a different emotion, and the journalist left chasing after something new, only to be heard from again one last time through a letter expressing his regrets that life had managed to prevent him from translating Bakhtin after all.

That happened a long time ago. We were determined to publish these interviews with Bakhtin, as we understood that his words, spoken in the midst of Brezhnev's deaf years and preserved on an old tape, would be of utmost importance to us today. It seemed to us that it was far more important in our brave new world to issue Bakhtin's tapes—rather than Lenin's. Our academic librarians and Bakhtin scholars prepared the text, added detailed comments to it, and published the interviews as a book. Since then, the conversations have been translated and printed in Japanese, Polish, and Italian. But there still was no English edition. Now, finally, thanks to the efforts of Professors Slav Gratchev and Margarita Marinova, we have a sophisticated and accurate translation, as well as a set of completely new commentaries, which immerse the reader in the true atmosphere of Russia at the turn of the twentieth century. It would be impossible to comprehend what or who Bakhtin is talking about without these comments, which are, by the way, simply wonderful. Finally, some forty years later, Bakhtin's word receives a new lease on life because of these fascinating interviews. And that is a truly happy occasion.

But what, exactly, do we have in those interviews with Bakhtin? Not only do they let us listen to his voice and his very interesting stories, but they also allow us to hear a different, free Russia: for the duration of those twelve hours Bakhtin speaks about what he wants and how he wants; he is at home, too old and too sick to be afraid of anything anymore. Most importantly: he is talking with someone who understands him well.

In this context Bakhtin's interlocutor, Viktor Duvakin (1909–1982), cuts a unique figure. He was a philologist, a connoisseur of Russian poetry of the now most famous and brilliant period—the avant-garde literature of the early twentieth century. He was also a scholar of the life and work of the Futurist poet Vladimir Mayakovsky. Following Mayakovsky's suicide in 1930, Duvakin became interested in collecting personal witness accounts of the poet's life, and thus ended up conducting a series of interviews in different cities, and recording reminiscences about his favorite author's biography and art. That is how he came to the idea of creating an oral repository of memories by interesting people, who managed to survive the horrors of Stalin's repressions. While still teaching at Moscow University, Duvakin offered a seminar—now remembered as one of the few islands of intellectual freedom during the 1940s–1960s—in which those enrolled got to read and discuss any poetic work by the Russian literary avant-garde.

But the Soviet State wanted to control everything, and artistic expression in particular. Bakhtin was arrested in 1929, and only luck and a serious disease saved him from being sent to the horrors of the concentration camps. Thus, Bakhtin was made to disappear. His teachers, his friends, his books were also forbidden. For thirty years he could not publish anything and lived in internal exile in various small towns where he taught at the local schools.

Much like whole fields of knowledge and historical epochs, Bakhtin, too, was erased from public Soviet discourse.

Duvakin's interviews with Bakhtin took place during the years, now most often referred to as "the long seventies" (1967–1982). During that time ordinary Soviet citizens stopped believing public language of any kind. The louder the speech, the less meaning it carried.

For many of Duvakin's interviewees (including Bakhtin among 295 others) private oral expression was the only thing that mattered, as it, alone, could hope to preserve the nation's historical memory, which the government strove to obliterate. Only in their Memory (including familial memory) could they exist and think freely, and avoid participating in the building of socialism, which nobody believed in anymore. The people of the 1970s engaged in the process of active remembrance and the humanization of the past. That, at least, was still possible.

Duvakin's former student, the literary critic Vadim Kozhinov, introduced him to Bakhtin. That the meeting could happen at all was also the result of pure luck. After many years of wandering, Bakhtin was finally allowed to take up residence in Moscow. He moved into his new Moscow apartment in September 1972; Duvakin recorded their conversations in February–March 1973; and on March 7, 1975, the great philosopher breathed his last breath.

Bakhtin agreed to the interviews despite the very difficult conditions following the death of his wife, and his worsening illness. He was eager for a real dialogue and was prepared to forgive his interlocutor the occasional ignorance about some complex questions they might be discussing; he was delighted to be heard and understood. They were creating a new history, a new memory, a sort of a humanization of the *chronotope*, if you will, which is so important to us today.

Bakhtin realized that the taping of his reminiscences and thoughts was an act of bravery with uncertain outcomes. The recordings could disappear at any moment. Duvakin could be fired from his job yet again; his work could have been forbidden, and the tapes could have been confiscated and destroyed. To our great fortune, everything worked out well, and now, in the twenty-first century, we finally have the chance to converse with Bakhtin. The present translation will expand the audience for the interviews to 20–30 million; at long last we'll hear the voice recorded especially for us, for our century.

The six interviews by Viktor Duvakin with Mikhail Bakhtin amount to six histories of the death and resurrection of the Word: Bakhtin was arrested because of his public lectures on Kant's philosophy, while Duvakin began to record his oral histories following his dismissal from the university due to his willingness to speak up in support of writers who fought for the freedom of their words. Bakhtin's ideas about poetry and poets, writers and philosophers, form the thematic center of these fascinating interviews. A large percentage of these men and women, whose work is now considered to be Russian culture's golden heritage, died in the concentration camps, their writings were not allowed to be published, their books were banned from public libraries. But the poetic anthologies from the distant 1910s and 1920s continued to be transmitted from one person to the next, copied and memorized like the Bible of the early Christians. The fight for the free Word was difficult and ongoing. This is what Bakhtin's interviews signify to us in Russia.

Acknowledgments

We would like to express our sincere gratitude to Moscow State University Scientific Library and the Department of Oral History, and the scholars there who allowed us to translate and publish this unique phono-document—Anna Pantsa and Dimitry Sporov. Without their support and understanding of the importance of this project—which will allow English speakers to experience an intimate encounter with Bakhtin's life and ideas—this project would not have been possible.

We also would like to express our gratitude to Caryl Emerson, professor emerita of Princeton University, whose careful reading of early drafts, valuable suggestions for revisions and additions to the present translation and notes to the text improved the overall quality of this volume in every way possible.

In addition, we would like to thank the publishing house Soglasie (Moscow, Russia) for their cooperation and permission to use their book *M. M. Bakhtin: Besedy s V. D. Duvakinym* [*M. M. Bakhtin: Conversations with Duvakin*] for consultation while we were translating the phono-document. In particular, we want to express our appreciation to the director of this publishing house, Dr. Tatiana Glazkova, who embraced our work and generously responded to all our questions and requests.

This work was partially supported by a grant from Christopher Newport University, Newport News, Virginia.

Notes

Translator's Introduction

1 Vitaly Makhlin, "Тоже разговор" [Also a conversation], *Voprosy literatury* 3 (2004), http://magazines.russ.ru/voplit/2004/3/mah1-pr.html. Makhlin also provides several reasons why the Duvakin interviews are instructive, the chief among those being that there was a complete generational gap between a person born in 1895 and 1909. The former envisioned himself as a "European," an intellectual who belonged to a larger, supra-national community, while the latter was already a "Soviet" man, whose experiences differed sharply from those of his Western counterparts.

2 Caryl Emerson makes a similar point in her assessment of the Russian response to the tapes. In chapter 1 of *The First Hundred Years of Mikhail Bakhtin* (Princeton, NJ: Princeton University Press, 1997), titled "The Russians Reclaim Bakhtin, 1975 to the Jubilee," she writes that "when the icon becomes a human being, the traits that make it accessible are also what makes it imperfect" (32). Ken Hirschkop agrees that incompatible but canonized myths can destroy even what little real-life knowledge we have of the man: "For a long time we knew very little about Bakhtin's life. Thanks to the efforts of post-*glasnost* scholarship, we now know even less" (*Mikhail Bakhtin. An Aesthetic for Democracy* [Oxford: Oxford University Press, 1999], 111).

3 To Bakhtin dialogue was a three-way conversation: the third participant embodying the speaker's a priori belief that he would be understood. In "Problema teksta" (Mikhail Bakhtin, *Sobranie sochinenii v semi tomakh*, vol. 5 [Moscow: Russkie Slovari], 1996), Bakhtin makes the following point: "Understanding constitutes a very important relationship (understanding can never be a tautology or mere repetition, as there are always two [participants], and a potential *third*) (323). Bakhtin clarifies his point about the importance of the *third* in "1961. Zametki" (*Sobranie sochinenii*): "Besides the addressee ("the second"), the author of the utterance anticipates—with a greater or lesser awareness of it—a higher

"superaddressee" (a "third"), whose absolutely just understanding is expected either in some metaphysical future, or in distant historical time" (337). Both Duvakin and Bakhtin were aware that the recordings would have to wait, possibly for a long time, in order to become available to an actual audience. Their conversations were thus meant for precisely the "distant historical time" that Bakhtin associates with the intended superaddressee of any utterance.

4 This is also why Bakhtin admired Khlebnikov's prophetic vision of universal future so much, while he himself remained dubious of anything that tries to reach beyond the particular and the embodied.

5 Emerson, *First Hundred Years*, 38.

6 Poetic performativity is a topic Dick McCaw focuses on in his *Bakhtin and Theatre: Dialogues with Stanislavski, Meyerhold and Grotowski* (New York: Routledge, 2015). McCaw explores the effect that Bakhtin's personal crippledness had on his relationship to performance, and points out that for Bakhtin, immobility was the norm. Because McCaw is a theater practitioner and trainer/counselor of actors, he grasps that for Bakhtin the body does not accumulate wisdom by moving, remembering, integrating (his categories of "horizon" and "surrounding" just swivel above the neck); the body is essentially a static placeholder with eyes. McCaw's ideas on this topic are developed even more fully in "Towards a Philosophy of the Moving Body," in *Bakhtin's Heritage in Literature, Arts, and Psychology*, ed. Viatcheslav Gratchev and Howard Mancing (Lanham, MD: Lexington Books, 2018).

7 Mikhail Bakhtin, *The Dialogic Imagination: Four Essays*, ed. Michael Holquist, trans. Michael Holquist and Caryl Emerson (Austin: University of Texas Press, 1981), 62.

8 Emerson, *First Hundred Years*, 5.

9 Such witness accounts appear in multiple volumes of the journal *Dialog. Karnaval. Khronotop* [Диалог. Карнавал. Хронотоп], published by the Vitebsk Pedagogical Institute. See, for example, the "Memorialia" sections of the following issues: 1992, vol. 1, no. 1 (109–122); 1995, vol. 12, no. 3 (59–78); 1996, vol. 15, no. 2 (78–82); 1997, vol. 18 , no. 1 (140–185); 1997, vol. 21, no. 4 (92–113); 1999, vol. 26, no. 1 (151–153); 2000, vol. 30, no. 1 (127–152). Bakhtin's excellent lectures in Saransk, recorded by his students, were collected in a recent book, *M.M. Bakhtin—Myslitel', Pedagog, Chelovek*, ed. by I. V. Klyueva and L. M. Lisunova (Saransk, 2010).

10 See S.G. Bocharov, "Ob odnom razgovore i vokrug nego," *Siuzhety russkoi literatury,* Moskva: Iazyki russkoi kul'tury (1999): 473–474.

Interview 1

In the notes to this interview I use the terms "Russian" and "Soviet" to distinguish between different epochs, using "Russian" to designate individuals whose main productive period falls before the Revolution of 1917, and "Soviet" for those whose main productive period falls after the Revolution. In instances in which the activities of an individual span the two epochs, I use the composite term "Russian-Soviet."

1 After the 1917 Revolution, the Bolsheviks replaced the Julian calendar with the Gregorian calendar, dropping the first thirteen days of February 1918, such that February 14 became February 1.

2 Orel, located about 220 miles southeast of Moscow, was in Bakhtin's time a provincial city with a population of less than 100,000.

3 Bakhtin's family belonged to Russian nobility dating back to the fourteenth century. After the Revolution, Bakhtin preferred not to talk about his family background since possible punishments for such an "offence" included internal exile or even the death penalty.

4 Duvakin misquotes Pushkin's poem "My Genealogy" ["Моя родословная"] (1830). The original reads "И присмирел наш род суровый" ["And my fierce clan became subdued"], not, as it is here, "И захирел наш род суровый."

5 In the Russian context, a gymnasium is a school with a strong emphasis on academic learning, which focuses on preparing students to enter a university for further advanced academic study, comparable to American preparatory high schools.

6 Ivan Georgievich Petrovsky (1901–1973) was a prominent mathematician, academic, and the president of the Moscow State University from 1951 until his death.

7 Antiochus Kantemir (1708–1744), often called "the Father of Russian poetry," was also one of the first Russian "men of the Enlightenment." He was an ambassador in London, where he became a close friend of Voltaire.

8 Dimitry Petrovich Svyatopolk-Mirsky (1890–1939), a prince by rank and a literary critic. He immigrated to England after the Revolution, where he published the famous *A History of Russian Literature: From the Earliest Times to the Death of Dostoyevsky (1881)* (New York: A. A. Knopf, 1927). Shortly after returning to Russia in 1932, he was arrested and sent to a concentration camp, where he perished.

9 Maxim Gorky [Aleksey Peshkov] (1868–1936) was a Russian-Soviet writer and literary bureaucrat, and the official spokesperson for Socialist Realism after 1934. He did much to save the lives of many fellow writers. In 1921, he left the USSR for Italy. After a personal invitation from Stalin in 1931, he returned to the USSR, but his relationship with Stalin soured after 1934, and in 1936 he was "hospitalized" and never returned home. Some scholars suspect that Gorky was poisoned following Stalin's orders.

10 Ivan Turgenev (1818–1883) was one of the most important Russian prose writers of the nineteenth century. His works shaped Russian prose in many ways, and some of his books were regarded as revolutionary.

11 Fyodor Plevako (1842–1909) defended the accused parties in about 200 judicial court cases, winning all of them. For his outstanding public service, Plevako was given a hereditary title and the honorary rank of Counselor of State.

12 After the 1917 October Revolution, people who came from the countryside to work in the cities were given the right to reside in the homes of the wealthy (for example, those of doctors, lawyers, and bankers). Private ownership was no longer protected by law, and individual properties were routinely subdivided without the owner's consent, sometimes resulting in two, three, or four families occupying the same premises.

13 Bakhtin's three sisters, his mother, and his adopted sister were living in Leningrad during World War II. They died from starvation during the Siege of Leningrad, which lasted almost 900 days, from 1941 through 1944. Their exact burial sites are unknown.

14 The Whites were all the forces fighting against the Bolsheviks (known as "The Reds") during the Russian Civil War (1918–1921).

15 Cheka (in Russian ЧК, an acronym for Extraordinary Commission), the first Soviet state security organization, was a special committee created in 1917 by Vladimir Lenin and headed by Felix Dzerzhinsky (1877–1926) until his mysterious death. When it was dissolved in 1922, the Ministry of State Security (MGB), later called the State Political Directorate or Administration (GPU), took over as the principal organization of Stalin's police state, until it was replaced by the People's Commissariat for Internal Affairs (NKVD) in 1934.

16 Vilnius (called Vilno, 1919–1939) is the capital of Lithuania (a former Soviet republic, now an independent nation). Vilnius was founded in the thirteenth century and became the capital of the Grand Duchy of Lithuania. Vilnius has always been known as a culturally vibrant city—very European, liberal, and independent.

17 M. Bakhtin lived in Vilno between 1905 and 1911.

18 Odessa was founded in 1794 by the order of Russian Empress, Catherine the Great. The Bakhtin family moved there in 1911.

19 Saint Petersburg University is one of the oldest, largest, and most prestigious universities in Russia. It has always been a center for classical education, Russian culture, and the sciences. Founded in 1724 by order of Peter the Great, by 1766 it had ceased to exist. It was officially reopened in 1819.

20 Vilnius University, the oldest university in Northern Europe, was founded in 1579 by Jesuits. It maintained its traditions for three and a half centuries until closed by the Communists in 1919. Later, it was reopened under Soviet administration—and under Soviet censorship.

21 Joachim Lelevel (1786–1861) was a Polish historian and patriot, and the ideological leader of the Cadet Revolution of 1830–1831.

22 Perhaps the most prominent Polish political figure of modern times, Józef Piłsudski (1867–1935) served as head of state and is considered the founder of the Polish Army, of which he became the first Marshal. In the USSR, Piłsudski was persona non grata, and one could be punished for even mentioning his name.

23 Adrian Krukovsky (1856–?) was a Russian historian, professor of literature, and prominent literary critic and translator. He wrote extensively about Russian and Western literature. The date of his death, as well as its cause, are unknown.

24 Nevel is a beautiful town on Lake Nevel, located near the Belarus border, some 400 miles southwest of Saint Petersburg. At the time Bakhtin lived there, Nevel had a population of about 20,000 people.

25 Bakhtin moved to Nevel in 1918.

26 Lev Vasilyevich Pumpyansky (1891–1940) was a philologist, historian of culture, and professor at Leningrad University during the 1930s. He belonged to the so-called "Bakhtin circle," which was formed in Vitebsk and later continued in Leningrad. He was arrested by the MGB and sentenced to death.

27 Vasily Trediakovsky (1703–1768) was a Russian poet, literary theoretician, and a playwright who, together with poet and scientist Mikhail Lomonosov (1711–1765), helped lay the foundation of classical Russian literature. He was the first Russian citizen of non-aristocratic birth to receive an education abroad, at the Sorbonne in Paris.

28 Nikolay Bakhtin (1894–1950) is the older brother of Mikhail Bakhtin. After the Revolution, he immigrated to France to save his life. He later defended his

doctoral dissertation at Cambridge University, where he eventually became a professor of literature. Later he was invited to teach at the University of Birmingham. Nikolay Bakhtin's talents have been overshadowed by his more famous brother Mikhail; Nikolay's important contributions to literary criticism still await study and acknowledgment.

29 Sergey Konovalov, the son of A. I. [Alexander Ivanovich] Konovalov (1874–1949), the millionaire and Minister of Commerce and Industry during the Provisionary Government in Russia after the February Revolution, was also a specialist in Russian history, literature, and culture. While a professor at Cambridge and Birmingham, he invited Nikolay Bakhtin to move to England.

30 Nikolay Gudzy (1887–1965) was a professor at Moscow State University who specialized in early Russian literature; he also was an expert on the works of Leo Tolstoy (1828–1910).

31 The Russian State Library (called the Lenin Library between 1925 and 1992) is the largest and most important library in Russia. Founded in 1862, its collection at present is the fifth largest in the world.

32 Nikolay Marr (1865–1934), one of the most prominent Russian linguists, was a specialist in the Middle East and its languages. He was able to speak and read about twenty-five Middle Eastern languages. Following the Revolution, Marr supported the Bolsheviks and became an apologist for Marxism. This weakened the value of his research, and many of his students who previously supported Marr broke ties with him.

33 Eduard Bagritsky (Dzuban) (1895–1934) was an excellent lyrical poet, translator, and dramaturg. He was born in Odessa to a Jewish family. While joining the Bolsheviks, many present-day critics agree that his works were highly allegorical and that he was unhappy with what he saw transpiring around him. He died in Moscow from lung disease. After his death, his wife was arrested and spent twenty years in exile. The street on which she lived in exile was, ironically, named after her husband.

34 Ilya Ilf (1897–1937) and Evgeny Petrov (1903–1942) were two Soviet humorist writers, both natives of Odessa. They are best remembered for two novels: respectively, *The Twelve Chairs* (1928) and *The Golden Calf* (1931). Ilya Ilf died in 1937 of tuberculosis that he contracted during an American trip, and Petrov, seriously depressed by the death of his colleague and best friend, wrote nothing of any significance afterward, becoming a frontline reporter during World War II. He was killed in 1942 near Sevastopol during a German air strike.

35 The Odessa National University (founded in 1865) is the oldest and best university of Ukraine.

36 Alexander Tomson (1860–1935) worked at the Novorossiisky [New Russian] University in Odessa from 1897 until his death. He specialized in Indo-European, Slavic, and Russian language studies.

37 Nikolay Lange (1858–1921) was a famous psychologist, the founder of one of the first Russian psychology labs at Novorossiisky University.

38 Wilhelm Wundt (1832–1920) was a German scientist, doctor, physiologist, and psychologist. He is best remembered as the founder of what he called Experimental Psychology.

39 *Confessions of an English Opium Eater* came out in Petersburg in 1834, but was not attributed to Thomas De Quincey, but to Charles Maturin, an Irish author of the

Gothic novel, *Melmoth the Wanderer* (1820). There were no other existing editions before Bakhtin's conversations with Duvakin. But the book was known in Russia, and it exercised a certain influence on Nikolay Gogol and Fyodor Dostoevsky.

40 *Revue des Deux Mondes* is the famous liberal French literary journal founded in 1829. Among the most notable contributors to the journal were Victor Hugo, George Sand, Honoré de Balzac, and Alexander Dumas. The *Revue des Deux Mondes* was conceived as an economic, political, and cultural bridge between Europe and the Americas.

41 Vasily Mochulsky (1856–1920) was a professor of Russian literature and culture.

42 Hermann Cohen (1842–1918), a German philosopher, was one of the main founders of the neo-Kantian Marburg school. He is known for his 1871 fundamental work, *Kant's Theorie der Erfahrung* [*Kant's Theory of Experience*]. Bakhtin acknowledges that Cohen exercised an enormous influence on him—an influence that remains to be studied in more detail.

43 An excerpt from Andrey Belyi's poem "Премудрость" ["Wisdom"] (1908).

44 Vladimir Solovyov (1853–1900) was a Russian philosopher, enormously erudite, a talented poet, and an influential literary critic. Many scholars have argued that he was the prototype for Alyosha Karamazov, the principal character of Dostoevsky's last novel *The Brothers Karamazov* (1880).

45 Here, given Bakhtin's knowledge of German, he argues that philosopher Søren Kierkegaard's last name should be pronounced *Kierkegor.*

46 Kierkegaard died in 1855; Dostoevsky in 1881.

47 Kierkegaard's collected works came out in twelve volumes, 1909–1924.

48 Both titles were among the best and most influential literary and philosophical journals published in the USSR. Due to the scope of their critical inquiry and exclusion of politics, they were relatively free from censorship, and the quality of the essays published was, in most cases, superb.

49 Alexander Pavlovich Kazansky (1859–?) was a renowned professor at Odessa University, and Bakhtin was one of his most dedicated students.

50 OPOJAZ (in Russian, ОПОЯЗ, Общество изучения Поэтического Языка [Society for the Study of Poetic Language]), a famous society of formalist literary scholars and linguists in Saint Petersburg, was founded in 1916 and dissolved by the early 1930s (*Wikipedia*).

51 Bakhtin refers to Boris Kazansky, a mediocre scholar and political chameleon. But below Bakhtin is mistaken: Boris Kazansky was not related to Alexander Kazansky.

52 LEF (in Russian, Левый фронт искусств [Left Front of the Arts]) was a wide-ranging association of avant-garde writers, photographers, critics, and designers in the Soviet Union during the 1920s. The organization published its own journal.

53 Oswald Külpe (1862–1915) was a German psychologist and philosopher. His handbook, *Introduction to Philosophy* (1897), was translated into Russian in 1901 and reissued in 1908.

54 Sergei Trubetskoy (1863–1905) was a Russian philosopher, a follower of Vladimir Solovyov, and for many years a professor at Moscow State University.

55 The Marburg School of neo-Kantian philosophy was a philosophical movement that started in Germany in the 1860s in response to the revival of philosophic materialism in Germany. Paul Natorp (1854–1924), together with Hermann Cohen, founded the school. Bakhtin, as seen above, was an admirer of Cohen.

56 Bakhtin is misremembering. The proper titles are: Cohen's *System of Philosophy* [*System der Philosophie*], which included *The Logic of Pure Knowledge* [*Logik der reinen Erkenntnis*] (1902), *The Ethics of Pure Will* [*Ethik der reinen Willens*] (1904), and *The Aesthetics of Pure Feeling* [*Ästhetik der reinen Gefühls*] (1912).

57 The brothers Nikolay (1889–1942) and Sergey Radlov (1892–1958) were sons of the prominent philosopher Ernst Radlov (1854–1928), a close friend of Vladimir Solovyov. Both brothers studied at Petersburg University at the same time as the Bakhtin brothers. Later Sergey became a well-known theater director. Nikolay became a famous artist, caricaturist, and art critic.

58 Matvey Kagan (1889–1937) was a Jewish intellectual and a close friend of Bakhtin. He studied philosophy in Germany, where he was one of Cohen's and Natorp's favorite students. Upon his return to Nevel, his hometown, he initiated the group that became known as the "Bakhtin circle." Like many other intellectuals, Kagan was arrested in 1937 and died soon after in a concentration camp.

59 Ernst Cassirer (1874–1945), a prominent German philosopher and historian of ideas, was a student of Cohen's. In 1933, he had to leave Germany due to Hitler's rise. He became a professor at Oxford, but in 1941 had to immigrate to the United States, where he became a professor at Yale and then at Columbia University.

60 Valery Bryusov (1873–1924) was one of the principal members of the Russian Symbolist movement. A prominent poet, writer, dramatist, translator, critic, and historian, he was one of the few of his circle who supported the Bolshevik government after the Revolution. He obtained a prominent position in the Ministry of Culture but in 1924 caught pneumonia and died shortly thereafter.

61 Peter Yakubovich (1860–1911) was most famous for the first translation into Russian of Charles Baudelaire's (1821–1867) *Les Fleurs du mal*, printed in Petersburg in 1909.

62 Fyodor Tyutchev (1803–1873) was a prominent poet, diplomat, and academic. He studied ancient poetry and conversed fluently in Latin. Although his poetry is often misunderstood or underappreciated, it would be fair to say that Tyutchev is one of the most refined and philosophical Russian poets.

63 Yevgeny Baratinsky (1800–1844) is one of the most striking and, at the same time, enigmatic and underrated figures of Russian literature. A soldier and a poet, he spent most of his life in the countryside, where he contemplated human existence in philosophical terms. He died unexpectedly while traveling in Italy.

64 Afanasy Fet [Shenshin] (1820–1892) was a Russian lyrical poet and academic. One of his last works was a translation of Arthur Schopenhauer's (1788–1860) philosophical essays into Russian.

65 Mikhail Lermontov (1814–1841) was the most significant Russian poet after Alexander Pushkin. A masterful prose writer as well as a poet, Lermontov's *A Hero of Our Time* (1840) inaugurated the Russian psychological novel.

66 See n61. Baudelaire's influence on the Russian Silver Age poets (Alexander Blok [1880–1921], Valery Bryusov, Marina Tsvetaeva [1892–1941], Anna Akhmatova [1889–1966], Osip Mandelstam [1891–1938], and others) was profound.

67 José-Maria de Heredia (1842–1905) was a Cuban-born poet. After obtaining French citizenship, he attained the great honor of membership in the French Academy. As a poet, he was not very prolific; the book that Bakhtin praises was his only collection. Heredia worked on *Les Trophées* (1893) for thirty years. Critics

and readers admired the perfection of its poetic form, and his work was translated into Russian by many distinguished poets.

68 Paul Éluard (1895–1952) was a French poet mostly remembered for cultivating Dadaism and Surrealism, and his relationship with Salvador Dalí (1904–1989).

69 Vyacheslav Ivanov (1866–1949) was a prominent Russian poet, playwright, scholar, and literary theorist. He was associated with the Russian Symbolist movement, and lived abroad between 1886 and 1905. After coming into conflict with the Bolshevik government, Ivanov left Russia permanently in 1924, eventually settling in Italy.

70 Innokenty Annensky (1855–1909), poet, critic, and translator, was representative of the first wave of Russian Symbolism. His influence on the post–Symbolist generation of Russian poets was significant. A brilliant translator, Annensky was the first to render successfully into Russian the authentic intonations of Charles Baudelaire and Paul Verlaine (1844–1896), two poets who later enjoyed enormous popularity in Russia.

71 Faddey Zelinsky (1859–1944) was a popular and influential classics professor at Saint Petersburg State University, a favorite of Bakhtin. He wrote *The History of Classical Religions* and revived Greek theater at the university. He personally knew Isadora Duncan (1877–1927), and when she was in Saint Petersburg in 1913, Zelinsky introduced her performances to all his students. Zelinsky held *doctor honoris causa* degrees from twelve European universities.

72 Mikhail Pokrovsky (1868–1932) was a literary scholar, translator, and author of many interesting essays about poetics, especially the poetics of the novel. Like many others, he suffered during the repression, and died in a concentration camp. His gravesite is unknown.

73 Bakhtin never officially graduated from any university. As he says, he attended courses at his own leisure, selected his own mentors, and learned best on his own. This lack of an official diploma was a major bureaucratic obstacle to receiving a doctoral degree after his dissertation defense in 1946.

74 Sergey Sobolevsky (1864–1963) was a historian of ancient languages, translator, and member of the Russian Academy of Science.

75 Sergey Radtsig (1882–1968) was a classics professor at Moscow University.

76 Vikenty Veresaev [Smidovich] (1867–1945) is a unique figure in Russian and Soviet literature. Like Anton Chekhov, a doctor by training, Veresaev loved literature and wrote about his medical experiences. His first book, *The Memoires of a Physician* (1901), had tremendous success. After traveling to Greece, Veresaev began translating *The Iliad* and *The Odyssey* into Russian. For his service to literature and education, Veresaev received the Stalin Prize—the highest award bestowed in the Soviet Union.

77 Fyodor Petrovsky (1890–1978) was a classics professor and translator. While his older brother was arrested, he was not; he managed to survive the repressions and live a long and productive life.

78 The title of the collection is *Antiquity and Modernity: In Honor of F. A. Petrovsky's 80th Anniversary* (Moscow: Nauka, 1972).

79 Aleksey Losev (1893–1988) was a prominent Russian philosopher, translator, literary scholar, and writer. Due to his religious views, he and his wife were arrested in 1930 and sent to the concentration camps. He managed to survive the Purge, and, when released, was allowed to return to Moscow University to teach again.

80 The surgery took place in February 1938.

81 The petty exhibitionism and bad taste denoted by the word "vulgar" was later made famous by Nabokov, who used it regularly in his writing and lectures. It is important to note that Bakhtin's use of the term here does not suggest any seriously crude behavior.

Interview 2

In the notes to this interview I use the terms "Russian" and "Soviet" to distinguish between different epochs, using "Russian" to designate individuals whose main productive period falls before the Revolution of 1917, and using "Soviet" for those whose main productive period falls after the Revolution. In instances in which the activities of an individual span the two epochs, I use the composite term "Russian-Soviet."

1 The Odessa Theater of Opera and Ballet is the oldest and most famous opera theater in Ukraine. It opened in 1810 and has staged performances by, among others, Tchaikovsky (as a conductor), Sergei Rachmaninov, Fyodor Chaliapin, Anna Pavlova, and Isadora Duncan.

2 Fyodor Chaliapin (1873–1938) was a Russian opera singer. He possessed the deepest and perhaps most expressive bass voice in opera history. He is remembered not only as a great singer but also as an accomplished performer, movie actor (adaptation of Miguel de Cervantes' *Don Quixote*, dir. G. W. Pabst, United Artists, 1933), artist, and sculptor.

3 Mikhail Lopatto (1892–1981) was a mediocre poet and literary critic who managed to publish a few books in Petersburg before leaving the Soviet Union.

4 Duvakin's joke is a play on words: "Lopatto" sounds like "lopata," which in Russian means "shovel."

5 The Shubravtsi Society (literally, "the society of loafers") appeared in Vilnius in 1817. It was formed by a group of Vilnian intellectuals who cared deeply about public education. The society existed until 1829, re-appearing in 1899.

6 Brambeus-Senkovskiy [Osip Senkovsky, b. Józef Sękowski] (1800–1858) was a Russian journalist, literary critic, and scholar of Middle Eastern studies. His literary nickname was "Baron Brambeus."

7 Bakhtin refers to Swift's *A Modest Proposal: For Preventing the Children of Poor People in Ireland from Being a Burden to Their Parents or Country, and for Making Them Beneficial to the Public* (1729). The essay, in the Roman rhetorical tradition of *Reductio ad absurdum*, suggests that it would be financially beneficial to sell poor Irish children as food to rich Englishmen.

8 Libertinism was a philosophical movement that appeared in France in the late seventeenth century, and continued in both France and Britain through the eighteenth century. Close to nihilism, Libertinism rejects the common moral norms of behavior, specifically sexual norms, and, perhaps, can be described as an extreme form of hedonism.

9 "Arzamas" was a literary society (1815–1818) of close friends, proponents of the so-called "New Literature" as opposed to the old, archaic forms of Russian literature that were still dominant. Alexander Pushkin was a member.

10 Unless otherwise noted, all poetry translations are by the translator of this volume.

The Russian text is as follows:

Я к вам пришел—провозвеститель веры
Таинственно святого omphalos'a
Познавший ласки вкрадчивой пантеры
И созерцавший оргии Лесбóса.
И женшины двухсот восьми племен
Меня ласкали вечно по-иному.
Я знал их страсти многоцветный сон,
Их упоенья тусклую истому . . .

11 On Vladimir Solovyev—see interview 1, n44.

12 On Faddey Zelinsky—see interview 1, n71.

13 Nikolay Lossky (1870–1965), a religious philosopher and the founder of "intuitivism," was a professor at Saint Petersburg University. After the Revolution, he left the USSR and taught in many countries, including the United States.

14 Alexander Vvedensky (1856–1925) was a prominent Russian neo-Kantian philosopher and psychologist. He chaired a philosophy department for many years and was also the founder and chair of the first Philosophical Society in Russia. He wrote a popular philosophy textbook that was in use until the 1980s.

15 Semyon Vengérov (1855–1920) was a literary critic and historian. He taught at the University of Saint Petersburg for some time, although he did not hold a PhD in philosophy. Bakhtin remembers him as a mediocre professor but brilliant bibliographer.

16 Ivan Lapshin (1870–1952) was a Russian philosopher. After the Revolution, he went to Czechoslovakia from which he never returned.

17 Stefan Srebrny (1890–1962) came to Russia as a student and became one of the favorite students of Faddey Zelinsky. After the Revolution, he returned to Poland in order to save his life.

18 Pavel Vinogradov (1854–1925) was a prominent medievalist. After the Revolution, he immigrated to England where he became a professor at Oxford.

19 Vasily Klyuchevsky (1841–1911) was a great Russian historian, a brilliant professor at Moscow University, who also served there as dean and provost. He was a member of the Imperial Academy of Science. His major work was the eighteen-volume *History of the Russian Empire* (London and New York, 1911–[1931]).

20 Jan Baudouin de Courtenay (1845–1929) was a Polish linguist who spoke and wrote fluently in ten European languages. He taught at the Saint Petersburg University from 1900 to 1918. After the Revolution, he returned to the newly independent Poland, where he worked until his death as a professor at the re-established University of Warsaw.

21 Victor Shklovsky (1893–1984) was a preeminent Russian literary theorist. To avoid arrest, he fled Russia in 1922 but later returned. A close friend of Sergey Eisenstein (1898–1948), the Russian filmmaker, Shklovsky wrote, probably, the most interesting study on Eisenstein and his filmography (*Eisenstein*, 1973). He died in Moscow.

22 Filip Fortunatov (1848–1914) was a prominent Russian linguist of the pre-Bolshevik era, a professor at Moscow University, and the founder of the Moscow School of Linguistics.

23 Ferdinand de Saussure (1857–1913) is considered to be the founder of modern linguistics and semiotics.

24 Boris Eikhenbaum (1886–1959) was an outstanding Soviet literary critic, one of the founders of the Formalist method. Eikhenbaum was an eminent scholar of Leo Tolstoy, Mikhail Lermontov, and Fyodor Tyutchev.

25 Evgeny Polivanov (1891–1938) was a scholar and linguist. He spoke eighteen languages but was able to read and write in more than fifty. After the Revolution, Polivanov worked with Leon Trotsky (1879–1940) and for that reason was arrested in 1937. A few months later and without a proper trial, Polivanov was sentenced to death.

26 Marrism is a linguistic theory concerned with the origins and "class-based nature" of language, first introduced by Nikolay Marr (1865–1934), and promoted by the Soviet state from the 1920s through the 1950s.

27 The Left Socialist Revolutionaries (Left SRs) was a political party in Russia between 1917 and 1923. They supported the Bolsheviks and helped them come to power, but a few months later they decided to join the opposition and tried to organize a coup. The Bolsheviks used this moment as a pretext for a "Red Terror" against the Left Socialists, and soon their party was decimated.

28 Lev Shcherba (1880–1944) was one of the most distinguished professors at Saint Petersburg University. He was a linguist and a member of Soviet Academy of Science.

29 Dmitry Petrov (1872–1925) was a professor of Romance languages at Saint Petersburg University.

30 Both brothers, Alexander Veselovsky (1838–1906) and Aleksey Veselovsky (1843–1918), were scholars of world literatures and professors at Moscow University.

31 Vladimir Shishmarev (1874–1957) was a French language professor at Moscow University.

32 *Pan Tadeusz* is an epic poem by the Polish poet, writer, and philosopher Adam Mickiewicz (1798–1855). Published in June 1834 in Paris, and considered by many to be the last great epic poem in European literature, *Pan Tadeusz* is Poland's national epic and required reading in Polish schools.

33 *Dziady* is a Romantic poetic drama by the Polish poet Adam Mickiewicz written in 1823–1860.

34 Semyon Vengérov (1855–1920) was professor of Russian literature at Saint Petersburg University. He prepared and published the complete works of many important Russian writers and personally wrote extensive commentaries, still possessing scholarly worth.

35 Vladimir Mayakovsky (1893–1930) was the foremost representative of the early twentieth-century Russian Futurism and is widely considered one of the most talented poets of the Soviet era. He was one of the few Soviet writers who were allowed to travel freely. After his suicide (or, possibly, assassination by the NKVD) in 1930, he was canonized by the Soviet authorities.

36 Velimir Khlebnikov (1885–1922) was a central figure of the Russian Futurist movement. He coined a great number of neologisms and explored the etymological roots of Russian words, seeking to find significance in the sounds of certain Cyrillic letters.

37 In the Russian academic system, a *dotsent* is a mid-level scholar with job security, roughly equivalent to an associate professor.

38 Traditional baked or fried buns stuffed with different fillings.

39 David Burliuk (1882–1967) is often called the Father of Russian Futurism. He was primarily a painter but also a poet. He did not accept the Revolution and in 1920, he immigrated to Japan, then to the United States, where he lived and worked until his death.

40 The infamous Anglo-Boer War (1899–1902) in South Africa between English colonizers and Boers—the descendants of emigrants from the Dutch Republic who colonized South Africa in the seventeenth century—ended with the victory of Great Britain.

41 The Stray Dog Café was a cult art cabaret located in downtown Saint Petersburg. It became famous when the most notable Silver Age poets and theater figures (Anna Akhmatova, Osip Mandelstam, Nikolay Gumilev, Vladimir Mayakovsky, Vsevolod Meyerhold, and Velimir Khlebnikov, among others) became frequent visitors there. The café existed from late December of 1911 until March 1915, when it closed on account of the war.

42 Duvakin is referring to Shklovsky here.

43 The Kadets were members of the Constitutional Democratic Party and were also referred to as Constitutional Democrats. The party originated as a liberal political party in the Russian Empire, encompassing constitutional monarchists and right-wing republicans.

44 Nevsky Prospect (Nevsky Avenue) is the main street in Saint Petersburg. It was planned by Peter the Great as the opening section of the highway to Moscow. Nevsky served as an inspiration for many Russian authors, most famously Nikolay Gogol and Fyodor Dostoevsky.

45 Lev Kasso (1865–1914) was a minister of education. Following the reforms initiated by Russian Prime Minister Peter Stolypin in 1906, he issued an order to expel university students whose activities were considered a threat to the civil order (see interview 3, n55).

46 Peter the Great's Table of Ranks (established in 1722) assigned a specific position to government members of the Russian Empire, according an equivalent civilian rank for each military one. The so-called Table of Civil Ranks started from the fourteenth rank (collegiate registrar, equal to cornet in military rank), and ended with the first rank as active privy councilor (equal to general lieutenant). University professors, who were employees in the imperial bureaucracy, normally held a fourth rank of active state councilor (equal to major general) and were highly respected.

47 Lev Petrazhitsky (1867–1931) was a law theoretician, founder of the sociology of law, and Chair of the Law Department at Saint Petersburg University. He emigrated from Russia after the Revolution. Bakhtin was influenced by his ideas, especially those about "official" and "unofficial" law.

48 Vol'fil is an abbreviation that stands for Free Philosophical Society. It existed at Saint Petersburg University from 1919 to 1924.

49 Andrey Bely (Boris Bugaev) (1880–1934) was a Russian writer, literary critic, poet, and one of the leaders of Russian Symbolism and Modernism. He was a close friend of Alexander Blok, Valery Bryusov, and Osip Mandelstam. He died of a heart attack.

50 Dmitry Merezhkovsky (1866–1941) was a prominent figure in the Silver Age of Russian literature. He was one of the founders of Russian Symbolism and the Russian historico-philosophical novel. He was nominated ten times for the Nobel

Prize but never received it. Even his enemies agreed that Merezhkovsky was an original philosophical thinker.

51 Zinaida Gippius (1869–1945) was one of the founders of Russian Symbolism. The wife of Dmitry Merezhkovsky, Gippius managed to preserve her own artistic identity and is remembered as a brilliant literary critic, poet, writer, and dramaturg. About Anton Kartashev (1875–1960), see interview 4, n4.

52 Dmitry Filosofov (1872–1940) was a Russian author and political activist. He became a close friend of Merezhkovsky and Gippius, with whom he was involved in a romantic ménage à trois for many years. After the Revolution, they together fled Communist Russia and escaped to Poland in 1919. The following year Merezhkovsky and Gippius moved on to Paris, but Filosofov stayed in Poland for the rest of his life.

53 The rector of a Russian university is equivalent to the president of a university in the West, while prorector is the equivalent to the provost.

54 Ivan Grevs (1860–1940) was an outstanding medievalist professor at Saint Petersburg University.

55 Eighty rubles in the early twentieth century was a considerable amount of money. Still, higher education was not very expensive when compared to Western tuitions at the time.

56 Grivennik was the equivalent of ten kopeks, or about ten cents.

57 Shchi (щи) is a traditional Russian cabbage soup that can be traced back to the ninth century.

58 The New Economic Policy (NEP) was the economic policy implemented by Lenin. It was in effect from 1921 to 1928 and offered a temporary suspension of the previous policy of extreme centralization and doctrinaire socialism. (See also interview 5, n17.)

59 Leonid Andreev (1871–1919) was considered to be among the first Expressionists in Russian prose. After the Revolution, he immigrated to Finland where he soon died from heart failure.

60 Moscow Art Theatre (MXAT) was founded in 1898 by the Russian theatre director and actor Konstantin Stanislavsky (see n66), together with Vladimir Nemirovish-Danchenko (1858–1943). The dramatic works of Anton Chekhov, Shakespeare, Ibsen, Gorky, and Hauptmann were closely associated with what would become the most famous Russian dramatic theater.

61 Leonid Sobinov (1872–1934) was an outstanding Russian-Soviet opera tenor. He started his career as a lawyer working with the famous Fyodor Plevako (1842–1908). While at the university, he began to sing, and by the age of twenty-five years, was already a leading tenor at Bolshoi Theatre.

62 Maria Venyaminovna Yudina (1899–1970), a famous Russian-Soviet piano player, was a close friend of Bakhtin's. A professor at the Saint Petersburg Conservatory, she was openly Christian and a follower of Saint Francis. Due to her religious views and her public sympathy for Igor Stravinsky (whose music was banned in the USSR), she lost her position and, after reading a controversial poem by Boris Pasternak during one of her own concerts, she was prohibited from giving public performances. She died alone, in her little apartment in Moscow, in dire poverty.

63 Vsevolod Meyerhold (1874–1940) was one of the most remarkable Russian actors and theater directors of all time. Starting on the stage of the Moscow Art Theater, he soon founded his own theater (the Meyerhold Theater). After the Revolution,

he had the opportunity to defect from the USSR while on tour in France, but he did not. After staging the famous *The Lady with the Camellias* (1934), which met with Stalin's disapproval, his theater was closed, and Meyerhold was arrested and sentenced to death.

64 The Bolshoi (which means "Large") Theatre, located in Moscow, is the most important opera and ballet theater in Russia. It opened in 1780; more than 800 operas and ballets were staged during its existence. After the Revolution, the theater was almost closed, but in 1921 the Bolsheviks decided to reconstruct the building and resurrect the company.

65 The Maly (which means "Little") Theatre in Moscow is the oldest dramatic theater in Russia, founded in 1756 by order of the Empress Elizabeth, daughter of Peter the Great. The official date of the inauguration of the theatrical building was 1824. It was then that the theater received its nickname—Maly—to distinguish it from the Bolshoi.

66 Konstantin Sergeyevich Stanislavsky (1863–1938) was the most famous Russian theater director, actor, and professor of dramatic art, best known today for his "system" of actor training, preparation, and rehearsal technique. He, together with Nemirovich-Danchenko, founded the Moscow Art Theater in 1898. His enormous fame was probably the reason why he managed to survive Stalin's Great Purge (1936–1938).

67 Henrik Ibsen's *Brand* (written 1865; performed 1867) was not popular in Norway, but when translated into Russian and staged at the Moscow Art Theater, it enjoyed tremendous success.

68 Vasily Kachalov (1875–1948) was a Russian-Soviet dramatic actor. He began his artistic career on the stage of MXAT as Stanislavsky's protégé and soon became a leading actor. Among his most famous roles were Hamlet, Ivan the Terrible, Ivan Karamazov, Don Juan, and Stavrogin (from Dostoevsky's *The Devils* [1871–1872]).

69 *The Lower Depths* (1902), perhaps Gorky's best-known play, centers on a group of impoverished characters living in a homeless shelter. This play for many years was misrepresented in the USSR as being pro-Revolution. In reality, this is Gorky's deepest philosophical inquiry into the meaning of human existence.

70 For Maxim Gorky, see interview 1, n9.

71 *The Cherry Orchard* (1903) is the last of Anton Chekhov's plays, and perhaps the most famous. It premiered in 1904 at MXAT with Stanislavsky as Gayev, the bumbling and eccentric brother of Lyubov Ranevskaya.

72 Vyacheslav Ivanov, see interview 1, n69.

73 Valentin Voloshinov (1895–1936) was a gifted Russian literary critic, philosopher, musicologist, and linguist. A close friend of Bakhtin's and a Marxist (which Bakhtin was not), Voloshinov wrote two books deeply influenced by ideas of the Bakhtin circle: *Freudianism, A Critical Sketch* (1927) and *Marxism and the Philosophy of Language* (1929). Voloshinov died from tuberculosis in 1936. His heritage fell into obscurity until it was revived in the West by Roman Jakobson.

74 Russian—similar to German and French—has two forms of direct address, a polite "you" (Вы) and the informal "you/thou" (ты). The choice of mode depends on how well you know the other person and whether you are superior or inferior in terms of age and position. The use of the informal "you" between two interlocutors suggests an intimate relationship/friendship.

75 Baku, the capital of Azerbaijan, is the largest city (population 3,000,000) on the Caspian Sea.

76 "Arbat" is the central and best-known street in Moscow. It is about a mile long, and is first mentioned in documents from the fifteenth century.

77 Ivan Alexeevich Bunin (1870–1953) was the first Russian writer to receive a Nobel Prize in Literature (1933). He immigrated to France in 1920.

78 Mikhail Gershenzon (1869–1925) was a literary critic, philosopher, and translator. His penetrating studies of Pushkin and Turgenev retain their critical value today. Together with Vyacheslav Ivanov, he co-authored *Correspondence across a Room* (1921).

79 *Correspondence across a Room* (1921) is a book written by Ivanov and Gershenzon in the form of epistles to each other. It is a philosophical discourse about God, freedom, life, and society.

80 Vladislav Khodasevich (1886–1939) was a highly influential Russian poet and literary critic. He immigrated to Berlin in 1922, where he published penetrating analyses of contemporary Soviet literature and encouraged the career of Vladimir Nabokov. Khodasevich's book *Necropolis* (1939) is invaluable for its characterizations of many prominent Soviet poets and writers, including Gorky and Blok.

81 About Innokenty Annensky—see interview 1, n70.

82 Here Bakhtin is referencing Khodasevich's book *Necropolis* (1939), which indeed presented a very negative picture of the Bryusov brothers.

83 Marina Tsvetaeva (1892–1941) is considered one of the greatest Russian poets of the twentieth century. She was famous not only for her brilliant and probing poetry but also for her excellent translations from French, German, Czech, and Italian—languages she spoke fluently. Many of her translations into Russian remain pre-eminent. Tsvetaeva's life ended tragically when she committed suicide during the first year of the Great Patriotic War.

84 Yuly Aykhenvald (1872–1928) was an influential literary critic. His most famous book, *Silhouettes of Russian Writers*, continues to be of interest to literary scholars today. After the Revolution he moved to Germany, where he translated all the major works of Schopenhauer into Russian. He tragically died in a train accident.

85 Ferdinand Hodler (1853–1918) was a Swiss painter known especially for his portraits. Influenced by Symbolism and Art Nouveau, he devised a highly personal style he called "parallelism."

86 Lev Kamenev (Rosenfeld) (1883–1936) was a Bolshevik revolutionary, a friend of Lenin, and a member of the Politburo. In 1936, he was arrested and sentenced to death for his support of Leon Trotsky (see interview 3, n49).

87 Olga Kameneva (Bronstein) (1883–1941) was Kamenev's wife and the sister of Leon Trotsky. When Kamenev was arrested and then shot and Trotsky was murdered in Mexico, Olga Kameneva was also arrested and sentenced to death in 1941. The location of her grave is unknown.

88 Bakhtin refers to Khodasevich's autobiographical work, *The White Corridor* [*Белый коридор*], which first appeared in Paris in 1925, after Khodasevich had immigrated to France.

89 In Russian, "Служенье муз не терпит суеты": from Pushkin's famous poem "October 19, 1827."

90 *Green Meadow* [*Луг зеленый*] was Andrey Bely's 1910 collection of critical and philosophical essays.

91 Sergey Solovyov (1885–1942) was a minor poet. He was a nephew of the famous philosopher Vladimir Solovyov.

92 Klobuk is the ecclesiastical headpiece that monks in the Orthodox church have worn since the twelfth century. The legend about the White Klobuk to which Bakhtin refers here became popular in the fifteenth century. It tells the story of how the White Klobuk came to Russia from Rome, through Constantinople, as a symbol of spiritual power, and thus helped transform Moscow into the "Third Rome." In 1564, the White Klobuk became the official headgear of the Russian Patriarch.

93 Duvakin is not correct here: Zinaida Gippius died in Paris at the age of seventy-six years.

94 Sergeyevich.

95 Merezhkovsky's "philosophical" explanation for their relationship was very well known. Quite often at those meetings he would argue—with great eloquence—that marriage in its traditional form was obsolete, that there had to be a new, better form of marriage, and that he and his wife were experimenting with these new forms.

96 Ivan Rukavishnikov (1877–1930) was a mediocre but prolific poet in the Symbolist movement—he published twenty volumes of works.

97 Stepan Skitalets (Petrov) (1869–1941) was a Russian poet, writer, musician, and friend of Maxim Gorky. His pen-name means "wanderer." After the Revolution, Skitalets immigrated to China, where he spent fifteen years. Then he returned to the USSR where, surprisingly, he was never arrested or prosecuted.

98 Alexander Meyer (1874–1939) was a notable religious philosopher. In 1928 he was arrested and sentenced to death, though his sentence was commuted to ten years in the gulag due to the intervention of a "connection."

99 Peter Lesgaft (1837–1909) was a Russian biologist, anatomist, anthropologist, surgeon, and professor of medicine. The only Soviet University of Physical Education was named after Lesgaft.

100 Both Bakhtin and Meyer received a ten-year sentence (later changed to five in Bakhtin's case) after a trial in 1929 for their participation in a supposedly right-wing, anti-Soviet organization called "Sunday," which existed in Leningrad from 1917 to 1928. Bakhtin never really participated in this circle, but he did personally know its leader, Meyer, and several of Bakhtin's close friends attended meetings of the organization as well.

101 "Christ Is Risen" was written in 1918 as a response to Blok's famous revolutionary poem *The Twelve.*

102 Alexander Blok (1880–1921) was among the greatest of the Russian Symbolist poets. Born to an aristocratic family, he accepted the Bolshevik Revolution in 1917, a move that surprised many of his admirers and friends. In 1921, he became ill and needed treatment abroad, but permission to leave Russia was only issued to him three days after his death.

103 Yevgeny Ivanov (1879–1942) was one of the most frequent visitors to the circle of Alexander Meyer. He was arrested together with Meyer and sentenced to five years in Siberia.

104 Vladimir Bonch-Bruyevich (1873–1955) was the close friend and personal secretary to Lenin. He actively participated in the first Bolshevik government. After Lenin's death, he wisely retired from politics and moved to neutral academic activities.

His passion was to manage archives and museums, which he succeeded in doing until his death.

105 The excerpt cited here is from Blok's poem *The Twelve* (1918). Some claim that it is the first literary demonstration of support for the Revolution of 1917. It is not typical of Blok's style: its strange rhythms and harsh, street-like language promptly alienated Blok from many of his admirers and friends who surmised that he was ingratiating himself to the new authorities. Yet the Bolsheviks were very suspicious of Blok's mysticism and asceticism. The appearance of Christ in a "revolutionary" poem was an issue of great controversy, one discussed by critics for many years.

106 The Russian text of the excerpt quoted here is as follows:

Впереди—с кровавым флагом,
И за вьюгой невидим,
И от пули невредим
Нежной поступью надвьюжной,
Снежной россыпью жемчужной,
В белом венчике из роз—
Впереди—Исус Христос.

107 They confuse the lines a little here. In the original it is: "Нежной поступью надвьюжной, / Снежной россыпью жемчужной, / В белом венчике из роз / Впереди—Исус Христос." ["With tender step, the storm below / Scattering up the pearl-like snow / His head adorned by roses iced / Ahead of them—goes Jesus Christ."]

108 *Verses about the Beautiful Lady* was published in 1904. This collection immediately put Blok at the forefront of the Russian Symbolist movement.

109 The excerpt, slightly misquoted, is from Blok's 1912 poem "My Friend's Life" ["Жизнь моего приятеля"]:

Таращил сочувственно с крыши
Глазищи обмызганный кот.
Ты думаешь, тоже свидетель?
Так он и ответит тебе!
В такой же гульбе
Его добродетель!

110 In Blok, the line reads: "Here's how he [the cat] will answer you."

111 Bakhtin references Blok's essay "Irony" ["Ирония"], which appeared in 1908.

112 The "Tower" that Bakhtin refers to here was Vyacheslav Ivanov's sixth-floor apartment in Saint Petersburg. The literary salon that met there every Wednesday from 1905 to 1909 attracted the most notable Petersburg intelligentsia and all sorts of artists, who came to listen to poetry and music, and to participate in philosophical discussions.

113 In Russian: "Есть в напевах твоих сокровенных . . ." ("К Музе," 1912).

114 In Russian:

Над тобой загорается вдруг
Тот неяркий, пурпурово-серый
И когда-то мной виденный круг.

115 Mikhail Vrubel (1856–1910), a Russian painter, is today considered to be the father of Russian Modernism. His artistic career was interrupted by the neurosis and deep depression that led to his decline and eventual death in 1910.

116 Bakhtin refers here to Blok's lecture titled "About the Present Condition of Russian Symbolism" ["О современном состоянии русского символизма"] that was delivered on March 26, 1910, and then published in *Apollo* [*Аполлон*] 8 (1910).

117 This is the beginning of Blok's 1913 poem, "The Artist" ["Художник"]: "В жаркое лето и в зиму метельную . . ."

118 Another excerpt from "My Friend's Life" (1912).

Пристал ко мне нищий дурак,
Идет по пятам, как знакомый.
"Где деньги твои?"—" Снес в кабак."
"Где сердце?"—"Закинуто в омут."

119 An excerpt from Blok's letter to Andrey Bely written in 1907. The entire text can be found in Blok's *Complete Works* (Moscow, 1963), vol. 8, 199.

120 The excerpt is from Blok's "Песня Гаетана" [The Song of Gaetan], in *The Rose and the Cross* (1913). In Russian: "Мира восторг беспредельный / Сердцу певучему дан . . ."

121 Tsarskoe Selo Lyceum (1811–1918) was perhaps the most prestigious college in the Russian Empire. It was founded specifically to produce highly educated people for key government positions. The most famous of its graduates was Alexander Pushkin, but during its existence the Lyceum produced hundreds of distinguished citizens in Russian history. In 1918 the Lyceum was permanently closed, and in 1925 its remaining graduates were systematically arrested and sentenced to either death, or 20 years in a concentrations camp (GULAG).

122 Nikolay Gumilev (1886–1921), a Russian poet, literary critic, and translator, was considered to be the founder of the Acmeist school of poetry, a school whose ideal was a compactness of verse and complete clarity of expression. He studied at Tsarskoe Selo Lyceum. Gumilev was married to Anna Akhmatova. He also traveled extensively and was also a notable explorer of Africa, from which he brought an invaluable collection of archeological rarities. In 1921, he was arrested by Cheka and executed shortly thereafter.

123 Anna Akhmatova (Gorenko) (1889–1966) is considered to be one of the best Soviet authors, as well as a seminal translator and literary critic. A woman of incredible will power—her two husbands were arrested and sentenced to death, and her only son (Lev Gumilev, who was to become a professor of history) spent more than ten years in a concentration camp—but she had the moral strength to continue her artistic activity until her very last days.

124 Rainer Maria Rilke (1875–1926), a great Modernist poet of the twentieth century, living in Prague and writing in German. Through Lou Salomé, a close friend of both Nietzsche and Freud, Rilke became acquainted with Russia, which he visited and where he got to know Leo Tolstoy, Ilya Repin, Boris Pasternak, and started a correspondence with Marina Tsvetaeva.

125 This excerpt is from the poem "У камина" ["By the Hearth"] (1910), by Nikolay Gumilev (1886–1921). Duvakin is slightly misremembering it (saying "Временами" instead of "Вечерами"). The original is as follows:

Вечерами к нам подходили львы.
Но трусливых душ не было меж нас,
Мы стреляли в них, целясь между глаз.

126 An excerpt from the poem "Наступление" ["The Attack"] (1914), by Gumilev. There are a couple of misremembered words here as well. The original Russian is as follows:

Мы четвертый день наступаем,
Мы не ели четыре дня.

Но не надо яства земного
В этот страшный и светлый час,
Оттого что Господне слово
Лучше хлеба питает нас.

И залитые кровью недели
Ослепительны и легки.

127 Alexey Surkov (1899–1983) was a minor Soviet poet, remembered for the famous song "Zemlyanka," written on the front in 1941 after an attack, and which became famous throughout the country. The plot of the song is simple: after an attack, the soldier is sitting beside the fire and is writing a letter to his wife. He tells her that every day Death walks only four steps behind.

128 Konstantin Simonov (1915–1979) was a Soviet poet, writer, and playwright. Bakhtin might be right: Simonov never was a great poet. But thanks to his tireless efforts Mikhail Bulgakov's novel, *The Master and Margarita* (1966), was finally published, and all the plays of Eugene O'Neill and Arthur Miller, as well as Hemingway's *For Whom the Bell Tolls*, were translated and published into Russian.

129 A hussar was a soldier of the light cavalry, a type of military originating in Hungary in the fifteenth century. The etymology of the word is unclear and perhaps means "corsair," that is, "someone who sits on a horse."

130 The Cross of Saint George was a state decoration established for soldiers and low-ranking officers in Imperial Russia. It was inaugurated in 1807 by the order of Alexander I.

131 The excerpt is from the poem "Память" ["Memory"] (1921), by Gumilev, one of his last poems, written right before he was arrested. The original Russian text is as follows: "Но святой Георгий тронул дважды / Пулею не тронутую грудь."

Interview 3

In the notes to this interview I use the terms "Russian" and "Soviet" to distinguish between different epochs, using "Russian" to designate individuals whose main productive period falls before the Revolution of 1917, and using "Soviet" for those whose main productive period falls after the Revolution. In instances in which the activities of an individual span the two epochs, I use the composite term "Russian-Soviet."

1 About Anna Akhmatova, see interview 2, n123.

2 Nikolay Gogol (1809–1852) was a preeminent Russian writer, poet, and dramaturg. His works, such as "Nevsky Prospekt," *Dead Souls* (1842), and the comedy *The*

Government Inspector (1836), inspired many future Russian authors, including the young Dostoevsky, who considered Gogol and Pushkin to be the greatest Russian writers.

3 *The Book of Snobs* (1846–1847) gave William Makepeace Thackeray (1811–1863) his first notoriety when it appeared as *The Snobs of England*, in *Punch*. The book introduced the modern meaning of the word "snob."

4 For the Table of Ranks, see interview 2, n46.

5 For Boris Eikhenbaum, see interview 2, n24.

6 Acmeism was a poetic school founded by Nikolay Gumilev and Sergey Gorodetsky around 1910–1912. Its most prominent poets were Anna Akhmatova (in her early years), Osip Mandelstam, and Mikhail Kuzmin. The group met in the Stray Dog Café in Saint Petersburg (see interview 2, n41), all of whom—except for Akhmatova, Gorodetsky, and Kuzmin—became victims of Stalin's repression and were arrested and killed.

7 Osip Mandelstam (1891–1938) was one of the most influential Russian poets of the twentieth century. He was, perhaps, the only one who dared to express openly his dissatisfaction with Stalin by writing the "Stalin Epigram" (1933). Although he read it only to a dozen of his closest friends, someone informed the authorities, and Mandelstam was arrested. After five years in the northern Urals, accompanied by his wife, Mandelstam returned to Moscow, only to be arrested again. This time his health suffered terribly, and he died somewhere near Sakhalin. His gravesite is unknown.

8 Sergey Gorodetsky (1884–1967) was a Russian-Soviet poet and translator. As a poet, Gorodetsky was mediocre, but as a translator, he was outstanding. He dedicated himself to the translation of librettos for operas; he was the first to translate into Russian Beethoven's *Fidelio* and Wagner's *The Mastersingers of Nuremberg* and *Lohengrin*. He also rewrote the libretto for the famous national opera by Mikhail Glinka (1804–1857), *A Life for the Tsar*.

9 Vladimir Narbut (1888–1938) was a Russian poet, writer, and literary critic. Because of his service in the army fighting against the Bolsheviks, he was arrested in 1936 by the НКВД [NKVD] (the Russian acronym stands for National Commissariat of Internal Affairs)—the future KGB—and exiled to Siberia. While in a concentration camp, he was resentenced to death.

10 Mikhail Kuzmin (1872–1936) was a Russian-Soviet poet, translator, and composer. He studied at the Saint Petersburg Conservatory under Rimsky-Korsakov. He was a close friend of Georgy Chicherin (1872–1936), the Minister of Foreign Affairs in the Bolshevik government, which perhaps helped him to survive the purges. Kuzmin is remembered in Russian literary history as a brilliant translator: Apuleius's *The Golden Ass* became a classic in Russia thanks to his efforts, as did the sonnets of Petrarch and Shakespeare, Shakespeare's plays, and Byron's *Don Juan*.

11 About Marina Tsvetaeva, see interview 2, n83.

12 About Vyacheslav Ivanov, see interview 1, n69.

13 *Cor ardens* [*The Burning Heart*] (Moscow, 1911) was Vyacheslav Ivanov's third published collection of poems, dedicated to his wife, Lydia Zinovieva-Annibal (1866–1907), who had recently passed away.

14 Bakhtin refers to the three-volume anthology, edited by his dedicated companion and lover, Olga Shor (pseud. Deschartes [1894–1978]).

15 Theodor Mommsen (1817–1903) was a German classical scholar, historian, journalist, and lawyer. His major work is the five-volume *History of Rome* (Leipzig, 1854–1856), for which he received the 1902 Nobel Prize in Literature.

16 Bakhtin refers here to the pianist Maria Yudina. See interview 2, n62.

17 Mikhail Zenkevich (1886–1973) was a Russian poet and translator. A mediocre poet, Zenkevich was an excellent translator. He translated many of Shakespeare's plays and novels by H. G. Wells. His most significant cultural contribution was perhaps the translation and publication of two volumes of American poetry.

18 Konstantin Balmont (1867–1942) was a prominent Russian Symbolist poet. Able to speak fluently in practically all European languages, he became a translator and a visiting professor at Oxford. After the Revolution, he immigrated to France where he lived until his death. His last years were darkened by a deepening depression and financial difficulties.

19 Lydia Zinovieva-Annibal (1866–1907), the wife of Vyacheslav Ivanov, was a minor writer. Together with her husband Ivanov, she organized her famous literary salon "The Tower" (see interview 2, n112). She died unexpectedly from scarlet fever.

20 Bakhtin here refers to the so-called ménage à trois—the philosophical experimentation with love and marriage that was very popular with Russian bohemians at the beginning of the twentieth century.

21 Duvakin is quoting from the beginning of Sergey Gorodetsky's poem "Адам" ["Adam"], which was published in the journal *Apollo* in 1913. The Russian text is as follows: "Прости, пленительная влага, / И первоздания туман!"

22 The Russian text is as follows: "В прозрачном ветре больше блага / Для сотворенных к жизни стран."

23 For Velimir Khlebnikov, see interview 2, n36.

24 For Vladimir Mayakovsky, see interview 2, n35.

25 For Stepan Skitalets, see interview 2, n97.

26 For Maxim Gorky, see interview 1, n9.

27 For Vladislav Khodasevich, see interview 2, n80.

28 Zoya Lodiy (1886–1957) was a famous Russian-Soviet soprano, a professor at the Saint Petersburg Music Conservatory. Her husband, Sergey Adrianov (1871–1942), was a professor at Saint Petersburg University. *Delo* [*Labor*] was a daily newspaper in Slovenia, left wing, founded in 1959.

29 Vladimir Lenin (1870–1924) knew Gorky personally and met with him many times. He immediately saw great talent in Gorky and strove to make him an emblem of the newly born Soviet literature.

30 The book Bakhtin refers to here is *Проблемы творчества Достоевского* [*Problems of Dostoevsky's Art*], published in 1929. It did not make Bakhtin famous, but it saved his life: Anatoly Lunacharsky (1875–1933), the Minister of Culture and Education of the first Bolshevik government, loved the book, and urged the proper authorities not to send Bakhtin to the GULAG, which would most likely have killed him, but to exile him internally to Kazakhstan. Gorky wrote on his behalf as well.

31 Created in 1934, the NKVD was the most feared Soviet organization, and was instrumental in Stalin's Great Purge (1936–1938).

32 Here and later, these three abbreviations were as Bakhtin and Duvakin used them. It is possible to equate the abbreviations GPU (interview 1, n15), MGB (interview 1, n15), and NKVD (interview 1, n15; interview 2, n36). However, the GPU and

MGB were parts of NKVD, the larger organization; yet they were all essentially doing the same thing: arresting people who were suspected of questioning Communist ideology.

33 Ekaterina Pavlovna Peshkova (1876–1965), the wife of Maxim Gorky, was the first human rights activist in the USSR. It was through her tireless and fearless efforts that the lives of many distinguished writers, artists, and poets were saved during Stalin's massive purges.

34 Vasily Rozanov (1856–1919), a Russian philosopher and the first to write about Dostoevsky's genius as a religious philosopher, made significant contributions to the study of Dostoevsky.

35 Georgy Gachev (1929–2008) was a Soviet literary critic, and a student and follower of Bakhtin. Gachev made significant contributions to the studies of Gorky's work. Due to his unorthodox views, which contradicted traditional Soviet ideology, his essays about Gorky were not published until the 1990s.

36 Vadim Kozhinov (1930–2001) was a prolific Soviet literary critic, and one of the three young scholars from the Gorky Institute in Moscow who "rediscovered" Bakhtin in the late 1950s (the other two were Gachev and Bocharov). His book on Tyutchev was an academic bestseller. Kozhinov helped Bakhtin publish his revised (1963) *Problems of Dostoevsky's Poetics* (first edition, 1929), and his book on Rabelais, *Rabelais and His World* (1965).

37 Sergey Bocharov (1929–2017) was a prominent Russian literary scholar. His first book was an analysis of Tolstoy's *War and Peace*, and he authored over 350 articles about such classic Russian writers as Khodasevich, Andreev, Gorky, Pushkin, Dostoevsky, and Gogol. Bocharov was consultant and lead research scholar for Bakhtin's collected works, *M. M. Bakhtin. Sobranie sochinenii* (Moscow, 1996–2011), in six volumes.

38 *The Life of Matvey Kozemyakin* (1910) is a novel Gorky wrote while living in Italy, re-thinking the meaning of his life and the possible negative repercussions of the upcoming revolution in Russia.

39 The unfinished, multivolume novel, *The Life of Klim Samgin* (1927–1937), is perhaps Gorky's most dramatic fiction. It is centered on the internal tragedy of Klim Samgin, the offspring of a family of Russian intellectuals, who is unable to find a place for himself in Russia's political climate at the turn of the twentieth century.

40 From the Greek ἀγέλαστος (agélastos, "not laughing").

41 Stepan Kutuzov is one of the important personages in Gorky's novel *The Life of Klim Samgin*.

42 For Gorky's play *The Lower Depths* (1902) (see interview 2, n69).

43 Luka is one of the most important characters in the play *The Lower Depths* (1902). The play, set in the late nineteenth century, focuses on social outcasts living in a shelter. The residents of the shelter are briefly uplifted by a newcomer, Luka, who listens carefully to their stories, offers advice, and engenders illusions, thus giving them hope. In the end, he disappears just as suddenly as he arrived. Broken by this fact, a drunkard actor commits suicide from despair.

44 It should be noted, again, that Bakhtin never officially graduated from university. He is telling a fib here (see also interview 1, n73).

45 The February Revolution (1917) was the first of two consecutive revolutions in Russia. On February 27, the spontaneous protests of soldiers and workers quickly

escalated into an actual revolution, which resulted in the abdication of Tsar Nicholas II and the election of a Provisional Government that was then overthrown in a Bolshevik coup in October of the same year.

46 Saint Petersburg was renamed Petrograd in 1914, when war was declared on Germany. In 1924, the city was renamed Leningrad to commemorate Vladimir Lenin. The name Saint Petersburg was restored to the city by popular referendum in 1991. So, the sequence runs: Saint Petersburg—Petrograd—Leningrad—Saint Petersburg.

47 The Socialist Revolutionaries were called "SRs" [эсеры]. They represented the Socialist Revolutionary Party, the largest political party from the pre-Revolution period, totaling 1,000,000 members after the February Revolution. But their success was short-lived: after the October Revolution, many party leaders were systematically repressed then killed; some of them voluntarily went into exile, to save their lives (see also n54).

48 Alexander Kerensky (1881–1970) was the head of the Provisional Government between the February Revolution and October Revolution. A lawyer by training, he knew how to speak well, but he did not know how to govern. Although warned many times about the coup that the Bolsheviks were preparing against him, he did nothing to prevent it, and lost everything. He escaped from the Winter Palace in the car of the U.S. ambassador under the U.S. flag. Then he fled to Finland, and later France. When Hitler took over France, Kerensky moved to the United States, where he taught for some time at Stanford University. He died at ninety years of age in New York.

49 Leon Trotsky (b. Leiba Bronshtein) (1879–1940) was the second most important figure in the Bolshevik government; he was the creator of the Russian Red Army. After Lenin's death in 1924, Trotsky's influence began to wane; by 1927 he was stripped of all previous appointments and, in 1929, forced into exile. In 1936, he settled in Mexico, where he was welcomed by Frida Kahlo and Diego Rivera. In 1940 an agent of NKVD, Ramon Mercader, snuck into Trotsky's villa and killed him with an axe.

50 Gregory Zinoviev (1883–1936) was an important figure in the Bolshevik government. It was he who warned Kerensky about the Bolshevik coup. His stand against the "red terror" distanced him from Lenin. After Lenin's death, Zinoviev helped Stalin rise to power. As an "Old Bolshevik" he was gradually stripped of all his positions in the 1930s, then arrested and shot, together with Lev Kamenev (see interview 2, n86).

51 Felix Dzerzhinsky (1877–1926) was the comrade-in-arms of Lenin; after the Revolution he became the head of Cheka ("Special Committee") that later would evolve into the NKVD, then the KGB (see interview 1, n15). He wielded significant power and was feared by Stalin himself. In 1926, while reporting to Party leaders about the corruption and bureaucracy that had taken over the country, he became ill and died the same day, presumably from a heart attack. However, some scholars suspect, perhaps with reason, that Stalin ordered his poisoning.

52 Andrey Vyshinsky (1883–1954) served as attorney general and was one of the major supporters of Stalin's Great Purge. At the 1945 post-war conference he attended in Yalta, he met Churchill and Roosevelt. Later he served as the USSR's representative to the UN.

53 Government by mob rule.

54 Pavel Milyukov (1859–1943) was a Minister of Foreign Affairs in the Provisional Government headed by Kerensky. Milyukov was the leader of the Constitutional Democratic Party (Kadets, see interview 2, n43) that was in opposition to the Bolsheviks; after the Revolution he fled to the West. He lived in France until his death.

55 Peter Stolypin (1862–1911) was a prime minister under the rule of the last Russian tsar, Nicholas II. Stolypin is remembered as one of the great reformers whose ideas, if developed in full, might have saved Russia from the Bolshevik Revolution. He fearlessly continued his reformist efforts in spite of eleven attempts to end his life. He was brutally assassinated in 1911, in Kiev (see also interview 2, n45).

56 The kolkhoz was a form of collective farming in the Soviet Union. Kolkhozes were not formed voluntarily but were coercively implemented from above: in 1929 the Communist Party ordered the collectivization of all free peasants' property. People were forced to become members of a kolkhoz whether they wanted to or not, and brutal methods were used to bring people into them. As a consequence, the productivity of these collective farms was very low, and in 1931–1933 the country went through the most terrible famine in Russian history, which led to about 7,000,000 deaths.

57 Grigori Rasputin (1869–1916), although a peasant, acquired world-wide fame as a personal friend of Tsar Nicholas II and an intimate confidant to his wife, the Empress Alexandra. He served as a "healer" for the tsar and his son, Alexey. Rasputin's power was most pronounced during World War I, when Nicholas left the palace to oversee the fighting of the Russian army on the front, leaving his wife in charge of domestic affairs. Rasputin acquired something of a free reign before his assassination by a group of disgruntled Russian nobility. His role in Russian history has been the subject of great debate for the last hundred years.

58 About this cabaret, see interview 2, n41.

59 This is what the guests who did not belong to the "circle" were called in those cafés.

60 The "Comedians' Resting Place" café followed the traditions of the closed "Stray Dog." It remained open from 1915 through 1919. Among its famous guests were Mayakovsky and Gumilev, Blok and Bryusov, Leonid Andreev and Anatoly Lunacharsky. Vsevolod Meyerhold staged there his famous comedy *Colombina's Scarf.* The café's walls were decorated by many talented artists, and the title of one of their artworks—the *Comedians' Resting Place,* created by Sudeykin—was chosen to be the café's official name.

61 On Kuzmin, see n10.

62 For Nevsky Prospect, see interview 2, n44.

63 This café did not exist for long.

64 For Ivan Rukavishnikov, see interview 2, n96.

65 Georgy Shengeli (1894–1956) was a Russian-Soviet poet, critic, and translator. He translated a great deal of French poetry into Russian, but not very skillfully. Due to political caution, Shengeli did not write any poetry for the last thirty years of his life, instead concentrating on literary translations.

66 Sergey Yesenin (1895–1925) was one of the most prominent Russian poets of the early twentieth century. A peasant by birth, he was decently educated and moved to Saint Petersburg, where he was welcomed by the artistic Bohemia. In 1921, he married Isadora Duncan and traveled with her to Europe and the United States (see also interview 1, n71). He returned disappointed with both his family life and

the West. But the NKVD never forgave Yesenin for this trip abroad: in 1925 he was forced into a psychiatric clinic, from which he escaped to Leningrad. A few days later, he was found dead in a room in hotel Astoria. Many scholars believe that Yesenin was murdered by the NKVD, but the official version was that the poet committed suicide.

67 Aleksey Kruchenykh (1886–1968) was a Futurist poet. He was the last of those who personally knew Vladimir Mayakovsky. After Mayakovsky's death and the massive repressions, Kruchenykh maintained a low profile and stopped writing poetry. Later, after Stalin's death, he conducted valuable research on Yesenin, whom he knew personally.

68 *Zaum* can be defined as experimental poetic language characterized by indeterminacy of meaning, often used by poets like Khlebnikov (see interview 2, n36) and Kruchenykh.

69 For David Burliuk, see interview 2, n39.

70 Vladimir Burliuk (1886–1916) was David's younger brother. He joined the avant-garde movement in his youth. Together with Kazimir Malevich, he illustrated many of his Futurist friends' books. Vladimir was drafted into military service when World War I started and was killed during an attack in 1916.

71 Pyotr Avdeevich Kuzko (1884–1969) was a literary critic and Soviet bureaucrat.

72 *LITO* was a Bolshevik literary journal issued by the Soviet Literary Department [Литературное отделение, ЛИТО] during the 1920s.

73 In Russian: "Иль в Советской Москве назначена / Klassische Walpurgisnacht" ("Klassische Walpurgisnacht," 1920).

74 In the pagan tradition, Walpurgis Night (falling between April 30 and May 1) is when witches gather on the top of a mountain for an orgiastic party. The legend originated in the eighth century, when pagans gathered at a sacred place to dance and collect herbs, which were supposed to acquire magic powers during Walpurgis Night.

75 "The Unusual Adventure . . ." [Необычайное приключение] (1920).

76 Mayakovsky, "A Cloud in Pants" (1914–1915) [Облако в штанах].

77 Mayakovsky, "War and Peace" (1916) [Война и мир].

78 Mayakovsky, "At the Top of My Voice" (1929–1930) [Во весь голос].

79 In Russian:

Я знаю силу слов, я знаю слов набат.
Они не те, которым рукоплещут ложи. (1928)

This is an unfinished poem by Mayakovsky.

80 In Russian, the poem continues:

От слов таких срываются гроба
шагать четверкою своих дубовых ножек.
Бывает, выбросят, не напечатав, не издав,
но слово мчится, подтянув подпруги,
звенит века, и подползают поезда
лобзать поэзии мозолистые руки.

Bakhtin is confusing "лобзать" [kiss] with "лизать" [lick].

81 In Russian, the poem-fragment ends with those lines:

Я знаю силу слов. Глядится пустяком,
опавшим лепестком под каблуками танца,
но человек душой губами костяком.

82 ROSTA (POCTA in Russian) existed between 1919 and 1921. Its members produced a series of satirical posters. Mayakovsky, who was a talented graphic artist, created a series of interesting posters himself. Kazimir Malevich also worked for ROSTA.

83 "A Slap in the Face of Public Taste" ["Пощёчина общественному вкусу"] (1912) was the official manifesto of the Russian Futurist movement that included poets such as Vladimir Mayakovsky, David Buriuk, Aleksey Kruchenykh, and Velimir Khlebnikov.

84 VHUTEMAS (ВХУТЕМАС in Russian) was the first art school founded by the Bolshevik government in 1920. Later, it became the Russian Academy of the Arts, Sculpture, and Architecture.

85 In Russian, the phrase Duvakin uses, "игровой момент ["the play aspect"] suggests two possible meanings: "playfulness," and as pertaining to a play on stage, "acting a role." Both are assumed in this instance.

86 Samuil Marshak (1887–1964) was one of the few fortunate Soviet authors who survived the Great Purge. In his youth, Marshak spent some years in England and studied at the University of London. After his return to the USSR, he created the first Soviet theater for children, for which he wrote frequently. He will always be remembered as the best translator of Shakespeare's sonnets and numerous plays into Russian. He also translated ballads by Robert Burns, the novels of Jane Austen, and the poetry of William Blake, William Wordsworth, John Keats, Robert Louis Stevenson, Lewis Carroll, Rudyard Kipling, among many others. Toward the end of his life, Marshak officially supported Alexander Solzhenitsyn's first novel, *One Day in the Life of Ivan Denisovich* (1962), and went to court to defend Joseph Brodsky.

87 For Lev Pumpyansky, see interview 1, n26.

88 The Novo-Sventsyansky Gymnasium [Свенцянская гимназия] was an institute of higher education in Nevel.

89 Vitebsk is the second oldest city (after Polotsk) in Belorussia, founded in 1021 by the Princess Olga on the River Vitba that gave the city its name. In Bakhtin's time, the city had a population of about 115,000 people. Mark Chagall was born in Vitebsk and spent the first half of his life there.

90 Marc Chagall (1887–1985) was perhaps the greatest representative of twentieth-century Russian avant-garde art.

91 Bakhtin's native city. About Orel, see interview 1, n2.

92 For Matvey Kagan, see interview 1, n58.

93 Georgy Koliubakin (1892–?) worked at the Unified Labor School in Nevel and ran the pharmacy at the local hospital.

94 The Siege of Leningrad (also called the Leningrad Blockade) by the Nazis started on September 8, 1941, and lasted until January 27, 1944, exactly 900 days. When the siege began, the city had very little food stored, so the famine started almost immediately. More than 1,000,000 civilians died. Leningrad never surrendered to the Germans and strove to maintain its cultural life despite the adversity: the 7th Symphony of Shostakovich was composed at this time. The continuous air strikes did not prevent the Leningrad libraries from remaining open during the siege. The city factories also continued to produce tanks that were immediately shipped to the front (see also interview 1, n13).

95 The Vitebsk Musical Conservatory opened in 1918. While in Vitebsk, Bakhtin was a professor, teaching courses on aesthetics.

96 Nikolay Malko (1883–1961) studied conducting with Rimsky-Korsakov, Lyadov, and Glazunov. He became the leading conductor of the Mariinsky Theatre (Saint Petersburg), but after the Revolution, due to the widespread famine, he relocated to Vitebsk, where he headed the Vitebsk Conservatory. In 1925, Malko left the USSR, established himself in Chicago, and then moved to Australia, where he became the chief conductor of the Sydney Symphonic Orchestra. He had many famous students, including Evgeny Mravinsky and Leo Ginzburg.

97 The Mariinsky Theatre is the second most important opera and ballet theater in Russia. It was founded in 1783 by order of the Empress Catherine the Great. Among its most notable twentieth-century ballet dancers were Rudolf Nureyev and Mikhail Baryshnikov.

98 Nikolay Dubasov (1869–1935) was a Russian pianist, the laureate of the first Anton Rubinstein Competition (the world's most prestigious musical competition at that time) in 1890. Later he became a professor at the Saint Petersburg Conservatory.

99 Valentin Presnyakov (1877–1966) was a Russian ballet master who worked at the Mariinsky Theatre, then retired and moved to Vitebsk. There, he founded the first Russian school for children with Down Syndrome and (together with Nikolay Malko) the Vitebsk Musical Conservatory.

100 Kazimir Malevich (1879–1935) was Russia's/USSR's most famous artist, founder of Suprematism—one of the earliest forms of abstract art of the new era. At Vitebsk, Malevich became the leading professor of the newly founded fine arts academy and practically directed the entire school.

101 "Suprematism" was an abstract art movement founded by Kazimir Malevich in 1913, focusing on geometric forms. Invented by Malevich, "Suprematism" (from Polish, Malevich's native language) signified for him the highest level in the development of painting in which the energy of light dominates everything else. Later, the word acquired a philosophical meaning as well. The famous triptych—*Black Square, Black Circle*, and *Black Cross*—was shown during the "Last Futurist Exhibition of Painting 0,10" in Saint Petersburg in 1915, and now it is considered to be the height of revolutionary art.

102 Ivan Vishnyak (1853–?) was a wealthy banker in Vitebsk. He built a luxurious house for himself and his family but had to flee after the Revolution. His house was nationalized by the Bolsheviks and later given to Marc Chagall to establish the People's College of the Arts.

103 Kazimir Malevich never finished school. He tried unsuccessfully three times to become a student at the Imperial Academy of Arts. When asked about his education, in all official forms he would write: "self-taught."

104 In fact, Malevich published seven books during his lifetime. All of them were dedicated to the theoretical explanation of the meaning of art as he understood it.

105 Bakhtin is mistaken here: by the end of his life Malevich indeed had some psychological problems, but he died at home, from prostate cancer.

106 "Supremats" is used by Bakhtin here to refer to Malevich's paintings.

107 Yehuda Pen (1854–1937) was an important leader of the so-called Jewish Renaissance in Russia at the beginning of the twentieth century. Although remembered as Marc Chagall's teacher, Pen had many distinguished students who later became internationally known. Pen himself lived quietly in Vitebsk, teaching painting. On a few occasions he organized exhibitions of some of his most talented students. Chagall, after founding the Art College, immediately invited Pen to serve as a

distinguished professor there. He was killed at home, at age eighty-two, perhaps by agents of the NKVD.

108 The Wanderers [Peredvizhniki] was a group of painters associated with the Russian Realism movement. The group was born in 1863 after fourteen rebellious artists left the Imperial Academy of the Arts to form the independent Artists' Cooperative Society. The Wanderers specialized in narrative genre paintings. Their work reflected populist themes that celebrated the beauty and honesty of the peasantry, the Russian countryside, and that were critical of the corruption permeating society at large.

109 Alexandra Azarh-Granovskaya (1892–1980) was a prominent Soviet theater director and professor.

110 Solomon Mikhoels (1890–1948) was a Soviet actor, the director of the Moscow State Jewish Theater, and chairman of the Jewish anti-fascist committee during World War II. In 1943, he traveled to the United States and Canada for fundraising purposes. Later, he wrote a letter to Stalin advocating for the creation of a new Jewish Autonomous region but never received a response. In 1948, while on a business trip in Belarus, he was murdered by NKVD agents, but the official version of his death was that he was hit by a truck while crossing the street.

111 Lilya Brik (Kagan) (1891–1978), known as the "Muse of the Russian Avant-garde," hosted one of the most famous literary salons of the twentieth century. Mayakovsky's "A Cloud in Pants" was dedicated to her. Until her last days, Brik maintained close contacts with some of the most interesting people of the twentieth century: Alexander Solzhenitsyn, Mstislav Rostropovich, Pablo Neruda, Fillip and Polina Rothschild, and Yves Saint Laurent. At the age of 87, immobilized after breaking her hip, she committed suicide in Moscow.

112 For Lossky, see interview 2, n13.

113 Anton Delvig (1798–1831) was a Russian poet of the Romantic period. He is best remembered for his close friendship with Alexander Pushkin. They both studied at the Tsarskoe Selo Lyceum, graduated in the same year, and remained intimate friends until Delvig's death from typhus.

114 Polotsk is the oldest city in Belarus.

115 Pavel Nikolayevich Medvedev (1892–1938) was a literary critic and theorist, and professor at Saint Petersburg University. While in Vitebsk, Medvedev was elected mayor of the city and helped establish both the Arts College and Vitebsk University. He worked closely with Chagall and Malevich. It was he who officially invited Lev Pumpyansky and Valentin Voloshinov to teach in Vitebsk. Medvedev and Bakhtin met there. In Saint Petersburg, Medvedev became one of the most popular professors. His public lectures on literature were very successful and attracted hundreds of people. In 1938, Medvedev was suddenly arrested by the NKVD, for unknown reasons, and within three weeks he was sentenced to death. His gravesite is unknown. The work on Blok, which Bakhtin mentions, *Aleksandr Blok's Creative Path* [*Tvorcheskii put A. A. Bloka*], was published in 1922.

116 For Valentin Voloshinov, see interview 2, n73.

117 Tatiana Shchepkina-Kupernik (1874–1952) was a famous Russian-Soviet actress, writer, and prominent translator. Her translations of Western classics are outstanding: Shakespeare, Lope de Vega, Calderón de la Barca, Moliere, and Lewis Carroll's *Alice in Wonderland* (1865) are especially worthy of note.

118 For Felix Dzerzhinsky, see n51.

119 Alexander Stromin (1902–1938) was one of the few honest and compassionate people who worked for the NKVD during the Great Purge. Later Bakhtin found out that Stromin was arrested and sentenced to death.

120 Sergey Kirov (1886–1934) was a prominent Bolshevik, the leader of the Leningrad Communist Party. His influence among Communist Party members was growing fast, which, presumably, angered Stalin who was always suspicious of his successful colleagues. Kirov was shot to death on December 1, 1934, by an unemployed worker, Leonid Nikolaev. Historians are still arguing over the real reasons behind Kirov's assassination: some believe that Nikolaev was given a secret order by the NKVD to kill Kirov, while others think that his reasons were personal (Nikolaev's wife was Kirov's secret lover). In any case, Kirov's death became the official pretext for the beginning of the Great Purge.

121 Bakhtin refers here to the article, written in accordance with Bolshevik orders whose aim was to "expose the truth" about those so-called religious and philosophical circles in Leningrad that dared to discuss Kant, Hegel, Plato, and Spinoza. The article condemned all those who organized and participated in such circles and called them nothing but "ashes of oaks" (that is, insignificant followers of ancient ideas that had outlived their purpose).

Interview 4

In the notes to this interview I use the terms "Russian" and "Soviet" to distinguish between different epochs, using "Russian" to designate individuals whose main productive period falls before the Revolution of 1917, and using "Soviet" for those whose main productive period falls after the Revolution. In instances in which the activities of an individual span the two epochs, I use the composite term "Russian-Soviet."

1 Academic Sergey Fyodorovich Platonov (1860–1933), together with his colleague Yevgeny Viktorovich Tarle (1874–1955), were accused by the NKVD of preparing a coup against the Soviet State. The NKVD "discovered" that Platonov aspired to become the prime minister, and Tarle the minister of foreign affairs. Both were arrested and exiled because of this presumed conspiracy to restore a capitalist government.

2 The Industrial Party Trial was a famous Soviet trial in 1930 in which a large number of academics and engineers were arrested for "sabotage." Platonov and Tarle happened to be in that group. Because Stalin was not yet in total control, all participants in this "counter-revolutionary organization" were only sentenced to ten years in concentration camps.

3 Lev Ramzin (1887–1948) was a professor of engineering who was also included in the Industrial Party Trial. He betrayed all his friends and colleagues.

4 Anton Kartashev (1875–1960) was the last Minister of Religion under the Provisional Government headed by Kerensky between February 27 and October 25, 1917.

5 For Alexander Kerensky, see interview 3, n48.

6 For Vladimir Solovyov, see interview 1, n44.

7 "The Brothers Tur" was the literary pseudonym of two critics, Leonid Davidovich Tubelsky (1905–1961) and Pyotr Lvovich Ryzhey (1908–1971); thus, the acronym:

Tubelsky and Ryzhey equals TuR. They often published sharp attacks on "suspicious" persons in government newspapers.

8 "Kukryniksy" ["Кукрыниксы"] was a group of three Soviet artists—Kupriyanov, Krylov, and Nikolay Sokolov. Their mostly satirical work became especially famous after the invasion of Hitler in 1941. They are considered to be classical representatives of Soviet political caricature. For a long time, it was rumored that they were connected with the GPU/NKVD, but now historians believe this was not the case.

9 The Lubyanka Building was the main headquarters of Cheka, GPU, NKVD, and the KGB between 1919 and 1991. Now it belongs to the FSB (Federal Security Bureau). The building is located in Moscow, not far from the Kremlin, on Lubyansky Square. The Lubyanka Building also housed an internal prison.

10 The DPZ was opened in 1875 as the first of Russia's "exemplary" preliminary prisons, where people were kept under arrest while the authorities were still preparing the evidence for the court hearings. One of the most famous prisoners of the DPZ on Shpalernaya Street was Vladimir Lenin.

11 Gorokhovaya Street is one of the longest and most important central roadways in Saint Petersburg. Following 1918, one of the buildings on Gorokhovaya housed the headquarters of Cheka (headed by Felix Dzerzhinsky).

12 For Felix Dzerzhinsky, see interview 3, n51.

13 Vyacheslav Menzhinsky (1874–1934) followed Dzerzhinsky as the head of NKVD. He was a very talented man, fluent in ten languages, including Arabic, who spent all his talent and energy on following Stalin's order to initiate the Great Purge (1936–1938) of the Russian intelligentsia, founding the system of concentration camps—GULAG (interview 2, n98). He died at home of heart failure.

14 Vasily Komarovich (1894–1942) was a Soviet historian of literature. His favorite writer was Fyodor Dostoevsky, and his contribution to Dostoevsky's scholarship is enormous. Komarovich also prepared the first complete works of Alexander Pushkin and Nikolay Gogol (1938). His erudition was extensive, and his lectures enthralled students, who filled up the auditorium, sitting even on the steps, or on folding chairs brought from home. Komarovich starved to death during the Nazi blockade of Leningrad. His gravesite is unknown.

15 The legend of Kitezh originated in the thirteenth century, when the Mongols conquered Russia. When they arrived at Kitezh, the locals did not prepare for a battle, but chose to pray instead. Suddenly, the entire city began to be submerged under water, and soon the land where the city used to be was replaced by a beautiful lake, now called Svetloyar. Kitezh is known as "The Russian Atlantis."

16 This novel by Dostoevsky (1875) is often seen as a failure. Komarovich rehabilitated the novel's reputation and explained its importance for the creative trajectory of Dostoevsky, and how it paved the way for *The Brothers Karamazov*.

17 Gorky was originally called Nizhny Novgorod. It is an ancient city in the center of Russia, founded in 1221. From 1932 until 1990 the city's name was "Gorky," in honor of Maxim Gorky.

18 Boris Engelhardt (1887–1942) was a Russian-Soviet literary critic and translator. During the 1930s he prudently focused on translations, but even that did not protect him from political persecution. He was arrested and sent to a concentra-

tion camp. At the moment of his arrest, his first wife, a niece of the famous Russian writer Vsevolod Garshin (see n19), committed suicide. Engelhardt, together with his second wife, who was a very talented poet, died from starvation during the Leningrad Blockade.

19 Vsevolod Garshin (1855–1888) was a prominent Russian writer, the creator of the Russian "long short story" or novella. Since childhood Garshin had experienced psychological problems, which became more pronounced by the time he reached his thirties. At the age of thirty-three years, he committed suicide.

20 Semyon Frank (1877–1950) was a Russian philosopher, religious thinker, and historian of Russian philosophy. In 1922, he was exiled from the USSR on the "Philosophical Ship." He then lived and died in Great Britain.

21 Ivan Ilyin (1883–1954) was a Russian philosopher, writer, and literary critic. From the beginning of the Revolution, Ilyin took a stand against the Bolsheviks, and in 1922, together with 245 other people, he left the USSR on a German boat called "The Philosophical Ship." The cream of the Russian intelligentsia was exiled by a special order by Lenin, who proposed to replace the massive death penalties with permanent exiles. Ilyin lived and died in Switzerland.

22 The Solovki Prison Camp was created in 1923 and soon became the largest in the series of northern concentration camps. The prison was housed in the Solovetsky Monastery—a Russian Orthodox monastery founded in 1420 on Solovetsky Island in the White Sea. During the ten years of its existence, about 7,500 prisoners died from starvation there.

23 Kem is a small town in the north of Russia, situated on the Kem River that flows into the White Sea. In 1920, the Bolsheviks founded the first prison camp there. The camp later became a middle transit point for those who were sent to Solovki.

24 Kazakhstan was the second largest Soviet republic (after the Russian Federation). During Soviet times Kazakhstan received hundreds of thousands of political prisoners. Bakhtin and his wife were exiled to the town of Kustanai in northwestern Kazakhstan, where he worked as an accountant for a pig farm.

25 Ivan Andreevsky (1894–1976) was a psychiatrist and a prominent religious philosopher. He was arrested multiple times. During World War II, he immigrated first to Germany, then to the United States. He died in New York.

26 OBERIU [ОБЭРИУ in Russian] was a group of writers and artists that existed between 1927 and 1930 in Leningrad. They proclaimed the beginning of a new era for the arts and refused to write in the standard forms. The most prominent in the group were Daniil Kharms (1905–1942), Nikolay Zabolotsky (1903–1958), and Konstantin Vaginov (1899–1934). Kharms was arrested in 1941 and died in a psychiatric clinic, intentionally starved to death. Zabolotsky spent ten years in concentration camps. Vaginov died in 1934 from tuberculosis.

27 Konstantin Vaginov (1899–1934) was a prominent Russian poet and writer whose works were forgotten during Soviet times. Vaginov belonged to many literary groups but managed to preserve his individuality. Mikhail Bakhtin had a high opinion of Vaginov's originality and invited him to the literary salon of Maria Yudina, where Vaginov met many interesting people: Sollertinsky, Pumpyansky, Medvedev, and others. Vaginov died from tuberculosis in 1934, but his prose found new readers in the 1990s when most of Vaginov's works were republished.

28 Nikolay Zabolotsky (1903–1958) was a lyrical poet. He could have become a great philosopher as well, if he had been born at the right time: the Revolution turned

Zabolotsky's life upside down. In 1932, his poetic book, the fruit of his philosophical inquiries, was stopped from publication. A few years later Zabolotsky was arrested and sent to concentration camps, where he spent ten years. After the exile, Zabolotsky returned to Moscow and continued his work. Unfortunately, his health was completely destroyed, and the poet died shortly after his 55th birthday.

29 Fyodor Sologub (1863–1927) was a Russian Symbolist poet, novelist, and essayist. On the Union of Soviet Writers, see interview 6, n83.

30 Anastasiya Chebotarevskaya (1876–1921) was a Russian writer, dramaturg, and translator. She translated many works by Stendhal, Maupassant, and Roman Rolland. During her marriage to Fyodor Sologub, she dedicated her life to him and his success. In 1921, frustrated with life in the USSR and her inability to leave the country, she committed suicide by jumping into the cold waters of the Neva River from a bridge.

31 The Neva River crosses Saint Petersburg and connects Lake Ladoga with the Gulf of Finland.

32 "The Monument" is Horace's *Odes*, Bk. 3, poem 30). The same motif was used by Derzhavin for his eighteenth-century ode of the same title; Pushkin used the same idea and wrote one of his most famous poems, "Памятник," in the early nineteenth century. For Lev Vasilyevich, see interview 1, n26.

33 Gavrila Derzhavin (1743–1816) was one of the greatest Russian poets before Alexander Pushkin, as well as an important statesman.

34 Akim Volynsky (1863–1926) was a prominent Russian literary and theatrical critic, the husband of the prima ballerina Olga Spessivtseva (1895–1991). Volynsky was a great connoisseur and admirer of Leonardo da Vinci and Dostoevsky; he wrote two excellent monographs about them. He died in dire poverty.

35 Fyodor Teternikov was the birth name of Fyodor Sologub. Sologub was indeed a poor provincial school teacher in his early years, barely able to make ends meet.

36 A selection of Volynsky's writings on ballet were translated into English by Stanley Rabinowitz as *Ballet's Magic Kingdom* (New Haven: Yale University Press, 2010).

37 *The Enchanted Goblet* [*Чародейная чаша*] (1922) and *Only Love* [*Одна любовь*] (1921) are two poetry collections by Fyodor Sologub.

38 Alexandra Chebotarevskaya (1869–1925) was the sister of Fyodor Sologub's wife, Anastasiya Chebotarevskaya. Like her sister, she also committed suicide by jumping into the Moscow River in February 1925.

39 *The Petty Demon* [*Мелкий бес*] (1905) is Sologub's most important novel. The book became a Russian bestseller, and during Sologub's life was published eleven times.

40 *Nav's spells* [*Навьи чары*] was the projected title for Sologub's trilogy, *The Created Legend* (1907). Critics received the novel coldly. The first who tried to defend the artistic qualities of it was Sologub's wife, Anastasiya, but even after her brilliant article the novel did not generate much interest.

41 *Bad Dreams* [*Тяжёлые сны*] (1895), Fyodor Sologub's first novel, is considered to be the first decadent novel in Russian literature.

42 Peredonov is the main character in *The Petty Demon*.

43 Mikhail Saltykov-Shchedrin (1826–1889) was a Russian satirical writer; his aphorisms are frequently quoted to this day.

44 Little Judas [*Иудушка*] is the nickname for the main character of Saltykov-Shchedrin's novel *The Golovlyov Family* (1880), the most perverse and amorally evil of the sons in the family.

45 Velikiye Luki, one of the oldest Russian cities, possesses a rich cultural history. It is located near the western border of Russia. In 2016, the city celebrated its 850th anniversary.

46 Duvakin is incorrect. The excerpt is from Nikolay Gumilev's poem "Умный дьявол" ["The Smart Devil"] (1906). The translation is adapted from Yevgeny Bonver's. The Russian text is as follows:

Мой старый друг, мой верный Дьявол,
Пропел мне песенку одну:
"Всю ночь моряк в пустыне плавал,
А на заре пошел ко дну."

Кругом вставали волны-стены,
Спадали, вспенивались вновь,
Пред ним неслась, белее пены,
Его великая любовь.
Он слышал зов, когда он плавал:

"О, верь мне, я не обману . . .
Но помни,- молвил умный Дьявол,-
Он на заре пошел ко дну."

47 The excerpt is from Sologub's poem "О смерть! я твой" (1894). The Russian text is as follows:

О смерть! я твой. Повсюду вижу
Одну тебя—и ненавижу
Очарования земли.

48 Bakhtin misremembers. There is one more stanza following the one he claims is the last. The Russian text of the quotation is as follows:

Не мне, обвеянному тайной
Твоей красы необычайной,
Не мне к ногам её упасть.

49 The actual ending of the poem reads in Russian:

Когда на них уже упала,
Прозрачней чистого кристалла,
Твоя холодная слеза.

50 Again, Bakhtin is misremembering the order of the lines (changing one of the words in the original: "запекшимся" instead of "томящимся"), which follows in Russian:

Что было, будет вновь,
Что было, будет не однажды.
С водой смешаю кровь
Устам, томящимся от жажды.

51 The excerpt is from the poem "Что было, будет вновь . . . ," from 1907.

52 Alexander Dobrolyubov (1876–1944) was a lesser known poet associated with the Russian Symbolist movement. Dobrolyubov could be called a "mystical" Russian Symbolist. After publishing a few books of poetry, and receiving some recognition for them, he suddenly renounced literature altogether, and spent the rest of his life traveling around Russia.

53 Convicts' squads [арестантские роты] were created by the Corps of Engineers in Russia in 1823 by an order of Tsar Nicholas I. During his reign, the prisons in Siberia became so full it was decided that it would be better to make them join convicts' squads, where they would work for the good of the country without pay. They built bridges and dams, paved roads, dug canals, etc.

54 For Zinaida Gippius, see interview 2, n51.

55 Nikolay Minsky (1855–1937) was a Russian poet and religious philosopher. Valery Bryusov and Alexander Blok both considered Minsky to be the first Russian Symbolist poet. He immigrated permanently to France before the Revolution.

56 Giacomo Leopardi (1798–1837) was an Italian lyrical poet, often seen as a forerunner of the Decadent literary movement. The poetry of Leopardi was brilliantly translated into Russian by Anna Akhmatova.

57 For Baudelaire in Russian, see interview 1, n61.

58 Théophile Gautier (1811–1872) was connected with the schools of Romanticism and Parnassus. He was called "magicien des lettres françaises" by Baudelaire, who dedicated his own book of poetry to Gautier—*Les Fleurs du mal* (1857).

59 Richard Wagner's (1813–1883) last opera, *Parsifal* (1882), had the greatest influence on German Romanticism.

60 For Innokenty Annensky, see interview 1, n70.

61 This is an excerpt from Paul Verlaine's poem "Languor" ["Томление"], translated by Annensky. The Russian text is as follows (Bakhtin changes "золотым" to "медленным" in his rendition):

Я—бледный римлянин эпохи Апостата.
Покуда портик мой от гула бойни тих,
Я стилем золотым слагаю акростих,
Где умирает блеск последнего заката заката.
Уже не розами, а скукой грудь объята . . .

62 The Russian reads:

Мира восторг беспредельный
Сердцу певучему дан.

63 The excerpt is from the poem, "Oh, spring without an end . . ." ["О, весна без конца и без краю . . ."] (1907) by Alexander Blok. The Russian is as follows:

За мученья, за гибель—я знаю -
Все равно: принимаю тебя.

Bakhtin replaces "мученья" with "паденье" in his quote.

64 Blok's words are: "Без конца и без краю мечта" ["Dream without an end or a beginning"]. Duvakin is misremembering it as "Без конца и без краю весна."

65 In Russian: "Узнаю тебя, жизнь! Принимаю! / И приветствую звоном щита!"

66 In Russian:

Чтобы вечным быть для песнопенья,
Надо в жизни этой пасть . . .

67 Here Bakhtin makes a factual mistake: the translation is not by Zhukovsky, but by Afanasy Fet. For Fet, see interview 1, n64.

68 Vasily Zhukovsky (1783–1852) was a distinguished Russian poet and the founder of Romanticism. Besides being an excellent poet, perhaps the best one before Alexander Pushkin, Zhukovsky was a brilliant translator. He was the first to translate Homer in Russian.

69 Friedrich Schiller (1759–1805). Here Bakhtin is referencing Schiller's *Die Götter Griechenlands* [The Gods of Greece] (1788).

70 The excerpt is from the poem "Хорошо!" ["Good!"], sometimes also known as "Октябрь" ["October"] (1927), by Vladimir Mayakovsky. The Russian text is as follows:

Я земной шар чуть не весь обошел—
И жизнь хороша, и жить хорошо!

71 In Russian, the lines Bakhtin is trying to remember are as follows:

А в нашей буче,
боевой, кипучей,-
и того лучше.

72 In Russian: "Моя милиция меня стережет."

73 Duvakin corrects Bakhtin: the militia is not looking out for the poet, "keeping watch" for him, but "protecting him" ["бережет"]. Bakhtin persists in remembering the verb in his own way.

74 In Russian: "Улица—моя, дома—мои . . ."

75 After the Revolution, it was prohibited to buy or sell apartments because they were nationalized and became the property of the state. So, the state gave free apartments to people who were "in need." For instance: a family with two children lived together in a three-bedroom apartment given to the parents by the state. After the children grew up and married, each new family submitted an application for an apartment and were placed on a waiting list. Eventually (in two years, or in five, depending on the urgency, the length of the waiting list, and other considerations), the "newlyweds" would receive their own apartment for free. With all the seeming advantages, the system was inherently flawed: it encouraged people to look for illegal solutions, such as bribing state officials in order to be placed at the top of the list.

76 In Russian:

За городом—
поле.
В полях
деревеньки.
В деревнях—
крестьяне.
Бороды
веники.
Сидят
папаши.
Каждый
хитр.
Землю попашет,
попишет
стихи.

77 For Vsevolod Meyerhold, see interview 2, n63.

78 The slogan in Russian rhymes: "Нигде кроме, как в Моссельпроме!" Mossel'prom [The Moscow Association of Enterprises Processing Agro-Industrial Products] was built by the architect David Kogan (1884–?) between 1923 and 1924. A ten-floor commercial building, it was one of the tallest structures in Moscow at

the time. It became famous through Vladimir Mayakovsky's advertising slogan: "Everything for everyone—at Mossel'prom."

79 The excerpt from Pushkin's novel-in-verse *Евгений Онегин* [*Eugene Onegin*], chap. 5, 42, translated by A. S. Kline. The Russian text is as follows:

Когда гремел мазурки гром,
В огромной зале все дрожало,
Паркет трещал под каблуком,
Тряслися, дребезжали рамы;
Теперь не то: и мы, как дамы,
Скользим по лаковым доскам.
Но в городах, по деревням
Еще мазурка сохранила
Первоначальные красы:
Припрыжки, каблуки, усы
Всё те же: их не изменила
Лихая мода, наш тиран,
Недуг новейших россиян.

80 This excerpt is from the 1925 poem "Домой!" ["Homeward!"]. The Russian text is as follows:

Уходите, мысли, восвояси,
Обнимись,
души и моря глубь.
Тот,
кто постоянно ясен—
тот,
по-моему,
просто глуп.

81 Lyubov Dmitrievna Mendeleeva-Blok (1881–1939) was the daughter of Dmitry Mendeleev (creator of the periodic table of chemical elements) and the wife of Alexander Blok. She was an actress and ballet historian. Her book about classical dance is fundamental for the history of Russian ballet.

82 The following excerpts are from Blok's 1911 poem, "Когда ты загнан и забит":

Когда ты загнан и забит
Людьми, заботой иль тоскою;
Когда под гробовой доскою
Все, что тебя пленяло, спит.

83 Duvakin is mistaken. This line (somewhat misquoted) is from a different poem, "Когда, вступая в мир огромный" [translation] (1909).

84 Bakhtin quotes here from Blok's famous poem "Возмездие" ["Retaliation"] (1911). The Russian text is as follows:

Когда ты загнан и забит
Людьми, заботой иль тоскою;
Когда под гробовой доскою
Все, что тебя пленяло, спит;
Когда по городской пустыне,
Отчаявшийся и больной,
Ты возвращаешься домой,

И тяжелит ресницы иней,-
Тогда—остановись на миг
Послушать тишину ночную:
Постигнешь слухом жизнь иную,
Которой днем ты не постиг;
По-новому окинешь взглядом
Даль снежных улиц, дым костра,
Ночь, тихо ждущую утра
Над белым запушенным садом,
И небо—книгу между книг;
Найдешь в душе опустошенной
Вновь образ матери склоненный,
И в этот несравненный миг -
Узоры на стекле фонарном,
Мороз, оледенивший кровь,
Твоя холодная любовь -
Все вспыхнет в сердце благодарном,
Ты все благословишь тогда,
Поняв, что жизнь—безмерно боле,
Чем quantum satis* Бранда воли,
А мир—прекрасен, как всегда.

85 For Lev Pumpyansky, a close friend of Bakhtin, see interview 1, n26.

86 Volkovo Cemetery is one of the oldest cemeteries in Saint Petersburg. Founded in 1753 by order of Empress Elizabeth, it became famous for its so-called Writers Corner—the part of the cemetery where many distinguished writers and scholars have been buried: Ivan Turgenev, Saltykov-Shchedrin, Dmitry Mendeleev, Alexander Blok, among others.

87 Smolensky Cemetery has been destroyed many times by flooding. In 1922, the Bolsheviks closed it due to lack of space and ordered the destruction of its main church. It was only in 1988 that the cemetery was re-opened; it is currently being reconstructed.

88 Anna Rugevich (1887–1958) was one of the closest friends of Bakhtin and his wife.

89 Anton Rubinstein (1829–1894) was a great Russian pianist, composer, and professor of music. As a pianist, Rubinstein was one of the most acclaimed performers of all time. In Saint Petersburg, he founded Russia's first music conservatory; among his numerous students was Peter Tchaikovsky.

90 *The Demon* (1875) is an opera by Anton Rubinstein. The libretto is based on the long narrative poem of the same name by Mikhail Lermontov. *The Demon* was first staged by the Mariinsky Theater in 1875, where it enjoyed tremendous success.

91 Nikolay Klyuev (1884–1937) was a Russian poet closely associated with Sergey Yesenin. He was greatly influenced by the Symbolist movement. His deep love for Russian folklore made him a unique and highly original poet. Klyuev tried to accept the Revolution, but soon realized that the Bolsheviks betrayed the Russian peasants and were destroying the country that he dearly loved. The open pessimism of his later poetry attracted the attention of the NKVD, which accused him of anti-Soviet propaganda. After the beginning of the Great Purge, Klyuev was

arrested and exiled; then, while in exile, he was arrested for the second time and sentenced to death. The location of his grave is unknown.

92 Nikolay Klyuev's *The Copper Whale* [*Медный кит*] came out at the end of 1919.

93 The excerpt is from the poem "Мать-суббота" ["Mother-Saturday"] (1922). The Russian text is as follows:

Ангел простых человеческих дел
В избу мою жаворонком влетел

94 Vasily Belov (1932–2012) was a Soviet writer considered one of the most influential writers of the so-called derevensky movement, i.e., the "small village" movement. The peak of his popularity in the USSR was in the 1970s, the time of the interviews with Bakhtin. He lived almost all his life and died in the same little town where he was born, near Vologda.

95 Alexander Belyaev (1884–1942) was an eminent Russian science fiction writer, often referred to as the "Russian Jules Verne." He published over seventy science fiction novels that were loved and read all across the USSR. During the Leningrad Blockade, Belyaev died from starvation in his apartment.

96 The excerpt is from the 1917 poem "Уму—республика, а сердцу—Матерь-Русь" ["The Republic Resides in the Brain, Mother Russia—in the Heart"], by Nikolay Klyuev. The original Russian text is as follows:

Но сердце—бубенец под свадебной дугой—
Глотает птичий грай и воздух золотой . . .

97 Sergey Antonovich Klychkov (1889–1937) was a Russian poet, novelist, and translator.

98 The quotation is from Yesenin's 1917 poem "О Русь, взмахни крылами" ["Spread Your Wings, Oh, Rus'"]: "И выбрал кличку Клюев, смиренный Миколай . . ." About Sergey Yesenin, see interview 3, n66.

99 Kirsha Danilov (1703–1776) was a worker at the factory of Russia's first millionaire, Prokofi Demidov (1710–1786). Danilov was a talented amateur folk musician and historian; he was the first to collect hundreds of Russian folk songs, stories, and ballades. His book served as an inspiration for Alexander Pushkin, Zhukovsky, and many other prominent Russian literary figures.

100 Bakhtin is quoting from Klyuev's 1925 poem "Плач о Сергее Есенине" ["Lamentation for Sergey Yesenin"]. It was negatively received by the Bolshevik government and contributed to Klyuev's arrest a few years later. In Russian, the quotation is as follows:

Помяни, чёртушко, Есенина
Кутьей из омылок банных!

101 He has. In the original, the line is: "Кутьей из углей да из омылок банных!" ["Funereal rice made of bits of coal and pieces of used up soap"].

102 According to Russian folklore, the Devil haunts bathhouses [банные], hence the additional connection to the bathhouse soap in the poem.

103 This sweetened rice-and-raisins dish in Russian is called "кутя." This traditional dish was served during the Christmas holidays, and also to commemorate a recently deceased relative.

104 In this conversation, Bakhtin remembers several prominent intellectuals who also happened to be homosexual: Nikolai Klyuev (1884–1937), Mikhail Kuzmin (1872–1936), Zubakin (1894–1938), and Peter Tchaikovsky (1840–1893). Homosexuals were regularly persecuted in the USSR and sent to the camps.

105 The fact that Peter Tchaikovsky was a homosexual was never discussed or publicly admitted during the Communist era. The Bolsheviks had difficulty admitting that the greatest Russian composer, internationally admired, was a homosexual.

106 Mikhail Kuzmin (1872–1936), in his *Wings*, was the first Russian novel to openly treat the topic of homosexuality. *Wings* was published in 1906 and produced a mixed response among the Russian literary intelligentsia. Maxim Gorky and Andrey Bely reacted very negatively. Zinaida Gippius called Kuzmin a "hooligan," and pronounced the topic completely inappropriate for serious literature. Alexander Blok, however, found the novel interesting and Kuzmin's prose excellent.

107 Mikhail Kozakov (1897–1954) was a Soviet writer and dramaturg.

108 Bakhtin is mistaken here: Kozakov was not exiled, but his wife was arrested, and Kozakov, as her husband, was under investigation for some time but later released.

109 Vsevolod Rozhdestvensky (1895–1977) was a Russian-Soviet poet and translator. As a poet he was, perhaps, not among the best. But Gorky's invitation to become an editor and translator for the newly established Soviet publishing house gave Rozhdestvensky a new passion in life—the translation of French poetry, in which he truly excelled.

110 For Tatiana Shchepkina-Kupernik, see interview 3, n117.

111 The excerpt is from a poem from Vsevolod Rozhdestvensky's collection of verses *Ursa Major* (1922). The text in Russian is as follows:

Была такая большая глупая страна
Но петь, как порой она певала,
Вам не удастся никогда!

112 An excerpt from "In the fields, suffused with starlight" ["О садах, согретых звездным светом . . ."], also from *Ursa Major.* The Russian text, slightly misquoted by Bakhtin, is as follows:

На полях, согретых звездным светом,
Горестно и трудно мы поем.
Оттого-то на пути земном
Ангелы приставлены к поэтам.

Водят, как слепых или детей,
И, неутомимые скитальцы,
Слышим мы внимательчые пальцы
Милых спутников в руке своей.

113 An excerpt from "Angel mine, so simple and demure" ["Ангел неразумный и простой"], also found in the same book of lyrics, *Ursa Major.* In Russian the text reads (Bakhtin misremembers several lines):

Ангел мой, такой простой,
Никогда не знающий, что надо,
Знаю: будеш ты моей женой,
Легкой девушкой земного сада.

Для земных неповторимых дней
Покидая . . . звуки клавиш,
В бестолковой комнате моей
Пыль сотрешь и вещи переставишь
А когда . . . —(что-то такое)–
Станешь человеческою лирой . . .

114 For *Doctor Zhivago* (1957) Boris Pasternak (1890–1960) received the Nobel Prize in Literature, the second Russian (after Ivan Bunin) to receive this award. During Stalin's reign, to save his life and to support his family, Pasternak focused on translation. His translations of Shakespeare, Goethe, Shiller, and Calderon are still among the very best. The publication of *Doctor Zhivago* in Italy (it was rejected by all publishers in the USSR) brought to Pasternak universal fame but created serious problems for him in his own country. The atmosphere of open animosity displayed by the official authorities ended up destroying Pasternak's health and contributed to his premature death in 1960.

115 Here Bakhtin tries to recall and recite the poem "In Memory of Alexander Blok" ["Памяти Александра Блока"] by Rozhdestvensky (1921), right after the poet's death. The Russian text reads:

. . . В первый раз . . . такой России . . .
Полустанками, телеграфистами, ночью,
Рудниками и зарей . . .
Первый раз . . .

116 In Russian:

Ночью . . .
Ты была его подругою . . .
Непутевой ночью . . .
Без креста
Первый раз . . . (какой-то) вьюгою . . .
Навсегда поцеловать в уста . . .

117 The original of the poem in Russian is:

Довелось ей быть твоей подругой,
Роковою ночью без креста,
В первый раз хмельной крещенской вьюгой
Навсегда поцеловать в уста . . .
Трех свечей глаза мутно-зеленые,
Дождь в окне, и острые, углом,
Вижу плечи—крылья преломленные—
Под измятым черным сюртуком.

Bakhtin is misremembering many of the lines.

118 For Konstantin Vaginov, see nn26–27.

119 For Maria Yudina, see interview 2, n62.

120 For Valentin Voloshinov, see interview 2, n73.

121 During his final years, after the death of his wife, Bakhtin had a caregiver, Galina Timofeevna Grevtsova, as a permanent member of his household.

122 Pavel Antokolsky (1896–1978) was a Russian-Soviet poet, dramaturg, and translator. His translations of Victor Hugo are among the best in the Russian language. For many years, Antokolsky was a theater director in Tomsk, where he was able to stage many of his own plays.

123 For Acmeism, see interview 3, n6.

124 For Nikolay Gumilev, see interview 2, n122.

125 For Anna Akhmatova, see interview 2, n123.

126 For OBERIU, see n26.

Interview 5

In the notes to this interview I use the terms "Russian" and "Soviet" to distinguish between different epochs, using "Russian" to designate individuals whose main productive period falls before the Revolution of 1917, and using "Soviet" for those whose main productive period falls after the Revolution. In instances in which the activities of an individual span the two epochs, I use the composite term "Russian-Soviet."

1 About Konstantin Vaginov, see interview 4, nn26–27.
2 Salvator Rosa (1615–1673) was a Baroque Italian painter, musician, and poet.
3 Ilya Gruzdev (1892–1960) was perhaps the most influential scholar of Maxim Gorky. He and Gorky maintained a personal friendship for many years and exchanged more than two-hundred letters. In his youth, Gruzdev hoped to become a poet and joined the notable poetic group called the "Serapion Brothers," formed in 1921. He later understood that his talent for poetry was quite limited and focused all his energy on scholarship instead.
4 Lengiz [Ленгиз] stands for the Leningrad State Publishing Company. In the USSR, private publishers were not allowed to exist. To ensure full control, all publishing houses belonged to, were subsidized by, and censored by the State.
5 Nikolay Tikhonov (1896–1979) was a Russian-Soviet poet. At first, Tikhonov considered himself to be a student of Nikolay Gumilev (see interview 2, n122). He later became a member of the "Serapion Brothers." However, perhaps frightened by what he saw around him, Tikhonov soon after became one of the most ardent supporters of the Communist ideology. Only toward the end of his life, in his last radio interview, did Tikhonov confess that all his life he had considered Gumilev to be one of the greatest Russian poets of the twentieth century.
6 "The Touring Theater" was founded in 1905 by Pavel Gaideburov. Its goal was to bring innovative plays to all parts of the Russian Empire. It mostly staged modern and lesser-known plays by Gorky, Chekhov, Ibsen, Bernard Shaw, and many others. The Touring Theater existed until 1928.
7 Pavel Gaideburov (1877–1960) was a prominent Russian-Soviet theater director, actor, writer, and a professor of scenic art.
8 Nadezhda Skarskaya (1868–1958) was a Russian/Soviet actress, wife of Pavel Gaideburov, and the co-founder of the Traveling Theater. During her long and active career in theater, Skarskaya played more than 200 roles. Toward the end of her life she published an excellent book about Soviet theater in the 1920s through the 1950s, *On Stage and In Life* (1959).
9 Vera Komissarzhevskaya (1864–1910) was a Russian superstar at the turn of the twentieth century. She performed all coveted female roles, including Ophelia from *Hamlet* and Margarita from *Faust*. Her most famous role was Nina, from Chekhov's *Seagull*. Komissarzhevskaya worked with Konstantin Stanislavsky (interview 2, n66), and then with Vsevolod Meyerhold (interview 2, n63). Eventually, in 1904, she founded her own theater—the Komissarzhevskaya Theater—which remains one of the most famous in Saint Petersburg. She died from smallpox, while on tour.
10 *The Wanderers* [*Peredvizhniki* in Russian] was a group of Russian realist artists that left the Academy of Arts in protest right before graduation, in 1863, and

formed a society of free and independent artists whose goal was to bring the art of painting to the masses. During the movement's almost fifty years of existence, it organized forty-eight itinerant exhibitions all over the Russian Empire. Almost all of their paintings were sold during those exhibitions, and now are parts of many invaluable collections of Russian realist art of the nineteenth century.

11 About Maly Theater, see interview 2, n65.

12 About Moscow Art Theater, see interview 2, n60.

13 "Ulyan" is a clear reference to Vladimir Lenin, whose last name was Ulyanov. This comparison of Lenin with Mahomet is revolutionary: in fact, not many people would think that Lenin was the first modern dictator. His model of ruling the country and manipulating the masses influenced Mussolini, Hitler, and Stalin.

14 Bakhtin is misremembering or skipping some lines from this poem. The complete text (which comes from the cycle "Petersburg Nights," collected in *Poems 1919–1923* [*Стихи 1919–1923*]) is as follows:

Отшельником живу, Екатерининский канал 105.
За окнами растет ромашка, клевер дикий,
Из-за разбитых каменных ворот
Я слышу Грузии, Азербайджана крики.

Из кукурузы хлеб, прогорклая вода.
Телесный храм разрушили.
В степях поет орда,
За красным знаменем летит она послушная.

Мне делать нечего пойду и помолюсь
И кипарисный крестик поцелую
Сегодня ты смердишь напропалую Русь
В Кремле твой Магомет по ступеням восходит

И на Кремле восходит Магомет Ульян:
"Иль иль Али, иль иль Али Рахман!"
И строятся полки, и снова вскачь
Зовут Китай поднять лихой кумач.

Мне ничего не надо: молод я
И горд своей душою неспокойной.
И вот смотрю закат, в котором жизнь моя,
Империи Великой и Просторной.

15 Vladimir Lenin died in 1924, from a second stroke. The first stroke, which happened in 1922, paralyzed the left part of his body, and he spent the next two years in bed, unable to take part in any political decisions, under the "care" of Stalin, who intentionally accelerated his death (see also interview 3, n29).

16 Bakhtin is mistaken here. Konstantin Vaginov's poem was published only once during his lifetime, in the journal *The Notes of the Wandering [Traveling] Theater*, in 1921.

17 The NEP [НЭП; New Economic Policy] was inaugurated by the Bolsheviks in 1921 to save a country threatened by economic collapse. The NEP allowed for

freedom of trade—essentially, capitalism. Lenin claimed that the NEP was only a temporary measure that was needed to save the Republic and would be abolished as soon as the communist revolution spread around the world. The NEP existed until 1931, but in spite of the visible economic improvements, it was abolished by Stalin, and any form of free trade was again prohibited in the Soviet Union for the next sixty years (see also interview 2, n58).

18 This is the beginning of Mayakovsky's poem "Me and Napoleon" ["Я и Наполеон"], published in 1915:

Я живу на Большой Пресне, 36, 24.
Место спокойненькое.
Тихонькое.
Ну?

19 World War I began on July 28, 1914 and ended on November 11, 1918.

20 This is the first half of a poem by Vaginov from 1924. Bakhtin is misremembering and skipping some lines. The original for this quotation is:

О, сделай статуей звенящей
Мою оболочку,
Чтоб после отверстого плена
Стояла и пела она
О жизни своей ненаглядной,
О чудной подруге своей,
Под сенью смарагдовой ночи,
У врат Вавилонской стены.

21 Memnon in Greek mythology is the Ethiopian king who enlisted to defend Troy. He was killed by Achilles, but later Zeus restored him to life and made him immortal. According to legend there was a beautiful statue of Memnon in Babylon, which Bakhtin refers to here.

22 Konstantin Vaginov was also a notable Modernist writer. His "absurdist" prose was forgotten for many years, and interest in it was revived only in the 1990s. His novels, *The Goat's Song* and *The Life and Works of Svistonov*, present an interesting combination of Surrealism and the Absurd (see also interview 4, nn26–27).

23 Teptelkin was modeled on the ideas and person of Bakhtin's classicist colleague and fellow Gogol scholar, Lev Pumpyansky (see interview 1, n26).

24 Peterhof Village was founded in 1710 by Peter the Great as his summer residence; it was a city of fountains intended to surpass Versailles. When Peterhof was built, it became the most popular place for Russian nobility to have their summer residencies or "dachas."

25 About Lev Pumpyansky, see interview 1, n26.

26 For Lyubov Mendeleeva-Blok, see interview 4, n81.

27 The prototype for this was Dostoevsky's "Dream of a Ridiculous Man" (1877).

28 Benedikt Livshits (1886–1938) was a prominent Russian poet, translator, and one of the first scholars of Futurism. A brilliant intellectual, Livshits was fluent in all European languages, including ancient Greek and Latin. At the age of eight he made his first translation of Horace. He was friends with almost all the most notable literary figures of the time, including Gumilev, Mandelstam, Akhmatova, Mayakovsky, and Yesenin. He was a frequent visitor at the "Stray Dog" literary café (see interview 2, n41). In 1938 he was arrested for "anti-Soviet propaganda,"

and shot a few days later. His relatives received a false letter that Livshits was exiled for ten years without the right to correspond.

29 Konstantin Fedin (1892–1977) was a prominent Soviet writer. Although favored by the Communist Party, he managed to maintain his integrity, wrote a number of novels, and published collections of essays about Gorky and many other writers of the 1920s.

30 For Georgy Shengeli, see interview 3, n65.

31 For Samuil Marshak, see interview 3, n86.

32 For Pavel Antokolsky, see interview 4, n122.

33 Located about twenty miles southwest of Moscow, Peredelkino is a village of small cottages, created in 1934 thanks to Maxim Gorky's idea that Soviet literary figures should be given free land on which to build their houses. Surrounded by a dense pine forest, Peredelkino was famous for its very healthy air. In just a few years, about fifty cottages were built. Boris Pasternak, Konstantin Fedin, Ilya Ilf, Evgeny Petrov, and many other Russian authors lived there.

34 For Vsevolod Meyerhold, see interview 2, n63.

35 *The Government Inspector* is Nikolay Gogol's most famous comedy, written in 1835 on the advice of Alexander Pushkin. Gogol himself said about his favorite comedy that he wanted to gather in one play all the injustices that he had seen in Russia.

36 *The Forest* (1875) by Alexander Ostrovsky (1823–1886) was one of the most frequently staged plays in Russia during the twentieth century (in more than 100 theaters).

37 Mikhail Chekhov (1891–1955) was a nephew of Anton Chekhov. The favorite student and friend of Konstantin Stanislavsky, Chekhov started performing at MXAT (Moscow Art Theatre). Chekhov's interpretation of Khlestakov in *The Government Inspector* is considered one of the best. In 1928, strongly opposed to the Bolsheviks, Mikhail Chekhov immigrated first to Germany, then to France, England, and, finally in 1939, to the United States, where he founded his own school of art. In 1945, Chekhov was invited by Alfred Hitchcock to play in *Spellbound* and was nominated for an Oscar.

38 *The Man from the Restaurant* (1927) was a black and white silent film by the Russian film director Yakov Protazanov (1881–1945). In this film, Mikhail Chekhov played the principal character—the waiter at a restaurant. This was the last movie in which Chekhov participated in the USSR before emigrating to Germany.

39 Sandro (Alexander) Moisiu [Moissi] (1879–1935) was a German actor of Albanian descent. His talent for embodying the characters he played was so powerful that he seemed to transcend the language he spoke: Moisiu's Romeo was not Italian; his Hamlet was not Danish; Faustus and Mephistopheles were not of any particular nation but conveyed universal human ambitions and concerns. In 1924–1925, Sandro Moisiu visited Moscow and Saint Petersburg, where he was celebrated by the Russian intelligentsia.

40 The Alexandrinsky Theater was founded in 1756 by the order of Empress Elizabeth, daughter of Peter the Great. It became the first public dramatic theater in Russia. It was only in 1832 that the already established theater received its own building, designed by the famous Italian architect Carlo Rossi.

41 Max Reinhardt (Goldmann) (1873–1943) was an Austrian theater director, actor, and one of the most notable theatrical innovators of the twentieth century.

Reinhardt headed the Deutsches Theater of Berlin from 1904 until the Nazis came into power in 1933, at which time he fled to the United States. His notable innovations included not using a footlight, bringing the dramatic action as close to the spectators as possible, and using a moving stage. Besides being a great director, Reinhardt was an excellent teacher: one of his most famous students was Marlene Dietrich (1901–1992).

42 Max Reinhardt cast Sandro Moisiu as Oedipus, and the success of the show in Moscow and Saint Petersburg was enormous.

43 The Tchaikovsky Concert Hall is a famous performance venue in Moscow. From 1922 to 1933 the building housed the Meyerhold Theater, the most innovative playhouse in the Russian capital. When Meyerhold was arrested and his theater closed, the building was abandoned. Then, in 1940 it became the home of the new Concert Hall, named after Tchaikovsky to honor his 100th anniversary.

44 During the Weimar Republic (1919–1933), the Republic passed through three different stages: overcoming the consequences of World War I (1919–1923); a period of relative stability (1924–1929); and the coming to power of the National Socialists (the Nazis) (1929–1933). With the Weimar Constitution, Germany for the first time became a representative democracy.

45 "Kaiser Germany" refers to the reign of the last German Emperor, Kaiser Wilhelm II (1859–1941; r. 1888–1918). His rule was marked by strong economic growth, which transformed Germany into a leading player on the world stage. Germany's humiliating defeat in World War I brought an end to the German monarchy: after the November Revolution of 1918, Kaiser Wilhelm was overthrown, and he fled to the Netherlands.

46 Georg Kaiser (1878–1945) was one of the most notable representatives of German Expressionism and one of the most important literary figures in Germany at the beginning of the twentieth century.

47 *Unfortunate Eugene* (more accurately, *The German Invalid* [*Der Deutsche Hinkemann*]) was Ernst Toller's most famous play; written in prison in 1923, it brought him world fame.

48 Ernst Toller (1893–1937) was a prominent German dramaturg and politician. He served for six days as President of the Bavarian Soviet Republic but then was arrested for his political activity and spent five years in prison, during which time he became a world-renowned playwright. His plays were staged in Europe, America, Australia, and the USSR. After Hitler came to power, Toller was forced to leave Germany. While living in the United States, he continued his active involvement in European affairs. (He tried to help European refugees and raised money to help the Republican fight against Franco.) After many years of fighting severe depression, Toller committed suicide in 1937.

49 Ivan Ermakov (1875–1942) was a pioneer of psychoanalysis in Russia. A professor of medicine and a psychiatrist, Ermakov was also a talented artist and the director of one of the most important Russian art museums—the Tretyakov Gallery in Moscow. He headed the publishing house that translated and published almost all works of Sigmund Freud in Russia. Ermakov founded the first State Psychoanalytic Institute in Moscow in 1921, closed by the Bolsheviks a few years later in 1925. Ermakov was also the first literary critic to analyze Pushkin, Gogol, and Dostoevsky from the perspective of psychoanalysis. In 1941, Ermakov was arrested and soon after died in a concentration camp.

50 "The Nose" (1832) is a satirical absurdist novella by Nikolay Gogol. Its influence on subsequent Russian and world authors is far reaching.

51 "The Little House in Kolomna" (1830) is a satirical poem by Alexander Pushkin written in octaves—a stanza rarely used in Russian prosody.

52 For Nikolay Zabolotsky, see interview 4, n28.

53 For Ekaterina Peshkova, see interview 3, n33.

54 Kustanay [Кустанай] is a city in northern Kazakhstan, about 3,500 miles east of Moscow, to which Bakhtin was sent into internal exile in 1929. The original name of the city was Nikolayevsk, in honor of Tsar Nicholas I. It was renamed Kustanay by the Bolsheviks.

55 Bakhtin worked as a bookkeeper during his years of internal exile in Kustanay. In Russian "an economist" can mean anyone who deals with numbers in their job.

56 Saransk is a regional city center (population 300,000 today), located about 400 miles southeast of Moscow. When Bakhtin arrived in Saransk there was a large Pedagogical Institute where he found a job as a professor of literature.

57 For the assassination of Sergey Kirov, see interview 3, n120.

58 At 2,200 miles, the Volga River is the longest in Europe and one of the five great rivers of Russia.

59 A Residence Permit, or Registration [прописка, in Russian], was mandatory in the USSR: every citizen had to have a special stamp in his/her passport showing that the individual resided at a certain address. To be able to legally live in any city in the USSR, a person had to receive this Residence Permit, or he/she would not be able to apply for a job, social security, etc., there. This was the Communists' way of "regulating" the population in order to make it spread more or less evenly throughout the country.

60 "Organs" here refers to the Security Police Organs, which had a certain number of people to arrest; once they had fulfilled their quota, they didn't care what happened to an arrested/exiled person.

61 The Gorky Institute of World Literature (often called IMLI) was the flagship Russian literary research institution. Founded in 1932, the IMLI played a preeminent role in translating, promoting, publishing, and researching world literature.

62 Bakhtin was invited by Professor Antonov, Rector of the Saransk Pedagogical Institute, to teach literature courses. The Dean, Professor Petrov, also supported Bakhtin by giving him the opportunity to teach as many classes as possible. But in 1937, when the Great Purge (1936–1938) started, Antonov was arrested and shot, and Petrov was dismissed from his position. Bakhtin, feeling himself at risk, asked to be officially released from his duties, and then secretly left for Moscow with his wife.

63 The money that Bakhtin had earned in Saransk was soon used up, and the real financial hardship began. The Bakhtins survived only thanks to the continuous help of his sisters, mother, and good friends.

64 Ivan Kanaev (1893–1984) was a Soviet biologist, one of the most prominent scholars of genetics, and a notable literary scholar. His works about Goethe interested Bakhtin, and his ideas have great value for Goethe scholars. Being a good friend and admirer of Bakhtin, Kanaev, at great personal risk, helped him obtain the books he needed for his research for many years. Without Kanaev, Bakhtin would have never been able to finish *Rabelais and His World* (1965). Some of Bakhtin's works were published under Kanaev's name.

65 Trofim Lysenko (1898–1976) was a Soviet biologist who, using his connections with Communist Party leaders, was able to hinder or even stop Soviet research into genetics for twenty-five years. As a result, Soviet genetics research fell well behind its Western counterparts. Only after Stalin's death was Lysenko removed from his positions and Soviet geneticists granted the financial support needed to continue their research.

66 "Morganist" was a derogatory term used by Lysenko and his supporters to refer to those Soviet scholars who insisted that the future of humanity depended upon the study of genetics. The term "morganist" was derived from the American biologist Thomas Morgan, a Nobel Prize laureate in Physiology (1933), who discovered the role chromosomes play in heredity.

67 The National Library of Russia was founded by order of Catherine the Great in 1795. It was one of the first public libraries in Eastern Europe. In 1932, the library was renamed the Saltykov-Shchedrin Public Library (in honor of the writer Saltykov-Shchedrin [1826–1889]). Its holdings are the second largest in Russia (after the State Library in Moscow), and the sixth largest in the world, with 37,000,000 volumes.

68 Savelovo is a small village near the city of Dmitrov, approximately 40 miles from Moscow, and a beautiful Russian city founded in 1154. At the time Bakhtin lived there, Dmitrov was about the same size and population as today—65,000. Bakhtin chose Savelovo due to its proximity to Moscow and because he could live there relatively cheaply on his small state pension.

69 Nadezhda Yakovlevna Mandelstam (1899–1980) was the wife and best friend of Osip Mandelstam (see interview 3, n7). She voluntarily followed her husband into exile. After he was arrested for the second time and later died in prison, Nadezhda sought to preserve his archive. Knowing that she could be arrested any moment and that the archive could be confiscated, she memorized all of Mandelstam's poems. Nadezhda Mandelstam made ends meet by teaching languages (she spoke four fluently). Toward the end of her life, she wrote about her husband in her *Memoirs*, a book that is invaluable to Mandelstam's scholars as well as to historians of Stalin's regime.

70 The city of Alexandrov belongs to the so-called Golden Ring of beautiful old Russian cities. It is located about seventy miles east of Moscow.

71 Josef Stalin died on March 1, 1953. He had a stroke, which left him paralyzed, and died a few days later without regaining consciousness. Many scholars today believe (and with good reason) that Stalin's closest companions—Khrushchev and Beria (the Head of NKVD)—ensured Stalin's death by not calling doctors in time.

72 For Vadim Kozhinov, see interview 3, n36.

73 Vladimir Turbin (1927–1993) was a close friend of Bakhtin's family and a professor at Moscow University.

74 Bakhtin refers to Leontina Melikhova, the close friend of Bakhtin and his wife. Leontina was a student of Vladimir Turbin, who also served as director of her PhD dissertation.

75 Mikhail Bulgakov (1891–1940) was a Russian writer, dramaturg, theater director, and essayist. A medical doctor by training, Bulgakov soon dedicated his life to literature. Although he wrote many excellent plays, he is best remembered as the author of one of Russia's best twentieth-century novels, *The Master and Margarita* (1940). Although very sick, Bulgakov dictated the last chapters of the novel to his

wife, who saved the manuscript for future generations. It was only many years later (1973) that Bulgakov's best work was officially published in Russia in full.

76 Bulgakov's novel, *The White Guard*, follows the fate of the Turbins (an old family of intellectuals and officers) in Kiev in the aftermath of 1917. His play, *The Days of the Turbins*, which he adapted from the novel, was staged by the Moscow Art Theater to great acclaim. It was also purportedly Stalin's favorite play.

77 Kiev is the capital of Ukraine.

78 Nikita Khrushchev (1894–1971) served as First Secretary of the Communist Party from 1953 to 1964, and as Premier from 1958 to 1964. This time was marked by the end of repressions, a political "thaw" in the country, and the revival of cultural life.

79 Professor Petrov, the former Dean of the Saransk Pedagogical Institute, once again helped Bakhtin obtain steady employment. In 1946, when the war with Germany was over, Petrov wrote a letter to the new rector of the Institute and recommended Bakhtin to him as a brilliant scholar who would teach the much-needed World Literature courses. Thanks to this letter, Bakhtin got the position.

80 Duvakin refers to the Sanatorium for Seniors in Peredelkino that was built in the 1950s for Soviet writers who became sick or disabled. They were placed under medical care at the sanatorium free of charge.

81 Bakhtin acknowledges his good fortune in acquiring an apartment, however small, just for his family, instead of living in a communal apartment.

82 For Sergey Bocharov, see interview 3, n37.

83 In 1966, Victor Duvakin was dismissed from his position at Moscow University because he defended his former student Andrei Sinyavsky (1925–1997), a prominent Soviet literary scholar and a writer. Sinyavsky was arrested for publishing his books in the West; after serving seven years as a political prisoner he was allowed to immigrate to France. Duvakin did not know that Vadim Kozhinov continuously defended Duvakin after his dismissal from the university (see interview 3, n36).

84 For Orel, see interview 1, n2.

85 Alexander Romanov II (1818–1881) was the Russian emperor (r. 1855–1881) whose reign oversaw the liberation of the serfs (1861). He is remembered as a great reformer (much like Peter the Great) who brought Russia to the height of its power and influence. He was killed by terrorists in 1881 in Saint Petersburg.

86 Yulian Sergeevich Seliu (1910–1995) was a veterinarian, biologist, and amateur writer. He wrote miniature-narratives. While visiting Bakhtin in the 1970s to treat his cat, Seliu read Bakhtin some of his miniatures, and Bakhtin was delighted with them.

87 Elena Guro (1877–1913) was a Russian poet, writer, and painter. She died young, at the age of thirty-nine years, from leukemia. Her work, a combination of poetry, prose, and impressionistic painting, secured her place in the history of Russian arts.

88 Mikhail Prishvin (1873–1954) was one of the most interesting Soviet writers, one who remains underappreciated. Prishvin wrote about Russian nature: Gorky called him "The Singer of Nature." Prishvin kept a life-long diary, which was only published in the 1990s. It reveals a deeply philosophical mind that searched for answers to the most burning human questions: the purpose of life, religion, gender relationships, and the inherent connection of humankind to nature.

89 This miniature, written in 1941, is reproduced in the book *Больной поросенок* [A sick piglet] (2002), 360. The story is two paragraphs long, and consists of static

detail: the flickering lamp, the sick piglet's blinking white eyelashes, the old people keeping watch, the other animals in the hut going about their business.

90 Ivan Turgenev's *Poems in Prose* [*Стихотворения в прозе*], trans. Constance Garnett, is a cycle of lyrical miniatures, written in 1879–1882, and originally titled by its author *Posthuma*, then *Senilia*. The latter title is sometimes used along with *Poems in Prose*, which appeared as late as in October 11, 1882, less than a year before Turgenev's death.

91 Vasily Vasilyevich Rozanov (also spelled Rosanov [1856–1919]), a Russian writer, religious thinker, and journalist, is best known for the originality and individuality of his prose works.

92 Lidia Evlampievna Sluchevskaya (1897–1979) was a philologist and acquaintance of Maria Yudina (see interview 2, n62), one of Bakhtin's most valued friends.

93 Igor Severyanin (Lotarev) (1887–1941) was a prominent Russian poet from the beginning of the twentieth century. During the Revolution, he immigrated to Estonia where he stayed until his death. Severyanin was the first to translate Estonian poetry into Russian.

Interview 6

In the notes to this interview I use the terms "Russian" and "Soviet" to distinguish between different epochs, using "Russian" to designate individuals whose main productive period falls before the Revolution of 1917, and using "Soviet" for those whose main productive period falls after the Revolution. In instances in which the activities of an individual span the two epochs, I use the composite term "Russian-Soviet."

1 For Maria Yudina, see interview 2, n62.

2 For Lev Pumpyansky, see interview 1, n26.

3 Doctor Veniamin Gavrilovitch Yudin (1864–1963) was Maria Yudina's father. He was a physician and a native of Nevel. A man of exceptional intelligence, he worked all his life to support his family and contribute to the community. For Kadets, see interview 2, n43.

4 The Mensheviks (meaning "minority" in Russian) was a faction of the Russian socialist movement. This faction emerged in 1904 at one of the Russian Social Democratic Labor Party's meetings, following a dispute between Vladimir Lenin (1870–1924) and Julius Martov (1873–1923). Lenin himself coined the term "Mensheviks" (as opposed to the "Bolsheviks," or the majority), referring to those who did not support him and his ideas. The faction existed until 1922, when most Mensheviks were arrested and forced into exile. Those who stayed in the USSR were murdered during the Great Purge (1936–1938).

5 For the Eseri (Social Democrats), see interview 3, n47.

6 Here Bakhtin refers to Maria Yudina's sister, Anna. She became a professional translator.

7 Neo-Kantianism was the so-called back to Kant movement, founded by Otto Liebmann (1840–1912) in 1865 as a reaction to the emerging materialism of the period. The Marburg School, founded by Hermann Cohen, Paul Natorp, and Ernst Cassirer, became the most accomplished exponent of neo-Kantianism (see interview 1, n42, n55).

8 Paul Natorp (1854–1924) was a prominent German philosopher, historian, scholar of classical languages, and a musician. Natorp was Cohen's best student and quickly became his teacher's friend and disciple.

9 For Ernst Cassirer, see interview 1, n59.

10 For Andrey Bely, see interview 2, n49.

11 Actually, Lev Pumpyansky's mother was Jewish and was born and raised in France. She spoke to her son only in French. Pumpyansky was fluent in French, as well as Latin, German, English, and Italian.

12 Slavophilism was the religious and cultural movement that originated in Moscow in the 1830s. Its main ideas were that the Russian Empire would soon become the "Third Rome," that Russian civilization was incompatible with European models, and that Peter the Great and Catherine the Great did a lot of harm to the country by allowing Europe to influence Russia. Among the most notable Slavophiles were Fyodor Dostoevsky, Mikhail Lomonosov, Fyodor Tyutchev, and Aleksey Khomyakov.

13 Aleksey Khomyakov (1804–1860) was a distinguished Russian philosopher, poet, and painter. Talented in many areas, Khomyakov became one of the founders and leaders of the Slavophilia movement. In his fundamental work, *Notes towards a Universal History*, which remained unfinished, Khomyakov argued that each nation has its own destiny, its own "absolute," preordained path. If the nation deviates from its "absolute," it will not be able to complete its mission. According to Khomyakov, Russia's mission was to become the spiritual leader of the world, something that the West had failed to accomplish. Khomyakov died from cholera while treating peasants during an outbreak of the disease.

14 The monastic vow [*постриг* in Russian] in the Eastern Orthodox Church is the process of becoming a monk or a nun. This procedure is very slow: the Church seeks to ensure that the probationers are sincere and fully committed to dedicating life to God. In the USSR, any relationship with the church was strongly discouraged, so those who decided to become a monk or a nun had to perform their vows in secret or they could be prosecuted.

15 In the Russian Orthodox Church, *panikhida* [панихида] is a memorial service first performed at the original burial site, and then repeated again, three, nine, and forty days after the death.

16 The Gnessin Institute, a prominent music school in Moscow, was established on February 15, 1895, by three sisters: Evgenia Fabianovna (1871–1940), Elena Fabianovna (1874–1967), and Maria Fabianovna Gnessin (1876–1918). Today it is a part of a group of educational institutions (including Gnessin State Musical College and Gnessin Russian Academy of Music) that offer formal musical instruction from primary- to graduate-level study.

17 Ivan Efimov (1878–1959) was a famous Russian sculptor, artist, illustrator, and puppeteer. Together with his wife, Nina Simonovich-Efimova (1877–1948), they laid the foundation of Soviet puppet-theater. Efimov's puppet designs, book illustrations, and sculpture were highly regarded during his lifetime.

18 Zlata Konstantinovna Yashina was the wife of the writer and poet Alexander Yashin.

19 During World War I, Pskov was the center of much activity behind the lines. After the Russo-German Brest-Litovsk Peace Conference (December 22, 1917–March 3, 1918), the Imperial German Army unexpectedly invaded the area but was forced to leave following the peace agreement on the Western front of November 11, 1918.

20 The Red Army was formed on February 23, 1918 by decree of Vladimir Lenin. In 1946, it was renamed the Soviet Army.

21 The Patriotic War of 1812 (as distinct from the War of 1812, between the United States and Great Britain) pitted Russia against Napoleon Bonaparte's French army. On June 24, a French force of 450,000 crossed the Russian border. Napoleon expected to finish the campaign in three months, but instead, on December 26, 1812, the war ended with the full surrender of the completely depleted French army: only about 30,000 soldiers went home alive. Napoleon, dressed as a woman, abandoned his troops.

22 "Funérailles" by Franz Liszt is considered a pinnacle of the piano repertoire in terms of technical difficulty.

23 Bakhtin is trying to remember Friedrich Schelling's (1775–1854) name. "Philosophy of Revelation" is a concept developed by Schelling between the 1830s and 1850s in a series of lectures delivered at different German universities. Bakhtin, being an admirer of Kant, valued Schelling and read his works in German.

24 Schelling is one of the first philosophers to develop a metaphysics based on the idea of true representation as transcending empirical and objective science. Bakhtin is trying to recall this final phase of Schelling's career.

25 Friedrich Schelling (1775–1854), a close friend of Hegel and Goethe, did not leave behind a specific school that could be connected with his name. Rather, he initiated three major directions in philosophy: subjective individualism, objective naturalism, and religious mysticism.

26 The first phase of Romanticism in German literature, centered in Jena from about 1798 to 1804. The most prominent members of this circle were August and Friedrich Schlegel, Ludwig Tieck, and Baron Georg von Hardenberg, known by his pen name "Novalis."

27 E. T. A. Hoffmann (1776–1822) was a German Romantic poet, writer, composer, lawyer, and music critic. He published his music critiques under the pen name "Johannes Kreisler."

28 Poet, writer, playwright, and translator, Johann Ludwig Tieck (1773–1853) believed that definite forms in literature could never exist, as the artist is endlessly engaged in a spiritual search. Still, he dedicated a considerable time to translating Shakespeare, Cervantes, and Luís de Camões, believing that good translations are needed as examples for the new art movement.

29 Clemens Brentano (1778–1842) was a German Romantic poet, writer, and eminent figure in the Heidelberg Romantic circle. Together with his friend and colleague Arnim, Brentano collected, edited, and published the first anthology of German folk songs.

30 Ludwig von Arnim (1781–1831) was the most prominent figure of the Heidelberg Romantic circle. A poet and writer, Arnim is most remembered for *Des Knaben Wunderhorn: Alte Deutsche Lieder* [*The Boy's Magic Horn: Old German Songs*], a collection of German folk poems and songs, published in three volumes between 1805 and 1808, which enjoyed great popularity in its country.

31 Leonid Nikolayev (1878–1942) was a Russian-Soviet pianist and one of the most prominent Soviet professors of music. Among his students were Dmitry Shostakovich, Vladimir Sofronitsky, and Maria Yudina.

32 For Anton Rubinstein, see interview 4, n89.

33 Nikolay Rubinstein (1835–1881) was a Russian pianist-virtuoso, conductor, professor of music and, most importantly, the first director of the Moscow

Conservatory, which he founded with his friend and benefactor, Nikolay Trubetskoy (1890–1938).

34 Dvortsovaya Neberezhnaya (often called "the Palace Quay" in English) is a famous street along the Neva River in Saint Petersburg. It contains the complex of the Hermitage Museum buildings (including the Winter Palace), the Hermitage Theatre, the Marble Palace, the Vladimir Palace, the New Michael Palace, the Saltykov Mansion, and the Summer Garden. Catherine the Great ordered the construction of the embankment out of granite in the late eighteenth century, thus creating one of the most beautiful streets in the city of Saint Petersburg.

35 The Peter and Paul Fortress was the first building in the newly born city of Saint Petersburg. The fortress was built in 1703 to protect the city from the Swedish army. Domenico Trezzini (c. 1670–1734), an Italian architect contracted by Peter the Great, built the beautiful Peter and Paul Cathedral, which to this day remains the tallest building in Saint Petersburg (101 meters, or 331 feet). The Fortress also became a famous political prison: at different times, among its famous prisoners were Peter the Great's son Aleksey, Fyodor Dostoevsky, and Leon Trotsky.

36 For academic Evgeny Tarle, see interview 4, n1.

37 Actually, Lev Pumpyansky was married in 1930, and remained happily married for ten years, until his arrest.

38 Lev Pumpyansky was the best friend of Nikolay Bakhtin, Mikhail's older brother. This is how they got to know each other and became friends.

39 Bakhtin refers to the young pianist Kirill Saltykov. He was a student of Maria Yudina's, and later became her fiancée. He died in an accident in 1939: he was an alpinist, and during one of his mountain climbs, he and two others tragically fell to their deaths. Saltykov was only twenty-five years old when he died.

40 Bakhtin refers here to the Romanov Tsars from 1613 to the February Revolution of 1917, when Nicholas II was forced to abdicate the throne.

41 After the death of her fiancé, Maria Yudina maintained a close relationship with his mother, Elena Saltykova (Kurakina) for the rest of her life.

42 "Saltychikha" was the nickname of Darya Saltykova (1730–1801)—a Russian noblewoman and a notorious sadist and serial killer. After discovering her atrocities (the investigation lasted over six years and revealed that Saltychikha had killed about seventy-five serfs, mainly women), Catherine the Great personally signed her sentence: life imprisonment. Saltychikha spent forty years in prison until her death.

43 For the writer Mikhail Saltykov-Shchedrin, see interview 4, n43.

44 Tsar Alexey Mikhailovich (1629–1676) was the second Russian tsar from the Romanov family, the father of Peter the Great.

45 Ivan the Terrible (1530–1584) is perhaps the most widely known, even mythic figure in Russian history. Historians continue to debate the significance of Ivan's rule, many, such as academic Sergey Platonov (see interview 4, n1), believing his politics to have been devastating for Russia.

46 Bakhtin is talking here about the father of Kirill Saltykov.

47 Nalchik is the capital of Kabardino-Balkaria, a part of the Russian Federation. It is located near the mountain range called the Greater Caucasus, which is a favorite alpinist location.

48 Bakhtin is misinformed: the bodies of all alpinists were found, and Kirill Saltykov was later buried in Moscow.

49 The Black Hundreds [черносотенцы in Russian] was an ultra-nationalist movement in Russia between 1905 and 1914. The movement was mainly characterized by its anti-Semitism and extreme advocacy of monarchism. Some scholars believe that it was the Black Hundreds who misled the last Russian Tsar Nicholas II and led him to believe that the Russian people loved him and were satisfied with the status quo; the organization constantly sent him letters, expressing love and admiration for him and his family. After the Revolution, the leaders of the Black Hundreds fled Russia.

50 Theodor Herzl (1860–1904) was a Jewish political activist, the leader of the Zionist Movement. He died without realizing his dream, but the Independent State of Israel was born in 1947.

51 For Boris Pasternak, see interview 4, n114.

52 John of Kronstadt (1829–1909) was one of the most well-known Russian Orthodox preachers. Kronstadt's popularity reached its peak when several people claimed to be cured after attending his services. People from all over Russia donated money to him—up to 50,000 rubles per year (the equivalent of US$1,000,000 today), which Kronstadt donated to those in need, or to build a school, or a hospital, or a chapel. After his death, Kronstadt was canonized.

53 Menahem Beilis (1874–1934) was a Russian Jew accused of the ritual murder of a boy in 1911, in Kiev. The "Beilis Trial" was the most notorious legal proceeding in the history of the Russian Empire. It lasted two years, and Beilis, who was eventually found innocent, left Russia, moving first to Palestine and then the United States.

54 For Viktor Shklovsky, see interview 2, n21.

55 Duvakin conducted a series of interviews with Shklovsky as well. These interviews, *Victor Shklovsky: The Duvakin Interviews of 1967–68*, edited and translated into English, will be published in 2019.

56 Heinrich Neuhaus (1888–1964) was perhaps the most famous Soviet professor of music and pianist in his day. He dedicated his life to the Moscow Conservatory of Music. To be a student of Neuhaus was to be known as a graduate from the best music school in the Soviet Union. Among his most notable students were Emil Gilels, Yakov Zak, Sviatoslav Richter, and Anton Ginsburg.

57 Vladimir Sofronitsky (1901–1961) was a preeminent Soviet pianist and professor at the Leningrad Conservatory of Music. The favorite student of Leonid Nikolayev (1904–1934), Sofronitsky studied with classmates Maria Yudina and Dmitry Shostakovich. Considered by many to be the best pianist in the Soviet Union, Sofronitsky was also celebrated as one of the best in the world (even though Stalin did not allow him to leave the USSR after 1930).

58 Bakhtin uses the German word *Fach*, which means "specialty," "particular subject," to suggest that she couldn't be easily pigeonholed.

59 For Rainer Rilke, see interview 2, n124.

60 Alongside Rilke, Stefan George (1868–1933) was the leader of the German Modernists. His work is often seen as providing a bridge between nineteenth-century German poetry and Modern art. George was also a notable translator, the first to render into German the poetry of Shakespeare, Dante, Baudelaire, and modern Italian and French poets. A born leader, George attracted a circle that existed for many years. He also published his own journal, *Blätter für die Kunst* [*Pages of Art*].

61 Friedrich Gundolf (1880–1931) was a poet, literary critic, and a close follower of Stefan George. He is the author of a monumental monograph on Goethe. Gundolf was arguably the most famous academic of the Weimar Republic. Among his students was the notorious Joseph Goebbels, Minister of Propaganda of Nazi Germany.

62 Ernst Bertram (1884–1957) wrote one of the best biographies of Friedrich Nietzsche, in which he tries to connect all of Nietzsche's major ideas with the ancient traditions of myth and mythological symbols, thus linking Nietzsche to classic European culture.

63 Duvakin refers here to an accident that happened to Maria Yudina in 1969, when she was hit by a car, and she lost the movement in her right hand, and thus the ability to perform again. However, after some time she recovered some mobility in her hand, and she was able to play privately for close friends.

64 The Suez Canal, built 1859–1869, is the major waterway connecting the Mediterranean with the Red Sea and the Indian Ocean. During the Suez Crisis of 1956 Britain, France, and Israel attempted to re-seize control of the canal after Egyptian President Gamal Nazar had nationalized it, only to be foiled by the intervention of the United States, the USSR, and the United Nations.

65 For Marina Tsvetaeva, see interview 2, n83.

66 Tsvetaeva's "Art in the Light of Conscience" ["Искусство при свете совести"] was first published in *Sovremennye zapiski* (Paris), 1932/1933, nos. 51 and 52.

67 Maria Yudina often interrupted her concerts in order to recite some of her favorite verses. In 1957, after reading the poetry of Boris Pasternak, she was forbidden from performing in public. The ban lasted for several years but was gradually lifted when Nikita Khrushchev was no longer in power.

68 Jakob Böhme (1575–1624) was a German mystic, philosopher, and theologian. He did not receive a formal education, and did not know Latin, the language of the educated elite. By profession, he was a shoemaker.

69 Boleslav Yavorsky (1877–1942) was a prominent Soviet theoretician of music, a pedagogue, and a professor at the Moscow Conservatory. At the request of the Soviet Minister of Education, Yavorsky traveled to the West, where he met with many important musicians. He convinced Sergey Prokofiev to return to the USSR. Yavorsky, while being on friendly terms with the Communist Party, managed to help many Soviet musicians, scholars, and artists. Yavorsky was the first to connect music with Clinical Psychology, and try to demonstrate the healing powers of music.

70 Avvakum Petrovich (1620–1682) was a Russian *protopope* (a priest of high rank in the Orthodox church), notorious for his polemics with Patriarch Nikon (1605–1681) and even the Russian tsar. After spending many years in exile and in prison, he was burnt at the stake—a very rare sentence in Russia.

71 Maria Yudina sometimes risked her own life by petitioning the NKVD and other Bolshevik leaders on behalf of many who were repressed, exiled, or condemned. Through her close friend Ekaterina Peshkova (see interview 3, n33), the wife of Maxim Gorky, Yudina was able to draw attention to many unlawfully arrested poets, writers, and artists, and she was able to save some of their lives. In Bakhtin's case, Peshkova's intervention helped convert his original sentence to five years of internal exile in Kazakhstan.

72 Bakhtin refers here to the short poem by Alexander Pushkin, "The Feast in Time of Plague" (1830). Walsingham, leader of a small company of young people during

the 1665 London plague epidemic, sets out a table in the middle of the city, where they defiantly eat and sing songs.

73 About Savelovo, the village where Bakhtin lived, see interview 5, n68.

74 Istra, founded in 1781, is a small, beautiful old Russian town located thirty miles northwest of Moscow. During the German invasion of 1941 through 1945, Istra found itself on the front line of the Russian defense.

75 Iksha is a small village near Istra, with a population of about 5,000. Iksha saw the fiercest battles between the Russians and the Nazis during the Moscow defense.

76 Ivan Sollertinsky (1902–1944) was a prominent theorist of music, a professor at the Leningrad Conservatory of Music, and friend and supporter of Dmitry Shostakovich. In his youth, Sollertinsky was a friend of Bakhtin's. The two of them met in Nevel, and he soon joined the Bakhtin circle. A polymath, Sollertinsky not only deeply influenced Soviet musicology but also delivered an enormous number of public lectures (over 1,000), almost always free of charge. He was the first musicologist to study and promote the music of Gustav Mahler in the USSR.

77 *Faust* (1808, revised 1828–1829) was first translated into Russian in 1838, by Edward Guber (1814–1847), a mediocre poet but an excellent translator. Pasternak's translation (1948–1953) is considered the best. He spent thirty years preparing it, and said that he considered the work to be his own tragedy.

78 Vladimir Favorsky (1886–1964) was a prominent Soviet graphic artist, portraitist, theorist, and art professor. He is known for his unique approach to book illustration, and he passed his passion for book illustration on to his numerous students at the Art Academy.

79 Konstantin Yuon (1875–1958) was a Russian-Soviet painter who, before the Revolution, became famous for his excellent landscapes. After the Revolution, he mainly worked as a theater designer and also became an art professor.

80 Pavel Shultz (1900–1983) was a notable Soviet archaeologist, who discovered the old Scythian settlement in Crimea: the Scythian Neapolis that existed between the third century BC and the sixth century AD. The settlement was located near present day Simferopol.

81 Zinaida Neuhaus (Pasternak) (1897–1966) was the first wife of the pianist Heinrich Neuhaus (1888–1964). While still married, Zinaida met Boris Pasternak (who was also married at the time) and fell under the spell of his personality. The two decided to divorce their current partners, but the process proved to be more difficult than expected. In 1932, Pasternak tried to commit suicide when Zinaida returned to her husband. Later, they finally married.

82 Byron wrote the poem "The Prisoner of Chillon" in 1816, after his visit to the Chillon Castle in Switzerland, near Lake Geneva. The Russian poet Vasily Zhukovsky (1783–1852) also visited the castle and then translated Byron's poem into Russian in 1821. His translation was highly praised by Pushkin and other Russian poets.

83 The Union of Soviet Writers was created by the Bolsheviks in 1934 as a vehicle of state control and censorship. Becoming a member of the Union meant gaining permission to publish books and to earn money by writing. The Union also supported its members in "good" standing (by giving them nice apartments, country cottages, excellent medical service, and money). To lose one's Union membership usually spelled disaster: the unfortunate writer would be prevented from publishing in the USSR and would lose all benefits, including, at times, their

apartment. In 1934, the Union consisted of 1,500 writers; in 1991 (the year the Union was dissolved) it had about 10,000 members.

84 A famous poem by Afanasy Fet, "The Night was Shining," was written on the evening of August 2, 1877. About Afanasy Fet, see interview 1, n64. Bakhtin misremembers some of the words in Fet's poem. The following is the original text:

Сияла ночь. Луной был полон сад. Лежали
Лучи у наших ног в гостиной без огней
Рояль был весь раскрыт, и струны в нем дрожали,
Как и сердца у нас за песнию твоей.

Ты пела до зари, в слезах изнемогая,
Что ты одна - любовь, что нет любви иной,
И так хотелось жить, чтоб, звуки не роняя,
Тебя любить, обнять и плакать над тобой.

И много лет прошло, томительных и скучных,
И вот в тиши ночной твой голос слышу вновь,
И веет, как тогда, во вздохах этих звучных,
Что ты одна - вся жизнь, что ты одна - любовь.
Что нет обид судьбы и сердца жгучей муки,
А жизни нет конца, и цели нет иной,
Как только веровать в рыдающие звуки,
Тебя любить, обнять и плакать над тобой!

85 For Fyodor Tyutchev, see interview 1, n62.

86 Henri Bergson (1859–1941), a prominent French philosopher and proponent of Intuitivism, was a professor at the French College, a member of the French Academy, and Nobel Prize Laureate in Literature (1927).

87 Duvakin quotes the first line of the poem "Память"/ "Только змеи сбрасывают кожи" ["Memory / Only Dragons Shed Their Skin"] (1921) by Nikolay Gumilev.

88 Vyacheslav Ivanov, *Songs from the Labyrinth*, written (1905). For Vyacheslav Ivanov, see interview 1, n69.

89 "Again you show yourselves, you wavering Forms,
Revealed, as you once were, to clouded vision.
Shall I attempt to hold you fast once more?
Heart's willing still to suffer that illusion?
You crowd so near! Well then, you shall endure,
And rouse me, from your mist and cloud's confusion:
My spirit feels so young again: it's shaken
By magic breezes that your breathings waken.

You bring with you the sight of joyful days,
And many a loved shade rises to the eye:
And like some other half-forgotten phrase,
First Love returns, and Friendship too is nigh . . ."
(http://www.poetryintranslation.com).

90 "What I possess seems far away from me, / And what is gone becomes . . ." (http://www.poetryintranslation.com).

91 "That Is Longing: Living in Turmoil," by Rainer Maria Rilke (1897), included in his poetry collection *Mir zur Feier* (1900).
That is longing: living in turmoil
and having no home in time
and those are wishes: gentle dialogs
of day's hours with eternity.
And that is life. Until out of a yesterday
the most lonely hour rises
which, smiling differently than the other sisters (hours)
silently encounters eternity.
(Translated by Jan and Allan van Assel; http://www.muurgedichten.nl/rilke.html)/

92 Bakhtin is quoting "La Mort des Amants," from Baudelaire's *Les Fleurs du Mal* (1857).
The Death of Lovers
beds of subtle fragrance shall be ours,
soft divans far deeper than a tomb,
fairer climes shall yield mysterious flowers
—flowers which for us were made to bloom.
lavishing our final amorous hours
there, our flaming hearts shall merge and loom
in the twin mirrors of these souls of ours
—torches vast which side by side consume.
then some evening, rose and mystic blue,
charged with the sobbing woe of our adieu,
Love shall link us in one lightning-spark;
later, shall the faithful angel fling
all the portals wide, illumining
the flameless torches and the mirrors dark. (Translated by Lewis Piaget Shanks, http://fleursdumal.org/poem/197).

93 Bakhtin recites Alexander Pushkin's poem "Reminiscence" (1828). The complete text of the poem in Russian is as follows:
Когда для смертного умолкнет шумный день,
И на немые стогны града
Полупрозрачная наляжет ночи тень
И сон, дневных трудов награда,
В то время для меня влачатся в тишине
Часы томительного бденья:
В бездействии ночном живей горят во мне
Змеи сердечной угрызенья;
Мечты кипят; в уме, подавленном тоской,
Теснится тяжких дум избыток;
Воспоминание безмолвно предо мной
Свой длинный развивает свиток;
И с отвращением читая жизнь мою,
Я трепещу и проклинаю,
И горько жалуюсь, и горько слезы лью,
Но строк печальных не смываю.

94 “Медный всадник” [“The Bronze Horseman”] (1833) is a long narrative poem by Alexander Pushkin. Though written in exile, it was published in Russia; but Tsar Nicholas I, who did not like Pushkin and had an affair with his wife, Natalya Goncharova (1812–1863), personally crossed out lines that were not to appear in print. The uncensored poem was only published in 1904.

95 Galina Timofeevna was Bakhtin’s housekeeper. She was helping Bakhtin after the death of his wife in 1971. See also interview 4, n121.

Bibliography

Bakhtin, M. M. [Mikhail]. *The Dialogic Imagination: Four Essays*. Edited by Michael Holquist. Translated by Michael Holquist and Caryl Emerson. Austin: University of Texas Press, 1981.

———. *Problems of Dostoevsky's Poetics*. Edited and translated by Caryl Emerson. Minneapolis: University of Minnesota Press, 1984.

———. *Sobranie sochinenii v semi tomakh*. Vol. 5. Moscow: Russkie Slovari, 1996.

———. *Dialog. Karnaval. Khronotop* [Диалог. Карнавал. Хронотоп]. Vitebsk: Vitebsk Pedagogical Institute (1992–2018).

Bocharov, S. G. "Ob odnom razgovore i vokrug nego," *Siuzhety russkoi literatury*. Moskva: Iazyki russkoi kul'tury (1999): 472–502.

Emerson, Caryl. "The Russians Reclaim Bakhtin, 1975 to the Jubilee." In *The First Hundred Years of Mikhail Bakhtin*, 31–72. Princeton, NJ: Princeton University Press, 1997.

Hirschkop, Ken. *Mikhail Bakhtin. An Aesthetic for Democracy*. Oxford: Oxford University Press, 1999.

Klyueva, L. V., and L. M. Lisunova, eds. *M. M. Bakhtin—Myslitel', Pedagog, Chelovek*. Saransk: Krasnyi Okti͡abr, 2010.

Makhlin, Vitaly. "Тоже разговор" [Also a Conversation]. *Voprosy Literatury* 2004, no. 3. http://magazines.russ.ru/voplit/2004/3/mah1-pr.html.

McCaw, Dick. *Bakhtin and Theatre: Dialogues with Stanislavski, Meyerhold and Grotowski*. New York: Routledge, 2015.

———. "Towards a Philosophy of the Moving Body." In *Bakhtin's Heritage in Literature, Arts, and Psychology*, edited by Viatcheslav Gratchev and Howard Mancing. Lanham, MD: Lexington Books, 2018.

Notes on Contributors

SLAV N. GRATCHEV is associate professor of Spanish at Marshall University, and the author of *The Polyphonic World of Cervantes and Dostoevsky* (2017) and coeditor with Howard Mancing of *Don Quixote: The Re-accentuation of the World's Greatest Literary Hero* (Bucknell, 2017). He has published numerous articles on Cervantes, Dostoevsky, and Bakhtin, and is coeditor with Howard Mancing on a volume dedicated to 100 years of Bakhtin's first scholarly publication—*Mikhail Bakhtin's Heritage in Literature, Arts, and Psychology: Art and Answerability* (2018).

MARGARITA MARINOVA is associate professor of English and comparative literature at Christopher Newport University, Virginia. Her translation of Mikhail Bulgakov's play *Don Quixote* (coedited with Scott Pollard, 2014) was nominated for a PEN award. She is also the author of *Transnational Russian-American Travel Writing* (2011), of articles about Russian and Soviet literature and culture, contemporary Bulgarian literature, and travel literature in various journals, including the *Slavic and East European Journal*, *Studies in Travel Writing*, *The Comparatist*, *Tulsa Studies in Women's Literature*, and also of chapters in *Global Cold War Literature: Western, Eastern and Postcolonial Perspectives* (2011) and *Don Quixote: The Re-accentuation of the World's Greatest Literary Hero* (Bucknell, 2017).

DMITRIY SPOROV is chair of the Department of Oral History at Moscow State University's Science Library, and a distinguished historian. He is also the president of the Foundation for Research in the Humanities; the chief editor for the book series, *Let's Remember Moscow: 1930s* (2015) and *Let's Remember Moscow: 1940s* (2016), a unique collection of oral memoirs about Moscow.

Index

Printed in the United States
By Bookmasters